The New Television Handbook

The New Television Handbook provides an exploration of the theory and practice of television at a time when the medium is undergoing radical changes. The book looks at television from the perspective of someone new to the industry, and explores the place of the medium within a constantly changing digital landscape.

This title discusses key skills involved in television production, including: producing, production management, directing, camera, sound, editing and visual effects. Each of these activities is placed within a wider context as it traces the production process from commissioning to post-production.

The book outlines the broad political and economic context of the television industry. It gives an account of television genres, in particular narrative, factual programmes and news, and it considers the academic discipline of media studies and the ways in which theorists have analysed and tried to understand the medium. It points to the interplay of theory and practice as it draws on the history of the medium and observes the ways in which the past continues to influence and invigorate the present.

The New Television Handbook includes:

- contributions from practitioners ranging from established producers to new entrants;
- a comprehensive list of key texts and television programmes;
- a revised glossary of specialist terms;
- a section on training and ways of getting into the industry.

By combining theory, real-world advice and a detailed overview of the industry and its history, *The New Television Handbook* is an ideal guide for students of media and television studies and young professionals entering the television industry.

Patricia Holland has worked as an independent filmmaker, a television editor and a freelance journalist. She is currently a writer and researcher specialising in television history, and lectures at Bournemouth University, UK. Her most recent book is *Broadcasting and the NHS in the Thatcherite 1980s* (2013). She is the author of the first and second editions of *The Television Handbook*.

Media Practice

Edited by James Curran, Goldsmiths College, University of London

The *Media Practice* handbooks are comprehensive resource books for students of media and journalism, and for anyone planning a career as a media professional. Each handbook combines a clear introduction to understanding how the media work with practical information about the structure, processes and skills involved in working in today's media industries, providing not only a guide on 'how to do it' but also a critical reflection on contemporary media practice.

The Advertising Handbook
3rd edition
Helen Powell, Jonathan Hardy,
Sarah Hawkin & Iain MacRury

The Alternative Media Handbook
Kate Coyer, Tony Dowmunt and
Alan Fountain

The Cyberspace Handbook
Jason Whittaker

The Digital Media Handbook
2nd edition
Andrew Dewdney and Peter Ride

The Documentary Handbook
Peter Lee-Wright

The Fashion Handbook
Tim Jackson and David Shaw

The Film Handbook
Mark de Valk with Sarah Arnold

**The Graphic Communication
Handbook**
Simon Downs

The Magazines Handbook
3rd edition
Jenny McKay

The Music Industry Handbook
2nd edition
Paul Rutter

The Newspapers Handbook
5th edition
Richard Keeble

The Photography Handbook
3rd edition
Terence Wright

The Public Relations Handbook
5th edition
Alison Theaker

The Radio Handbook
3rd edition
Carole Fleming

The Sound Handbook
Tim Crook

The New Television Handbook
5th edition
Patricia Holland

The New Television Handbook

Fifth edition

Patricia Holland

Routledge
Taylor & Francis Group

LONDON AND NEW YORK

Fifth edition published 2017
by Routledge
2 Park Square, Milton Park, Abingdon, Oxon, OX14 4RN

and by Routledge
711 Third Avenue, New York, NY 10017

Routledge is an imprint of the Taylor & Francis Group, an informa business

First edition published by Routledge 1997

Second edition published by Routledge 2000

Third edition published by Routledge 2005

Fourth edition published by Routledge 2011

British Library Cataloguing in Publication Data
A catalogue record for this book is available from the British Library

Library of Congress Cataloging in Publication Data
Names: Holland, Patricia, 1936– author.
Title: The new television handbook / Patricia Holland.
Other titles: Television handbook
Description: Fifth edition. | London ; New York : Routledge, 2016. |
Series: Media practice | Originally published under the title:
The television handbook (2000). |
Includes bibliographical references and index.
Identifiers: LCCN 2016025369| ISBN 9781138833500
(hardback : alk. paper) | ISBN 9781138833517 (pbk. : alk. paper) |
ISBN 9781315724836 (ebook)
Subjects: LCSH: Television – Production and direction – Handbooks,
manuals, etc. | Television broadcasting--Handbooks, manuals, etc.
Classification: LCC PN1992.5 .H63 2016 | DDC 791.4302/32 – dc23
LC record available at https://lccn.loc.gov/2016025369

ISBN: 978-1-138-83350-0 (hbk)
ISBN: 978-1-138-83351-7 (pbk)
ISBN: 978-1-315-72483-6 (ebk)

Typeset in Helvetica Neue and Avant Garde
by Florence Production Ltd, Stoodleigh, Devon, UK

Printed and bound in Great Britain by
TJ International Ltd, Padstow, Cornwall

Contents

List of figures   *x*
Acknowledgements   *xi*
Introduction   *xii*

PART 1
ON TELEVISION AND TELEVISION STUDIES   **1**

1   Television and tele-literacy   3

Television today   3
Tele-literacy   5

2   The history of television in the United Kingdom   10

Conditions of possibility   10

3   The contemporary landscape: UK channels
    and public service   18

The three ages of television   18
The BBC and its future   19
Commercial UK broadcasters and public service   22
Ofcom and regulation   25
Other UK-based channels   28
Independent production companies   28
Kate Beal: Woodcut Media   32

4   The contemporary landscape: globalisation,
    multichannel and multiplatform   35

    Globalisation and multichannel   35
    Online and multiplatform   37

5   The landscape of television in the
    United Kingdom: text   41

    The age of superabundance: interstitials and paratexts   41
    The linear flow: scheduling and branding   42
    Cross-platform, paratexts and interactivity   45
    About genres   47
    Overview of the main television genres   48
    A note on ratings, funding and formats   52

6   Studying television   54

    Studying television: an overview   54
    Mapping the field   55

PART 2
THE PRACTITIONERS' PERSPECTIVE   65

7   Working in television: an overview   67

    Working in television   67
    Programme production types   69
    Production processes   72
    Television work areas   74

8   Producing and production management   76

    Producers   76
    Production management   78

    Abigail McKenzie: Talent Team Assistant, BBC
        Children's Department   84

9   The director's concerns   86

    Director and crew   86
    The director's concerns   89
    Types of shot   94
    A fresh perception of the world   102

10   The visual dimension: cameras, lighting and
     the cinematographer   104

     Cameras and recording media   104
     Cameras and digital cinematography   107
     Visions of light   111
     Lighting: basic principles   113

11   Sound recording and the audio space   119

     Television and the flow of sound   119
     Sound recording and audio design   122
     Sound quality   127

12   Studios and studio work   136

     'Live' and 'as live'   136
     Working in the studio   137
     Studios   144
     QVC: the shopping channel   145

13   Post-production processes: editing   151

     Editing and post-production   151
     The work of editing   154
     Editing processes   157
     Styles of editing   159
     The final stages   163

14   Sound, visual effects and preparing for
     broadcast   165

     The aural dimension: creating the audio space   165
     Sound editing   168
     Graphics and visual effects   172
     Post-production: preparing for broadcast and distribution   179
     Luke Sothinathan: VT technician   181

PART 3
PROGRAMMES AND GENRES   **183**

15   Drama and television narrative   185

     Thinking about narrative   185

Fictional narratives: drama 186
Narrative theory 192
Narrative realism and other realisms 200
Identity and narration 204

16 From documentary to factual entertainment   207

Contemporary factual programming 207
*Brief history of UK documentary: the creative treatment
    of actuality* 209
Documentary and contemporary subgenres 212
Research for factual programmes 215
Interview techniques 219
Documentary and factual ethics 223
Anne Parisio: Parisio Productions 229
Note 229

17 News, politics and television as information   232
LISETTE JOHNSTON

History 232
Types of news and current affairs 233
Television news teams 235
The news agenda 240
Producing the news 242
Gio Ulleri: journalist/filmmaker 245

PART 4
TRAINING AND INDUSTRY CONTEXTS   **249**

18 Training, education and getting into the
   industry   251

Training and getting into the industry 251
RedBalloon and Solent Productions 254

19 Opening up the industry: diversity and access   257

Diversity and access 257
Relevant documents 260
MAMA Youth Project 260
Bob Clarke: Executive Producer, MAMA Youth Project 262

Jonny Yapi – my story   264
Training and opportunities: a list of useful references   266

20   Hannah's diary   **268**

Hannah's diary: April–November 2015   268
Contacts for entry-level jobs   275

21   Making programmes: pitching and commissioning   **276**

Turning an idea into a commission   276
Opportunities and funds   281

Glossary   285
Bibliography   301
Programme references   308
Index   323

Figures

1.1 Live election broadcast from the studio at Bournemouth University   8
3.1 Filming for Woodcut Media in South Korea   31
6.1 Television studies: mapping the field   56
7.1 Location filming   68
7.2 Inside an OB van   74
9.1 'Crossing the line'   92
9.2 Classification of shots   95
9.3 Framing   97
9.4 Camera angles   98
9.5 Filming with a Steadicam on location   101
10.1 Filming with a Panasonic P2 Varicam   105
10.2 Filming with an Arri Alexa   107
10.3 The relationship between focal length and angle of vision   110
10.4 Zooming   111
10.5 Three-point lighting   116
11.1 Sound recordist and cinematographer filming the Queen's visit
to Malta, 2015   127
11.2 The acoustics of a room   128
11.3 Sound presence   129
11.4 Polar diagram   131
11.5 Cardioid pick-up pattern   131
12.1 Filming with a studio camera   140
12.2 Studio gallery at QVC   144
12.3 Floor manager and assistant sorting the product   147
17.1 Outside broadcast from the Dhaka World Debate   236
18.1 Filming at Glastonbury 2015   252
18.2 The interactive globe at Salisbury Cathedral   255
19.1 Filming for *What's Up* Season 9   261

Acknowledgements

There are many people to thank for advice and support during the writing of this book. I am particularly indebted to my friends and colleagues, television practitioners and teachers, who have shared their expertise with me, especially those who have allowed me to transcribe their accounts of their television experiences. They range from experienced producers to new entrants to the industry and are credited in each of the relevant chapters. Particular thanks go to Mark Bond, Maike Helmers, Karl Rawstrone, Phil Spicer and Tim Putnam of Bournemouth University for advice on cinematography, editing, video effects and studio work; to Joy Monks and Elke Weissmann of Edge Hill University and to Robin Small for advice on production management; to Gisela Kraus for advice on sound recording; to Lisette Johnston, of the BBC and City University, for writing the chapter on news; and to Trevor Hearing for reading through and making comments on Part 2 of the book. I would also like to thank Alex Kann of the Community Channel, Mark Longhurst of Sky News, Bob Clarke of the Mama Youth Project and Vanessa Ridley of QVC among others, for allowing me to visit, question and observe, and everyone who took the trouble to hunt down appropriate pictures for the book. Special thanks go to the students and trainees who have shared their experiences with me, and to generations of students at Bournemouth University for their insights and enthusiasm. In addition I'd like to thank Manda Clarke for help in formatting the pictures.

Finally, thanks to the Centre for Media History Research at Bournemouth University for support in writing the book, and to Series Editor, James Curran, for insisting that I undertook to write this latest version of the *Television Handbook*.

Introduction

This is a book about television in the second decade of the twenty-first century, written from the point of view of practitioners and those who are aiming to become practitioners. However, it comes at a time when television itself is in a state of flux. Indeed, we must begin by asking whether it is still possible to speak of 'television' as a single, coherent medium. As the transformations brought by the digital revolution bring ever more innovations, television continues to overflow its boundaries. Broadcast programmes are only part of an ever-developing group of media available across many platforms. Content, which used to be seen as specifically televisual, can now be accessed on numerous different devices, from the tiny screen of a mobile phone to ultra-high-definition television sets that can dominate a room. The familiar flow of the television output is accompanied by a mass of supplementary material: websites, 'red button' information, producer's blogs, fan sites, cross-platform narratives and more. Television is mutating – oozing amoeba-like before our very eyes. Young people starting out on their careers may take the traditional route through the industry, or they may abandon broadcast and work with online media, or they may combine the two. And it is easier than ever to create engaging content, using a mobile phone if no camera is available, and to put it on YouTube or elsewhere online. This book will explore these challenges as it deals with the cluster of media grouped around television production, which is why we describe it as *'New'* Television.

From the point of view of those who work in television, many long-established principles and practices remain, but they must be reinterpreted for the digital era. Constantly developing and highly sophisticated equipment demands new skills and new types of understanding from cinematographers, editors, video technicians and many others. The structure of a narrative can be explored and analysed, as it has been since the days of Aristotle back in the fifth-century BCE, but the creation of a contemporary television narrative frequently involves highly complex plot structures woven across episodes and across platforms, referring back and forth between websites, paratexts and fan texts.

In addition, the institutions of UK television, which evolved slowly over the second half of the twentieth century, have become transformed in the first decades of the twenty-first century. The principles that were established when access to the airwaves (the electromagnetic spectrum that carries the broadcast signal) was restricted are under challenge now that cable, satellite, streaming and digital compression have made hundreds of channels possible and are replacing linear schedules with on-demand viewing and expanded choice. Television has become globalised. Those who enter the industry in the 20teens find themselves working within a very different set of organisational structures from those who started work in the 1990s.

This book will consider this changing landscape from the perspective of someone new to the industry, and will take on board a number of different aspects. On the one hand it will look at the broader political and economic context of the television industry, and on the other it will consider the detail of the daily lives of practitioners, ranging from established producers to new entrants. It will argue that practical experience cannot be understood without looking at the wider picture. It will also consider the academic discipline of media studies, and the ways in which theorists have analysed and tried to understand the phenomenon we still refer to as television, and will consider the practice of programme-making in the light of this analysis. It will argue that an understanding of practice illuminates theoretical insights, while, at the same time, a critical approach has driven much innovation in television and the moving image. Throughout the book we will take on board the history of the medium, and will note the ways in which the past continues to influence and invigorate the present. Whether we are discussing how to direct a studio show or how to edit a documentary, the history of the craft remains important.

Part 1 of this book, 'On television and television studies', gives greater depth to this all-important context. It sets out the institutional framework of UK television: the UK's public-service ecology and the shift to a multichannel, globally based, commercialised landscape. It then describes the range of television texts and the cross-platform landscape, and finally looks at the ways in which television has been, and currently is being, studied.

At the centre of the book, Part 2, 'The practitioners' perspective' discusses key skills: producing, production management, directing, camera, sound and editing, placing each of them within a wider context.

Part 3, called 'Programmes and genres', looks in detail at three key genres, once more from the perspective of practitioners in those fields. We look at drama and the role of scripted narrative; factual genres, ranging from classic documentary to 'factual entertainment'; and news, considering the techniques and practices involved.

Finally, Part 4 'Training and industry contexts', outlines forms of training and industry contexts, including the approaches of commissioning editors, issues of diversity and the processes of getting into the industry. In this section, and throughout the book, a number of practitioners, from new entrants to established producers, will give an account of their experiences.

This is a book that is intended to be *used* rather than read from cover to cover. It should be dipped into as needed, referring to the index as well as the contents page. For that reason there will be a certain amount of repetition as key points will recur under several headings. There are also many cross-references, which means that themes can be traced across the different sections of the book. Practical advice and theoretical ideas about television are not rigidly separated. The aim is to always illustrate the interrelationship between the two. That means that, in the 'practitioners' section, there is much discussion of the nature of television, differences of opinion and relevant debates, while the theoretical sections never lose sight of the practitioner's viewpoint.

The literature on television is expanding as commentators come to grips with the evolving multiplatform landscape. Throughout the book we will refer to recent publications in the particular areas and to more general studies of the medium. We will prioritise UK writers as this book focuses on UK television. But American programmes are an important part of the televisual experience, and many American scholars have led the way in television studies. Their work will be discussed, while bearing in mind the differences between the British and American experience. Two or three key texts are referred to at the end of each chapter; a longer bibliography at the end of the book gives details of all the books cited. All programmes referred to are listed with dates and relevant details (pp. 308–322).

Finally, to reiterate, this is a book from the perspective of practitioners, and throughout it assumes that an understanding of the history of the medium and its wider context can only enhance their work. Many debates from earlier eras of film and the moving image are startlingly current. Indeed the early decades of the twenty-first century echo the early decades of the twentieth century for innovation and experiment. Over the century, practitioners have contributed to theoretical ideas, while theorists have influenced practice. A division between them is artificial.

Part 1

On television and television studies

CHAPTER 1

Television and tele-literacy

TELEVISION TODAY

Television is a transnational business and a national institution. It remains our most-watched form of entertainment and our most important source of information. It is an outlet for creativity and a medium through which social concern and political views may be expressed. It is a substantial employer of administrators and office workers as well as skilled engineers, technicians, programme-makers and performers. Yet changes in recent years have been so great that it has been questioned whether 'television' as a separate medium is still a viable concept. That will be a question we come back to repeatedly in this book as we focus attention on different aspects of the contemporary scene.

At the same time, we should be wary of putting too much stress on 'newness' for its own sake – exciting though the prospect of unpredictable change may be. Technologies and structures may be evolving, but many of the trends we see today have longer roots in the history of the medium. Television has long pushed beyond the domestic screen in dialogue with proliferating technologies and cultural practices. Back in 1974, the great theorist Raymond Williams described the medium as a combination of 'technology' and 'cultural form'. He, too, was writing at a time of change, and noted that new technologies are constantly emerging, but that aspects of the old ones always linger. He argued that we must always take into account these 'residual' technologies as well as the 'emergent' ones, while focusing on those that are 'dominant' in the contemporary scene (Williams 1974). Taking our cue from Williams, we will be discussing both the technological and the cultural aspects of television and observing how they interrelate. We will be careful not to fall into the trap of 'technological determinism', and assume that technology is the most important factor. Instead we will be paying careful attention to all those social, cultural, economic and political forces that are shaping the way technologies are used. All these aspects are important to today's practitioners.

Since the 1950s, television has been a central and much loved part of British culture. It has developed from a comfortable, home-based medium – that warm glow in the corner of the living room still celebrated by programmes such as *Gogglebox* – to the multiscreen, cross-platform phenomenon we know today. Arguably, its contemporary manifestations still provide a companionate voice and a circle of friends old and new – Ena Sharples of *Coronation Street*; Brian Cox on the solar system; the ever-changing *Dr Who*; the anarchic disruptions of a Miranda Hart or of Ant and Dec; the antics of celebrities holed up in the *Big Brother* house and many more. Now that they are available beyond their domestic context and at any time of day on catch-up and on mobile screens, their appeal is, if anything, enhanced. At the same time, television aims to offer a 'window on the world' (*Panorama*'s first description of itself). Documentaries and factual programmes probe behind the headlines, while television news and its associated websites provide a major source from which most of us get to learn about and interpret domestic politics and world affairs. Those who work, and aspire to work, in the medium may aim to contribute to any one of many diverse areas.

Those who produce television programmes tend to inhabit what Jeremy Tunstall described as a genre-specific world, absorbed in their own very different fields, whether sport or children's programming (Tunstall 1993: 2). However, a special characteristic of television in the United Kingdom has been that it has not allowed those diverse areas to drift too far apart, arguing that audiences do not always know in advance what it is they want to see, so they should be offered something of everything. The proliferation of formats, the constant invention of new genres, the ways in which disparate expectations are allowed to rub up against each other, has given UK television a richness that remains unique and valuable, alongside the increase in specialist, globally based channels. Across its free-to-air terrestrial broadcasters, UK television still maintains a balance between its commitments to entertainment and to politics; to information and to relaxation. The pressure to address only the biggest audience is moderated within a regulated public-service system. Variety, diversity and unexpected juxtapositions have been at the core of a television service that has taken seriously the privilege of entry into people's homes.

However, the expansion of the multichannel landscape has meant that UK television is now part of a global, largely American-based, system. The twentieth-century pattern, with a number of well-established and familiar channels, where most production was UK-funded and UK-based, has given way to the expanding universe of multiple channels and multinational business interests. The advantages of the new, global landscape are that programme-makers have access to international commissions and international funding, while broadcasters can sell their programmes worldwide. Meanwhile audiences can view numerous channels offering a wide range of international programming – from hugely popular drama series, such as *Breaking Bad*, *Lost*, *Game of Thrones* – through to news from other perspectives, say from Al-Jazeera or CNN.

At the same time, questions about the social value and function of television have become more intense under pressure from economic and political changes. The lightening of UK regulation has made control of broadcast television a rich prize for multinational media companies. At the same time television has become a platform for entrepreneurs, advertisers, sponsors, celebrity agents, public relations organisations and marketing people. Television has become brand-conscious (Johnson 2012). We now hear talk of 'product' where once we spoke of programmes, and of 'consumers' and 'the market' where once we meant the audience. The future of the BBC as the publicly funded cornerstone of British television has come under attack. These trends towards a more commercial environment have long been present, but have been held in check by regulation and legislation. However, in the 20teens television is undoubtedly more commercial and more troubled. Old principles have been shaken and new ones are unsure. Chapter 2 will explore the contemporary landscape of UK television in greater detail.

In addition a generation gap is opening up. The under-30s (often referred to as the 'millennials') tend to take global content for granted. They regularly access multiple sources, and do not identify 'television' as their most important source of entertainment or information. The older generation, by contrast, prefer scheduled programming and rely on television listings (Ofcom 2014: 1.15).

We will trace the mutating television medium throughout this book, observing the landscape as it heaves and resettles. We will note the ways in which digital and online platforms interact with broadcast television so that it is unclear whether they make up a completely new medium or are part of a revolution within television itself. Either way, as time goes on, it will be those now entering the media professions who will be instrumental in developing these new structures. The need for a dialogue between those who think about television and those who make it has never been more acute.

TELE-LITERACY

This is a handbook for the tele-literate and those who aim to be tele-literate. We have deliberately stuck with the term *tele-literacy* here, rather than the more common 'media literacy', as this book is focused on television with its own specificity and history, as well as its contemporary extensions. We use the term to combine a knowledge of the skills of television practice with a critical appraisal of the content of television and an enthusiasm for the medium in all its responsible and irresponsible proliferations, from *TOWIE* to *Newsnight*; from *The Great British Bake-off* to major events such as the Queen's 90th Birthday. This book puts practical advice on 'how to do it' within the context of academic theory, debates between television professionals, and issues that concern the public at large.

In recent years, many academics and others concerned with media education have turned their attention to the production of television, and have begun to grapple with the implications of an interplay between theory and practice. The days are past when television professionals and those who study the medium brought different perspectives that seemed totally at odds with each other. Yet there are still some who work in the industry who argue that 'media studies' are irrelevant, since television theory has nothing to do with the real world of production. Media theory is abstract and sceptical, they say; it attacks rather than helps practitioners. Although there is some justice in these criticisms, in many ways they miss the point. To make useful critical judgements, television studies can never simply take the perspective of the broadcasters. As two researchers into television talk shows wrote:

> Whatever the intentions of broadcasters in making these programmes . . ., these do not determine the nature of the product. This must be revealed through textual analysis, and the programmes have many unintended consequences which only audience research can discover.
>
> (Livingstone and Lunt 1994: 2)

Television studies have their own history, which is explored in Chapter 6, where we argue that practitioners have made an important contribution to critical ideas, and sometimes to the most abstract realms of theory. Meanwhile contemporary television theory increasingly takes into account the concerns of television practice. This involves reflecting on the context of programme production and the institutional constraints on practitioners, and has frequently led to the evolution of forms of critical practice.

Nevertheless, for many years, education and practical training had little to do with each other. Training in practical skills tended to be on the job, oriented to technical expertise and with the prospect of a secure career ahead. Meanwhile a degree from an élite university, in almost any subject, often qualified young men (and they were almost all men) for graduate training schemes at the BBC, which would lead to producer and management jobs. But the structures of employment have changed. The hierarchies have (almost all) broken down (women and particularly people from black, Asian and minority ethnic (BAME) backgrounds are still under-represented), and much of television has become an industry for entrepreneurs and a casualised workforce. Universities and colleges have increasingly stepped in to offer practical training alongside their more critical teaching and have set about building closer links with the industry. Extended periods of work experience, both in small production companies and large organisations including the BBC, are now a regular and expected part of a university curriculum. Many universities have their own television studios and some have set up their own production companies. Southampton Solent University's production unit contributes to the BBC's coverage of the Glastonbury Festival (Figure 18.1), while RedBalloon, based at Bournemouth University, won an award for its contribution to the 800th anniversary of Magna Carta (see Chapter 18). Within these units students can do paid production work on real projects. They deal with budgets and a client brief as they would in any production company.

Beyond the universities there are many other opportunities for training to a professional standard. A number of organisations run short courses: they range from the British Academy of Film and Television Arts (BAFTA) to specialised projects such as the MAMA Youth Project. We look at these in more detail in Chapter 19. Meanwhile the digital revolution means that the paraphernalia of filming and editing has become more easily available and simpler to use, and a wider group of people is gaining access to television skills. An individual can own a camcorder, buy an editing programme for their computer and learn the basics of the craft from an expanding range of online tutorials.

Thinking about television and promoting tele-literacy is also an activity that is carried on in many forums, from the pub to the starchiest of academic journals. People new to the industry and all who seek to be tele-literate are now able to follow and take part in a debate that is more than just 'did you see?' It can be found on online discussion boards, Facebook pages and Twitter feeds – to say nothing of programmes that go behind the scenes of the blockbuster hits, such as *The Xtra Factor* and *The Apprentice: You're Fired*. Debates may be superficial and chiefly concerned with gossip about celebrities, but these are also spaces where programme-makers may engage with viewers.

The daily and weekly broadsheet press carry extensive comment on topics as varied as personalities, technology and legislation. They report on the economics of the industry on the business pages, while the media pages follow the deliberations of channel controllers, as well as issues including scheduling, commissioning and other matters that arouse public concern. Trade magazines such as *Broadcast* follow industry trends, while academic journals such as *Critical Studies in Television* run a regular blog as well as their published journal. In addition, public meetings and seminars are organised by educational institutions, pressure groups and bodies such as the British Film Institute. The regulator, Office of Communications (Ofcom), carries out detailed research into the media and audiences, all of which is available online, while the government publishes public consultation papers on television policy.

In this way debates around television and the wider media are increasingly accessible to the general public. Knowledge of the medium has never been so widespread. We will be drawing on these various sources throughout this book.

In today's media-saturated society, practical training, formal academic study and a wider social conversation all overlap. But there still remains an important difference between studying television in a spirit of disinterested and critical enquiry and making television programmes. Independent intellectual values should not be abandoned in the face of an onslaught from those who feel that, in the new competitive atmosphere, only the most pragmatic of approaches will do. In this book, references to the sort of theoretical ideas that inform television studies are threaded through the chapters on practical approaches. For example, in considering the capacities of modern cameras, Dziga Vertov's writings on the 'camera-eye' are startlingly relevant (Chapter 10); when looking at advice about narrative structure, the formal explorations of writers such as David Bordwell and Roland Barthes are as useful as the down-to-earth advice offered by Syd Field and Robert McKee (Chapter 15); when we come to new media and the world of digital communications, postmodern theory offers some provocative insights (Chapter 5).

This book does not suggest that theory and practice should collapse into each other, but that they should *inform* each other. It looks at examples of good practice as well as showing how some theoretical perspectives have illuminated day-to-day production norms within a number of television genres. In addition, the politics of television and the changing structure of the *institution* of television inevitably influence the experience of all who work in the medium, and concern all who care about it. That is why Chapters 2–4 will deal with the institution of television and its history.

FIGURE 1.1
Live election broadcast from the studio at Bournemouth University, May 2015

Photograph: Neil Goridge

The practitioners who have contributed to the book, some as written pieces, some in the form of extended interviews, are all aware of the contribution that *thinking* about television and engaging with the politics of television has made to their careers. They range from newly graduated students seeking jobs, to experienced producers and educators. They include policy-makers and commissioning editors as well as those who are making their way through the expanding television jungle.

KEY TEXTS

Bennett, J. and Strange, N. (2011) *Television as Digital Media*, Durham, NC: Duke University Press.

Ofcom (2014) *Public Service Content in a Connected Society: Ofcom's Third Review of Public Service Broadcasting*, London: Ofcom.

CHAPTER 2

The history of television in the United Kingdom

CONDITIONS OF POSSIBILITY

As we have argued in Chapter 1, to understand the *practice* of television, it is not enough simply to consider the programmes and the way they are made. It is also important to ask what are the economic, cultural, technological and political circumstances which made those particular programmes possible at that particular moment in time. Changing technologies have contributed to constant innovation, but political and social factors have been equally influential. Historical developments do not reflect inevitable progress but are the results of campaigns, arguments and economic pressures. Television is an all-inclusive, highly popular medium that is also a business, so it is not surprising that it has regularly been at the centre of political disputes and conflicts. Only by understanding its history can we understand the special qualities of the medium and the ways in which it is developing and changing. Knowing about the past throws a new light on the present.

That is why we begin this chapter with an account of the changes to the *institution* of television in the United Kingdom. A brief paragraph on each decade will summarise the relevant factors, including government legislation, the funding and ownership of media organisations and the technological innovations that have made changes possible. Together these provide the historical *conditions of possibility*, as well as the roots of our present highly complex television landscape.

1920s: the birth of the BBC

The British Broadcasting Company, which broadcast the first radio programme to the nation, received a Royal Charter in 1927 and changed from being a commercial company to a public corporation. This was mainly a solution to the technical problem of broadcasting frequencies. A corporation with a monopoly on broadcasting could expand its radio services in a planned way, and avoid the situation in which 'tuning in' would be difficult because a free-for-all on the radio spectrum would lead to interference between the channels. So broadcasting was established as a *public service*. The BBC was granted a Royal Charter, which must be periodically renewed by the government of the day, and it was funded by a levy on those who owned equipment to receive the broadcast signal. This was known as a licence fee and its level was determined by the government of the day in consultation with the Corporation. The BBC negotiated a position that ensured it was independent from both government and commercial pressures. Its income came directly from the licence fee, rather than from general taxation, and it was controlled by an independent Board of Governors.

The BBC's first charismatic Director General, John Reith, had ambitions that went way beyond achieving a clear audio signal. At a time when the school-leaving age was 14, Reith used the Corporation's freedom from commercial pressures to plan a range of programming that would broaden the horizons of a population that had not had the advantage of a wide education. His famous formula was that the purpose of broadcasting was to 'educate and inform', as well as to 'entertain'. The BBC was publicly funded and saw itself as responsible to the public 'as a whole'. It was a public service.

During the 1920s and 1930s there were a number of experiments by enthusiasts and entrepreneurs to find ways of broadcasting images as well as sound, but television – the word is derived from Greek and means 'seeing from a distance' – as a popular medium did not yet exist.

1930s: the BBC's first experiments

The BBC established experimental television studios at Alexandra Palace, a vast Victorian entertainment centre in North London. Perched high on a hill, it was a suitable location for a television transmitter mast. There were studios for two competing television technologies, as the Corporation was uncertain which to adopt, but its first public broadcast, on 2 November 1936, used the EMI-Marconi system, which became the established system. In that first broadcast, the glamorous Adele Dixon sang of a 'mighty maze of mystic, magic rays, which bring television to you'.

The first transmissions reached only a small number of viewers around London, who were within range of the transmitter and wealthy enough to buy a new-fangled television set. Transmissions were cancelled when the Second World War began in 1939, chiefly because of fears that the signals from the transmitters could be picked up by enemy bombers.

1940s: relaunch

In 1946, when the war ended, BBC television was re-established and the public service model was extended. From the beginning the BBC was more than just programmes. It was also responsible for the broadcasting infrastructure, developed by the Corporation's engineering department. Transmitter masts were built across the United Kingdom as an intrinsic part of the commitment to make the signal available to everyone equally.

1950s: expansion and the arrival of ITV

Live pictures of the young Queen Elizabeth's coronation in 1953 led to television sets being purchased in unprecedented numbers. But there was a significant campaign to break the BBC's monopoly of the airwaves. It was dominated by advertisers and entrepreneurs who wanted a share of the action, but joined by many who thought that the BBC was too narrow and there was a need for a greater diversity. The Television Act of 1954 enabled a number of regionally based commercial television companies to be granted the licence to broadcast. Together they contributed to the Independent Television (ITV) network. The first of the 15 separate companies began broadcasting in September 1955, and then new companies were added across the nations and regions of the United Kingdom. They were funded by advertising and made programmes that would appeal to their individual regions as well as to the ITV network. Together the companies funded a separate company, Independent Television News (ITN), which was committed, like the BBC, to objective and impartial news reporting. ITV companies were responsible to a new body, the Independent Television Authority (ITA).

After a shaky start the companies soon became financially secure, as they had a monopoly of broadcast advertising. They brought an attractive new range of popular entertainment shows and American imports, but the ITA ensured that they too followed a public service remit and commissioned a broad range of programming. ITV franchises only ran for a limited period, so the companies had to be constantly on their toes, ensuring that they complied with the ITA requirements for fear of losing their licence to broadcast in the next round of applications.

Most historians accept that competition between the two channels was a productive one. The BBC became less elite and stuffy, while regulation meant that ITV would not only seek out the most profitable programmes.

1960s: the launch of BBC2 and the coming of colour

The 1960s saw an expansion of creative broadcasting and innovation at both the BBC and ITV. At the BBC, Director General Hugh Carlton Green was an innovative maverick who supported satirical programmes, such as the notorious *That Was The Week That Was*, and created a space for radical playwrights. But in response the moral purity campaigner Mary Whitehouse set up a high-profile 'Clean Up Television Campaign' against what she saw as a corrupting medium.

At the same time, the report of the Pilkington Committee of 1962 criticised the ITV companies for being too populist (their programmes were 'candy floss', wrote Richard Hoggart, one of the Committee's members (Holland 2006: 37–8)). The Committee awarded the third broadcast channel to the BBC. BBC2 launched in 1964. It was not expected to compete for the largest audiences, but was free to innovate and schedule programmes that were more demanding on audience attention. Meanwhile the ITA laid down that the companies must broadcast certain genres, including current affairs and children's, even if they did not attract the advertisers. When the ITV franchises were reviewed in 1968, some companies lost their licence to broadcast and new companies took over. For the next decade it was accepted that competition between ITV and the BBC was for quality in programming rather than for revenue.

In 1967 BBC2 began broadcasting in colour and by the end of the decade all UK television was in colour.

1970s: radical campaigning

The 1970s saw a number of new approaches, and there were pressures to appeal to a more diverse audience. The BBC and ITV were highly exclusive institutions, both in terms of those who worked for them and those who were able to express their opinions through them. Regional accents were rarely heard, women and members of the black and minority ethnic communities were seriously under-represented. Jobs were hard to get. They were either craft-based, controlled by unions who operated a rigid closed shop, or they were seen as gentlemanly occupations, part of the civil service, suitable for those highly educated in the liberal traditions of Oxford and Cambridge. Consequently, over the 1970s, there was some vigorous campaigning by film- and video-makers from outside the television establishment. In response the BBC set up a Community Programme Unit which allowed 'ordinary people' and campaigning groups to make their own programmes (Oakley and Lee-Wright 2016). In 1977, the Annan Report recommended the setting up of a fourth channel to provide space for independent programme-makers.

In 1972, the ITA became the Independent Broadcasting Authority (IBA) and took on responsibility for commercial radio channels.

1980–86: the launch of Channel Four

Channel Four was launched in 1982 and was required to 'cater for tastes, interests and audiences not served by ITV (or other television channels) and to innovate in the form and content of programmes'. This was achieved through a new model of how a television station could be run. Channel Four was a 'publisher' rather than a producer and commissioned its programmes from independent production companies. Although it was commercially funded and showed advertisements, it did not compete for advertising funding, but received an agreed amount from the

ITV companies. That meant that it did not have to seek out the largest audience and could serve minority interests. Its first chief executive, Jeremy Isaacs, wrote, 'we're a channel which some of the audience will watch all of the time, and all of the audience some of the time' (Isaacs 1989).

Channel Four was not privately owned, but a subsidiary of the IBA (which had taken over from the ITA as regulator). In Wales, the relevant frequencies were granted to the Welsh language channel, Sianel Pedwar Cymru (S4C; broadcaster for Wales).

Numerous independent production companies, some of them just two or three people working from a small office, were set up to provide programmes for Channel Four. The channel also commissioned programmes from radical and minority programme-makers and locally based 'workshops', groups of filmmakers sometimes regionally based and sometimes, like Broadsides, an all-woman feminist collective, around a particular issue.

The public service ecology

This arrangement of four channels, competing in the friendliest of ways, but largely complementary, established what has been described as a 'delicate television ecology striking a balance between commercial forces and public commitments'. Since they were not competing for funding, they could compete for quality and audiences. Together they subscribed to the principles of public service broadcasting as expressed by the various government committees up to the Annan Committee (1977), which recommended the establishment of Channel Four.
These principles were codified as:

- Geographical universality. Broadcast programmes should be available to the whole population.
- Universality of appeal. Broadcast programmes should cater for all tastes and interests.
- There should be special provision for minorities, especially disadvantaged minorities.
- Broadcasters should recognise their special relationship to the sense of national identity and community.
- Broadcasting should be distanced from all vested interests, and in particular from those of the government of the day.
- Universality of payment. One main instrument of broadcasting should be directly funded by the corpus of users.
- Broadcasting should be structured so as to encourage competition in good programming rather than competition for numbers.
- The public guidelines for broadcasting should liberate rather than restrict broadcasters (Broadcasting Research Unit 1985).

- It is considered that public service addresses viewers as 'citizens' to be involved and informed, whereas a market system sees its audience as 'consumers', whose 'demands' must be satisfied.

1986–89: the Peacock Committee and marketisation

The non-commercial priorities of public service broadcasting became the centre of a heated political debate, which intensified in the mid-1980s when Margaret Thatcher's Conservative government was committed to deregulation and a free market. Until the 1980s, it had not been technically feasible to challenge the four-channel arrangement, because of the limited space on the radio spectrum that carries the broadcast signal. But by the mid-1980s, the cable industry was developing and there were satellites in place which could potentially broadcast hundreds of channels, either directly to people's homes through their own private satellite dishes, or via the cables. In 1989, Sky Television, owned by Rupert Murdoch, who also controlled UK newspapers and other media enterprises around the globe, launched four satellite channels aimed at the United Kingdom. The rival British Satellite Broadcasting (BSB) launched in 1990, but later in the year they merged to become BSkyB. It was effectively a take-over by Sky.

With the arrival of satellite broadcasting there were no more physical restrictions on the number of channels. In addition, channels originating outside the United Kingdom were not subject to UK regulation. It was questioned whether the public service system, depending on regulation as a defence against commercial pressures, could survive. Media moguls were at the forefront of a campaign to let market forces rip.

Rupert Murdoch, in a speech at the Edinburgh Television Festival in 1989, declared that:

> This public service television system has had, in my view, debilitating effects on British society, by producing a television output which is so often obsessed with class, dominated by anti-commercial attitudes and with a tendency to hark back to the past.

His argument, and that of the politicians who agreed with him, was that audiences should be free to choose from among as many channels as possible, and that commercial channels should not be required to broadcast programmes that did not attract the biggest audiences.

In 1986, the Peacock Report considered whether the BBC should give up the licence fee and take advertising instead. It decided that it should not, as there was not enough advertising to go round, but argued that the BBC should not broadcast popular genres, but only those that the commercial channels did not find profitable.

The task of the BBC was to compensate for 'market failure' (30 years later, another Conservative government would make some very similar proposals).

1990s: the expansion of satellite broadcasting: the launch of Channel 5

The Broadcasting Act of 1990 replaced the IBA with the Independent Television Commission (ITC) to regulate 'with a lighter touch'. For the first time ITV franchises were 'put up for auction', and were awarded partly on how much they were prepared to bid for the licence to broadcast. In addition, the limits on ownership were lifted, so that owners could control more than one ITV company. In addition, all broadcasters were required to award 25 per cent of their production to independent producers. This would give greater opportunities to the small companies that had been set up to make programmes for Channel Four. Channel Four itself was no longer protected from commercial competition but was required to sell its own advertising, although it remained a not-for-profit public trust. The BBC set up an 'internal market' known as 'Producer Choice', which meant that departments and facilities must compete with each other and with outside providers. Channel 5 was launched in 1997 as a fully commercial channel. The marketisation of British television was under way.

From the beginning of the decade, satellite broadcasting began to compete with the terrestrial channels. Unlike 'free-to-air' television, funded by the licence fee or advertising, satellite programmes were 'pay-TV' funded by a regular subscription. Across the decade increasing numbers of satellite channels became available, some dedicated to a particular type of output, such as Sky Sports and The Cartoon Network, some directed at a particular audience, such as the children's channel, Nickelodeon. Most were based outside the United Kingdom, the majority in the United States.

Cable broadcasting also expanded, but, despite some early experimentation, cable companies rarely produced their own material. Soon their main task was to distribute the signals from satellite companies. And there were experiments with digital broadcasting.

2000s: the expansion of multichannel: the establishment of Ofcom

The multichannel system continued to expand. All the terrestrial broadcasters launched 'families' of digital channels, often genre-specific and targeted at particular audiences, such as the BBC's CBeebies for children up to the age of six, and Children's BBC, CBBC, for six to twelve year-olds. These vied for attention with literally hundreds of other channels and different ways of accessing content. More American and global broadcasters designed their output for international audiences. During the 2003 Gulf War, UK viewers could access US-based channels, including CNN International and Fox News, as well as the Qatar-based Al Jazeera.

The 2003 Communications Act set up the Office of Communications (Ofcom) as a regulator to cover telecoms as well as broadcasting. It replaced the ITC and its remit covers the commercial free-to-air, terrestrial channels that continue to have public service obligations (see regulation: p. 25). However, since restrictions on ownership were lifted, the regional ITV companies continued to merge and take each other over, and in 2004 ITV plc became a single company, owning eleven of the fifteen regional licences.

20teens: the digital switch-over and multiplatform

By 2012 all television sets in the United Kingdom had been converted to digital, and the analogue signals were switched off. Various types of set-top box now give access to the established channels and to 'on-demand' programmes streamed via the internet on channels such as Netflix and Amazon Prime. The introduction of the 'smart' television, integrated with the internet, has increased the range of material available and further blurred the distinction between television and other media. Viewing is no longer linear.

Today we take it for granted that television is one among many digital media, received on a number of different platforms, from mobile phones to television screens. And any review of the contemporary television landscape must take note of the multiplatform material which complements and interacts with the programmes.

New entrants to the industry now need to engage with a medium that is both rooted in its long history and at the same time appears to be changing almost daily.

KEY TEXTS

Brown, M. (2007) A *Licence to Be Different: The Story of Channel 4*, London: BFI.
Curran, J. and Seaton, J. (2009) *Power Without Responsibility*, 7th edn, London: Routledge.
Higgins, C. (2015) *This New Noise: The Extraordinary Birth and Troubled Life of the BBC*, London: Faber.

CHAPTER 3

The contemporary landscape: UK channels and public service

THE THREE AGES OF TELEVISION

Over its history, television has gone through three main phases: the first has been described as *'the age of scarcity'*, since very few channels were available. Channels were tangible things, fixed and identifiable, each with its own character. Each was provided by a broadcaster which was responsible for the totality of the content and the flow of programmes throughout the day. A carefully planned mix of programmes was scheduled to match the day and time – undemanding chat in the mornings, horror films late at night and sports on Saturdays. Appointment viewing was the norm. If you missed the appointment, you missed the programme.

In some respects that pattern has continued, but it ceased to be the only one when the expansion of satellite and cable brought *'the age of plenty'* and put increasing choice before the viewers. Since many new channels, such as Nickelodeon for children and Discovery for documentaries, were genre-specific, a schedule planned to match the time of day became less relevant. The traditional broadcasters produced less of their own output and commissioned more from independent companies, many of them globally based.

In the twenty-first century, the digital revolution has moved one step further and brought what could be called *'the age of superabundance'*, bringing apparently limitless choice. With a multitude of channels on many different platforms and a disappearing schedule, viewing on demand is becoming the norm. And the age of superabundance is global. To understand the scope of television in the 20teens it is clear that we must look both beyond the television screen and beyond the United Kingdom.

And yet . . . the domestic landscape is still dominated by the core terrestrial channels with their roots in the national psyche and their millions of loyal viewers (Ofcom 2015a). BBC 1 and 2, ITV and Channels 4 and 5 have pride of place on the electronic programme guide (EPG), and occupy the main pages in the *Radio Times* and other listings. They are free-to-air, subject to regulation by Ofcom or the BBC Trust, and are committed to public service principles in different ways. At the same time their 'family' of channels, their streaming catch-up services, websites, extensive online material and global reach means that they are an important part of the age of superabundance. They remain national cultural institutions, but at the same time are keenly aware of their role as competitive businesses in a global market-place. Marketing and promotional content is an increasingly important part of their output (Johnson 2012).

In this overview of the contemporary landscape of UK television, we will bear in mind the role of government policy on the one hand, and commercial, global pressures on the other. We will consider funding, ownership and legislation, and will look at the BBC, the commercial UK broadcasters, the role of regulation and the independent production companies. Chapter 4 will then consider the contribution of the online and multiplatform world and the effect of globalisation.

Chapter 5 will move from the *institution* to the *text*, and will look in greater detail at the content of television, considering genres, schedules, ratings and the television flow.

THE BBC AND ITS FUTURE

The BBC is the key British broadcaster. In 2012 it commanded almost one-third of the UK's television viewing (Tunstall 2015: 3). At the time of writing, it has seven domestic television channels as well as BBC World, a network of overseas channels. Its marketing arm, BBC Worldwide, is run on a commercial basis. It has an extensive online operation, including news sites, interactive sites, background information and websites expanding on and contributing to its programmes. In addition there's a BBC YouTube channel, and in 2016 the youth-oriented BBC3 became online only. Programmes can be viewed as catch-up on BBC iPlayer, and many programmes from the BBC's extensive archives are being made available online.

The BBC is a publicly funded broadcaster, which does not take commercial advertising on its domestic channels. Its 2006 Charter Review formalised its six 'public purposes':

1   Sustaining citizenship and civil society
2   Promoting education and learning
3   Stimulating creativity and cultural excellence
4   Representing the United Kingdom, its nations, regions and communities

5   Bringing the United Kingdom to the world and the world to the United Kingdom

6   Delivering to the public the benefit of emerging communications technologies and services.

The aspiration to provide education, information and entertainment to the population as a whole, expressed by its first Director General, John Reith, remains an important reference point. Against this background, BBC1 and BBC2 both schedule a wide range of genres, with BBC1 aiming for a more popular audience with hugely successful entertainment shows, such as *Strictly Come Dancing* and *EastEnders*, while BBC2 aims for greater depth and includes a substantial input of news and current affairs, from *Victoria Derbyshire* in the mornings to *Newsnight* in the evenings every weekday. BBC3 was launched to target the under-35s, at a time when the BBC had been criticised for appealing chiefly to the over-40s. It was used to try out new comedy, such as *Little Britain*, as well as innovative reality formats such as *Tough Young Teachers* and *Don't Tell the Bride*. Despite a considerable campaign to keep it on air, the channel became online only in early 2016. Other channels include: BBC4 with programmes for more specialised tastes, such as substantial documentaries, history and arts coverage; CBeebies for children from one to six; CBBC (Children's BBC) for children from six to twelve. Then there is the News Channel, with 24-hour news, the Parliament Channel, an HD channel and the internationally respected BBC World. In 2008, the BBC set up a Scottish Gaelic language channel, BBC Alba, jointly with the Gaelic Media Service. Finally, in 2010 it was required to take responsibility for the Welsh language channel S4C (Sianel Pedwar Cymru: Broadcaster for Wales), which had previously been independent and funded by a grant from the government. The requirement to fund S4C is one example of the ways in which the government has required the BBC to take on a number of new commitments in the last few years.

The BBC derives a proportion of its income from its commercial activities, such as overseas sales and marketing spin-offs, including DVDs, books, games and toys. Nevertheless its unique status comes from its funding by a licence fee paid by the public on the ownership of radio and television sets. This is not part of general taxation, but a fee that goes directly to the BBC and gives the right to view anything on the free-to-air channels at any time at no extra cost. This independent funding underpins the BBC's obligation to address the whole population and has helped to protect the Corporation from the commercial pressures that affect other broadcasters. It also guarantees independence from government. This is especially important as there are times when governments around the world have used their national broadcasters as a mouthpiece for their views. The Corporation is free to criticise the government, and has, over its history, become embroiled in some notable confrontations.

However, the government of the day has an important hold over the BBC. The Corporation was set up by a Royal Charter, which the government must renew at regular intervals, most recently in 2016. In addition, it has the power to set the level of the licence fee. At such times the BBC becomes vulnerable to the political views of the party in power. Over the years, governments have tended to become more interventionist and successive Directors General have felt the need to appease them. In particular, during the 20teens, the BBC has come under pressure from a government that is unsympathetic to public funding. In 2010 and 2015 extra obligations were imposed on the Corporation while the licence fee was frozen (at £145.50 per household). This meant a substantial reduction in income, and the Corporation has had to implement substantial cuts across the board.

Although it is widely accepted that the BBC remains at the heart of British cultural life and national identity, there have long been criticisms from those opposed to public funding, including from much of the press. Many argue that the BBC's success in competing with the commercial channels is unfair because of its secure funding. They argue that the BBC should stick to providing only those minority programmes the commercial channels do not find profitable. In other words, it should provide for 'market failure'. This means that the BBC must constantly justify its popular success, especially at difficult moments such as Charter Renewal. Despite its independence and huge popularity, the BBC continues to be subject to political pressures.

From the 1990s the structure of the BBC changed to become more like a commercial company. Since the 1990 Broadcasting Act, quotas had been laid down for independent production companies to make programmes for the Corporation. Then, in 2016, the BBC's production department became BBC Studios, which may compete with independent producers for the whole of the BBC's output (see below on independent production companies).

At the same time, over the last few years the BBC has continued to innovate, expanding its public commitments by developing the iPlayer and its substantial online operations as an essential contribution to its services. Programmes invite audiences to participate through tweets and e-mails. They can engage with news items through the BBC News App or the phone messaging service WhatsApp, and visit each programme's web page for interviews, discussion and extra video material. There is a move towards streaming original material online, as the youth-oriented BBC3 is now online only.

Despite the changes, the BBC remains a unique organisation, committed to a broad range of programming, from the frivolous to the powerful; drawing the nation to-gether through its spectacular entertainment as well as through its presentation of major public events; committed to the arts, to in-depth, impartial news and current affairs, to major dramas and to children's programmes, as well as to innovation. It continues to provide a provocative and diverse range of material that sets a standard in an environment with a decreasing commitment to public service.

COMMERCIAL UK BROADCASTERS AND PUBLIC SERVICE

Channels with public service obligations

Within the diverse UK television ecology, the BBC is not the only broadcaster with public commitments. While satellite and digital platforms pose an ever-increasing challenge to the long-established public service system, ITV and Channels 4 and 5, funded by advertising, have continued to be designated 'public service broadcasters' (often abbreviated as 'PSBs'). They have the right to broadcast over the radio spectrum and to come at the top of the EPG. In exchange, they are subject to regulation by Ofcom and have statutory obligations to broadcast 'an appropriate amount' of public service content.

The specific requirements have changed over the years, and are different for each broadcaster, but the objectives of public service content were summarised in the 2003 Communications Act as to:

- inform an understanding of the world
- stimulate knowledge and learning
- reflect cultural identity
- represent diversity and alternative viewpoints. (Ofcom 2014 para 2.4)

In a recent review of public service broadcasting, Ofcom calculated that, despite the proliferation of channels, the 'PSB channels still account for over half of all viewing' (2015 para 1.13).

However, that same review reported that, although most respondents to their survey thought public service *principles* were important, many of them, especially younger people, did not recognise the concept of a 'public service' *channel* (2.47). For them, programmes were more important than providers. Broadcasters have therefore made considerable efforts to communicate their identities and values to their viewers. 'Idents, promos and trailers contribute to the tone of voice and identity of television channels and are a key tool in helping them to stand out within a competitive marketplace', writes Catherine Johnson, who has made an extensive study of the role of branding on television (blog 2015).

The fact that the terrestrial commercial broadcasters are funded by advertising means that their main business is not just to attract audiences to programmes, but to *sell audiences* to advertisers. In other words, they must make programmes that will appeal not just to large audiences, but to the sort of audiences the advertisers want to address – those who are likely to buy the cars, cosmetics, electronics and household goods which dominate the ad breaks. This commercial requirement may come into conflict with their public service commitments.

ITV plc

The longest running of the commercial PSBs, ITV has engaged in healthy competition with the BBC since 1955, and has an impressive history of diverse, high-quality programming. Now a single plc, instead of the original network of regional companies, ITV is divided into ITV Broadcasting Limited, which operates the television networks; its production arm, called ITV Studios, which includes Global Entertainment dealing with overseas sales and distribution; and ITV Commercial and Online, which runs the catch-up service ITV Hub, as well as being responsible for advertising and business activities.

ITV is a substantial producer of UK programmes, made both by ITV Studios and the independent sector. It specialises in smash hit entertainment: *The X-Factor, I'm a Celebrity: Get Me Out of Here*; popular dramas: *Downton Abbey, Midsomer Murders, Jekyll and Hyde* and many more, as well as news from ITN and a wide range of factual and other formats.

For many years the ITV companies were immensely wealthy as they had a monopoly on broadcast advertising. But in the current multichannel, multiplatform landscape, that monopoly is no more. The commercial channels must compete with each other for funding, and also with the internet, which now takes up almost half of all UK advertising (Tunstall 2015: 61). As their profits are squeezed, there is less incentive for the commercial public service channels to schedule 'public service' programmes that will not attract a profitable audience. ITV's occasional current affairs series *Tonight* does not have the budget nor the journalistic edge that the high-profile series *This Week* and *World in Action* once had. A ban on advertising unhealthy foods to children has meant that programmes for children would not be profitable. Consequently, ITV has virtually abandoned commissioning them, much to the consternation of the independent production companies that specialise in children's programmes. ITV's children's channel, CITV, like most of ITV's family of channels, depends on repeats and American programmes.

In the early days, the various ITV companies prided themselves on conveying the flavour of their particular region. Granada, based in Manchester, created 'Granadaland' and was proud of the northern voices of *Coronation Street*, first broadcast in 1960. Although *Corrie*, with its title sequence of the Manchester rooftops, is still going strong, ITV plc now has its headquarters in London and has largely lost its varied regional flavours. Once thriving headquarters and studios in Yorkshire, Birmingham and elsewhere have closed down and many of those who had worked for the separate companies lost their jobs.

In addition, ITV has bought a number of American production companies. Jeremy Tunstall writes: 'ITV may be in danger of losing some of its UK identity by doing so much importing of made-in-USA productions, by owning Hollywood independent production companies and by participating in high-profile ITV-US co-productions' (Tunstall 2015: 36).

Channel 5

Channel 5, whose public service obligations are lighter than those of ITV, also carries a substantial amount of Hollywood programming, and since 2014 has been owned by the American media giant Viacom. It is largely given over to entertainment, and schedules a number of provocative factual formats, such as *Can't Pay? We'll Take it Away*. At the time of writing, *Celebrity Big Brother* is its main attraction.

Channel Four

Channel Four (C4C, Channel Four Corporation) is rather different. Despite its dependence on advertising, the channel remains a not-for-profit statutory corporation, with its profits ploughed back into the output. Its historian, Maggie Brown, described its brief as 'a licence to be different' (Brown 2007).

Channel Four has more obligations than the other commercial channels, including supporting creative talent and working with cultural organisations.

The channel's website outlines its requirements to:

- be innovative and distinctive
- stimulate public debate on contemporary issues
- reflect the cultural diversity of the United Kingdom
- champion alternative points of view
- inspire change in people's lives
- nurture new and existing talent.

www.channel4.com/info/corporate/about/channel-4s-remit

The channel was originally set up as a 'publisher' rather than a producer of programmes. This was intended to make space for alternative points of view, and to widen the opportunities for filmmakers at a time when almost all BBC and ITV programmes were made in-house. Today the channel still commissions from small UK-based companies as well as the larger independents. However, many of the companies that were set up to contribute to the channel back in the 1980s have now become major international players (see Indies p. 28 below).

Its other initiatives include Film4, which contributed significantly to the British film industry when it was set up in the 1980s, and still funds and co-funds a number of films, including the Oscar-winning *12 Years a Slave* (2014). The channel was a pioneer of docu-soaps and reality shows; it triumphantly launched *Big Brother* in 2000 and recent innovations include the impressive series of 'fixed-rig' documentaries such as *Educating Yorkshire* and *24 Hours in A&E*. And it has continued to seek out innovative formats. It was the first UK channel to schedule the new type of high-budget, continuing dramas produced by Home Box Office (HBO) in the United States, which have become so popular in recent years. Over the years it has prided itself on breaking taboos and has pushed at the limits of what is acceptable on television, with recurring programmes on sex education and medical conditions, with provocative titles such as *Embarrassing Bodies*. The remit to be innovative and challenging may sometimes become a licence to shock.

C4C has a family of channels, including E4, More4, 4Seven and Film4, which are mostly given over to movies and repeats. In addition, there is a wide range of websites and online material, including the on-demand service, 4oD.

Despite Channel Four's long-established independence, at the time of writing the government has suggested that the channel may be privatised.

Other local and national channels

As well as channels addressed to the United Kingdom as a whole, digital switchover also freed up spectrum for *local* channels. Ofcom invited applicants to 'facilitate civic understanding and fair and well-informed debate through coverage of local news and current affairs'. About nineteen licences were granted in 2013, from Brighton in the South to Leeds, Liverpool and Newcastle in the North. Partly launched with funding from the BBC, they are nevertheless privately owned – not always locally – and funded by advertising. They are accompanied by substantial websites with local content, but, at the time of writing, are having difficulty in funding their commitment to broadcast a number of hours of original, local programming.

There are also *national* commercial channels: Northern Ireland has Ulster Television (UTV). In 2015 UTV became part of ITV plc. Wales is served by ITV Wales and S4C (Sianel Pedwar Cymru: Broadcaster for Wales), which has been funded by the BBC since 2010; and Scotland has Scottish Television (STV), the one remaining independent ITV company.

In addition, the non-commercial Community Channel is supported by the major broadcasters, and is 'dedicated to highlighting issues from the community, voluntary and charitable sector, both locally and internationally' www.communitychannel.org/info/.

OFCOM AND REGULATION

To fully understand the landscape of UK television, and the importance of the commercial public service channels, it is necessary to understand the role of the regulator. The UK's public service system continues to depend on the broadcasters conforming to certain statutory requirements, enshrined in the various Broadcasting Acts, and supervised by the regulator of the day. Just as the licence fee is intended to ensure that the government does not assert undue influence on the BBC, so regulation is intended to ensure that commercial pressures do not assert undue influence on the commercial channels. Or, as the distinguished broadcaster David Attenborough put it: '. . . the fundamental proposition that there should be broadcasting uninfluenced by either commercialism on one hand or politics on the other remains, and that's what's called public service broadcasting' (*Evening Standard* 7 September 2015).

The idea of 'regulation' is often greeted with suspicion – particularly in the popular press. Regulators – in all fields – are seen as those who lay down unnecessary rules, who stifle initiative and put limits on enterprise. For broadcasting, 'regulation' tends to be seen as negative, equivalent to 'censorship', interfering with free communication, *preventing* material from being shown. The idea of *'enabling* regulation', which ensures that a wide range of material *is* shown, seems alien. But this has been a central role of the various UK television regulators over the years.

Advocates of a free market system argue that the only regulation needed is customer satisfaction: if viewers don't like it, they'll simply turn off. Many who run television companies and find any restraint on commercial aims irksome, agree. However, a large body of opinion recognises that, left to market forces alone, certain types of audience, such as children or those seeking education, may not be served at all. In addition creative programme-makers do not always want to be limited by commercial factors. Therefore, to ensure that a wide range of programmes is available, including those that do not attract profitable audiences, the right conditions must be created by legislation and regulation. A political debate has raged for many years between those who advocate a market system and see their audience as 'customers' or 'consumers', and those who advocate a regulated public service system, which will serve a wide audience in their capacity as 'citizens'. In the 20teens, as technologies change, the role of the regulator continues to be challenged. However, it remains key to the UK public service system.

The right to broadcast on the airwaves, the radio spectrum, is granted to the BBC, ITV and Channels 4 and 5 by various Acts of Parliament which, in return, lay down certain conditions. To ensure that the broadcasting organisations stay within the law and abide by their remit, their activities are regulated by Ofcom, which grants their licence to broadcast. It is Ofcom's job to supervise a diverse range of media, including telecoms, postal services and radio as well as television (but, significantly, not the internet). It was thought that the twenty-first-century digital landscape would require less regulation, so Ofcom, which took over the role in 2003, was described as a 'light touch' regulator.

Ofcom oversees the television industry on behalf of the viewing public. One of its most important roles is to investigate viewers' complaints and hold the broadcasters to account. Its main tasks are set out on its website.

It must ensure that the *infrastructure* is in place and that:

- the United Kingdom has a wide range of electronic communications services, including high-speed services such as broadband;
- the radio spectrum (the airwaves used by everyone from taxi firms to mobile-phone companies and broadcasters) is used in the most effective way (see p. 132 to see how this affects sound recordists using radio mics).

For *programmes* on the free-to-air channels, it must ensure that:

- a wide range of high-quality television and radio programmes is provided, appealing to a range of tastes and interests;
- television and radio services are provided by a range of different organisations.

And for the *audience* its concern is that:

- people who watch television and listen to the radio, especially children, are protected from harmful or offensive material;
- people are protected from being treated unfairly in television and radio programmes, and from having their privacy invaded.

It publishes a Broadcasting Code for programme-makers, which deals with such ethical issues (2015b).

What is relevant here is that Ofcom oversees the public service system and produces regular reviews that assess how well the broadcasters have fulfilled their obligations. This is not an on-high value judgement made by the regulator, but is based on specific factors: the *amount spent* on programmes in the relevant genres; the *number* of programmes broadcast; *viewing figures*; and, importantly, a detailed *survey of audience* opinions. This means it is one of the most important sources of information on the current state of the broadcasting industries.

In its regular Public Service Reviews, Ofcom is chiefly concerned with the provision of 'public service *content'*. This is different from the broader concept of 'public service', which envisages a universal provision, offering entertainment as well as education and information, arguing that they all interact with each other. This is still an important part of the ethos that has underpinned UK broadcasting.

However, in its 2015 review, Ofcom has noted that a great deal of material which fits the objectives of public service content can be found in many forms on the internet. There are services from cultural institutions such as the Tate Gallery and the National Theatre, as well as television-like services from streaming news channels such as Vice Media and BuzzFeed (2015a para 2.13). With this change to the landscape in mind, in April 2015 it was reported that Ofcom was 'contemplating a deregulation of the television industry to reflect shifts in how people watch' (*Advanced Television* 17 April 2015 http://advanced-television.com/2015/04/17/ofcom-considering-deregulation-of-tv/).

These differences of approach are part of the important political debates that affect the structure, funding and regulation of UK broadcasting. Hence they affect everyone who works in the industry, whether for established broadcasters or, increasingly, for independent production companies.

OTHER UK-BASED CHANNELS

Some UK-based channels are not seen as part of the public service system, and not referred to as 'PSBs' although they accept Ofcom's Broadcasting Code. They include the 'families' of channels run by ITV and Channels 4 and 5. Also:

UKTV

UKTV is a group of 11 genre-specific channels. Their output is made up of reruns of BBC productions and American programmes. The content of each of the channels is indicated by their names: Drama, Good Food, Home and Yesterday – although some channels such as Alibi (crime drama), Really (reality and lifestyle programmes) and Dave (comedy) are rather more obscure. In fact, in order to attract bigger audiences, these channels have been renamed several times since their launch in 1992. They each attract a very small audience share. UKTV is half-owned by the BBC and half by the American Scripps Networks Interactive company.

Sky UK

Also UK-based are the satellite channels run by Sky UK, funded by subscription, among them Sky News, Sky 1, Sky Atlantic and Sky Arts, which broadcast a range of genres, and a number of channels from the popular Sky Sports. Sky has become a major UK broadcaster. In terms of its revenue, it is bigger than the BBC. Its UK operation began when Rupert Murdoch's News International (now called News UK) launched four channels in 1989, before merging with BSB to become BSkyB. BSkyB gradually expanded and was given a significant boost when it bought the exclusive rights to broadcast premier league football in 1992. Sky dishes sprouted on rooftops across the country. Today the broadcaster occupies a site in Isleworth, West London, with substantial buildings and studios where Sky News, Sky Sports and the rest are produced. The huge American-based parent company, News Corp, broadcasts across the globe, and News UK recently expanded across Europe, acquiring Sky Italia and Sky Deutschland in 2014. At this point the UK operation was renamed Sky UK.

Most of the channels broadcast international content, but Sky News has long been a respected competitor to BBC and ITN and accepts Ofcom guidelines (see Chapter 17 for news). In addition, Sky 1 is increasingly commissioning dramas from UK production companies, while Sky Academy is a project that supports aspirant television-makers (see Chapter 19).

INDEPENDENT PRODUCTION COMPANIES

Independent production companies are a major part of the UK television landscape. Many new entrants to the industry will find their first job with an 'indie', probably working as a freelancer and contributing to programmes for a number of different broadcasters. Channel Four commissions all its new programming from independents while the BBC and ITV must fulfil production quotas. UK independents may also make programmes for Sky and non-UK, global channels such as Discovery and Al Jazeera (see Kate Beal p. 32; Gio Ulleri p. 245). Productions range from programmes with a modest budget to high-profile productions sold to an international market.

The UK independent sector was established in the 1980s, following a vigorous campaign by filmmakers who argued that there should be space for more diverse and radical views on the television screens. In response, Channel Four was launched as a 'publisher' rather than a producer, and numerous independent companies set themselves up to provide programmes for the new outlet. Channel Four took programmes from ITV and from established filmmakers, but it also commissioned new companies, which were sometimes as small as three or four enthusiasts working from a backroom office, or a loosely knit group of campaigners with a message to get across, or possibly one of the regionally based 'workshops'. Many of those commissioned were the sort of programme-makers who would today be putting their films on YouTube or creating their own internet channels.

Many of the new companies were short-lived, but others thrived, especially when the 1990 Broadcasting Act introduced quotas for independents on the BBC and ITV. An 'independent' company was defined as one that was not owned by a broadcaster, nor linked to a broadcaster by owning shares (Ofcom 2014 para 6.51). It was a definition that would become more flexible as time went on.

Once established, the independents were soon making a major creative contribution to UK television. They were producing programmes in every genre: drama, comedy, current affairs, factual entertainment, historical documentaries – the whole range. There has been a regular exchange of talent as experienced executives, producers and technicians move between the broadcasters and the independent companies. It was the UK/Dutch company Endemol, under the charismatic producer Peter Bazalgette, which introduced *Big Brother* to Channel Four.

At first the broadcasters retained the distribution and marketing rights to the programmes they commissioned. But from 2003 the companies were allowed to keep their intellectual property and the independent sector took off. Successful marketing, overseas sales, a growing reputation and more expensive commissions began to bring in substantial profits. Meanwhile larger established media organisations began seeing UK independents as ripe for investment. One pervasive narrative over the last decade has been the tendency or need for smaller companies to merge or sell-out in the interests of survival in a market increasingly dominated by larger players.

Today, some companies are small and UK-based, such as Kate Beal's Woodcut Media (see p. 32), while others have become substantial international outfits owned by American majors. Endemol is now part of the Endemol-Shine Group, describing itself as a 'global content creator, producer and distributor with creative companies in over 30 markets'. The company is 50 percent owned by Rupert Murdoch's 21st Century Fox. Wall to Wall is owned by the Shed Media Group, based in Los Angeles and ultimately owned by the American giant Warner Brothers. Leanne Klein, who described her work researching and directing Channel Four programmes for Wall to Wall in the first edition of *The Television Handbook* (1996), was recently appointed chief executive officer (CEO) of the company.

Media commentator Mark Sweney wrote in *The Observer*: 'British indies are victims of their own success. From the makers of *Downton Abbey* and *The Voice* to *The Apprentice* and *MasterChef*, their parents are foreign giants, mostly from the United States, including NBC Universal, Warner Bros, Sony and Rupert Murdoch's 21st Century Fox' (10 August 2014). The trade press now divides the independents into the smaller *micro-indies*; the larger *super-indies*, created when the smaller companies engage in partnerships or mergers; and finally, the *mega-indies*, created when a super-indie is acquired by an international broadcaster or distributor.

This situation has led to considerable debate about the role of production companies that are no longer 'independent' but are part of global organisations bigger than the broadcasters themselves. 'While UK production is an undoubted commercial success story, I wonder if it will continue to be a creative one. Scale demands an increased focus on cost cutting and margins', said David Abraham, chief executive of Channel Four, in a speech to the Edinburgh Television Festival in 2014. And a senior industry executive added: 'There is also the question of national identity. People are now looking for international hits: in some ways, you create the sort of content that doesn't work precisely for the home nation.'

In a survey published in 2012, James Bennett and his colleagues discussed the 'compact' between the UK broadcasters, especially the BBC and Channel Four who are committed to public service, and the independent sector. On the one hand, when they interviewed a range of people working for large independents, they reported that, from company directors to producers and researchers, most of them valued public service principles. These act as a motivation and affect 'the kinds of content produced, the kinds of content producers want to make, and the way in which it is made' (p. 11). But, on the other hand, the report concludes that increasing commercial pressures are making that compact increasingly fragile. As the broadcasters face cuts in budgets, and the independents become part of larger conglomerates, there is more emphasis on safe formats and international sales (pp. 28–31).

In response to the growing power of the independents, the broadcasters are beginning to behave like independents themselves. ITV has been buying up American production companies in what John Ellis described as a 'spending spree' (2014 CST blog), while the BBC has changed the BBC production department into a separate company, called BBC Studios. Director General Tony Hall argued that 'this is to combat the "domination" of programme making in the hands of a small group of super-producers' www.bbc.co.uk/mediacentre/speeches/2014/dg-city-university.

From the point of view of those who make the programmes, like so much in the current television picture, the story of independent producers is a story of the very small and the very large. As Giovanni Ullieri writes, as a self-shooting journalist-producer he usually works alone, or with one other person. As a freelancer he was employed by Wall to Wall for the series *Drugs Inc*, broadcast on the National Geographic channel. Ultimately he, as an individual programme-maker, is working for Wall to Wall's parent company, the American giant Warner Brothers (see below, p. 245).

So, in this competitive global context, is the familiar landscape of UK television disappearing? Is it possible to sustain a commitment to public service across the board? Perhaps we need not be concerned, since a wide range of programming in many genres reaches our screens, and the smaller, UK-based independents still have an important presence. Below Kate Beal describes her experiences setting up and running the UK-based Woodcut Media. Then in the following chapter we will consider the phenomenon of globalisation and the multichannel, landscape.

FIGURE 3.1
Filming for a series with travelling magician 'Magical Bones' in Seoul, South Korea.
Courtesy Woodcut Media

PROFILE

Kate Beal: Woodcut Media

Kate Beal is the CEO and joint creative director of Woodcut Media, which she set up in 2014. The company makes documentaries and factual programmes for UK and international broadcasters.

'I went to York University, where I did a degree in Politics and English, but I've actually been working in television since I was 15! My mother worked at Meridian (the ITV company that held the franchise to broadcast to the South and Southeast of England from 1993), so I got to do work experience there. I remember helping out on a local access programme called *Freescreen*, a late night show. Of course, that couldn't happen now, as no-one under 18 can be alone with a member of staff who hasn't been CRB-checked (i.e. checked by the Criminal Records Bureau to confirm that they don't have a record and pose no threat to a young person). That means that although I'm a strong believer in young people doing work experience, we can't employ anyone until they are 18.

When I started I did numerous runners' jobs. I worked on *Countdown to Christmas with Maggie Philbin* and at one point I looked after Esther Rantzen's handbag. Later I had the brief of befriending the 13-year-old actress, Brooke Kinsella, in *No Child of Mine* (1997), who played a child who had been abused, in a docu-drama directed by Peter Kosminsky. Peter Kosminsky later got me a job as a runner, then third assistant director (AD) on a drama called *Walking on the Moon* (1999) for Meridian. I gained a great deal of experience and became a series producer at Meridian by the age of 25, when I produced *Firefighters* in 2003. I've worked on both documentaries and drama, but, as time went on, I felt I had to choose. I'd always been more interested in factual – basically because I wanted to make a difference.

In 2005, when Meridian was taken over by ITV plc, I decided to start my own company and take on some of Meridian's factual output. There was no need for bank loans as I used my redundancy money to buy the kit – three cameras and an edit suite – and to rent an office. I called it KMB (my initials) and was able to take on some of the other redundant staff. We had two commissions for ITV Meridian, as the local station was now called. These were *Pets and Their Vets*, which is still sold internationally, and a gardening show, *Coming Up Roses*.

It was a time when the indies' terms of trade were changing. They were now allowed to keep the intellectual property (IP) rights to the programmes they produced, whereas previously those rights had belonged to the broadcasters who had commissioned the programmes. That meant that independent companies could make a bigger profit by marketing their programmes and by selling them to more than one broadcaster. This was when many of the companies began to grow much larger – some of them very large indeed (see p. 28 for more about indies). The broadcasters are pulling back a bit now. They're beginning to distinguish between smaller and larger independent companies.

In 2008 I was approached by Talent Television, based in London, who offered to buy the company as they were expanding their business. They said 'we don't just want the company, we want you'! I agreed and we became Talent South. For the next few years I produced numerous programmes and series. In 2014 Talent was restructuring, so I relaunched Talent South as Woodcut Media, and hired Derren Lawford, who was a commissioner at London Live and had been online producer for BBC3's *Our War*. Independent companies like ours tend to specialise in either factual or drama, and we have always specialised in factual. Our investor, a media advisory firm called Bob and Co, recently launched another company, Duchess Street Productions, which specialises in drama.

As Talent South and as Woodcut, we've made a number of documentaries. We produced *Mandela, My Dad and Me* with Idris Elba; *The Krays: The Prison Years* for Discovery; *Tina Malone: Pregnant at 50* for TLC; and a ten-part series about the airfields that saved Britain. What do I look for in a programme idea? At one level the first question is 'will this sell?' But really it's the story. I like to learn something, and I want to know what format works best for the story. Is this story serious or does it work in an entertaining way? I'm currently thinking of ideas for factual entertainment.

I take many roles. Basically I'm a producer, but I'm also a storyteller, a project manager and a business person. I'm good at the business side. On many of my shows, such as *Firefighters*, I was also the director, and when we did a twenty-part series, *Children's Ward*, in 2002 I did the filming as well. After all, I'm of that generation when cameras became smaller and more access-ible – and I was self-tutored. I suppose I was among the first of the new guard.

The programmes sometimes have websites and other supplementary material, but these are controlled by the channel and not by the indie. Sometimes there are separate teams. Commissioners don't expect the production companies to provide the second screen stuff.

I find that British broadcasters value creativity more, but 60 per cent of our commissions come from the international channels who tend to be a bit more rigid in their requirements. I think that plurality must be maintained in television production.

PROFILE

So, my career has gone from runner to researcher, to assistant producer with some filming, to television directing, location directing, producer/director, series producer and now executive producer. I'm multiskilled: I can carry out an in-depth interview, and do camera or research – but I can also do budgets and organise the business side.

In my view people aspiring to enter the profession need to know what it is they want to do. At Woodcut we take students on work experience, and, when they're with us, it's the real world. First they send us their CV, then we interview them. They usually stay for one or two weeks and during that time they're a valuable member of the team. There's no point in doing work experience if what you do doesn't matter. We pay their travel – I believe in equal opportunities and I don't just want to employ rich kids. I have also employed some students on zero-hours contracts as occasional runners and that sort of thing. I was paid as a student, and I believe in paying. And students have moved on to full-time jobs in the industry. In fact one of them went straight from us to a job at the Disney Channel'.

KEY TEXTS

Bennett, J., Kerr, P., Strange, N. and Medrado, A. (2012) *Multiplatforming Public Service Broadcasting: The Economic and Cultural Role of UK Digital and TV Independents*, http://eprints.bournemouth.ac.uk/21021/1/bennett-strange-kerr-medrado-2012-multiplatforming-psb-industry-report.pdf.
Ofcom (2015a) *Public Service Broadcasting in the Internet Age: Ofcom's Third Review of Public Service Broadcasting*, London: Ofcom.
Tunstall, J. (2015) *The BBC and Television Genres in Jeopardy*, Bern: Peter Lang.

CHAPTER 4

The contemporary landscape: globalisation, multichannel and multiplatform

GLOBALISATION AND MULTICHANNEL

Globalisation is the most significant factor in the television landscape of the 20teens. Of course, television has always looked beyond the UK's borders. A Mickey Mouse cartoon was the first programme when television restarted in 1946; *Dallas* and *Dynasty* helped define the 1980s, well before 'Nordic noir' caught the imagination of the 20teens. And the United Kingdom has produced programmes, from *Dr Who* to *Teletubbies*, which have been marketed across the world. Since *Brideshead Revisited* and before, dramas that exude 'Britishness' have been made with an eye on the international market. But today a globalised landscape is a multichannel landscape. Increasingly, over the 2000s, viewers have gained access to hundreds of television and internet channels that circulate the globe with little respect for territorial boundaries. They arrive on our screens via digital satellite and cable technology, and by streaming on the internet, targeted at a global audience. It is difficult to see television as a self-contained national industry controlled by national legislation when global players such as Google, Amazon, Apple and Netflix are providing easily accessible streams of content.

When we discuss globalisation from the point of view of production, we must also bear in mind that most prestigious UK series could not be made without co-production money, and that many UK companies are ultimately owned by American/global conglomerates. 'There has been a gradual shift in the balance of power, away from the broadcasters towards the global producers', wrote the BBC

Trust in its review of its supply of programmes (2015 para 2.1.4). As quoted in the previous chapter, Jeremy Tunstall recently drew attention to changes at ITV, which 'may be in danger of losing some of its UK identity by doing so much importing of made-in-USA productions, by owning Hollywood independent production companies and by participating in high-profile ITV-US co-productions' (Tunstall 2015: 36).

Reviewing the television landscape, we can consider three major aspects of globalisation: content, ownership and influence.

Content: Channels based outside the United Kingdom, beyond UK regulation, are part of our regular viewing diet. Hollywood has around twenty major television networks, each of which has numerous channels, most of which are available in the United Kingdom. In addition, an increasing number of American programmes are shown on UK channels as well as a large number of co-productions. Jeremy Tunstall estimates that 'made in US programming takes up 40 percent of UK audience viewing time' (2015: 62). Series such as *Breaking Bad* and *Game of Thrones* are an important part of the UK television experience. In addition, non-Western channels including Al-Jazeera and Russia Today (RT) can be accessed on Freeview, giving an alternative perspective on the news. Globalisation also means internet access across the globe. YouTube videos from the Middle East and other conflict zones can give an immediate insight, and are drawn on by the mainstream news channels.

Ownership is of prime importance. Some of the most important UK media organisations are American-owned or part-American-owned, while British television organisations, such as ITV, are buying American companies. Huge multinational corporations have long been anxious to buy into the UK television market. Since the Thatcher government of the 1980s, a conviction that the global free market is the way forward has meant that restrictions on foreign ownership have been progressively lifted. This is why Sky UK can be ultimately controlled by 21st Century Fox, the American company owned by the media mogul Rupert Murdoch, even though he also owns 33 per cent of the national newspaper circulation – owning the prestigious *Times* and *Sunday Times* as well as the populist *Sun*. Murdoch owns 39 per cent of Sky UK and has made no secret of his desire to take over the whole outfit. Indeed, he almost achieved this with the agreement of the UK government in 2013, if the scandal over serious wrongdoing by his newspaper, the *News of the World* had not intervened, leading to the closure of that paper (Davies 2014).

Across the rest of the UK television landscape, the monopoly cable distributor Virgin is American-owned, UKTV is half-American-owned, while Channel 5 is owned by the global media giant Viacom. In addition, seven of the biggest 'independent' UK production companies are also owned by American majors, while 'Google and other American internet companies have a huge impact on the British media and UK scene', writes Jeremy Tunstall, who points out that American-owned companies account for around 28 per cent of all UK viewing (2015: 60, 62).

Influence: Ironically, the 'free market' has led to a concentration of ownership, and this has given rise to issues around plurality. There is concern over the political power potentially exercised by the powerful corporations that own a significant proportion of the UK media, if only because the government fears to offend them. The example of Rupert Murdoch illustrates this, as his newspapers are strident in their political views and their desire to influence public opinion.

There are also issues around plurality of content. When owners are competing for the biggest audiences and the highest revenues, they will tend to produce the same, most popular, genres and avoid minority, experimental or oppositional spaces.

Jeremy Tunstall has pointed out that both Hollywood and Silicon Valley (i.e. American/ global companies involved in programme production and marketing, and companies involved in digital innovation) have chosen London as a 'hub location for their global strategies', including advertising, international law and political lobbying. He writes: 'London is no longer a world media and TV hub, but is rapidly becoming a colonial media outpost of the United States (Tunstall 2015: 2). On the whole, as far as the UK media are concerned, globalisation means American domination. This is true for content, ownership and influence.

ONLINE AND MULTIPLATFORM

The online screenscape is an important part of the television landscape in the twenty-first century, both from the point of view of the audience and the programme-makers. We have moved beyond multichannel to multiplatform. Here, too, the very small is balanced against the very large. A click of the mouse may take the viewer from a major Hollywood production, streamed via Netflix, to a YouTube video made by a 15-year-old who thought it would be fun to do. The global scope of the internet offers a platform both for multinational media giants and for new companies set up on a shoestring. And, like television production companies, when internet producers become successful, they too may become part of a global conglomerate.

Although internet-based media are distinct from television, a review of the television landscape would be incomplete without considering the role of online material. The internet expands the scope of television in three ways: first, as a *distribution* facility, enabling programmes made for television to be viewed through streaming on a variety of platforms, including tablets and mobile phones; second, as a *supplement* to popular programmes, expanding on them and providing extra material – videos, interviews, updates interactive fan sites and more. These are the *paratexts* that interact with the main programme (Gray 2010 and see Chapter 5 for more on paratexts). Third, there is the *television-like* material made for the internet, including videos made for YouTube as well as dedicated websites. Internet filmmakers range from YouTube stars such as Zoella and PewDiePie, to local community groups. They may have little relationship to mainstream television.

Of course, the online landscape includes a vast amount of material provided by the established UK broadcasters. The BBC has its own YouTube channel, and has set up initiatives such as *The Space*, an online digital arts project that the Corporation runs together with Arts Council England (www.thespace.org/), and BBC Taster that previews experimental ideas (www.bbc.co.uk/taster/about). As part of the *distribution* function of the internet, programmes from all UK channels are available for catch-up viewing, streamed on All 4, BBC iPlayer, ITV Hub, UKTV Play and the rest.

However, video on demand (VoD) also gives access to a wide range of global programming. A subscription to Netflix, Now TV, YouView or one of the other services buys access to a library of cinema films from across the world as well as highly popular international television series. Increasingly these distributors are also becoming producers as they commission new series, such as Netflix's *House of Cards*. This was one of the first times a television-like series was not premiered on linear TV. It is a trend that is likely to be followed by the broadcasters. New programmes and series are likely to be made available online first, or even exclusively, especially following the move online of BBC3. BBC Director General Tony Hall is on record as saying that the iPlayer could become the 'front door' for BBC content rather than just a catch-up service (*Guardian* 5 April 2014). Channel Four's All 4 mixes catch-up with exclusive content, including live streaming and premieres of shows such as *Made in Chelsea* before they're broadcast on television.

Twitter has made a major contribution to audience interaction. A *Radio Times* survey in October 2015 showed *The X Factor* as topping the list of most-tweeted (*Radio Times* 27 October 2015). Factual entertainment followed, with a considerable number of tweeters debating *The Apprentice* and *Made in Chelsea*. 'Tweets can change what happens the next week, because we're influenced by what the tweeters say,' said Stephen Lambert, producer of *Gogglebox*. 'Now we can feel the audience's reaction, second by second.' But politics also engaged the tweeters: the BBC's *Question Time* was also on the most-tweeted list.

This type of 'cross-media consumption', using more than one medium simultaneously, is increasingly important. As far back as 2006, Mark Thompson, then Director General of the BBC, pronounced during a Royal Television Society Lecture: 'We can deliver much more public value when we think in a 360 degree way, rather than focusing separately on different platforms or channels. Wherever possible we need to think cross-platform: in our commissioning, our making, our distribution.'

Online content that runs alongside broadcast programmes is often supplied by independent digital companies who are commissioned to work in parallel to the programme-makers. However, as James Bennett and his colleagues found, collaboration may be problematic because of the different cultures and time-scales of the two disciplines. Whereas for a broadcast programme everything builds up to the transmission date, the online material has a longer life span, and may continue to be developed over time (2012). We will look more closely at the interaction between texts and paratexts in Chapter 5.

The online landscape also includes a great deal of *television-like* factual material, including live-streaming, with reports of news and current events and numerous celebrity items. These are found on the websites of major newspapers, as well as in online channels such as Vice Media and BuzzFeed, two companies that have moved from small beginnings to global prominence. Vice Media began as a print magazine in Montreal and is now a multimedia network based in New York. It produces a suite of channels covering a number of genres, such as sport and food. Its news channel, Vice News, produces long-form journalism, and, by commissioning filmmakers from around the world, is able to cover stories the broadcasters will not touch. These include a Middle East report from behind the lines of Al-Qaeda, and *The Road to Mosul*, which followed the Kurdish peshmerger forces as they tried to resist Islamic State (IS/Daesh). When Ofcom reported that 'public service content' is available beyond the broadcasters, the media regulator quoted BuzzFeed and Vice Media, as well as online channels run by charities and arts organisations, such as Tate Britain and the National Theatre (2015a para 2.13).

Independent filmmakers today, the inheritors of the radical and independent sectors who campaigned for Channel Four in the 1970s, are likely to be involved in small production companies, making films for the arts or voluntary sectors, distributed both on DVD and the internet. Little Fish Films, for example, based in Bristol and South London, specialises in video projects for artists and performers, as well as local community and health groups. It partners with local councils, the Environment Agency and other community groups. (The People's Voice web channel describes itself as 'news the mainstream doesn't broadcast'.)

A major contribution to the online landscape is, of course, YouTube, which can act both as an outlet for new work, and as an archive, a depository for previously broadcast material. Anyone can upload a one-off video onto YouTube, or can decide to create a continuing 'channel'. Some celebrated YouTubers have built up huge followings for their blogs and personal videos, frequently by just sharing their thoughts with whoever cares to click on them. The personal diary format was devised by the BBC's Community Programme Unit when they gave cameras to ordinary people to record their everyday lives (Oakley and Lee-Wright 2016). Today's diarists may have begun as unknowns, but many have become major celebrities and have built up a substantial income from their work. Zoe Sugg, known as Zoella, is among many diarists who have founded lucrative businesses based around their YouTube presence, as is Felix Kjellberg, known as PewDiePie. Reportedly his YouTube gained 10 billion views in September 2015 – many of them watching him playing video games www.tubefilter.com/2015/09/06/pewdiepie-youtube-10-billion-views/ (*Guardian* 22 October 2015).

A number of companies, known as multichannel networks (MCNs), have been set up to act as agents for YouTubers, promoting them and seeking out sponsors. Some MCNs specialise in content areas, for example, DanceOn for the dance community, while others are more general http://digiday.com/publishers/wtf-mcn/.

'Fans and hobbyists are the new publishers,' claims Maker Studios, an MCN that specialises in videos for children and young people. Its promotion states that this is 'the next generation media company' as it represents small-scale creators. It argues that 'content should not be restricted to one destination' so its marketing programmes are worldwide. In 2014, Maker Studios was bought by the American giant Disney, which meant that it was able to access Disney material. 'What a difference a year makes,' said Maker's president Ynon Kreiz. 'Being part of the Walt Disney Company, the world's largest media organization, has given us access to some of the most beloved brands and franchises in the universe' http://variety.com/2015/digital/news/newfronts-2015-maker-studios-to-tout-disney-synergies-with-marvel-espn-alliances-1201481222/.

Once more the very small individual creators have become linked to one of the largest of all global media companies.

KEY TEXTS

Iosifidis, P. (2016) 'Media ownership and concentration in the United Kingdom' in E. Noam (ed.) *Who Owns the World's Media*, Oxford: OUP.
Ofcom (2015a) *Public Service Broadcasting in the Internet Age: Ofcom's Third Review of Public Service Broadcasting*, London: Ofcom (July 2015).
Tunstall, J. (2015) *The BBC and Television Genres in Jeopardy*, Bern: Peter Lang.

CHAPTER 5

The landscape of television in the United Kingdom: text

THE AGE OF SUPERABUNDANCE: INTERSTITIALS AND PARATEXTS

The changing institutional landscape has brought an age of superabundance, both in broadcast television itself and in the expanding online media, which affects and interacts with broadcast programmes at every point. In Chapters 3 and 4 we considered the *institutional aspects* of this contemporary media landscape. Now we will look at the media *text* – the content available in these screen-based worlds that interweave with our own. In some ways the linear *flow* of visual and aural content scheduled by the broadcasters is more important than it ever has been. As well as the programmes, it includes advertisements, channel idents, trailers, sponsors' messages and other material, much of it associated with branding (together known as the *interstitials*), which all contribute to the viewing experience. Yet, at the same time, linear television is becoming irrelevant. Content is dispersed. No longer confined to the sequential flow, it is available on a range of platforms and screens and can be selected and reorganised by the viewer (Johnson 2012: 165). Some argue that the material that supplements and accompanies the texts is becoming as important as the programmes themselves (Gray 2010). Websites, books, DVDs, games and numerous other products (collectively known as the *paratexts*) enhance and interact with the television experience. The television flow continues to overflow. This means that we must consider the television output itself, but also reconsider the definition of a 'programme'.

In this chapter we will also give an overview of the *genres* that make up the output in this superabundant age. We will note that genres established in the early days of television are still strong, and they reflect something of their history, especially as an increasing number of outlets make classic programmes from the archive easily available. For those working in television, the culture of news will be very different from the culture of drama or comedy. However, genres are constantly mutating and evolving, and they tend to overlap and interact. For example, there are many comedy programmes that reflect and comment on the news, while the hybrid 'factual entertainment' has become a dominant contemporary genre. We give an account of the major genres below and will be looking more closely at some of the most important in Part 3 of this book.

THE LINEAR FLOW: SCHEDULING AND BRANDING

Interstitials and the linear flow

When BBC television began in the 1940s, programmes were seen as separate events and there were restful breaks between them. These were the 'Interludes' when the screen was filled with gentle images such as goldfish floating lazily around in their bowl. The 1950s brought commercial television, where the gaps between programmes were filled with lively advertisements, often as attractive as the programmes themselves. Developing competition between two channels meant that each channel strove to keep viewers hooked into the flow of *their* channel, rather than thinking 'let's see what's on the other side'. *Scheduling* became important. By the 20teens, now that competition has intensified beyond the imagination of those early schedulers, organising the flow has become crucial for the linear channels. Today gaps between and within the programmes are filled by numerous eye-catching events, all aiming to grab the viewer's attention. These interstitials are of several types, each with a specific purpose. *Advertisements* and sponsors' messages promote their wares and, importantly, finance their channel, as they take up an increasing amount of air time. *Channel identifications* brand their channels and aim to promote viewer loyalty. *Trailers* and *promotional material* attract viewers to future programmes, while eye-catching *opening sequences* are designed to hook them in and ensure that they do not turn off or switch channels. Overall, the interstitials provide what Catherine Johnson described as a 'continuous flow of "promotainment"' (2012: 155). Producing a flow of programmes, paced through the day, with promotional interstitial material that will keep a reasonably sized audience tuned to your channel, while bearing in mind what rival channels are showing, is an art in itself.

Scheduling and the flow

In 1974, the great cultural critic Raymond Williams described the *flow* of programmes as 'perhaps the defining characteristic of broadcasting, simultaneously as a technology and as a cultural form' (Williams 1974, Chapter 4). Television has been distinguished by its time-based linear nature, respecting the progression of the hours, marking the movement of the day from breakfast chat to late night satire and adult comedy. And, despite on-demand and catch-up viewing, to a large extent this cultural pattern remains.

Linear channels organise the day with a range of different genres across the schedule. In the early days, broadcasts were only in the evenings, but as the hours of transmission were expanded to include first afternoons, then mornings, new genres were evolved to suit the new time slots. 'Housewife-friendly' soap operas were launched in the afternoons, and topical chat on the breakfast-time sofa became a familiar way to start the day. Despite its low prestige, it has been in this flow of 'everyday television' in the off-peak hours that many characteristically televisual approaches have evolved. They include the development of the presenter as a friend, with a relaxed and easy address directly to the audience; the celebrity interview, often referring to other programmes in the schedule; the low key, continuous format, mixing conversation and entertainment, with weak boundaries between items.

In the mid-1990s, Steve Morrison, Managing Director of London Weekend Television, described ITV's schedule thus:

> Like the architecture of a house, the viewer can watch *This Morning* in the kitchen, *Coronation Street* with the family in the living room; later the kids go off to bed and Mum and Dad settle down to strong narrative drama at nine; *News at Ten* is there for the late working professional and the set's still on in the bedroom after 10.30 for the teenage kids.
>
> (Hargrave 1995: 120)

In the 20teens, this strongly built house is becoming more like a flexible space with sliding doors leading in all directions. However, much of this description still holds true.

Until the late 1980s the channels had ambled along together more or less amiably, but as channels multiplied and the competitive market culture caught hold, things changed. When he was Controller of Programmes at BBC1, Michael Grade acquired a reputation for 'aggressive scheduling', defined by Jeremy Bugler, at the time Editor of LWT's *London Programme*, as the 'law' that says:

> The scheduler should pitch his most popular programmes against his opponents weakest. He (*sic*) will then scoop the pool and possibly ruin his opponent's ratings for the rest of the evening
>
> (*Guardian* 15 August 1985)

Alternatively, schedulers may compete by putting like against like, or they may give audiences the benefit of complementarity, allowing the viewer to follow their favourite genre across the channels. The BBC was recently strongly criticised for competing, by scheduling *Strictly Come Dancing* against ITV's *The X-Factor*.

However, 'Viewers aren't as loyal to a channel as they were 10 years ago, so big titles, topicality and genres that are a little unexpected are likely to hit the sweet spot for us', Channel Four's head of Drama, Piers Wenger, told *Broadcast* magazine in January 2016 (14 January 2016), 'there's a sense of event . . . and a need to watch them live.' Ever since 1955, when *Sunday Night at the London Palladium* became the weekly blockbuster for the ITV network, it has been recognised that audiences respond to 'events'. Schedulers still aim to create 'appointment viewing' for their block-buster shows. *Strictly Come Dancing, The X-Factor, The Great British Bake-Off, The Apprentice, I'm a Celebrity: Get Me Out of Here* are just a few of those that have captured substantial audiences in the 20teens. Crucially, viewers are invited to interact with the programmes, and affect their outcome, through voting either by telephone or online. In addition, all of them are backed up by numerous websites, Twitter feeds and articles in newspapers and magazines, as well as spin-off programmes throughout the week. 'Creating paratexts is a key task for media producers' writes Jonathan Gray (2010: 207). It all helps to build the tension and draw in the audiences for the main event.

Although this scheduled structure is largely still in place on the main terrestrial channels, within the multichannel landscape the arrival of genre-specific channels has created a different pattern. Children no longer had to be catered for on Saturday mornings and in the space between school and bedtime, when CBeebies could run from 6am to 7pm and the Disney Channel was available at any time of the day and night. In the age of superabundance, streaming channels, on-demand viewing and DVDs can be viewed at any time. Rather than being paced in weekly episodes, an indulgent day of binge viewing can run through a whole series of *Mad Men* or *The Sopranos* at one sitting. In this situation 'flow' has gained a different meaning. Flow has become overflow.

As viewing has fragmented, and as competition has intensified in the age of super-abundance, broadcasters have needed to make greater efforts to attract viewers to their channels through various devices, including the use of branding and interstitials.

Branding and promotional material

'Branding is not simply a means of financially exploiting programmes. Rather it can be understood as a response to the new conditions emerging with the television industry', writes Catherine Johnson (2012: 165).

As the television landscape became more competitive, more attention was applied to promoting the distinctive qualities of each of the channels, and their brands were promoted across families of channels as well as in marketing spin-offs, such as books and DVDs. Graphic design had long made an important contribution to the television experience, but the arrival of digital technologies brought innovative station idents such as Channel Four's children's bricks flying though three-dimensional space and the extraordinary 2s that metamorphosed into squidgy toys or metallic objects that marked BBC2. These were the forerunners of the complex sequences of the 20teens, such as Channel Four's exploration of landscapes – rocky coast-lines, dock-side cranes, council estates – which miraculously reconfigure themselves into the figure 4. Although Channel Four's newest design smashes the famous 4 symbol into pieces, 4s and 2s continue to serve the function of branding, while at the same time entertaining and amusing the viewers (see Chapter 14 for more on visual effects).

Programmes of a certain type are frequently branded by being grouped under a series title. Channel Four has *Dispatches* for current affairs, while the BBC groups major international documentaries under the heading of *Storyville*. They mark out the kind of programme viewers can expect at that point in the schedule. The disadvantage, loudly voiced by some programme-makers, is that programme editors come to expect a more standardised product. Themed seasons, such as recent seasons on the First World War and the BBC's 2015 *Make it Digital* season, are a way of grouping a varied range of formats – dramas, documentaries, infotainment – together. The one-off programme made outside a strand or a familiar series is now a rare creature.

Popular programmes are now themselves treated as 'brands', promoted across a range of merchandise and developing across several media. Catherine Johnson writes: 'The broadcast text is just one aspect of a more dynamic and open-ended context of production and consumption for programme brands that have a much longer life across a far wider range of texts' (2012: 165).

(The BBC's obsession with branding was mocked by the comedy *W1A*. In one episode, brand advisers were happy to reduce the initials 'BBC' to a mere 'lll'. In 2016 this actually happened when BBC3 online became lll!)

As programme brands proliferate across the screenscape and beyond, numerous related experiences cluster around a broadcast programme or series, sometimes becoming as important as the 'tentpole' programme itself (Gray 2010). These are the *paratexts* that we will consider in the following section.

CROSS-PLATFORM, PARATEXTS AND INTERACTIVITY

The *paratexts* and extra materials created by the broadcasters to enhance their programmes make a major contribution to the contemporary television experience. Back in 2000, *Big Brother* was a pioneer of the cross-platform format, when it first confined a group of 'ordinary people' to the 'Big Brother house' and placed them under 24-hour surveillance. Its nightly transmission on Channel Four was a conventionally edited half-hour programme, made up of material selected from events in the previous 24 hours. Meanwhile E4 offered four broadcast options: 24-hour live coverage; live with a ten-minute delay; events from two hours ago or events from four hours ago. Then there was live streaming on the web. In addition, viewers could receive SMS texts on their mobiles, and were invited to vote by telephone which house member to evict. This was the way forward for television in the new millennium, declared producer Peter Bazalgette: a big event, exploited on many media, involving audience interaction (Royal Television Society speech 2001). His message was taken up with enthusiasm by the broadcasters. 'Event TV' continues to draw its audience to the live programme (more than 12 million people watched the final of *Strictly Come Dancing* in December 2015) and has multiplied the number of websites, related programmes, celebrity interviews, glimpses behind the scenes and other spin-offs, ranging from the traditional to the most current. *Big Brother* itself, currently on Channel 5, gained new formats with *Celebrity Big Brother*; *Big Brother's Little Brother* and *Big Brother's Big Mouth.*

In his book on paratexts, Jonathan Gray argues that they should not simply be seen as supplementary to a programme, since, in many cases, they have become as important as the programme itself. In every case, paratexts are in *dialogue* with a text and affect its meaning and how it is interpreted. He argues that they negotiate between the industry, which sees them as promotional material and a source of finance, the text, and the audience (2010: 23). He distinguishes three types of paratext:

Entryway. Trailers, interviews, newspaper items, which *prepare* an audience for viewing a text (p. 35). These include the opening credits, which indicate the genre, character and tone of a programme and prepare the viewers for what they will be watching (p. 73).

In media res (Latin for 'in the middle of things'). This includes parallel websites, related programmes, Twitter feeds, including material created by viewers and performers. This interaction with participants is especially important in 'constructed factual' programmes. Viewers are often expected to watch more than one screen simultaneously, in what Gray describes as an 'intertextual dialogue'. Programmes such as *The Only Way is Essex* spill over into the web pages of the participants, discussing their activities and promoting their personal merchandise. Medical programmes such as *Embarrassing Bodies* are presented on television in a light-hearted way, but are accompanied online by reliable medical advice, including health tips for teenagers and a health checker.

Discussing *Lost*, a long-running fictional series with a highly complex plot, Jonathan Gray describes how regular viewers turn to the internet to see how it's interpreted by others. 'The fan community pools its knowledge' (p. 136).

Textual overflow. A show does not stop when the screening ends. The websites and commentary continue. Programmes are remembered through repeats and DVDs as well as sequels. As some series run for a very long time and are regularly reprised, some fan communities have a long life. Henry Jenkins, who has studied fandom for many years, describes websites created by individual fans and fan communities running parallel to particular programmes (2012). Such viewer-created paratexts include fan art, fan sites, fan fiction, videos and other creative material.

In discussing 'unofficial' fan-created paratexts, Gray suggests that fan fiction, fan art and fan video are capable of 'challenging or supplementing those created by the industry' and 'carving out alternative pathways through texts' (2010: 143). For Henry Jenkins, fans 'cease to be simply an audience for popular texts; instead, they become active participants in the construction and circulation of meanings' (1992: 23–4).

ABOUT GENRES

Television programmes are conveniently classified into genres. It is a classification which, on the one hand, structures the organisation of production and, on the other, indicates to viewers the nature of the programme they are about to see. Jonathan Gray argues that a genre provides a 'set of rules for interpreting a text' (2010: 50). Each genre has its own style, its own norms, its own grammar of programme-making, its own history and culture. On the one hand, television genres are based on rules and conventions that are rooted in the history of the medium, but on the other, they have evolved and changed over the years. An important factor in locating a genre is who appears on the screen and in what capacity. Each has its own range of on-screen personalities: who may be actors, journalists, presenters or sports people. At the same time, with the increasing importance of celebrity, prominent figures in all genres appear across a range of programmes: news readers, musicians, comedians appear on panel shows and quizzes, learn to dance on *Strictly Come Dancing*, or are abandoned in the jungle in *I'm a Celebrity: Get Me Out of Here*. Discussions of popular programmes spread across the schedule in endless self-reference, as soap opera actors go on chat shows to discuss how their character is doing, comics do impersonations of other television personalities, contestants in game shows discuss their success or failure in a range of spin-off programmes, while competing programmes trade sly digs with each other.

However, within the broadcast organisations, programme-makers tend to work in genre-based departments that also function as career ladders. In his recent book on genres and their producers, Jeremy Tunstall wrote that they continue to inhabit a 'genre-specific' world, where the tone and policy tends to be set by the head of the relevant department (2015: 16). The skills and approaches involved for each genre are different and production teams work to different timetables. Those who work in news departments see themselves as journalists with a daily turnaround: they look to the press and other news media. Those who work in drama tend to be part of networks with links to the theatre and feature film industries. Their production timetables extend over months.

Within each of the departments, established genres are recognised, which are common not only to television but also to cinema, book publishing and other cultural forms. Familiarity with a genre means building up a set of expectations about style and content, both on the part of the producers and their regular audience. Certain conventions are recognised, like the audience laughter punctuating a sitcom.

In addition, there are many subgenres with their own conventions: for example, fantasy need not stick to the natural rules of the biological world – indeed a series such as *Doctor Who* relishes breaking them. On the other hand, a courtroom drama would be ruined if strict logic were not followed in the sequence of cause and effect (for more on drama and narrative, see Chapter 15).

Although the genres appear distinct, over their history the ways in which they have been organised has constantly changed in response to changing tastes and needs. In the 1950s the BBC had a Women's Programmes Unit, which was abolished in the 1960s in favour of a Family Programmes Department (Leman 1987). Specialised units have been created, such as the BBC's Disability Programme Unit (1998–2002) and Asian Programmes Unit (1965–2009). Both Channel Four and the BBC have branched into cinema: Channel Four launched Film4 in the 1980s, the BBC followed with Screen 2. In today's converged, digital universe, genres are aware of each other and often overlap into each other's territory, as the recent emergence of 'factual entertainment' demonstrates.

While most of the satellite and cable channels are genre-specific, the main terrestrial UK broadcasters are expected to provide a wide range of genres. However, because of increasing competition, there is pressure on the broadcasters to neglect genres that cater for smaller audiences. In his recent survey, Jeremy Tunstall noted a number of 'public service' genres that are in decline (see p. 51).

Below we give an overview of genres that are part of the contemporary television landscape, outlining four main categories: drama, news, entertainment and factual, noting some of the prominent subgenres. In Part 3 we discuss some important genres in greater detail from the point of view of those who make them.

OVERVIEW OF THE MAIN TELEVISION GENRES

Drama includes single dramas, series, serials and soap operas.

Programmes that are classified as drama are normally scripted and performed by actors. They include:

- One-off dramas, although single dramas are now very rare.
- *Serials*, which have a given number of episodes. The plot develops across the episodes and resolves at the end.
- *Drama series*: have tended to return over three to five years, sometimes much longer. Plots may be contained in a single episode, or may continue across a series. Either way the basic situation leaves open the possibility of another series.
- *Serials and series* are themselves subdivided into many subgenres, each with its own conventions and audience expectations. These include police

series, medical series, fantasy/sci-fi series, adaptations, costume dramas and more.

- *Soap operas*, known as continuing drama. Several episodes a week follow the daily lives of a number of characters, and develop in real time over many years.

(See Chapter 15 for more on drama.)

News and current affairs are journalist-led. They include daily bulletins and 24-hour news channels. In addition, news departments tend to produce:

- *News magazines*, including programmes such as *Newsnight*, which offer background to the news in the form of short filmed reports and discussions with reporters, experts and protagonists.
- *Current affairs*, described as 'long-form journalism', it occupies a space between news and documentary. It includes regular investigatory series such as *Panorama*, and documentary-style current affairs as in *Dispatches*.
- Series such as *Question Time* and *Crimewatch*, which have news-based content.

(See Chapter 17 for more on news.)

Comedy and entertainment include a range of scripted and partially scripted shows. They may be performed by comic actors; comedians skilled at ad-libbing; and a range of other entertainers such as musicians, singers and dancers. Members of the public may also be involved.

A wide variety of entertainment shows includes:

- *Sitcoms*: situation comedies. Dramas based on jokes and comic situations, often performed in front of a studio audience.
- *Quiz shows and games shows*: usually enlivened by jokes and witty responses.
- *Talent contests*: either involving celebrities, such as *Strictly Come Dancing*, or selected members of the public, such as *Big Brother*. These may become spectacular 'big entertainment'.
- *Popular music*
- *Chat shows* in which a celebrity host interviews other performers or personalities
- *Stand-ups*
- *Variety shows*
- *Satire*

The new genre of 'factual entertainment' is listed below.

'Factual' is a general label covering an expanding genre, which mixes scripted with unscripted elements and ranges from classic observational documentaries involving 'ordinary people' in the United Kingdom or overseas; through presenter-led programmes on wildlife, the arts and many other topics; to highly constructed 'factual entertainment' formats where participants, who are usually not television professionals, collaborate in a performance.

Factual subgenres include:

Presenter-led genres, in which the presenter plays an active role. These usually seek to inform and educate as well as to entertain. They include:

- *Arts*: covering theatre, music, dance, cinema, visual arts, photography and literature.
- *Wildlife*.
- *Science*: astronomy is popular here.
- *History*: some programmes are archive-based; in others the presenter often acts out the costumes and manners of the period under discussion.
- *Travel*

'Observational' genres, based on everyday life and interaction. In these genres the people who appear on screen are 'ordinary people', usually going about their everyday lives.

- *Behind the scenes*: in a hotel, a department store or other institution – often described as 'access' programmes.
- *Fixed-rig documentaries*: cameras are permanently fixed in a hospital, police station, school or other institution.
- *Social observation*: often following police or enforcement officers. Frequently using mobile phone footage or surveillance cameras, capturing nuisance neighbours or arguments in the street.

Consumer programmes: these are presenter-led and often involve 'ordinary people'. These tend to be concerned with selling or improving your house, selling your antiques, improving your business, fashion and style, and so on.

- *Cookery*
- *Antiques*
- *Gardening*

Factual entertainment: including formatted series. 'Ordinary people' are followed, apparently in their everyday lives. Participants are frequently coached and situations are set up. Programmes include:

- *'Reality' genres* – in which the participants take part in a contrived situation: helping a 'hoarder' to clear their house; going on a blind date etc.

- *Medical factual* – identifying medical conditions: obesity, sexual problems, helping to deal with them.

- *Contests* – celebrities or members of the public take part in a challenge, whether fending for yourself on a remote island (*The Island with Bear Grylls*) or pitching a business idea (*Dragons' Den*). These tend to be hybrids between game shows and factual.

(See Chapter 16 for more on factual programmes.)

Other programme groupings

- Sport is a major input to television programming. It includes live coverage of sports events, and magazine and news programmes. Sports coverage tends to be dominated by the genre-specific channels such as Sky Sports and BT Sport.

- Children's, including drama, animation, information and entertainment.

- Religion, including issues of morality, faith and belief as well as acts of worship.

- Youth programmes.

- Education, including programmes made for use in schools, and adult education, such as the BBC's Learning Zone made together with the Open University.

- Daytime programmes.

- 'Ordinary television' is a useful categorisation for the low-key flow of conversation that does not use fireworks to trap the audience's attention, but acts as a familiar, background companion: sofa shows; breakfast shows; low-key chat and similar. This is sometimes described as 'ephemeral TV' (Bonner 2003). These programmes are not part of the canon and are rarely discussed in television histories and academic writing (but see Brett Mills in Creeber (2015) and *TV Handbook* 2nd edition).

Jeremy Tunstall's 21 genres

In 2015 Jeremy Tunstall identified 21 prominent UK genres (under the above classification, many of these are, in fact, subgenres). He divided them according to their performance in the current media climate. Seven are declining, six are in better health, and seven are in 'goodish health'. The 21st is sport, which he did not consider in detail as it is dominated by Sky and BT.

Seven declining genres: these, according to Tunstall, are now in jeopardy: Education, natural history, science, arts, children's, religion and current affairs.

This group is predominantly factual, with strong public service broadcasting traditions. They tend to be strong on the BBC.

Six genres 'in better health':
Soap, big entertainment, talk, homes, quiz/game shows and reality.
These are strong on the commercial channels.

Seven genres are 'in goodish health':
Drama, news, documentary, travel, comedy, history and cooking.
Of these the most prestigious are drama and news. These genres are primarily on the BBC but are also strong on the other public service channels.

A NOTE ON RATINGS, FUNDING AND FORMATS

At this time of intense competition across so many channels, broadcasters and producers are even more concerned with ratings than in the past when only a few channels were competing. Now that there is so much on offer, the numbers viewing terrestrial television have fallen drastically. The development of popular genres and decisions about which genres to schedule at what time of day are affected as never before by audience numbers.

Audience sizes are calculated by the broadcasting organisations themselves and by the Broadcasters' Audience Research Board (BARB), using a variety of overlapping methods, including monitoring the switching on of television sets and conducting polls among the public. Weekly figures are published in the trade magazine *Broadcast* and are the subject of much discussion. Press comment tends to play up the competition between channels, especially at peak viewing times like Christmas.

Over the years, programme-makers have valued the Audience Appreciation Index (AI) equally highly. This is a survey of viewers' opinions on programmes, and gives some sense of an audience's evaluation of the output. But commercial pressures are causing priorities to change. Jeremy Tunstall writes: 'Unlike their 1990 predecessors [producers] are very serious about audience research numbers.' Today's executive producers regularly quote such numbers as 'cost-per audience member' (2015: 69). He described 'the speeding up of research findings by a new regime of "overnights"'. This means that data on last night's programming is available at 9.30am seven days a week. Producers anxiously follow the measurements of audience movement across 24 hours. 'In a cautious industry with few opportunities to take commercial decisions on the basis of hard evidence, the effect of these developments is to significantly influence content, format and, ultimately genre', writes Graeme Turner in *The Television Genre Book* (Creeber 2015: 9).

Genres are also influenced by the need for overseas sales and by the need to raise co-production money (Tunstall 2015: 134). This means that formats are favoured which will be popular with overseas audiences and co-producers. In 2016, Channel Four's Head of Drama, Piers Wenger, told *Broadcast* magazine that five years previously, co-production was almost unheard of for Channel Four drama. By 2017 he forecast that at least 80 per cent of its peak-time drama will be co-produced (14 January 2016). The need for overseas sales has also led to the prioritising of a *format* to the extent that some argue that the format has become as important as the genre (Chalaby 2016).

A format is a set of specifications that are essential to a show. (e.g. *Have I Got News for You* is a quiz show based on questions about recent news items. It is played in front of an audience, by two teams made up of a resident comedian/satirist and a visiting celebrity). The details of a format are enshrined in a 'bible', which can be sold in many different markets. This is more effective than selling the original programmes, which contain local idioms and references which may not be understood by a new audience. Once a format is purchased local participants can be recruited. Quiz shows and reality shows are the most obviously formatted programmes, but dramas and comedies may also be formatted. For example, the format for *The Office* has sold in 80 countries (see p. 214 for more on formats).

George Ritzer has argued that this sort of approach leads to 'Macdonaldisation'; in other words, to a boring standardisation of output. Others have responded that it allows for flexibility across cultures (Ritzer 2000; Creeber 2015: 11).

KEY TEXTS

Creeber, G. (ed.) (2015) *The Television Genre Book*, 3rd edn, London: BFI.
Gray, J. (2010) *Show Sold Separately: Promos, Spoilers, and Other Media Paratexts*, New York: New York University Press.
Johnson, C. (2012) *Branding Television*, London: Routledge.
Tunstall, J. (2015) *The BBC and Television Genres in Jeopardy*, Bern: Peter Lang.

CHAPTER 6

Studying television

STUDYING TELEVISION: AN OVERVIEW

Television studies have had a contentious history. Despite its central role in global culture, politics and economics, for many years the 'box in the corner' was treated with amused condescension if not contempt by an academic community unwilling to take popular culture seriously. Now that television is part of a powerful global media and communications industry, it cannot be ignored. However, it is increasingly difficult to pin down exactly *what* is being studied. In the age of 'convergence culture' (Jenkins 2008), television can only be properly understood if its many different aspects are taken into account. However, it is difficult to encompass in one simple conceptual framework television's disparate facets as entertainer, storyteller, educator, home companion, medium for advertising and marketing, democratic forum, global industry and key player in the information economy.

The preceding chapters have considered the history and the contemporary landscape of the television medium, both global and within the United Kingdom, and have reflected on the changing nature of television texts. This chapter will look at the ways in which television scholars have approached this phenomenon we call television, and will look at debates about *how* television should be studied.

This book is intended, above all, to consider television as a *practice*, and there has long been an uneasy relationship between making television and theorising about it. Theoretical work is sometimes expressed in abstract terms that seem to have little purchase on real life. New entrants to the industry are still sometimes told that they must forget what they learnt at university. Yet, television studies, in all their various forms, have, over their history, been interwoven with contributions from practitioners, sometimes in ways that are unexpected and not always recognised. One of the aims of this chapter will be to highlight traces of those influences as they contribute to the interplay between theory and practice. In other words, asking questions about television and approaching it from a theoretical perspective (which is different from simply learning about 'media theory') is important in itself, and particularly important for media practitioners. Therefore, we will speak of 'theoretical approaches', or 'thinking critically', rather than attempting to outline cut and dried 'theories'. Thinking critically about a medium is a continuous practice. This book echoes the view of Graham Roberts who argues that 'a serious multi-disciplinary historical study of television ... must begin with a dialogue between practitioners and theorists, and indeed should involve theorists who *are* practitioners and vice versa' (Roberts 2001: 2).

In a short chapter like this, any account of the many disparate methods and approaches to studying television is bound to be inadequate and may well give the impression of a coherence that is not there. It will only be possible to mention a few key texts, and it is helpful to refer to the various introductions to the field, such as *Television Studies: The Key Concepts* (Calvert *et al.* 2007) and *Critical Ideas in Television Studies* (Corner 1999). *Channels of Discourse Reassembled* (Allen (ed.) 1992) has chapters illustrating a number of the powerful theoretical approaches that have influenced television studies, including ideology, psychoanalysis and narrative theory.

MAPPING THE FIELD

Our map of the field (Figure 6.1) illustrates the place of television within the wider social and global landscape. We refer to many of these aspects throughout the book. However, we should note the three main areas within which television tends to be studied: *production, text* and *reception.*

Studying *production* means understanding the everyday practices of television production and the experiences of those who work within it (Mayer *et al.* 2009). But it also involves looking more widely at those factors that make production possible, tracing the cultural, social, political, technological and economic conditions within which creative writers, producers and technicians are placed. Particularly important is a study of the *institutions* that employ them, the structure of the industry and the regulation and legislation that affect their work. We explored this broader landscape and its upheavals in Chapter 3.

Studying the television *text* means giving an account of the *content* available on the various channels and online platforms. Primarily this includes analysing and understanding programme genres (Creeber 2015). Numerous publications reflect on drama, documentary, factual entertainment, comedy and the newer formats. But a study of the television text is about more than programmes. It involves understanding the broad scope of the television output, including the multiple platforms, paratexts and interstitials which characterise contemporary media. We considered

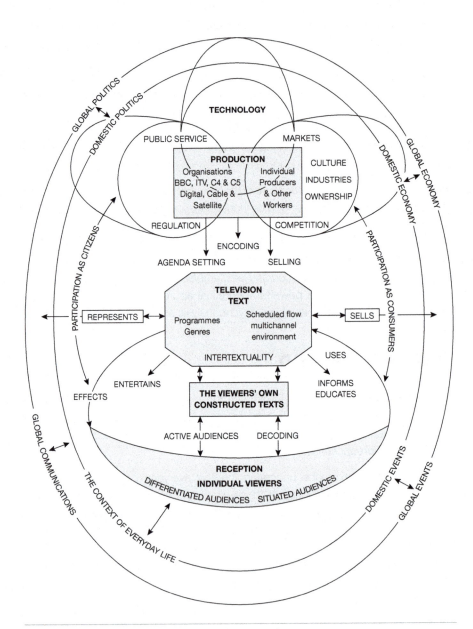

FIGURE 6.1
Television studies: mapping the field

With thanks to Sonia Livingstone

this textual landscape in Chapter 4, and various aspects of particular genres will be looked at in Chapters 15 to 17.

Finally, studying *audiences* involves counting heads – or, to use the jargon, eyeballs – to produce the viewing figures and ratings that drive competition between the channels, and attract advertisers. It also includes studying the preferences and opinions of individual viewers. The broader context of audience studies looks at how content is accessed, what viewers make of it and the role of media use within the wider culture. The regulator Ofcom produces regular reports that cover these areas, and there is a considerable literature on the ways in which audiences respond to and make use of television, much of it based on empirical studies, observing and listening to television viewers (Livingstone 1998). As this book focuses on practice, detailed work on audience reception is beyond its scope.

The three-part map is contained within widening circles, where each aspect of television reflects and is affected by the economic and social sphere which has given rise to it. There is reciprocal movement and interaction at every point.

Over the years, different methodologies have evolved for different parts of the map, and a range of theoretical perspectives has evolved. This means that some acrimonious disputes have occurred – particularly between the advocates of research, which is empirically based, using surveys, experiments and documentation, and those who prefer theoretically driven approaches.

With this in mind we will look at each of the three areas, focusing on how they have been studied.

Production/institution

Studies in the area that we have characterised as 'production' range from broad social, technological and economic generalities, to blow-by-blow, nitty-gritty accounts of daily experience. Accounts of globalisation, economics and media policy give an understanding of the macro-context within which programmes are produced, and programme-makers work, while at the micro level studies such as Georgina Born's ethnographic observation within the BBC, carried out in the late 1990s, can give an immediate and detailed insight into the daily lives of those working for the Corporation (2005). Equally, Jeremy Tunstall's regularly updated studies of the professional values of television producers, based on extensive interviews and ranging across channels and production companies, offer an invaluable insight into the practices of a group of key personnel (Tunstall 1993, 2015). In addition there has been a renewed interest in studies of television production practices (Mayer *et al.* 2009).

A closer understanding of the institutions of the media is gained by a study of their history – understanding how they came to be as they are. (In Chapters 2 and 3 we outlined the history and contemporary status of television institutions in the United Kingdom.) Official histories of ITV and the BBC have been written giving a valuable overview of their changing organisational and production practices, as well as an insight into the personalities who influenced them. These official researchers were given special access to the archives of the organisations. Historians value the opportunity to carry out detailed archive research, revealing much about the lives of those who have been part of broadcasting history. In addition, many of the major players in UK television have published their own accounts of their time in office, for example, Jeremy Isaacs, the first chief executive of Channel Four (Isaacs 1989). As the role of independent producers becomes more important, a number of studies have been conducted into their organisation and approaches (Bennett *et al.* 2012). Government inquiries and reports, such as those produced in the run-up to the BBC's 2016 licence renewal, are an invaluable source of information, as are Ofcom's regular reports on issues including public service broadcasting, children and the media and so on. In addition, all the broadcasters have detailed websites that describe their structure and history.

Theorising media power

Meanwhile, many historians and media theorists have argued that understanding contemporary media depends on a wider understanding of social theory and the global political economy (Curran and Seaton 2009; Freedman 2014). This body of work considers issues of economic and political power, as well as the ideologies that drive them. The theme of democratic accountability has been strong, with theorisations of the nature of public service broadcasting, and an eagle eye on censorship. Of great strategic importance at a theoretical level have been the debates around the concept of the 'public sphere' with its suggestion that broadcasting can offer a real space for democratic debate (Dahlgren 1995).

However, while studying media history, there have been tensions between the approaches of historians and social and cultural theorists: between empirically grounded studies, based on information from archives and interviews, and the more theoretical ways of interpreting the media. John Corner writes:

> Theory is essential to most academic enquiry because it indicates a level at which evidence, analysis and concepts are connected together to form a generalised explanatory account, however provisional and partial, which can be applied to a given range of phenomena and conditions.
>
> (2011: 3)

This desire for a 'generalised explanatory account' has underpinned much theorising since the surge of interest in 'theory' in the 1960s and 1970s. And a campaigning spirit was behind the evolution of much media theory, which partly accounts for its critical reflexes. In particular the radical 1960s gave rise to an influential neo-marxist critical tradition. Concerned about élite dominance and looking to make good exclusions and redress wrongs, many writers felt that broader explanations were needed to account for the role of media in capitalist society. It was an approach drawn on by the Centre for Contemporary Cultural Studies (CCCS) at Birmingham, which published influential studies of youth culture and race relations, as well as many other areas (Hall *et al.* 1980).

However, theorising came to rely on some rather abstract generalisations and was strongly criticised by those who argued that accounts of the media should only be based on a close attention to properly conducted surveys and extant records rather than philosophical ideas. Nevertheless, attempts to explain 'media power' have continued to draw on writers including Michel Foucault, who traced the exercise of power through the structure of institutions; Pierre Bourdieu, a sociologist who analysed culture and its links to social privilege, and Noam Chomsky, who deconstructed media messages as propaganda. This is not the place to go into the complexities and subtleties of these influential works but to note their importance for media studies, in particular looking at the place of media within broader social structures.

Texts: theorising flow and overflow

In the words of Charlotte Brunsdon, there was a moment when the study of television became 'textualised' and attention was paid to a range of genres that had not previously been considered worthy of study, such as soaps and sitcom (Brunsdon 1998: 105). And the exultant introduction of *semiotic* textual analysis by writers around the journal *Screen* was also part of the theoretical 'turn' in the 1970s. It meant that the older style of literary criticism, which had focused on judgements of quality and interpretations of character and plot, was discredited. This was thought to be value-laden, subjective and élitist. In contrast, semiology aimed to be like a science. Ed Buscombe quotes the French writer Christian Metz – characteristically from a campaigning pamphlet rather than a published book – on the 'great capacity for demystification' of a semiotic approach. 'It is a necessary emergence out of religion,' wrote Buscombe (1974: 13). The aim was to demonstrate how 'texts', including television texts, construct their message. They are built up of 'signs', each of which carries a meaning: the camera angles, the use of colour, the accents of the performers – for a semiotic analysis, every detail is significant. This means that all texts can be analysed in a similar way, regardless of whether they are prestigious offerings or low-brow entertainment (see also Chapter 15 on narrative). The refusal to make straightforward value judgements is one of the aspects of television studies that outraged the traditionalists.

As we have discussed in Chapter 5, to say that the television text is an object of study is not enough, since it is by no means clear which part of the television output *is* the text. It cannot simply be 'programmes', since each programme is embedded in a mass of other material. Back in 1974, Raymond Williams had observed that 'the central television experience is the fact of *flow*'. A programme flows into the ads, the trailers and the next programme. Today a 'text' is likely to be a multidimensional overflow, expanded across several screens as viewers seek out supplementary material, blogs and websites, or engage in a Twitter conversation with friends or with the programme itself (Bennett and Strange 2011).

Another complication is that texts are multifaceted. They are more like a rotating, mirrored ball in a dance hall, reflecting shards of light in many directions, than a linear sequence of clear-cut information. An analysis of any text will reveal aspects that toss our attention well beyond the text itself. One face will reveal something about the conditions in which the text was produced – from the signs of an authorial voice to the visibility of lavish spending. Another will suggest something about the relationship between the text and the world it claims to represent – it may be a realistic portrayal, may exaggerate for the sake of humour, and so on. A third will reflect expectations of the intended audience – inviting us to ask who this programme is designed for. These are all factors that those creating new texts must take into account.

When taking the first approach, and looking at the ways in which texts convey signs of their *production*, some critics, particularly in the neo-marxist mode, have noted the ways that a text may *encode* the 'ideology' of its makers or of its context, and hence convey the 'dominant ideology' of its times (Hall 1977). The concept of the 'ideological effect' became important as critical media theorists scrutinised texts for bias, signs of bureaucratic control, and the hidden hand of power (Glasgow University Media Group 1976; Hall *et al.* 1980). Although this has been a hugely influential approach, it is one that most producers and other practitioners vigorously resist, refusing to see themselves as mere ideological agents.

Considering how texts look outwards to the *real world* has led to other important areas of study, in particular analyses of '*representation*' (Hall 1997) – identifying ways in which various groups, including women and people from ethnic minorities, are portrayed, sometimes stereotypically, sometimes narrowly, sometimes negatively. In combating stereotypes, the theoretical work of feminist writers on film and television has been embedded in political activism. Many women filmmakers have argued that theory and practice must evolve together and inform each other. Laura Mulvey's seminal article on the male gaze, written in 1975, went alongside her own independent filmmaking, and was part of an attempt to link a changing practice to a theoretical challenge (Mulvey 1989). Her aim was to use psychoanalytic theory to help understand the relationship between film and audience, and hence to challenge what she saw as the inherently sexist structure of cinema itself. The feminist independent film movement of the 1970s united women practitioners and writers well before its theoretical ideas were generally taken up by university departments. Today organisations such as Women in Film and Television continue to campaign against discrimination in portrayal and also in employment. Meanwhile the literature on misrepresented identities and communities continues to expand, focusing on sexuality, ethnicity, disability and other forms of discrimination (see also p. 227 for more on stereotyping and Chapter 19 for more on diversity).

More broadly, especially when considering documentary and factual programming, scholars have needed to ask how a television programme can give a truthful image of reality. This has led to the rich literature of debates around theories of documentary realism, as well as a provocative consideration of the newer genres of 'constructed reality' (Winston 1995; Kilborn and Izod 1997; Biressi and Nunn 2007). (See also Chapter 16.)

Finally, texts look outwards to their *audience*, to their 'readers'. Analysis can demonstrate that texts encode within themselves certain expectations of what their audience will be like. To give an obvious example, a children's programme is constructed and presented in quite a different way from an adult one. The 2015 version of *Jekyll and Hyde* was, according to its makers, designed for 'family viewing', but it also addressed a young adult audience, and contained scenes of horror and violence thought to appeal to this age group. As it was transmitted at 7pm, before the 9pm watershed, it came in for a certain amount of criticism as younger children are also expected to be watching at that time. However, we should not confuse this projected 'reader', constructed by the 'text', with actual audiences made up of real flesh and blood individuals.

Audience/reception

The BAFTA-winning 'constructed factual' series *Gogglebox* turns the cameras back on the audience as families and groups of friends across the United Kingdom gather in front of their television sets to respond to the week's programmes. From the ebullient Jamaican ladies to the snobbish couple who fancy a drink and live in a mansion, these are engaged viewers: collapsing in hysterical laughter, cringing at the intimacy of *Embarrassing Bodies* or declaring 'I don't believe a word of it . . . it's just set up for the television'. In contrast, when a famous audience study placed spy cameras on top of television sets, rather than the lively and engaged households who feature in *Gogglebox*, it revealed people on the sofa snoozing, canoodling, reading the newspaper, arguing and very rarely giving full attention to the television flow (Collet and Lamb 1986). And this was well before the arrival of Twitter and the second screen actually *expected* a distracted audience.

Audience research serves a number of purposes. On the one hand, it can provide useful data for a heavily commercialised media. Broadcasters need to know which programmes are engaging their viewers. Commercial companies need to trace the audience demographic as their income depends on attracting the social groups who can be targeted by their advertisers. Seen in this light, audiences are commodities to be packaged and sold. The 'ratings' are published daily by the Broadcasters' Audience Research Board (BARB), and a consolidated total, which includes catch-up viewing, appears at the end of each week.

Audience research carried out by the regulatory body Ofcom has a different purpose. The regulator's brief is to map the landscape of television provision, to monitor important aspects, such as public service broadcasting, and to represent the interests of audiences. Work of this sort is used by governments to influence media policy. For example, Ofcom has traced the decline of linear viewing and found it to be slower than many had predicted.

Finally there is academic research that seeks to go beyond counting heads (or eyeballs) and simpler measurements of responses, like the Audience Appreciation Index (AI) used by the BBC and BARB. In a discipline that has largely grown out of social psychology, researchers are more interested in what viewers make of television and what part it plays in their lives (Livingstone 1998). This has included a long-term concern with the 'effects' of television – which can be traced back to the deep suspicion of the 'mass media' among intellectuals in the early part of the twentieth century. Many with an élite education who valued 'culture' scorned 'mass culture' as crude and corrupting. In particular, children, if exposed to violent images, were thought likely to become violent adults (Davies 2010). It is a strand of research from social psychology which continues to this day.

The early history of audience studies was part of an empirical tradition in American communications studies which flourished from the early years of the twentieth century. The simple 'effects' model on which much of that work was based is often referred to as a 'hypodermic needle' model, since it assumes that passive audiences are 'injected' with predetermined meanings. The model has been challenged by a variety of approaches to audience studies. George Gerbner and Larry Gross's concept of 'cultivation' argued that recurrent messages 'cultivate' social ideas. This research tradition had a number of aims, including to identify media influence and media power (Gerbner 1998). On the other hand, the 'uses and gratifications' approach developed by Jay Blumler and Elihu Katz looked at how people actually *use* television – perhaps as a companionable presence around the house, or a convenient way of keeping the kids quiet (Blumler and Katz 1974). The theme was: 'we should not ask what media does to the people, but what people do to the media.'

The idea that messages 'encoded' by producers were then 'decoded' by viewers led many researchers to insist that audiences are in fact 'active'.

The insistence on an 'active audience' anticipated contemporary work on multichannel activity. DVDs, websites, the use of a phone or a tablet all modify the ways in which viewers engage with television text. Henry Jenkins was a pioneer in this field. His studies of fan culture point out that engagement through fan conventions, acting out and so on have long preceded the complex multiplatform media use of today (Jenkins 1992). In many ways audiences can have a real influence on production and on the text.

It is here that we can close the circle and put the individual act of watching and actively responding back into the broader context of politics, economics and society. Television and its allied media are an indispensable part of modern social living.

While they are an important part of the global economy, they are also at the heart of personal life.

As the landscape of television takes on new and unfamiliar forms, it is not surprising that the study of the medium continues to shift between these multiple aspects.

KEY TEXTS

Allen, R. (ed.) (1992) *Channels of Discourse, Reassembled*, 2nd edn, London: Routledge.
Calvert, B., Casey, N., Casey, B., French, L. and Lewis, J. (2007) *Television Studies: The Key Concepts*, London: Routledge.
Corner, J. (1999) *Critical Ideas in Television Studies*, Oxford: Clarendon Press.
Mayer, V., Banks, M. and Caldwell, J. T. (eds) (2009) *Production Studies: Cultural Studies of Media Industries*, New York: Routledge.

Part 2

The practitioners' perspective

CHAPTER 7

Working in television: an overview

WORKING IN TELEVISION

This handbook on television production comes at a time when production is in a state of flux, as traditional craft skills are transformed by evolving technologies. Someone trained in digital media may decide to work on video effects or advertising, or may produce material for one of the many websites associated with programmes. YouTube and the internet are providing an alternative outlet for both aspiring and established filmmakers, while jobs are opening up in companies providing internet streaming for conferences and events. Yet all of these are related to the medium of television in various ways, and make an important contribution to the television experience. While much programme-making continues within the rules and practices that are well established within each genre, changing technology means that practices shift in unexpected ways. A different type of training is needed, together with adaptability and regular retraining, as new techniques are introduced with remarkable frequency. In addition, the secure careers that characterised earlier decades are no longer common practice, and those who wish to work in the industry find themselves on uncertain ground. Yet part of the excitement about being new to television is the opportunity to make a contribution to the changing shape of the medium.

Part 2 of this handbook will be looking at television production from the practitioners' perspective. After outlining the main work areas in the industry it will look in detail at the key skills involved in pre-production, production and post-production. Each of the chapters will be introduced by a discussion of the ideas and changing circumstances which have contributed to its history and development, from practical everyday demands to creative challenges. Part 2 will also include case studies in which practitioners describe their own experience, and we will look at particular examples of work in the television industry.

Working in television involves jobs that range from exercising traditional skills to developing the newest technology; from routine administration to exceptional creativity; from hard-working assistants to highly trained technicians. Television needs accountants as well as presenters; carpenters as well as news producers; skilled electricians as well as comedy writers. It needs camera assistants, commissioning editors, production managers, visual effects supervisors and more. One recent graduate who was offered administrative work at the BBC's Salford studios said how surprised she was at the variety of jobs available. The people who do those jobs are as diverse as the jobs themselves. They come from different backgrounds, require different types of training, have different professional and technical skills, use different jargons and are accustomed to different working environments. But all contribute to the television experience. Inevitably, some jobs that are important to television are beyond the scope of this book, including administration, areas such as wardrobe and make-up, and high-level technical and engineering expertise. We note the ways in which these are essential to creating the television output, but here our focus will be on the basic production skills.

FIGURE 7.1
Crew on location setting up for a shot. The camera is an Arri Alexa. The cinematographer is supported by a grip

Photograph: Lewis Kahn

The creation of a programme for broadcast television moves through four major phases. Each involves many different people and requires a wide range of tasks to be undertaken. In Part 2 we will be looking at: *pre-production*, which involves getting a programme commissioned, financed, organised and up and running; the *production* period, when the technical skills of directing, camera work and sound recording are needed; and *post-production*, when the skills of editing the picture and sound come into play, when visual effects are created and the programme is prepared for broadcast. Once a programme is completed, the tasks of *marketing* and *promotion* take over. Although we will refer to this as a fourth phase, considerations of how a programme will be marketed tend to be part of the calculations from its inception, affecting its commissioning and financing. However, a detailed discussion of marketing is beyond the scope of this book.

Working in television can be very demanding. Long hours, stress, a highly competitive atmosphere, dealing with difficult colleagues and inflated egos; it's all par for the course. This book contains several first-hand accounts from practitioners on coping with the day-to-day problems that are inseparable from practical work. At the same time, we will be arguing that, in a changing environment, the next generation of programme-makers will need to arrive in the medium with a critical understanding not only of the mechanics of television, but of the broader context within which they are carried out.

PROGRAMME PRODUCTION TYPES

For convenience, we can make a broad distinction between *types* of material that are part of the daily television output. This is a different sort of classification from the 'genres' discussed in Chapter 5, as it is based on the practicalities of the production processes and hence affects the type of skills and equipment required. Below we describe the differences between 'live' programmes and 'filmed' programmes, and the processes that construct them, and we note the ways in which the two processes overlap. Then we discuss 'segmented' programmes, which include both 'live' and 'filmed' elements. In addition, we note those inputs to the television experience which surround or supplement the programmes, referred to as 'paratexts' and 'interstitials'. All of these are made by skilled professionals working in different parts of the industry.

'Live' programmes: studio and OB

These may either be broadcast simultaneously with the action, or they may be 'as live', recorded, then broadcast later. Sometimes they are broadcast without change only minutes later, sometimes, following some editing to heighten the impact of the programme, at a later scheduled date. 'Live' programmes originate either from a studio or an outside broadcast (OB) unit. Typically they use multiple camera set-ups in which as many as five cameras feed simultaneous signals into a studio gallery, a control room or an OB truck. There, a director, together with a gallery team, selects the shots that are instantaneously edited to create the broadcast programme. Unlike filmed programmes, 'live' programmes are recorded in the order of final transmission. A rare example of a daily live output is QVC, the shopping channel (see Chapter 12).

Originally it was liveness that distinguished the naturalness and immediacy of television from the worked-over sophistication of cinema. Its particular magic lay in the fact that these people you could see on the screen were actually talking to you, *now*, although they were many miles away. Live programmes still seek to create that sense of immediacy and straightforward communication; these include sporting events, the Proms, public ceremonies such as the Queen's ninetieth birthday celebrations and regular news broadcasts. In addition, a stand-up comedy show, such as *Sarah Millican Live* installs its OB cameras in major theatres around the country to convey the sense of being present at the show as it happens. Many live programmes include an audience, whose members contribute to its sense of immediacy. Studio sitcoms gain energy from audience laughter. In *Question Time* politicians and commentators respond to questions, while mobile cameras seek out audience reactions.

At a time when viewing is streamed 'on demand', recorded on hard disc or viewed on catch-up or DVD, schedulers are anxious to find formats that will engage an audience at the moment of transmission. For the commercial channels this means that advertisers are assured that there will be an audience for the advertisements; for all broadcasters it preserves that sense of a communal event, a national talking point, which was an important characteristic of television in its early days. There was much hype around *EastEnders*, when the soap opera, normally recorded well in advance of transmission, broadcast a week of live programmes to mark its thirtieth anniversary in February 2015. For formats with a competitive element, in which viewers are invited to participate by voting, from *Big Brother* to *Strictly Come Dancing*, liveness is of the essence.

However, as television changes, the meaning of 'live' is changing. Now that 'on demand' is a normal way of watching, the description 'live television' is coming to refer to programmes *as scheduled*, whether transmitted live or pre-filmed. However, the process of producing a live, or 'as live', programme in a studio or as an OB still retains significant differences from producing filmed programmes. Elements of liveness remain in a number of formats. Meanwhile the special characteristics of genuinely live programmes – viewed as they are performed – remain.

Filmed programmes and hybrids

These include programmes filmed on location or in a studio designed for film rather than television production. Although the use of digital recording is changing some of the practices, usually filmed programmes use a single camera and are edited after filming is completed. Unlike live programmes, the shots will not be recorded in the order in which they finally appear, and many 'takes' of each shot may be provided for the editor to select between. The filmed materials – the 'rushes' – are transferred to an editing suite where they are shaped and enhanced with sound and video effects to create the final production. Many programmes, ranging from major dramas and documentaries to the proliferating subgenres of factual entertainment, are made in this way.

However, developing technologies are enabling some genres to draw on the two basic types. 'Fixed-rig' documentaries, such as *Educating Essex* and *24 Hours in Police Custody*, bridge between them. They are 'live' in the sense that they record the action on multiple cameras as it unfolds, and 'filmed' in the sense that a final selection is made elsewhere. The fixed-rig itself involves up to 100 cameras placed around a location, usually an institution, such as a school, a hospital or a police station. A director in a special facility that acts as a gallery – it may be an OB van, a temporary hut or a specially prepared and wired-up room – will select which cameras to activate, and will assemble 'live' sequences as the action develops. The shape of the overall programme is later constructed in an editing suite.

Similarly, live programmes such as *The X-Factor* and *Strictly Come Dancing* include significant amounts of pre-recorded, edited material. Soap operas such as *EastEnders* and long-running dramas such as *Casualty* are produced in a permanent set specially constructed with cameras in place and facilities organised so that, effectively, there is a great deal in common with the studio set-up.

Segmented television and the overflow

Back in the 1960s, the influential commentator Raymond Williams pointed out that the structure of television consisted of a *flow* of information, but this is divided into *segments* (Ellis 1982). Dramas and documentaries are themselves segmented, made up of sequences linked to create the whole, while many programme formats depend on a segmented structure. Magazine programmes, sofa shows, news broadcasts are collaged and bricollaged. They are made up of loosely related items, often combining both live and filmed elements, frequently linked together by studio presenters. Inputs may come from many sources, including specially filmed items, and sometimes 'captured' material from the wide range of imagery available in the contemporary world, such as CCTV and smart phones. In fact, some programmes are given over to short sequences of this sort of footage. ITV's *Britain Sees Red: Caught on Camera* tracks down mobile phone footage and raids the internet for moments of confrontation and bursts of anger. Like many programmes, its segments are linked by startling graphics – in this case expressive bursts of angry red.

Television is, in itself, a segmented experience. The cracks between the programmes are designed to link together its continuous flow with segments that include trailers, advertisements and increasingly complex station identifications. They are the *inter-stitials* that surround and interrupt the programmes, each of which is, in itself, a polished self-contained segment. In the early days of live television, the links between programmes took the form of captions, with voice-over information. They were prepared by a department known as 'presentation' and had very low prestige. Now the interstitials have become the height of spectacle and gems of contemporary visual and aural design. They are prepared by highly skilled creative teams and are relevant to a discussion of working in the medium. All are part of the television experience (see Chapter 5).

However, as we have frequently noted in this book, television is itself breaching its boundaries. It is no longer a linear flow, but an *over*flow, with material found on multiple channels, on DVDs, and online, as well as in a variety of programme spin-offs, such as books, video games and numerous other forms. These are what Jonathan Gray describes as *paratexts*, by which he means those additional 'texts', wherever they are found, which enhance or expand the original 'text' of a programme (Gray 2010). He has conducted a detailed analysis of these spin-offs, identifying several types of paratext including title sequences, trailers, promos, as well as toys, video games and the multiple websites and fan sites which develop alongside favourite programmes (see Chapter 5). In many cases, online material both contributes to and enhances a text, and is valuable in its own right. The remarkable BBC3 documentary series *Our War*, made from material filmed by the helmet cameras worn by young soldiers in Afghanistan, was supplemented by a website that included a range of short films which broadened the scope of the programme. Some feature the soldiers themselves, speaking of their personal responses to the events; some trace the experiences of young Afghans. A number were filmed by a young woman Afghan filmmaker, currently living in Canada, who was able to record the stories of women and young people caught up in the conflict. Perhaps most inventively, accounts of experiences recorded in Afghanistan were animated by sixth formers at a number of schools around the United Kingdom. This was the work of an online team, coordinated by producer Darren Lawford. This online work, together with the whole range of broadcast material, is an integral part of contemporary television and involves the input of specialised, skilled and creative practitioners.

PRODUCTION PROCESSES

Whether drama or documentary, entertainment or arts, 'live', 'filmed' or 'segmented', a number of processes are common to all programmes:

- Most programmes are carefully researched, and as far as possible the production work is pre-planned. In the case of a drama, this will usually mean that every word is scripted and the shooting is carefully storyboarded; in the case of a current affairs documentary, it may mean that research has revealed a line of investigation and determined which locations should be filmed and which people should be interviewed. In the case of a fixed-rig documentary, the planning involves research into the institutions, building relationships with the participants and the careful positioning of the cameras.

- Before production begins there is what is described as a 'pro-filmic event'. This is the scene that the cameras will film. This 'event' may be highly contrived by the programme-makers: for costume drama sets, props and costumes are all carefully designed, lit and put into place. On the other hand, the filmmakers may aim to intervene as little as possible with events as they unfold. A fly-on-the-wall documentary seeks to record life *as it happens*. Between the two, the 'constructed factual' genre, such as *The Only Way is Essex*, involves a great deal of planning, as well as some observational filming and input from the people being filmed. These different genres need different sorts of preparation, and different kinds of expertise will be drawn on. For the documentary there will be researchers, advisors and specialist experts, for the drama there will be set and costume designers, historical experts; casting experts, wig-makers and others. Work on the pro-filmic event prepares the 'mise-en-scene' – the characteristic 'look' of the programme.

- All programmes are made up of a number of discrete shots as the scene is recorded by the cameras. In a live studio programme the shots will be assembled as the action progresses, in the order of the final transmission. The programme will be recorded as a whole. For a filmed programme, the shots will almost never be recorded in the sequence which the audience finally sees. Instead the shots will be set up one by one, then assembled at the post-production stage to create a filmic whole (see Chapter 13).

- All programmes first combine *shots* into *sequences*, then assemble the sequences to create the whole programme. For a studio programme this is done in real time by the vision mixer in the studio gallery; for a filmed programme the work is carried out in an editing suite. Editing is crucial to the construction of a programme. At this stage programmes are shaped with titles and credits and often enhanced with visual effects (see Chapter 14 for visual effects).

- The sound track will be constructed separately. For a 'live' programme a sound engineer balances the input from the microphones in the studio or OB set up. For a filmed programme, an audio designer combines the recorded sound with other audio effects at the editing stage. Sound design is an important element, offering the possibility of music, commentary and special effects, in addition to the natural sounds recorded during filming (see Chapters 11 and 14).

TELEVISION WORK AREAS

Planning and producing a programme from the initial idea to the final transmission can involve many different roles and skills. For some large-scale spectaculars or sports events there will be hundreds of people involved, while on smaller productions the work may be shared between a few individuals. The following chapters on the practitioners' perspective will recognise these differences as we go on to discuss the major television roles. We will refer both to 'live' and filmed programmes, and will take into account segments, paratexts and interstitials as we outline some of the principles of production, production management, directing, camerawork, lighting, sound recording, editing and visual effects. These underlying principles apply both to those aiming for full-time employment in the industry and those who, in the present casualised structure, aim either to get freelance work or to make their own programmes independent of the television institutions.

The breadth of different skills involved in producing broadcast material will be clear from any list of credits that follows a television programme. Although we will refer to many of them here, it is impossible to cover them all. However, there are a number of organisations that give an account of the work areas in television and offer information about where to train and how to apply for jobs. In particular,

FIGURE 7.2
Working in Solent Productions' outside broadcasting truck

Courtesy: Solent Productions

Creative Skillset was originally set up to promote training within the television industry. It now has a wider remit, but continues to monitor the industry and provides useful information on the range on work available. http://creativeskillset.org/search/59? tags%5B%5D=TV&tags%5B%5D=&tags%5B%5D=&q=.

(See Chapters 18 and 19, and p. 266 for a list of training opportunities.)

KEY TEXT

Dismore, J. (2011) *TV: An Insider's Guide*, Evesham, UK: Hothive Books.

CHAPTER 8

Producing and production management

PRODUCERS

British television is a producer-led medium, states Jeremy Tunstall, who has studied the work of producers across three decades (Tunstall 1993, 2015). Within the broadcasting institutions it is they who have the greatest control over the creative output, and it has been executive producers who have risen to become programme controllers and heads of channels. Most of today's independent production companies were launched by people who had production experience in the big broadcasting organisations, and those who aspire to run their own companies definitely need to acquire production skills.

Tunstall's books are based on interviews with working producers and he observes that there is no simple, clear-cut definition as the experience varies a great deal with different genres. However, whatever the genre, producing a programme or a series is a demanding job:

> The producer's role encompasses elements not only of the civil servant but of a latter-day Renaissance man, capable of playing all parts. . . . He or she needs some basic grasp of television technology . . . of sound, lighting and sets; requires (usually extensive) specialist knowledge of the particular programme genre, such as drama or news; needs to be able to juggle ideas against finance; needs plenty of sheer energy; needs some performance skills – the ability to enthuse and activate others during a long working day; and needs diplomatic skills to smooth ruffled egos and to persuade others to do things at different times and for less money than they would prefer.
>
> (1993: 6)

Many innovations and initiatives that have contributed to the development of the television medium over its history have come from remarkable producers pursuing their own vision: people such as Tony Garnett who launched the celebrated *Wednesday Play* on the BBC in the 1960s; Phil Redmond who set up the Liverpool-based Mersey Television to make the soap opera *Brookside* when Channel Four first began to commission independent production companies; Peter Bazalgette who innovated with audience participation and the multichannel experience for *Big Brother* in 2000. But being an established producer in a television organisation or a large independent company, with all the long-term responsibility that entails, is not necessarily the same thing as producing a single programme or series, which largely involves common sense, persistence and hard work.

Producers are the people who get the whole thing under way, and bear ultimate responsibility. Producers deal with logistics and money. Some independent producers may be risking their own money, most must negotiate with the broadcaster who commissions them (see Kate Beal p. 32 for more on the experience of an independent producer). Producers who are employed by a television company must argue for resources and justify their budgets within their respective organisations, and must frequently negotiate partnership deals in order to fund a production. In addition, they must bear in mind issues concerning distribution, marketing and the production of promotional material: taking account of overseas sales is a significant factor in the original planning. In addition the producer must be aware of relevant legislation, must liaise with the company's lawyers and ensure at every stage that a programme complies with Ofcom's broadcasting code. This covers issues such as harm and offence, protecting the under-18s, due impartiality, commercial references and product placement, and is updated every year.

It is usually the producer who selects the writer, director and crew, although sometimes the commission to make a programme may depend on the use of a particular director, actor or presenter who is part of the 'package'. Choosing with whom to work, ensuring harmonious working relationships and making sure that the crew get on well together as a team can be more important in the production of everyday television than a burning talent. Above all, a producer must be a facilitator.

Any programme is the result of team action, and the producers' input will vary with the circumstances. In a smaller production the director or the writer may also do the producing, or the whole team may work collaboratively. Larger productions may also employ an edit producer (often described as a 'preditor'), which may mean that the director will not supervise the editing process (see Anne Parisio p. 229), and a digital producer for the websites and online videos which accompany most programmes. For major productions there will be several layers of producers. The ITV series *Jekyll and Hyde*, for example, has an Executive Producer, who is the Director of Drama at ITV Studios, and bears the ultimate responsibility for the studios' drama output; responsible to him is Charlie Higson, who conceived the series and is chief writer. His title is Creator/Executive Producer and he points out that he is in charge of creativity. He commissions the other writers who work on the series and is on the set as much as possible. His is the role that is frequently referred to as the 'showrunner'. Then there is the Series Producer, who describes his work as being 'at the coal face', and a Line Producer. However, they explain that their responsibilities 'all cross over' (interviews at the British Film Institute 22 October 2015). Many productions credit numerous producers, and their precise titles may differ.

There are few rules on how to go about getting a programme off the ground, but training in financial skills, budgeting and knowledge of the law as it relates to programme-making are all now making an appearance on television courses.

While the *producer* supervises the whole production, he or she works closely with the *production manager* who also needs to be aware of these diverse areas, and shares the work of budgeting, planning the schedule, contracting the cast and crew, and other organisational matters. This chapter will now look at the production process, from pre-production to distribution, from the point of the view of the production manager.

PRODUCTION MANAGEMENT

In the complex industry which is television today, a production manager, just like a producer, needs to have a broad understanding of the medium in our global, convergent era. This ranges from the business perspective of how productions are financed and how staff are employed, to the creative aspect of how the different genres are approached and how audiences are addressed.

There was a time when production managers trained on the job, beginning as a runner, moving to production assistant or floor manager, then working their way up. Now there are a number of courses, some of them at BA level, where the skills of production management can be learned and put into practice in the professional world through work experience and short contracts. However, in today's casualised industry, many production managers, even very experienced ones, are freelancers. They must build up their contacts and are constantly on the look-out for the next job.

From a practical perspective, when working on a specific project, the production manager must deal with the overall process as it moves through its four major stages: pre-production; the production period; post-production; and distribution (see Tunstall 2015: 66–7). Production manager Robin Small says:

> These steps flow logically from the beginning of a film to the end. Unless you are very rich or very reckless, it is not possible to start shooting until the programme idea has been thoroughly researched, the production is financed

and the budget is in place. The film cannot be edited until rushes have been shot, and it cannot be distributed until there is a completed film to market. The production manager needs a thorough knowledge of all four stages, and must understand how each stage relates to the others. This means that they must know something about everyone else's job. The aim is total coordination of all aspects of the production.

The production manager's work will vary according to whether they are employed by a large organisation, such as the BBC, where they may be part of a substantial production management team, or whether they are working for a small production company where their role overlaps with that of the producer and director. Usually the production manager will deal with the organisation from the office, while the production team does the day-to-day coordination and the first assistant director ensures that everything goes smoothly on location. The tasks will differ according to the genre of the programme. Dealing with professional actors who are accustomed to the daily routine of call sheets and make-up sessions is very different from organising the 'ordinary people' who make up the 'cast' of a 'constructed factual' programme such as *Benefits Street* or *Long Lost Family*. Different again are large events like a major football match where the team will include many production assistants and specialists such as health and safety advisers.

Despite the differences, there are certain basic tasks that must be carried out on all productions, before, during and after the production period. 'In an ideal world production management is a planned activity requiring much anticipation and preparation', says Robin Small, who continues:

> This is fine in theory, but in practice production for television has always in-volved tight deadlines and budgets. This demands a balancing act between the creative aims of the production team, the practical requirements of exe-cutive producers who want a finished programme delivered on time, and the programme accountants who want it delivered on budget. These conflicting pressures mean that an essential skill for a production manager is to be able to prioritise on a daily basis. The skills of planning can be learnt, but it would be foolish to pretend that this is all you need to be a good production manager. There is no substitute for experience. Over time a production manager begins to anticipate potential crisis scenarios and learns how to react to them.

Throughout the process the balance between practicality and creativity remains key, and it is the production manager whose job it is to keep everyone's feet on the ground. Creativity is essential, but without practicality it will not get anywhere. This means that the production manager needs a meticulous attention to detail, including the ability to note down and make available all the elements that go into preparing and running a production smoothly. Above all, the production must come in on time and on budget. We will bear these points in mind as we look at the production manager's involvement in the stages of production.

Pre-production

The production manager may be involved in the research and development stage of a programme project. Their expertise will help to ensure that a proposal goes to a commissioning editor with a well-worked out and carefully costed script. For some programmes it is also important that locations, artists, production team and relevant permissions are already in place (see also p. 279 on pitching).

Once the programme has been commissioned, the first priority is a suitable production office. There needs to be enough space to store heavy equipment and a quiet area for briefings and interviews. It should be properly equipped with computers and printers, as well as plenty of tea and coffee. At crisis points the smallest details can become important.

Working with the director and the producer, the production manager's first task is to produce:

A production schedule: planning the time to be spent in the various phases of production, taking into account editing and visual effects.

A detailed budget: using the script to estimate every cost. Budget templates are available from commissioning broadcasters and organisations such as PACT, the trade association for UK independent production companies. These break down the different cost areas, from wages and hire of equipment through to location costs and such essential items as insurance, office overheads and production stills. It is important to work backwards from the first shooting date to construct a realistic timetable and budget, identifying all the elements that the production will need.

Together with the producer and director, the next tasks will be:

- Booking the relevant personnel, including crew and artists

  This entails being aware of employment practices and employment rights. It means checking the current rates and *drawing up contracts*. The large broadcasters and many independent companies employ lawyers, sometimes on a part-time basis, to deal with the legal aspects of this. The production manager should keep a master list of contacts for artists and crew with addresses, phone numbers and the contact number of their agent or representative if they have one. A separate emergency list should include national insurance numbers, and the phone numbers of their doctor and next of kin. It is a good idea to make a note of any health or diet requirements.

- Booking the necessary equipment

  The production manager should keep a contact list of suppliers, and a list of all equipment bought in or hired, including electrical machinery, ropes, chains, scaffolding, lighting and plant. It is important to check that it is safe and has the appropriate test certificates. Make sure any operatives hold current qualifications.

- Finding suitable locations

  Locations may be chosen with the help of a specialised location finder. As soon as they have been decided on, it is up to the production manager to make sure that permissions are in place and insurance is arranged. Health and safety is an essential part of the production manager's job, safeguarding the crew, artists, visitors, contractors and the public. There should be a risk assessment for each location. If there are any special effects, proper experts such as stunt artists, pyrotechnic specialists and fight arrangers should be employed. Always make sure they have their own insurance and check their credentials before filming starts.

  At this stage it is also important to involve the visual effects supervisors, to ensure that the effects are planned and that suitable material is provided for them to work with (see Chapter 14).

- Overseas filming

  This requires extra arrangements, including making a note of everyone's passport numbers. Medical insurance should be arranged and vaccination and visa requirements should be checked. The Foreign and Commonwealth Office publishes a regular update advice list for visitors to hazardous countries. Make sure your insurance covers the level of risk involved.

- Travel and accommodation

  This should be arranged well in advance, as should location support, including catering and first aid. Inform the relevant bodies, such as the police, of what you are doing and when.

The production period

The production manager's main concerns during the production period are:

- Logistics and cash flow

  It is up to them to arrange that the production has what it needs, when and where it is wanted. This means keeping the show on the road on a daily basis, ensuring that immediate needs are met with flexibility and speed, and dealing with emergencies. But this must be balanced with planning the following days' or weeks' activity, bearing in mind long-term deadlines and overall costs. Pragmatism and patience are essential, plus the ability to conjure a balanced weekly budget out of that changing animal experience called the shoot.

- Accommodation, catering, communication and transport

  These should be in place and timed, so that the crew can get where they need to go, can communicate vital information to each other, and are able to eat and rest with proper breaks.

- Call lists

  All crew and cast should have *call lists* showing what time they are needed and where. For fiction shoots the actors should have three calls: a transport/pick-up call; a makeup/costume call; and the on-set call to ensure that they are ready when the director needs them. For non-fiction shoots the crew need to know when and where they are meeting. Work backwards from the time of the shoot and allow time for setting up, moving equipment, parking, travel and rest stops. Remember that things take twice as long in the dark, and a small problem such as lack of parking can play havoc with a schedule.

Close liaison with the director and the production coordinator during the production period will ensure that the shoot goes smoothly and that everyone is fully informed about the timetable and what their commitments are.

The production manager should ensure that all the post-production facilities are booked and prepared, including editing, sound editing and video effects facilities, and the needs of post-production should be borne in mind throughout the production period. An editor may be present at the shoot, to help select takes and put together some rough assemblies, and a visual effects supervisor may also be present, advising on what original material will be needed to create the desired effects (see Chapter 14 for visual effects).

Post-production

The key points at this stage are the rough cut, the fine cut, the sound edit and the completion of the master, edited programme. A timetable must be worked out so that all these processes link smoothly with each other. The production manager will need to work backwards from the deadlines for the fine cut and the online master (for more on editing see Chapters 13 and 14).

The production manager should ensure that:

- Post-production staff and facilities are *booked and prepared*. This may be in an established editing facility, or, for smaller productions, editing equipment may be hired in to the production office.
- All material is properly *logged*.
- Extra material, such as archive footage and music, is cleared for *copyright*.
- Originally composed music may be commissioned and created.
- A *narrator* or voice-over artist may be employed.

The delivery of a commissioned programme, complying with the required technical standards, is the editor's responsibility (see Chapter 13 on editing).

Distribution

The production manager's final task is to organise and supervise the distribution of the final programme. Even if it is made for a scheduled slot for the BBC or other broadcaster, there is frequently the question of foreign sales and promotional activities. This involves checking the *technical requirements* and *compliance requirements* for foreign sales, as well as providing copies for publicity or for sale (for more on compliance and overseas sales, see p. 181 on post-production).

At this stage any legal problems should be cleared up, and all copyright and contract agreements should be finalised. This is essential to prevent any future claims or liability, and is especially important for documentary or archive-based programmes (Crone *et al.* 2002).

Production managers should ask themselves:

- Did you remember to get signed waivers and consent forms from anybody who was interviewed?

- Was anything that was said libellous or was there any music playing in the background from which a future claim could arise?

- Do the people who may be doing interviews know of their commitments and are they available as part of their contract?

- Have you checked up on the residuals such as book rights and secondary sales?

Robin Small concludes:

> Winding down the production office can begin once the programme is finally delivered. Any outstanding financial matters should also be resolved, including paying off outstanding bills and contributors.

> Publicity should include programme billing, providing stills, arranging interviews with the director or cast, press previews, advance screenings, advertisements on radio, press and television and, if you still have the energy, getting the launch and final night party in place. Before you turn the light out, did you remember to bring a bottle opener, order the wine and a taxi home so that you can start all over again tomorrow – once the headache tablets you managed to forget finally take effect!

Thanks to production manager Robin Small for contributing to this chapter, and also to all involved in the Production Management BA at Edge Hill University.

PROFILE

Abigail McKenzie: Talent Team Assistant, BBC Children's Department

Abi McKenzie graduated from Edge Hill University with a BA in Television Production Management in 2015. She was appointed to the post of Talent Team Assistant in the BBC Children's Department at Media City, Salford, in May 2015. Here she describes how her work experience and her university course led to her full-time employment.

'While I was doing my degree I also did a work experience placement, followed by numerous casual contracts. My work experience was with BBC Sport as part of the production management team working towards BBC *Sports Personality of the Year, 2014* (SPOTY14). I went out on several shoots and found it to be a brilliant experience!

This is a huge event: a week of broadcasts, then a three-hour presentation ceremony transmitted live on BBC1. It takes place in November or December every year in different cities around the United Kingdom. In 2014 it was in Glasgow in the new SSE Hydro arena. As it was an OB we had to set everything up.

There was an audience of 16,000, with special places for guests, and the BBC had around 500 people working towards the event. There was a production manager, production executive, three production assistants, an accountant, a health and safety advisor and two production coordinators who worked together to coordinate the logistics for pre-event filming and the event itself. The production team collaborated with two event managers from an external company as well as working hard alongside the team situated at the arena itself. I reported to the production manager and shadowed the production assistants.

Several weeks after my placement came to an end, I was contacted by the Talent Team within BBC Sport and offered my first casual contract as a runner on *Football Focus*, *Final Score* and *Match of the Day* (broadcast on Saturdays during the football season on BBC1). Following this role, I was invited back to work as a production management assistant on the BBC Sport News team and then as a team assistant on the BBC Sport Multi Media team. Overall I did three freelance stints across BBC Sport, gaining experience across television production, news and interactive.

Since I was coming to the end of my time at the university, I applied for several fixed-term positions at the BBC in Salford (vacancies are advertised on the BBC Careers Hub website) and was successful in a number of interviews.

PROFILE

PROFILE

As I'm a mother of a two-year old, I did not want a job that involved travelling or time away from home, so I accepted the job in Talent and HR, working with the 'Talent Team', which recruits and supports staff for BBC Children's. As well as the more routine work, I go to screenings and visit productions. As a mother, this job suits me perfectly.

Once I was in the BBC I was surprised how many varied jobs there are available for new applicants.'

KEY TEXTS

Crone, T., Alberstat, P., Cassels, C. and Overs, E. (2002) *Law and the Media – An Everyday Guide for Professionals*, Oxford: Focal Press.

Kellison, C. (2009) *Producing for TV and New Media: A Real World Approach for Producers*, Oxford: Focal Press.

Ofcom (2015b) *Broadcasting Code*, London: Ofcom, http://stakeholders.ofcom. org.uk/binaries/broadcast/code-july-15/Ofcom_Broadcast_Code_July_2015. pdf.

Owens, J. and Millerson, G. (2012) *Television Production*, 15th edn, Oxford: Focal Press.

Small, R. (1999) *Production Safety for Film and Television*, Oxford: Focal Press.

CHAPTER 9

The director's concerns

DIRECTOR AND CREW

Television is a time-based visual and aural medium. Creators of television, whether working on sport or crime dramas, *The Great British Bake-Off* or a sofa show, are dealing with three basic aspects: a developing *narrative structure* as the programme moves through time, a rich and informative *sound track* which will enhance the narrative and create its own particular qualities, and a pleasurable or striking *visual* impression. Directors are concerned with all three as they focus on creating a programme that will appeal to their audience. We will be discussing narrative in Chapter 15 and sound in Chapters 11 and 14. In this chapter and the next we will focus on the visual aspects from the point of view of the director and the cinematographer.

Over the years the position of director has been glamorised. On the one hand there is the mythology surrounding larger-than-life Hollywood figures, and on the other there are the 'auteur' theories developed in France in the 1950s, which argued that a cinema film is a total work of art and it is the director who is the artist. Both approaches seriously underestimate the contribution made by the whole group of programme-makers, from skilled technicians to performers and support staff, and are far from appropriate to the routine task of producing daily television. Even so, the attraction lingers, given a boost by the prominence of the big-name directors, or sometimes the creative 'showrunners', on websites and DVD extras. This is 'resurrecting the TV author' writes Jonathan Gray, 'authorship adds style and substance' (2010: 108). However, on UK television, the list of people noted for their innovative contribution to the medium includes engineers, channel controllers, newscasters, scriptwriters, cinematographers, digital effects artists, editors, animators, production assistants and many others as well as directors.

In addition, many stylistic approaches will be pre-determined by the genre and institutional placing of a programme, especially for long-running series. The soap-opera naturalism of *Coronation St* or the casual approach of *Countryfile* may look obvious, but they are carefully constructed nonetheless, developed over the years by successive makers of the series. A fresh director may add something of their own approach, but unless, like *Dr Who*, a series is constantly reshaped, they may not make radical changes. That said, the director retains a pivotal role in the production of a programme and there are those who have placed their personal stamp on their work: Peter Kosminsky has evolved a particular style of drama-documentary; Adam Curtis makes personal documentary essays, developing complex arguments using archive material. Balancing creativity with craft, many directors seek to express their own creative vision, and all directors aim to capture the attention and stir the emotions of the audience.

In television there are several different types of directors. The person who controls a live news broadcast in a studio gallery has a very different job from the director in charge of filming and editing a year-long observational series or from the team of directors who work on a long-running soap opera. Different production types and different genres pose their own challenges. Dramas require special skills in working with actors and an understanding of performance. At the same time, the period reconstruction of a series such as *Downton Abbey* contrasts with the up-to-date urgency of, for example, *Casualty*. In longer documentaries and current affairs, directors may be concerned as much with the journalistic as the televisual impact of a programme, while 'factual entertainment' shows such as *The Only Way is Essex*, and 'formatted' programmes such as *Don't Tell the Bride* involve a particular relationship with their subjects (see Chapter 16 for more on formatted programmes). However, whether working on location or in a studio, on a high-end drama or a sofa show, during the shoot the authority lies with the director. He or she must plan which shots will be taken and in which order, and what their content will be. Within certain limits, it is up to them to make things work, and that includes the smooth running of the production period as well as the content of the final programme.

Programmes differ enormously in their budgets, from feature films designed for cinema release costing many millions of pounds, through high-budget commercials made by specialist companies, to relatively low-budget programmes made by smaller companies and independent producers. Size of budget and scale of production inevitably affects crewing and the relationships between those who bring their different skills to the job. At all levels it remains a director's task to know as much as possible about those different skills, whether they are carried out by individuals or substantial teams. They should recognise the implications of what their crew is being asked to achieve, and understand something of the technical problems their creative decisions are posing. Teamwork is all important. Directors must gain the trust of their crew, and very often crew members will be chosen for their flexibility and ability to fit in as well as for the quality of their work. A shoot can be disastrous if those who are working closely together, often under conditions of considerable stress, do not get on. A great deal of nervous energy may be used up in trying to keep the peace. Not causing upsets or creating scenes, the ability to work long hours and cope with all eventualities, these are the tough demands that are made of television directors and crews.

In addition to the director, key roles during the production period include the *assistant director (first AD)*, the *sound engineer* and the *cinematographer.* Depending on the size of the production, each of these may either work alone or with a single assistant, or they may head a substantial team. In the case of the *first AD*, there may be a second and third AD, each with specific roles. It is the AD who represents the production manager during the shoot. Often known as the 'sergeant major', he or she is responsible for the organisation, making sure everything is in place and on time, and ensuring that things happen as they should, leaving the director free to concentrate on the creative aspects. The *sound engineer* contributes to the 'audio design' of a programme and is responsible for producing sound that is clear and faithfully represents the dialogue or music that is being recorded (see Chapter 11 for more on sound recording). The chief responsibility of the *cinematographer* is to produce the images the director asks for. In most cases the overall style and effect will have been decided well before shooting begins, and their concern will be with the types of camera used, as well as the control of the lighting and the content and composition of the shots (see Chapter 10 for more on cinematography and lighting).

Currently, due to the greater accessibility of cameras and recording equipment and a less rigid attitude towards craft skills, which were once closely guarded fiefdoms, it is becoming more common for programme-makers to be multiskilled. It is not unusual for the same person to produce and direct a programme, and sometimes to film it, too, using a portable single camera (PSC) (see Gio Ulleri p. 245; Anne Parisio p. 229). Many freelance directors have bought their own camera gear and gained some training in its use. Especially in news, documentaries and other factual genres, many directors feel that filming their own material brings them closer to their subjects. In this case, the person with the camera is also the person who decides which shots will be taken and in which order, as well as the aesthetic effect desired. Many cameras can record sound simultaneously with the filming, in which case the person who is doing the filming must also keep an eye on sound levels. However, the best quality sound tends to be separately recorded and monitored by a skilled sound recordist.

Over the years there have been some remarkable examples of documentary directors who are also experienced cinematographers. They include Molly Dineen who filmed and directed *The Ark*, a moving and sympathetic look at the life of London Zoo, and Chris Terrill who was among the first to use lightweight digital equipment for his series, including *Soho Stories* and *The Cruise*. In addition, long established directors began to realise that there are circumstances in which it is more appropriate to do their own filming. Paul Watson, who made his reputation in 1974 with what was arguably the first docu-soap, *The Family*, did his own shooting for *Malcolm and Barbara: A Love Story*. Over a period of four years, he followed the life of a couple as the husband deteriorated from the dreadful, mind-destroying, Alzheimer's disease.

By contrast, a larger production will employ a director of photography (DOP) who directs the lighting and may supervise a number of camera operators and assistants. There may be a 'focus puller' (helping the camera operator by adjusting the focus as the camera tracks in or out) and a 'clapper/loader' (in charge of the clapper board used to synchronise picture and sound). In addition, a digital imaging technician (DIT) will be in charge of the memory cards and will liaise with the editor. In a fixed-rig set up and some studios the cameras are controlled remotely from the gallery. Chapter 12 will look at studio work, but in this and the next two chapters we will discuss the production period from the point of view of 'filmed' programmes and segments, beginning with the visual element and the work of the director and the cinematographer. Despite the changes of recent years, there remain certain competencies without which the basic structures of television simply would not work.

THE DIRECTOR'S CONCERNS

Alan Wurtzel and John Rosenbaum use the concepts of 'video space' and 'audio space' to describe the imaginary worlds created for television viewers:

> The only measure of reality for the television viewer is what they see and hear through the television receiver. A 'real life' event that unfolds before the cameras does not exist for viewers until that reality is translated through the television realities and on to their sets.
>
> (1995: 39)

Those video and audio spaces, the overall effect created by the myriad of inputs that make up a television programme, are conjured up by the work of the director.

Programmes are usually constructed from relatively self-contained sequences. A sequence will typically be shot in a single location and will have some form of internal coherence. Bearing in mind that each shot is only a small segment of the sequence, thought must be given to how the shots will cut together at the editing stage to create the whole. For example, without enough planning there is a temptation to shoot large quantities of material, such as long, rambling interviews that are hard to edit.

As well as creating the emotional and aesthetic atmosphere of each sequence, the director has certain practical tasks:

Preparation and planning

The patterning of shots must be pre-prepared, and the shooting schedule planned and timed (see Production Management p. 80 above). In a drama, the sequence will be carefully prepared and sometimes storyboarded beforehand. A documentary is more likely to be more spontaneously shot and constructed at the editing stage.

The presenter Mary Beard described the balance between planning and improvisation in her series on ancient Rome.

> There's a detailed road map which plots the running order of how the argument is to develop and in what locations across the 60 minutes. But when I face the camera the words are mine – more or less spontaneous. They have been carefully considered but never learned by heart.
>
> (*Guardian* 13 July 2013)

For the greatest efficiency, shots will inevitably be filmed in a different order from that in which they appear in the final sequence. Since changes in camera position may entail considerable disruption, involving the readjustment of lights, microphones and other paraphernalia, it is more efficient to take all necessary shots from a single camera set up at one go. This means that, when the beginning and end of a programme take place in the same location – beside a river, on top of a tower block – it's likely that the beginning and end will be shot at the same time, even though this may be difficult for the actors.

The director must also:

- Make sure the crew are properly briefed so that they can make their own creative contribution.

- Ensure continuity throughout a sequence (see visual grammar below).

- Ensure that a sufficient variety of shots is provided to give flexibility in the editing room. It is important to provide wide shots and covering material, and also 'cutaways'. These are shots that can be used to shorten the main action, such as someone listening while the protagonist is talking. In a documentary situation where the crew have to keep up with fast-moving action, the cinematographer must be briefed about what sort of cutaways are needed, as they must be captured while the action is happening.

- Control the number of takes of any given shot. Apart from some forms of observational documentary filming, it is customary to repeat the action several times to ensure that the desired result is achieved. An actor may forget their lines, an aeroplane may pass overhead obliterating the sound, a microphone shadow may be seen in shot, or the director or cinematographer may simply think the whole thing could be done more effectively. Even in spontaneous interviews, if the interviewee feels they could express a particular idea better or temporarily runs out of ideas, the director will call 'cut' and another take will be set up.

- Oversee the technical production of the scene. In an established organisation with regular procedures, say sports programmes or an ongoing soap opera, the picture and sound quality will also be monitored by specialised technicians. But ultimately problems such as unwanted microphones in shot or lapses in continuity are the director's responsibility.

Visual grammar

For a smooth flow that does not jolt the audience out of the illusion of continuity, certain conventions are followed. These are devices by which the actual space that exists between each shot is smoothed out in the finished film and in the audience's mind. It has often been stressed that such continuity is, indeed, an illusion, as the video space is carefully created.

Continuity

To maintain continuity between shots the director must ensure that:

- *Visual detail is consistent*. For example, clothing should not be rearranged between shots – jackets should stay open or done up; hair should not suddenly change its style; spectacles should be consistently on or off; objects in the room should not change their position, and so on.

- *Movement is continuous*. A hand gesture begun in the long shot should be continued in the close up; an entrance through a door should not show the door knob being turned in both the exterior and interior shots; if a character is running when they leave one shot, they should not be walking in the next – unless, of course, continuity is deliberately broken to achieve a special effect. A turn of the head, a gesture, the crossing of a car across the action temporarily blanking out the screen may all serve to carry over, to 'suture' (this clinical term, meaning to stitch up a wound, has been used by film theorists) the real gap between two shots, and to make the audience perceive them as continuous.

Of course the decision may be made to use other forms of editing, which do not rely on continuity, such as parallel editing, but these, too, must be prepared at the shooting stage (see Chapter 13).

The 180 degree rule

Crossing the imaginary 'line' that runs between the characters in a scene will involve a sense of discontinuity, as the person facing right will suddenly appear to be facing left, and hence away from their companion. In a football match, all the cameras

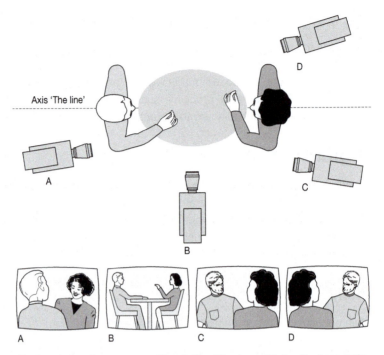

The three images from camera positions A, B and C cut smoothly together because the characters maintain their screen directions. Position D, however, has 'crossed the line'. It reverses the characters' eyelines and so does not intercut with the other angles.

FIGURE 9.1
'Crossing the line'

must be on the same side of the pitch, or else there will be confusion about which team is running in which direction. If the 'line' is crossed, a cutaway will be necessary to bridge the gap, or there may be a shot in which a camera movement allows the audience to observe the participants in the scene changing position in relation to each other. With hand-held, observational shooting, camera movements are often fluid and undefined. These conventions then come into play at the editing stage, when the editor selects which sections of the shots to cut together.

Similarly, if several shots show a character travelling, say walking along a street, they must consistently enter camera right and exit camera left, or else there will be the impression of reverse or random movement.

Shot, reverse shot structure

This is a basic sequence in classical continuity narrative construction. For example, shots of two characters engaged in dialogue will favour first one and then the other. The camera will frame on one person facing right and on the other facing left.

Edited together, this gives the illusion of two people facing each other and enables cutting back and forth between the characters who appear to be interacting. The audience 'read' the alternation as a link between them, whether or not they were *actually* together when the shots were taken. For example, an interviewer's questions will often be filmed when the interviewee is no longer in the room. In this case, it will be important to ensure that the eyelines of the two characters match. If their eyes do not appear to engage with each other, the effect is strange and disorienting. This is the sort of detail a good cinematographer will be able to recognise.

The principle of motivation

A movement within a scene may prompt, or 'motivate', a camera movement or a cut. The camera may pan to follow the glance of a character, or the editor may cut to the object the character has noticed.

An intensification of emotion may motivate a cut to a closer shot, feeding the audiences desire to observe more closely. Classic examples are the *Man Alive* series, produced by Desmond Wilcox in the 1960s, and the probing *Face to Face* interviews conducted by John Freeman in the 1960s and revived by Jeremy Isaacs in the 1990s, which used very big close shots to reveal the flickers of emotion in their interviewees' faces.

The patterning of shots

Too many shots taken from a similar distance from the subject are difficult to edit into a smooth sequence and tiring for the audience. Usually a wide shot will establish the scene, showing something of the setting and ambience, followed by closer shots, so that the characters' facial expressions become clearer and the viewer can follow their thoughts as well as their actions.

Two shots on the same person should involve a significant change of angle. A minimal change is read as a 'jump cut', an awkward twitch, rather than a deliberate perceptual shift (see Chapter 13 for a consideration of these principles from the point of view of the editor).

Shots as material for visual effects

When visual effects will be used in a scene, the director and cinematographer must provide some shots that the effects team will use as the basis of their work. These may include:

Clean plate

A 'clean plate' for a sequence that will be enhanced at the post-production stage. This may be a background shot within which the digitally created action will take place, or a second take of a shot without actors or events to provide additional information for the visual effects team.

Survey references

Shots that include 'survey references', such as markers and measuring sticks, give a clear idea of the dimensions of a scene, and examples for light matching, material matching and camera matching. Often the visual effects supervisors will be present at the shoot to help the crews understand what will be required for the effects sequence to work properly.

Green screen (or blue screen)

One frequently used effect is to film the action – presenter, actor – against a plain green backdrop. The background may then be filmed quite separately, whether at a distant location, or a computer-generated fantasy world as *Dr Who* travels through time. The two images can then be combined through a process called chroma key. In a studio recording, this can be done in the gallery by the vision mixer. It is a frequently used effect for news programmes and news magazines.

Most television studios have a green curtain available for chroma key work. Some have special studios available with all green floor and walls. The move from the use of blue to green screen was, allegedly, because so many presenters were wearing blue jeans. This meant that when the image was superimposed, their legs simply dissolved into the background!

Within visual effects new techniques and processes are constantly developing (see Chapter 14).

TYPES OF SHOT

During the production period, the director, together with the cinematographer, must arrange each of the *shots* that will be assembled to create the *sequences* that will structure the *programme*. The shots are patiently created, one by one, each carefully designed with its own characteristics, and each making a different set of demands on the performers and technicians involved.

Shots may be categorised according to:

- usage
- content of the shot
- camera angle
- camera movement

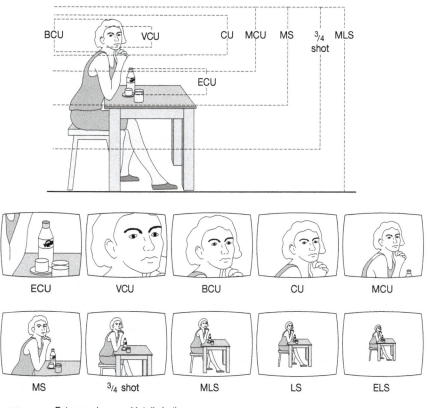

ECU	Extreme close-up (detail shot)
VCU	Very close shot (face shot) from mid-forehead to above the chin
BCU	Big close-up (full head). The head nearly fills the screen
CU	Close-up. Just above the head to the upper chest
MCU	Medium close shot. Cuts the body at the lower chest, just below the armpit
MS	Medium shot (mid-shot, waist shot). Cuts the body just below the waist
$^3/_4$ shot	Cuts just below the knees
MLS	Medium long shot (full length shot). The entire body, plus a short distance above and below
LS	Long shot. The person occupies around two-thirds of screen height
ELS	Extra long shot or extreme long shot

FIGURE 9.2
Shots classified by the amount of a person included within the frame

A sequence of shots will be planned, perhaps storyboarded, and it will be up to the DOP and his or her crew to achieve them. For simplicity, we will just refer to the cinematographer from now on.

Shots classified by usage

From the point of view of the director and editor, shots can be classified according to their eventual use in the programme:

- *Master shot*: a wide shot in which an entire sequence is played out. Close shots and other angles may be shot later and edited into the master shot. This is an objective shot, taken from the point of view of an imaginary viewer outside the scene.

- *Point of view shot*: a shot from the viewpoint of one of the actors in a scene. This is described as a subjective shot.

- *Over-the-shoulder shot*: this may usefully link two or more participants in a conversation, as a partial view of the back of each person's head while the other is speaking reminds us of their presence.

- *Cutaway*: a shot that is not directly connected to the content of a scene, but which may be inserted to speed up the editing or to cover a hiatus in the action. During a routine interview, shots of the interviewer or of the interviewee's hands, of objects around the room or objects to which the interviewee is referring, may be used to condense an hour or so of material into a manageable ten minutes or whatever length is required.

- *Clean plate*: for a sequence that will be created at the post-production stage. This is usually a second take of the shot without actors or events.

Shots classified by content

Shots may be described according to how they divide up their subjects, in other words, by the amount of person included within the frame:

Certain aesthetic preferences have controlled what tends to be seen as an acceptable framing for routine use. Although such rules are often broken, the breaking of them usually serves to draw attention to the convention.

When more than one person is included within the frame they may be referred to as two shots, three shots and so on, up to 'crowd shots'.

A shot with a wide angle lens, which includes a broad view of the action, is called a wide shot.

Too much headroom can be as bad as too little

The longer the shot, the more headroom is needed

Certain aesthetic preferences have controlled what tends to be seen as an acceptable framing for routine use. Although such rules are often broken, the breaking of them usually serves to draw attention to the convention.

FIGURE 9.3
Framing

Shots classified by camera angle

To achieve the desired angle within the frame, the camera must be placed at the appropriate level. Shots are described according to the possible positions of the camera in relation to normal eye-level.

Viewpoints carry their own emotional impact and influence the way subjects are seen. If the camera is at eye-level, the gaze of the person within the frame meets that of the audience. Low-angle or high-angle shots each create a specific effect. If the camera is low, looking up, the audience has the impression of a dominant character towering over them. For extreme low angles, such as those in *Citizen Kane* (1941) – a film that is in itself a university course for cinematographers – Orson Welles needed help from the set builders. For the notorious shots showing Kane looming over his wife against an expanse of ceiling, the stage itself was built up, allowing the camera to be positioned well below floor level (Kael 1971).

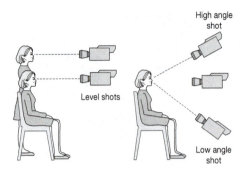

FIGURE 9.4
Camera angles

By contrast, if the camera is high, looking down, the character appears diminished within the frame. The angle increases a sense of their vulnerability. In the Channel Four series *The Secret Life of the Four, Five and Six Year Olds*, the camera avoided this effect by remaining at the children's eye-level, about two feet from the ground.

Hollywood film noir of the 1930s and 1940s experimented with camera angles, which derived from German expressionist cinema of the 1920s. In the Soviet Union, documentary filmmaker Dziga Vertov and others were experimenting with the medium of film itself. Their aim was to 'make the image strange'. One way of doing this was to show familiar things from unfamiliar angles. 'Always avoid the navel position', they declared. By contrast, the British documentarist Edgar Anstey felt that the most straightforward way of shooting showed most respect to those he was portraying. In his film *Housing Problems* (1935), he and Ruby Grierson pioneered the interview form. 'We always had the camera four feet off the ground (i.e. at eye-level)' he wrote, 'because it was *not our film.*'

Shots classified by movement

Camera movements reframe a scene as it develops. This gives a very different effect from the movement of figures within a static frame. In a drama, one of the jobs of the director is to design the movement of the actors in interaction with the movement of the frame. Camera movements are described as 'motivated' when they follow an action or are prompted by an event within the scene – for example, a pan may follow a character as they cross a room, a tilt down may follow the direction of the character's gaze as they notice something on the floor, a track moves alongside two characters as they walk together. A camera movement that follows no logic but its own is described as 'unmotivated'.

- *Static shots*: a director may decide to keep the camera still and to move the characters within the frame. When the camera comes to rest after a series of moving shots, or when a film is composed without camera movement – Patrick Keiller's *London* (1994) and Chantal Akerman's *Jeanne Dielman, 23 Quai du Commerce, 1080 Bruxelles* (1975) are two celebrated but very different examples – a lack of movement can have a striking effect.

- *Pans and tilts*: when the camera head makes a pivoting movement from side to side, it is described as a pan; when it pivots up or down, it is a tilt.

- *Tracking*: a movement that takes its name from the tracks, similar to railway tracks, along which the camera moves. The use of tracks ensures a smooth movement, but a 'tracking shot' may be any travelling shot in which the camera is moving along with the action.

- *Crabbing*: a sideways movement.

- *Zoom*: a movement just of the lens. A zoom lens can move from wide shot to close up without losing focus. The introduction of a long zoom lens in the 1960s greatly enhanced the flexibility of hand-held cameras. The crash zoom – a sudden, unexpected closing in on a person or object – became a favourite device.

Camera mountings

Apart from the zoom, camera movements are achieved largely through different kinds of mountings. In the early days of cinema, cameras strapped to the front of trains gave exciting travelling views to audiences at the music halls and variety shows where they formed part of the bill. Travelling shots may use any form of mounting, from aerial shots from a drone, to road shots from the window of a car, or simply a camera operator pushed on a trolley to achieve greater smoothness. Together with the cameras themselves, mountings are constantly developing, and becoming lighter and more manipulable. The possibility of remote control has introduced many new devices, and has enabled a wide range of movements, from a small-scale track across a table-top, to a broad, sweeping aerial view.

Television studios are equipped with cameras mounted on a pedestal or a jib. The camera operator may either work from the studio floor or cameras may be controlled remotely from the gallery (see Chapter 12). Film studios and major location set-ups may use a substantial dolly or crane. The opening shot of Orson Welles's *Touch of Evil* (1958) is remembered as a virtuoso use of a moving crane shot choreographed with developing action. The bigger the mounting, the bigger the crew required to operate it, including at least one grip – the person who controls the dolly, moving it along steadily so that no jolt or hesitation will be visible in the shot.

For television location crews, a range of readily available and manipulable mountings is available:

- The camera may be *hand-held*, which usually means securely balanced on the shoulder of the cinematographer, although now many cameras are small enough to be literally held in the hand. A hand-held – or rather shoulder-held – camera may be kept rigid, as if on a tripod, or may make a variety of informal movements as the operator moves it around, adjusting focus in imitation of the human eye. Sometimes derisively referred to as 'wobblyscope', this is a modified version of the 'direct cinema' style evolved by Richard Leacock and the Maysles brothers in the United States in the 1960s, which was made possible by the development of a 16mm portable film camera. They aimed for a fluid and continuous sequence that followed the action in real time, rather than being broken down into discrete shots. Although today's cameras may be much smaller and more lightweight, hand-held movements of long duration still need a great deal of skill to achieve.

- A *tripod* is part of the regular equipment of a camera crew. A good tripod is stable with a fluid 'head' on which the camera is mounted. This gives a steady, controllable frame, allowing varied movements without unwanted jolts or judders. It is usually the job of the camera assistant to move and place the tripod, as well as, when necessary, to operate the clapper board.

- A *jimmy jib* has a long extension arm with the camera suspended at one end and a monitor and camera controls at the other. A 'hot head' supports the camera and enables it to be controlled remotely. However, the jib needs a van to transport it and at least two people to manipulate it, including a trained operator. Lighter weight jibs are also available, which can be assembled even in difficult territory.

- A *dolly or a crane*: mounting on a dolly allows for controlled tracking. The addition of a crane makes rising and descending movements possible, too. The cinematographer, and sometimes the assistant, ride on the dolly and operate the camera directly. However, a large crane is rarely used on location. Instead a range of camera jibs provide flexible movements and can be mounted on a dolly if necessary.

- *Sliders and skaters*: the camera may slide along a rail suspended between two tripods, achieving a smooth tracking shot, or it may be placed on a small platform on wheels. This can be used for fine table-top work – allowing the camera to circle smoothly around objects as small as a bottle of wine or a vase of flowers.

- *Skycam*: for a large event, such as a music festival, a camera can be mounted on a telescopic mast for a high shot. Alternatively a sturdy wire can be suspended between towers on either side of a venue, so that a remotely controlled camera can glide over the heads of the crowd.

FIGURE 9.5
Filming with a Steadicam on location. The camera operator can achieve steady
pictures even while moving or shooting from difficult positions

Photograph: Lewis Kahn

- *Steadicam*: this mounting straps the camera supports to the body of the
  operator and incorporates a device to keep the image steady. A skilled
  operator can move or run while they are shooting with virtually no camera
  shake. Phil Redmond claims that he was the first to introduce the use of
  Steadicam into British television. When the quiet, suburban Brookside Close
  was converted into a set for a new soap opera in 1982, this was part
  of his strategy to create a naturalistic style, filmed within the four walls of
  real houses rather than a studio set (Redmond 2000). Operating a Steadicam is a difficult and specialised skill; the cameras are heavy and the
  harness cumbersome. Recently a newer lighter form of harness has been
  developed which can be used by less experienced operators, helping to
  keep lighter cameras steady.

- A *MoVI* is a portable frame with two handles which allows the camera to
  be balanced on a giro-controlled gimbal mounting. This enables movement
  through three axes, and can give a similar effect to a Steadicam. It is
  popular for use with DSLR and smaller cameras, but, once again, its
  operation requires skill and experience.

- *Aerial shots*: finally, mountings are needed for those spectacular aerial
  shots which sweep over the landscape and follow the action from above.

For many years these were achieved by filming from a helicopter, and often entailed precarious acrobatics by a well-strapped-in cinematographer. The arrival of 'unmanned aerial vehicles' (UAVs), popularly known as 'drones', has changed this. The use of drones has given rise to a range of new risks and problems, including legal ones. Drone operators, usually from specialist companies, must now be aware of the Civil Aviation Authority (CAA) regulations, which control their use.

In an article for the Royal Television Society (February 2015), Andrew Sheldon, Creative Director of the independent production company True North, described the drone as 'the gadget of the moment', which 'brings a little bit of Hollywood to even the most mundane corners of the EPG' (the electronic programme guide). However, he pointed out that their use gives rise to human rights as well as public safety issues, as they can be used for covert and investigative programmes, and for reporting the news from conflict zones.

Nevertheless, he added, they are now 'part of the grammar of television' www.rts. org.uk/magazine/article/send-drones.

A FRESH PERCEPTION OF THE WORLD

A director's desire to make the most of all available techniques is not new. In Moscow in 1929 Denis Kaufman, who chose to be known as Dziga Vertov because it sounded like the incessant cranking of a camera turned by hand, made *Man with a Movie Camera*, the film in which the camera takes a bow. He was determined to use 'every cinematic technique, every cinematic invention, every device and method' for this documentary of urban life in the Soviet Union. Aiming to exploit to the full the resources of the camera, pushing it beyond what the human eye can perceive, he wrote:

> I am the cinema-eye. I am a mechanical eye. I, a machine, can show you the world as only I can see it. From today I liberate myself forever from human immobility. *I am in perpetual motion*, I approach and move away from objects, I creep up to them, I climb on to them, I move alongside the muzzle of a running horse, I tear into the crowd at full speed, I run before the fleeing soldiers, I tip over on to my back, I ascend with aeroplanes, I fall and rise together with falling and rising bodies. . . . My way leads to the creation of a fresh perception of the world. And this is how I can decipher a world unknown to you.
>
> (Enzenberger 1972: 3)

The modern reader will recognise many of the shots Vertov describes here. Some of them have become clichés in the intervening years, but the exuberance of this description reflects an enthusiasm for seeing things in a new way: the sheer pleasure of the inventive image, the 'fresh perception of the world'. Of course Vertov was criticised, notably by the greatest filmmaker of his generation, Sergei Eisenstein, who called some of his tricks 'unmotivated camera mischief' (Vertov 1984: xxi). That debate between the two virtuosos of early Soviet cinema stakes out positions that are still defended, and will underlie much of the information presented in this book as we consider different forms of technology and what it is possible to do with them. Are there rules appropriate to each genre, so that what you do with the camera must be 'motivated' by the structures of the genre? Or does anything go? It seems that today, 'camera mischief' is definitely in fashion.

Of course, for twenty-first-century mischief, a camera is effectively 'a computer with a lens', and it is used in collaboration with numerous other computers to create the effects that enhance contemporary programmes and interstitials. Sophisticated visual effects may add fantasy and spectacle to the programmes, as well as to the advertisements, title sequences and other material, which come between them. Alternatively they may make imperceptible adjustments to the image without disrupting the impression of realism. The television image was once thought of as a direct source of 'reality', but now manipulation and illusion pervade every part. 'Reality' has retreated as television continues to push at the boundaries of the visual (for visual effects, see Chapter 14).

All the techniques discussed in the following chapters create *meaning* of some sort or another. Every difference, whether it be a difference of acting style, a difference of camera angle, a deliberate imperfection in the image or a difference in sound quality, carries its own sets of implications, connotations and meanings. Part of the pleasure of both making and watching television is in the fluidity of these meanings.

KEY TEXTS

Bamford, N. (2012) *Directing Television: A Professional Survival Guide*, London: Bloomsbury.
Rabiger, M. (2015) *Directing the Documentary*, 6th edn, Oxford: Focal Press.
Wurtzel, A. and Rosenbaum, J. (1995) *Television Production*, 4th edn, New York: McGraw-Hill.

CHAPTER 10

The visual dimension: cameras, lighting and the cinematographer

CAMERAS AND RECORDING MEDIA

Since the American inventor Thomas Edison first patented his motion-picture camera, the Kinetograph, in 1891, the desire to do something more with moving images has driven technological invention. From a simple wooden box with a handle to wind the roll of film and a device to hold each frame steady behind the lens for long enough to make an exposure, a huge range of cameras and other devices has developed. Now, more than a century after the first moving pictures, digital cameras come in many shapes and sizes, from mobile phones through to cameras for 3D, high-definition television (HDTV) and ultra-high-definition (4K) images. In the 20teens new developments follow each other with remarkable speed. Over the decades each new technical development has brought new forms of aesthetic experimentation. From time to time these hardened into 'rules', only to be broken when the next development came along. Now, in the twenty-first century, digital photography together with computer-generated imagery (CGI) and digital effects have combined to produce the startling visual variety which makes today's television and its accompanying online media so endlessly fascinating.

From the early days of cinema it has been possible to capture a filmed image on perforated celluloid stock. This passes behind the lens where it is held momentarily in position to create a static frame. The image is recorded on the film emulsion through a photo-chemical process. The earliest cameras were hand-cranked, but with the arrival of sound and mechanical cameras, the speed became fixed at 24 or 25 frames per second. Several different gauges, based on the width of the stock, have been in use, originally creating a black and white image, then, before long, colour. Usually a negative image is produced in the camera, and this is sent to specialised laboratories to be processed and printed.

FIGURE 10.1
Natalie Brown filming with a Panasonic P2 Varicam for Sky 1's *What's Up* Season 9

Photograph: Lyle Ashun. Courtesy: Licklemor Productions

The arrival of television (the word means 'viewing from a distance'), first broadcast to the UK public in 1936, meant that the image was not recorded, but was an immediate experience, like sound radio, transmitted through the invisible radio spectrum. It was celebrated in that very first programme by the glamorous Adele Dixon who sang of the 'mighty maze of mystic magic rays . . . which bring television to you'. The moment was filmed, and the clip on the BBC website shows the cameras and the array of controls involved in creating that first public broadcast www.bbc.co.uk/programmes/p00lkqyq.

Television cameras were electronic, the image was transitory and at first every effort was made to create a type of programme that would be specifically televisual. For example, early documentaries experimented with live studio reconstructions rather than being shot on film. But there were concerns about the ephemeral nature of television, and film made a comeback. Live studio programmes were preserved by 'telerecording' – effectively by placing a film camera in front of a television screen.

As we have seen throughout this book, across the history of moving image media, aesthetic choices have been linked to developing technology, and many of the styles of the past contribute to the range of visual options available today. For example, the introduction of high-quality 16mm stock in the early 1960s meant that cameras could be smaller and light enough to be carried on the shoulder, instead of using the weighty tripods necessary to support a bulky 35mm camera. This gave rise to the new and urgent documentary style developed by Robert Drew and Richard Leacock in the United States (called 'direct cinema') and, in a different way by Jean Rouch in France (called 'cinema verité') (see Chapter 16).

The arrival of video tape changed the options once more. Without the need to send the material to a laboratory to be processed, this was a medium that was not just used by established professionals. When Channel Four was set up in 1982 with a brief to commission independent companies and a wider range of pro-gramming (see Chapter 2), video tape came into its own. Many different formats were developed, some for high-end professional use, others for semi-professional use. Many small, independent collectives and campaigning groups used video. One of its most innovative uses was in the early 1990s, when the BBC's Community Programme Unit launched the *Video Diaries* series, followed by the *Video Nation* project, in which hundreds of ordinary people were given High-8 tape camcorders to record their everyday lives. These were the broadcast forerunners of the YouTube channels and vloggers of today. Indeed, some of them can now be found on YouTube (Colonel Gordon Hensher shares his thoughts on looking in the mirror: www.youtube.com/watch?v=DML3VMrcLgM).

This gave rise to a new genre and a completely new 'look' on television, in which the informality of the presentation and the roughness of the image conveyed its own sense of spontaneity.

The earliest digital formats were on tape, but now the image is almost always file-based, captured on a solid-state memory card or hard disc, although, for archive purposes, material tends to be stored on a 3/4-inch digital tape. Contemporary technology can be confusing, as digital formats are constantly developing and are difficult to standardise. However, the BBC issues recommendations for crews making programmes for the Corporation.

The resources of digital technology have vastly expanded the scope of the image, both during filming and at the post-production stage. For example, new proces-ses offer higher and higher resolution, giving, among other things, a greater range of colour and greater sensitivity. A single candle can produce enough light for a modern camera to record two people in an intimate candle-lit dinner. Digital cameras have a great deal of flexibility, with sophisticated ways of manipulating the image within the camera itself. At the same time, film stock manufacturers Kodak continue to produce celluloid film, as some directors prefer film for aesthetic reasons. Quentin Tarantino is said to have rejected digital cinematography as 'television in public'.

Kodak now describe their concern as 'motion picture imaging', since digital work and film are now so closely interrelated. As usual, aesthetic choices and developing technology are working together.

CAMERAS AND DIGITAL CINEMATOGRAPHY

Cameras

A digital camera has been described as a computer with a lens. Contemporary digital cameras used for television production come with a wide range of features. Most are technically 'camcorders' as they have the ability to record picture and sound. A complex system will record more information per frame, a less expensive system less information. However, today even the smallest and least expensive can, when necessary, produce a broadcast-quality image. Technology continues to develop at a rapid pace with companies such as Sony, Arri, Canon, JVC and Panasonic all competing with each other. Constant new developments mean that the situation remains ever changing.

Most professional cameras produce a high definition (HD) 2K image with a wide-screen aspect ratio (2K refers to a horizontal resolution of 2,048 pixels). However, 'HD' does not necessarily mean the best quality, as the information can be compressed and the quality of the image also depends on factors such as the quality of the lens. Meanwhile, as technology advances, the size of the sensor, the device that converts the optical image to an electric signal, continues to increase.

FIGURE 10.2
Mark Bond filming with an Arri Alexa

Courtesy: RedBalloon Productions

The 2015 wildlife series *The Hunt* was filmed in the highest resolution available, 4K. The reason, said the producer, was to 'future-proof' the series (*Radio Times* 31 October 2015: 10). At the time no broadcaster could transmit that degree of detail, but many predict that 4K is likely to become standard.

Many cameras are modular, built of individual parts that can be configured in various ways. However, the size of the sensor is of crucial importance. Cameras that are described as 'digital cinematography' cameras have large sensors, similar to those used for cinema films, while standard digital cameras have smaller sensors.

Some game-changing developments have included:

1   *Canon 5D Mark 2* developed in 2008 is a stills camera with video capacity. This proved to be a game changer as it was high quality with a large, full frame, sensor (bigger than 35mm celluloid stock).

2   *Panasonic AG AF101* was the first fully modular camera to be developed. It has a large 'four thirds' sensor. In other words, it gives a four-by-three aspect ratio (four units width to three units height) designed for a filmic look.

3   *Canon C300*. This was another game changer, producing an image equivalent to super-35mm celluloid stock. It has been the most popular choice in the mid-20teens.

Meanwhile the Arri Alexa and Red camera ranges continue to be used for high-end television and feature films.

For choice of camera, the important issues are:

- resolution
- bytes per second – the read and write speed
- codec – the 'file wrapper' system to code and decode the images and other information. On a cheaper system some information may be lost (Stump 2014: 374)
- format – this refers to the horizontal resolution, for example, 2K is 2,048 pixels wide, UHD 4K is 3,840.

Although the type of camera has a strong relation to the nature of the image, within the television industry the choice is more often than not a pragmatic one, controlled by decisions already made by the programme series or by the equipment available. In addition, the size of the budget will inevitably influence what system is used. *The Hunt* had a multimillion-pound budget.

By contrast, for some news crews the newest innovation is a 'live app' for a smart phone or tablet. Crews can carry a lightweight backpack containing a number of sim cards to link to the mobile phone networks over which they transmit their signal.

LiveU's website describes this as 'the next level in mobile newsgathering'. The facility was used by Sky News in its extensive 2015 election coverage, with student broadcasters operating the units at each polling station www.liveu.tv/sky-150.

But digital cinematography is not completely standardised. The BBC operates a tiering system, in which certain tiers are considered appropriate for different types of programme. Top-end drama and top-end documentaries come in the highest tier, while electronic news gathering (ENG) may come in the lowest. The Corporation's commissioning website lays down requirements for cinematographers in each tier www.bbc.co.uk/commissioning/tv/production/articles/technical-requirements.

The Digital Production Partnership, set up by ITV, the BBC and Channel Four, 'to maximise the potential of digital', are major players in establishing standards across the industry. www.digitalproductionpartnership.co.uk/what-we-do/technical-standards/.

Full access to its services is for members only, but numerous other organisations offer advice and consultation.

Lenses

Contemporary lenses have been tailored to the requirements of digital sensors, which means that they tend to be smaller and lighter than previously. However, the basic principles remain; with all cameras, the use of different lenses produces different types of shot and different sets of relationships between background and foreground figures within the frame.

Lenses on studio cameras are described in terms of the angle of vision; lenses on film cameras in terms of their focal length. The effect is the same:

- The longer the focal length of the lens, the narrower the angle of vision – sometimes described as the 'angle of acceptance' – the less there will be in the picture. That means the individual subjects will be larger. A long lens is known as a telephoto lens.

- The shorter the lens, the wider the angle of vision, the more there will be in the picture. In this case the individual subjects appear smaller. Short lenses are referred to as wide angle.

- A telephoto lens will give a crushed up effect between a foreground figure and the background.

- A wide angle lens will give a wide panorama behind the same-sized foreground figure.

If a telephoto lens is used to produce a close-up head, the camera will need to be further away than if a wide angle is used. However, the face will appear differently for each of the two lenses. The wide angle will distort the image by spreading out the features. Horror movies and scary children's programmes use this distortion to great effect. This can be pushed even further by using the ultra-wide angle fisheye lens. Between these two extremes, a standard lens gives a relationship between foreground and background which is close to normal vision.

- A zoom lens is a single lens with variable focal lengths. The size of the figure in shot changes as the lens is zoomed in or out. A zoom lens tends to be described by the ratio between its longest and shortest focal length, for example, a 'ten to one'. Similarly a 'ten by twenty five' is a zoom whose minimum focal length is 25mm and longest multiplies that by ten, that is, 250mm.

But, however sensitive the camera, the lighting of a scene is crucial. Without careful lighting, the desired effect cannot be achieved. The cinematographer/DOP is aware of the light falling on the scene and is in charge of the arrangement of the lights that are part of a location kit. The next sections will deal with the basic principles of lighting a scene (for cameras in 'live' studio set-ups, see Chapter 12).

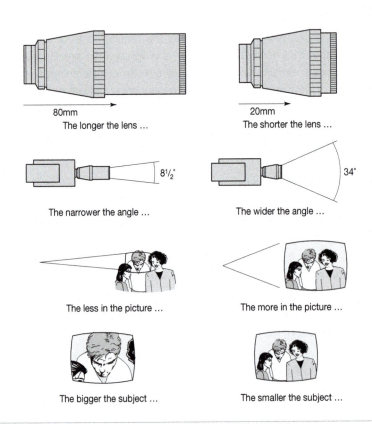

FIGURE 10.3
The relationship between focal length and angle of vision

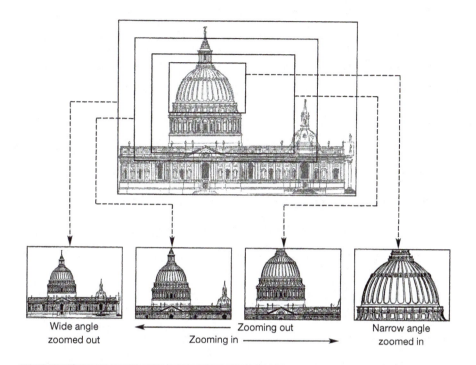

| Wide angle | ← Zooming out | Narrow angle |
| zoomed out | Zooming in → | zoomed in |

FIGURE 10.4
Zooming

VISIONS OF LIGHT

The first and unavoidable principle of lighting is that there should be enough illumination for the image to register. Since contemporary cameras are more sensitive than ever before, the second principle has become even more important: the way a scene is illuminated should express the mood and atmosphere which suits the theme. Someone making an observational documentary filmed in the street, a home or a workplace will want to preserve as faithfully as possible the light they are observing. In contrast, the DOP and lighting director working on a drama will set out to create atmospheric effects to reflect the mood.

Programmes shot on location will draw chiefly on the light which is available, whether from sunlight or artificial sources. It is possible to find ways of shooting under a wide variety of circumstances without adding to the available light. Alternatively, the natural lighting may be enhanced – dark corners illuminated, shadows created or sunlight redirected by reflective screens. However, cinematographer Nick Hale writes:

In my view, scenes should not be over lit. It's not necessary to reveal everything in full detail. It's wrong to think that it's not possible to shoot a scene if you can't get a light on the character's face. If the audience already knows what a character looks like, they are able to recognise their voice and shape so there's no reason why they should not be seen in silhouette.

(Hale 2000)

In contrast to location work, a studio gives total lighting control, with an array of light sources already in place, mounted in ceiling gantries as well as on movable stands.

When shooting with small crews, the cinematographer, sometimes helped by an assistant, is responsible for moving and fixing the lights, as well as for deciding where they are to be placed. But on bigger productions it is the specialist lighting electricians (the 'sparks') who take responsibility for the practicalities of rigging, wiring and making sure that electrical power is available.

Over the history of cinema and then of television and digital media, different lighting styles have been used to dramatic effect. In the early days of the twentieth century, the move to Hollywood was partly determined by the brilliance and clarity of the year-long Californian sunlight. But filming out of doors lost its popularity as techniques became more sophisticated and specialist studios gave greater control over the design of sets and lighting. The variations in studio lighting that developed became part of the artistry of the moving image, and they constitute a rich body of work to which the makers of television as well as cinema still refer. In Germany, the expressionist films of the 1920s used a dramatic chiaroscuro, with intense and exaggerated black and white, giving deep shadows and clear highlights. The style was taken up by Hollywood, influenced by the influx of German émigrés fleeing from Nazism, and developed into the celebrated black and white 'film noir', which, in the 1990s, was recalled by the style known as neo-noir. The style has been imitated on television many times in crime and thriller dramas. Recently, dramas from Denmark and Sweden, described as Nordic-noir, have used a much flatter, greyer monotone to convey the bleakness of their topics. Street scenes avoid the warm colours of brick and use 'glass, concrete and hard materials', said Henrick Georgsson, director of *The Bridge*. 'We try to make a cold world around the actions of the characters' (*Radio Times* 21 November 2015: 47). By contrast, soap operas and sitcoms have inherited the brighter and more even lighting used in the domestic melodramas of 1950s Hollywood.

In the early days of television, the black and white tube could only tolerate a narrow range of contrasts, so dramatic lighting effects were of necessity less common than in the cinema. By the 1960s, developing technology, including the availability of 16mm film, meant that many programme-makers were excited by the possibility of shooting out of doors, using minimal lighting and aiming to interfere as little as possible with the activity they were recording. With the coming of colour, the *effects* produced by lighting, as opposed to the mere illumination of the scene, became both more difficult to deal with and broader in scope. The sheer volume of visual information in any given shot was now huge, with the colour temperature – the warmth or coldness, redness or blueness – of the light adding a whole new range of possible variations.

By the 2000s, both drama and documentary producers were experimenting with a wider range of visual styles. Television drama had become more cinematic, and documentary was developing a 'deco-doc' style, interested in visual effects and reconstructions as well as actuality filming. Now, in the 20teens, it is taken for granted that the effects created in the original shoot will be enhanced at the post-production stage. Many of the filmed set-ups will be planned in consultation with the effects designer. The fantasy genre so popular on contemporary television (*Dr Who*; *Game of Thrones*) draws heavily on effects of this sort. At the same time, creative programme-makers are still anxious to explore the possibilities of location lighting. The 2014 drama *Wolf Hall*, largely filmed in authentic Tudor locations, recreated the impression of a sixteenth-century interior by filming as much as possible by the light of candles – the only illumination that would have been available in the 1530s. This was partly made possible by using specially sensitive cameras. It also caused considerable controversy among viewers, who are accustomed to a clearly lit image, even at the expense of authenticity www.telegraph.co.uk/news/bbc/11361855/Wolf-Hall-viewers-complain-naturally-lit-scenes-left-them-in-the-dark.html.

As with all technical areas, the task of lighting ranges from the simple exercise of common sense through to the sophisticated knowledge and sensitivity brought by an experienced DOP and lighting crew.

LIGHTING: BASIC PRINCIPLES

Reasons for artificial lighting

To provide visibility

Despite the increasing sensitivity of digital cameras, for the majority of set-ups, extra light is needed. It is often necessary to lower the contrast between the highest and lowest illumination levels in the scene in order to give the desired range of contrast in the image.

For routine interviews or documentary filming, where the crew wants to remain as unobtrusive as possible, the aim may be to use the minimum lighting necessary, especially to put the people being filmed at their ease. Michael Rabiger points out that 'the discomfort caused by injudicious lighting serves to inhibit the nervous' (Rabiger 1992: 119) and that the heat from the lights can be as uncomfortable as the unusually brilliant illumination. Those being filmed should be given the chance to get accustomed to the lighting, especially in their own homes. Bill Sims and Karen Wilson had bright lights arranged in every room of their home over a period of six years, as Jennifer Fox filmed her ten-part observational series, *An American Love Story.* They said they quickly got used to them, and even came to miss them when they were turned off. Similarly, the school students, hospital patients and others who have taken part in 'fixed-rig' documentaries have quickly grown accustomed to an unusually bright environment.

To provide information

The quality of light tells us something about time of day: twilight is very different from morning light, moonlight from sunlight. It can tell us about location, from the kaleidoscopic dazzle of a twenty-first-century city at night, to the whiteness of a snowbound landscape. Lighting can contribute to the creation of the video space within a scene: the shadow from a window where actually no window exists; 'sunlight' streaming in through a door, which in reality has nothing behind it but a 2 kilowatt light. It contributes to the illusion of three-dimensionality in the flat image on the screen.

To enhance a scene

Given that extra lighting is necessary, it can be manipulated for emotional or aesthetic effect. One approach is to exaggerate the lighting found at the scene – a cosy corner lamp, a foreboding dark shadow and so on.

As a 'functional' light within the scene

A door opens letting light through; a torch illuminates a dark corridor; a lamp is switched on. In Alfred Hitchcock's *Rear Window* (1954), the introduction of Grace Kelly is contrived through an elegant use of the soft illumination from table lamps. She illuminates her own face as she brightens the room of invalid James Stewart, by switching on three lamps, one for each of her three names (Lisa Carol Fremont).

To create effects

Effects that are non-naturalistic or impressionistic heighten the atmosphere of a scene or to mark changes in mood or mode. The changing colours of a game show, or of a rock group in late night entertainment or the swirling lights and dramatic effects of *Strictly Come Dancing,* are purely for visual pleasure.

Light sources

These include:

Available light – from windows, artificial interior lighting, lamps – even candles in the period drama *Wolf Hall.*

Key lights – scenes that are brightly lit and colourful have a low contrast factor and are referred to as high key. They may exploit the use of colour – as with the bright reds and yellows of breakfast time programmes. The assumption is that these suggest youth, energy and happiness. Low-key images have a high-contrast factor and create a sombre and more dramatic mood. Large areas of darkness revealing no detail are contrasted with strong highlights and splashes of light.

- *High key* – low contrast (bright, cheerful, energetic)
- *Low key* – high contrast (sombre, dramatic)

Three-point lighting – this basic lighting set up for a presenter, an interview or a simple set involves:

- *A key light* – provides the 'key' to the scene's appearance, and defines the main shadows to be seen on a face. It may be hard, providing clear, modelling shadows, or soft, giving a more glamorous, gentler appearance. A shift in the position of the key may alter the lighting from naturalistic illumination to one with strange, unnaturalistic shadows.
- *A fill light* – reduces the harshness and contrast provided by the key. This will usually be a soft light, possibly softened further by a diffusion filter. If lighting a single figure, it will usually be positioned below the eye-line. Some experienced women politicians have been known to insist on a low light for their interviews, so as to reduce the ageing effect of bags under the eyes. The low angle of the light can produce glints in the subjects' eyes, which gives animation to their face. In a television studio, with lights suspended from a ceiling grid, a low position is not always possible, so a dark triangle may remain unlit beneath the chin.
- *A backlight* – a hard backlight can provide a highlight effect to the hair and shoulders, and separate the subject from their background. If it is diagonally opposite the key it can give a balance to the shape of the face. A woman with long black hair will need more light, a bald man, less.

Bouncing light – light that is 'bounced' off a surface, either within the scene – say a light-coloured wall – or outside it, where a sheet of white or reflective material can be held in an appropriate position. This gives an effect that is more diffused and general than direct lighting.

Note on continuity – lights will inevitably be moved and lighting set-ups adjusted between shots to provide the maximum effect. For example, as the camera moves in from a wide shot to a close shot, the light sources will also need to come closer or the face is likely to be under-lit. Even so, an illusion of continuity must be maintained between the shots.

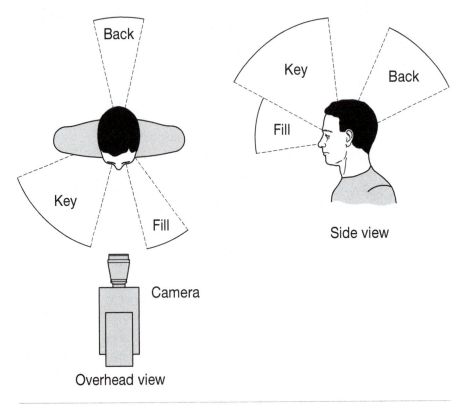

FIGURE 10.5
Three-point lighting

Light quality: intensity and colour

Hard and soft lighting

Lighting is described as hard or soft depending on whether it gives shadows that are hard- or soft-edged.

Hard light – the light source is small in relation to the subject, giving hard shadows.

Soft light – the light source is large in relation to the subject, giving soft shadows.

Light spread – spot and flood

This describes the area covered by a light.

A *spot* is an intense, narrow-angled beam of light.

A *flood* describes a wide beam with a broader spread.

Some lights are fitted with a 'Fresnel' lens, which enables a light to be adjusted between a wider or narrower beam. Side flaps, or 'barn doors', may be used to blank off part of the light and control its spread and direction.

Daylight and tungsten colour bias

There is a difference in colour bias between natural *daylight* and artificial (*tungsten*) light. If the two different sources are illuminating a single scene, coloured gelatine sheets on the windows and the light sources help match the blue of daylight with the redder quality of artificial lighting and bring the colour temperature into balance.

Colour conversion filters on the camera will affect the colour temperature of the whole scene. Electronic cameras have an adjustment that allows them to find an optimal colour rendition. Before shooting each scene the camera must be 'white balanced'. This means using a sheet of paper or some other white surface to 'tell' the camera what counts as white in these particular lighting conditions.

Gels, diffusers and reflectors

Gels: coloured gelatine sheets may be placed in front of the lights to create different intensities of reds, yellows and blues. Other colours and textures are available for effects.

Diffusers: flame-proof 'spun' fibre glass sheets may be fixed over the lamp, or some material such as 'scrim', a heat-proof opaque paper supported in a large frame, will diffuse the light, making it softer and reducing its intensity.

Reflectors: including white umbrellas and huge circular white sheets will add a filling of light, reflecting it gently back from its source. Many camera crews carry a fold-up type of reflector that is white or silver on one side and gold on the other.

Which lights?

Studio lights are fixed in position and are controlled from the studio gallery.

The portable lights most frequently in use on location for programmes such as documentaries, interviews and short sequences are:

'External reflector' or lens-less spotlights, varying from 250 watt to 3 kilowatt. The most common are 800 watt tungsten halogen lamps, sometimes known as *Redheads*, which are light and easily moved. They can be mounted on stands or clipped onto a shelf or other object in the location.

HMI (Hydrargyrum Medium Arc Iodide) is a large intense lamp, balanced for daylight. It has a high light-to-heat ratio.

Sungun is a hand-held light, around 250 watt, which runs from belt batteries and can give an intense beam. Useful on location when other forms of lighting are impossible to be set up.

Nick Hale writes: 'I don't like the powerful sungun that is so often brought out by camera crews in an emergency. I find that the light it gives is white and glaring, creating burnt out faces against a black background.'

Low-energy lights

LED (light-emitting diode): low-energy light sources can cover both daylight and tungsten. They have the advantage of consuming very little power and emitting a good level of light output while generating very little heat. Since LEDs are small, the lighting units are compact, lightweight and easy to handle. The BBC has launched a low-energy lighting project. Its new, specially designed studio in Wales for the hospital drama series *Casualty* uses 100 per cent low-energy lights http://downloads.bbc.co.uk/outreach/BBC_LEL_Guidelines.pdf.

LEDs are constantly improving, and it is predicted that eventually all light sources for television production will use low-energy LEDs.

With thanks to DOP Mark Bond, lecturer in cinematography, Bournemouth University.

KEY TEXTS

Ballinger, A. (2004) *New Cinematographers*, London: Lawrence King.
Brown, B. (2011) *Cinematography: Theory and Practice: Image Making for Cinematographers, Directors, and Videographers*, 2nd edn, Oxford: Focal Press.
Brown, B. (2015) *The Filmmakers' Guide to Digital Imaging,* Oxford: Focal Press.
Stump, D. (2014) *Digital Cinematography: Fundamentals, Tools, Techniques and Workflows*, London: Routledge.

CHAPTER 11

Sound recording and the audio space

TELEVISION AND THE FLOW OF SOUND

The flow of sound holds television together, yet sound, the creation of an 'audio space', is often neglected in studies of this intensely visual medium. But television is heir to radio, as well as to cinema, theatre and the music hall, and, unlike cinema, television began life with the expectation that its pictures would be accompanied by natural sound. Indeed, when BBC television first set up its headquarters in the majestic Alexandra Palace in North London, the radio grandees at Broadcasting House saw it as an inferior medium. They thought its pictures would simply illustrate their radio programmes. The earliest news bulletins consisted of an anonymous voice accompanied by some rather uninspiring still images. Newsreaders were not permitted to be *seen* speaking to the cameras as it was thought that their facial expression might add a biased interpretation to the neutrality of the news.

Yet in the early days of television, in the 1930s and 1940s, audiences were accustomed to 'talking pictures' in the cinema. From crime dramas to musicals, a powerful and inventive sound track was an important part of the experience. But some major differences developed between the use of sound in cinema and in television. The first is the direct address of the 'talking head'. Unlike the stars of the cinema screen, television personalities speak out of the screen to us, the audience, in a very personal way. The other difference is television's continuous flow of sound. Whereas cinema is viewed in a darkened auditorium, with all attention on the brilliantly illuminated screen and its surround-sound track, television is an everyday object, a moving image on a portable screen, which chatters and sings. It may be experienced as much as a form of company, an extra voice in the corner of the room, as a medium that needs careful attention. John Ellis has argued that cinema is the object of the audience's 'gaze', whereas television can be taken in by the occasional 'glance' (Ellis 1982: 164–5). Arguably this makes the flow of sound even more important. Television has to demand our attention, and frequently it is the sound that issues that demand.

The sound track interweaves three major dimensions: music, with its ability to create a mood and stir the emotions; sound effects, whether the naturalistic sounds of the everyday world, or the heightened impact of constructed noises; and, above all, the flow of the human voice, whose meanings and communicative power drive the flow of the broadcast material.

The voice

The 'talking head' remains the basic building block of television output. Major television genres, including news broadcasts, chat shows and documentaries that range from David Attenborough's natural history travels to Michael Portillo's train journeys, are presenter-led. They feature a charismatic individual whose speech defines the programme and who addresses the audience intimately and directly. The interview is another major factor in constructing programmes. Individuals, from politicians and celebrities to ordinary people from across the world, address the audience through the medium of an interviewer (see p. 219 for more on interviews). Their varied voices contribute to the extraordinary complexity of television's 'audio space'. And not all speakers are visible. Many programmes are commentary-led, built up by a flow of speech from an anonymous, but usually reassuring, speaker, who carries forward a narrative and occasionally comments on the action. Television is driven by the variety, flexibility, expressiveness and interest of the human voice.

In the early days of the BBC, voices were extremely formal, delivering 'Standard', educated English with all the authority of a school-teacherly medium. To today's ears, those accents sound affected and even laughable. But the founder of the BBC, John Reith, claimed that Standard English was a democratising force, able to overcome the class divisions inherent in regional accents. Yet the BBC also aimed to speak to the *whole* population; consequently many argued that broad-casting should address the public *as they were*, in all their variety. Some producers, especially in the regions, tried to broaden the range of voices that could be heard. Radio producer Olive Shapley has described her excitement when the mobile recording van was developed in the 1930s and, for the first time, microphones could be taken onto the streets to record ordinary people talking in their everyday style. These were the regional and working-class accents that were for many years considered inappropriate for the airwaves (Shapley 1996).

When television began to establish itself as the major public medium, the contest over which voices were suitable grew, if anything, more intense. For many years, women's voices were thought to be too lightweight for the authority required to be a newsreader (Holland 1987). Regional accents crept only slowly into the 'serious' parts of national television, but, from 1955, the fact that the first ITV companies were regionally based helped. Granada, based in Manchester, declared that it represented Granadaland and launched *Coronation Street* with its northern voices in 1960. Channel Four was set up with a brief to widen the range of voices heard on television. It commissioned regionally based companies and workshops, and broadcast the Merseyside-based *Brookside* from 1982. As late as 1995, the snobbish *Daily Telegraph* criticised that long-running soap for its 'unremitting dialect', stating that it preferred the accents of BBC English to 'the strangulated syllables of Liverpool or Rastafaria' (Leader column 16 February 1995). Now, despite some notable exceptions, such as presenter and television executive Melvyn Bragg (Lord Bragg), who, over his long career, stubbornly refused to lose his Cumbrian accent, it still tends to be the respondents who speak with class or regional accents rather than the interviewers.

There remain powerful arguments that UK television should be more diverse, and the question of accents is a symptom of this. However, the movement towards 'access' programming, where 'ordinary people' get to make their own programmes, such as the BBC's *Video Diaries* in the 1990s, has expanded. The arrival of YouTube has brought a cacophony of voices, and this has had a knock-on effect on mainstream media, especially television. With the popularity of docu-soaps and 'constructed factual' programmes such as *Don't Tell the Bride* and *The Only Way is Essex*, together with the celebrity status of characters such as 'White Dee' of *Benefits Street*, the variety of voices on television has continued to increase. That increase has been linked both with changing expectations and with increasing flexibility in the technology that records their voices.

Sound effects and music

Sound of many sorts makes a crucial contribution to the mood, the emotional setting and the illusion of reality conveyed by a programme. Accompanying the flow of the human voice are the sound effects – the slamming door or the barking dog – which may either be kept discreetly in the background, or may make an important contribution to the action. Above all there is music. This is central to the broadcast experience, whether featuring a performance or adding to the soundtrack. Music is at the centre of popular contests such as *The Voice* and *Britain's Got Talent*. Musical performance ranges from the newest rock band to the most sophisticated classical or jazz events, from *Later with Jools Holland* to *The Proms*. The 'Promenade Concerts' started in 1895 to make 'élite' classical music available to everyone, and they remain a highlight of the BBC's summer schedule.

Music enhances the sound track of the majority of programmes, whether drama or entertainment. It drives the advertisements, draws attention to station idents and trailers, and plays a part in almost every genre, setting a mood over opening titles, emphasising dramatic moments, adding a pulsating heartbeat to the moment when the contestant in a game show waits to hear who has been eliminated, and moving a programme to its final climax. In a radical change from their austere beginnings, even the news headlines are now backed by urgent, pulsating music in some of the daily bulletins. Fanfares and stings attract attention and form a punctuation throughout the television day as well as offering their own particular pleasures.

Audio space

Many different elements go to make up what Alan Wurtzel and John Rosenbaum describe as the 'audio space' that those who make a television programme create to accompany the 'videospace' on the screen (1995: 47). Natural sounds are recorded at the filming stage, but these are manipulated and others are added later during post-production. For the post-production work of audio design, see Chapter 14. In this chapter, we will discuss the production stage and the work of those whose job it is to record the sound in the studio or on location.

SOUND RECORDING AND AUDIO DESIGN

Mary Beard, presenter of many entertaining programmes about the ancient world, began an article about her filming experiences with a complaint about the rigours of a schedule, and especially the sound recordist's search for perfection. She writes:

> Imagine it, you've just, on your third go, got the words to sound absolutely right, when the engineer with the boom explains that a rubbish lorry could clearly be heard trundling along in the background and you have to do it all over again and (probably) again. Try suggesting to the director that the noise doesn't really matter and you get a horrified look back. . . . I still find it slightly strange how elaborately TV conceals the intrusions of the 'real world' on to our screens.
>
> (*Guardian* 13 July 2015: 13)

So, is this a question of maintaining the desired 'audio space' or of deceiving the audience?

A sound engineer's basic job is to record good quality sound, which will be consistent throughout a programme, even though, as Mary Beard's comments show, the principles behind this may be questioned. Meanwhile, experienced recordists complain that many directors, especially in news, do not care about sound quality. Sometimes the urgency of the situation takes priority: there may not be the time to film three or more takes. We will be taking these practical issues into account as we look at the principles and consider the conventions that underlie television sound recording. As we will see, while filming is actually going on, there may be a number of practical options open, and an experienced recordist will make decisions depending on the circumstances of the particular shoot.

As technology has evolved, sound recording has, as with so many aspects of programme-making, become on the one hand more complex and specialised, and on the other simpler and more widely available. Currently anyone can purchase a stereo microphone to attach to an i-phone and produce good quality sound (www. ixymic.com/). Cameras with microphones attached are often the first choice for location shooting, and are essential for journalists or documentary directors who operate alone, without a specialist sound recordist (see Gio Ulleri: p. 245). Although this chapter focuses on the work of the sound recordist or audio supervisor, the self-shooting director will need to bear many of its points in mind. Either way the basic principles remain: ensuring that the audio is *appropriate to the needs* of the programme, and controlling the sound quality through the *selection* and *placement* of the microphones.

Decisions on which microphones to use and where they should be placed are made for both aesthetic and acoustic reasons. In general, the closer a microphone can be to the source of the sound, the richer and more flexible that sound will be. But their placement is always limited by the position of the camera and usually by the need to keep the microphone out of shot. However, conventions change and develop, including ideas concerning the use and visibility of microphones. In some genres, particularly in a drama, the intrusion of even the shadow of a boom will break the illusion and mean a call for another take. But people approached in the street, whether attention-seeking celebrities or random individuals approached for a 'vox pop' sound bite (the name comes from the Latin 'vox populi', meaning 'voice of the people'), are not surprised when a microphone is thrust towards them. Visible radio mics, clipped to a collar or lapel, are also taken for granted.

In these more knowing days, a number of television programmes in various genres accept that microphones can be seen in vision. In *The Sky at Night* microphones and cameras frequently appear in shot, and in one episode (BBC4 20 July 2015) we even saw presenter Chris Lintott clapping his hands in front of the camera. Some viewers may have been puzzled, but those who understand the principles of location filming would know that this was to create that sharp thwack that will be used to match the image to its separately recorded sound track. Traditionally the familiar clapper board does this task, and for many years trainees have found that dealing with the clapper board is their first job on location. The clapper board names the shot and counts the takes. A hand clap is less informative but fine when the board has been mislaid.

There are many examples where the microphone is part of the action. The celebrated documentary director Nick Broomfield features in his own films, and is his own sound recordist. He carries his microphone like a weapon as he pursues his subjects, ranging from apartheid leader Eugene Terre Blanche in *The Leader, his Driver and the Driver's Wife* (1991) to brothel keeper Heidi Fleiss (*Heidi Fleiss Hollywood Madam* 1995) and American Vice-Presidential candidate Sarah Palin (*Sarah Palin: You Betcha* 2011).

Paradoxically, the more 'naturalistic' the genre, the more artifice must be employed, as the techniques and tools of the television industry must be kept out of sight and not allowed to interfere with the audience's immersion in the programme.

Drama and many documentaries depend on the illusion that the action is taking place without the mediation of a television crew. Some dramas employ devices that ensure good quality sound by introducing a microphone into the narrative. CBS's *Northern Exposure* (1990–5) centres on a local radio station, K-Bear Radio. Chris, the announcer (played by John Corbett), speaks straight into a microphone, which is part of the action. It allows him to provide narrative links and commentary on the storyline with a rich and intimate sound.

Sound engineers often complain that they are the last people to be considered in the design of a set or the planning of a shot. This is probably true, but the fact remains that sound is of crucial importance, whether we are considering the clarity essential for audience comprehension, or the overall package that creates the 'audio design' of a scene. Gerald Millerson lists possible problems with sound. It may be

> sibilant, muffled, distorted, of variable volume with random noise and distracting background sounds. [It] may not match the picture, voices may be inaudible or confusingly jumbled together. . . . Little wonder that the professional audio man (*sic*) takes so much trouble to achieve the 'obvious'.
>
> (Millerson 1990: 269)

Francis Ford Coppola's film *The Conversation* (1974) is a tribute to all sound engineers. Although made well before digital technology, it illustrates, within the context of a thriller, both the ways in which different sound elements in a single scene can be isolated and prioritised, and the way in which the interpretation of spoken words can effectively change the way an action is understood.

Sound in relation to the image

From the carefully controlled environment of the studio to the unpredictable circumstances of documentary location shooting, television sound can be classified by its relation to the image. Each of these poses its own problems for the sound recordist.

Synchronised 'natural' sound that is an intrinsic part of the content of a scene

Synchronised (or sync) sound, recorded simultaneously with the pictures, is natural to television, which began as a live broadcast. Of central importance is dialogue and speech. The audience also expects to hear sounds created by any visible action – footsteps, the movement of furniture, the opening and shutting of doors, cars passing in the background of a street interview and so on.

Over the years, a major problem has been to keep sound and vision 'in sync'. If we watch a speaker on our television screens it is deeply disturbing if the sound of their voice trails behind or anticipates the movement of their lips, even by a fraction of a second. Contemporary digital technology offers a number of options. Sometimes the sound signal is recorded together with the picture on the same disc or card, in which case it will be automatically in sync. But increasingly it is found that better quality sound is produced if it is recorded separately – or it may simply be more convenient to do it this way. In this case, there needs to be a link from the microphone to the sound mixer and from the mixer to the internal or external recording device. This may be a radio link, but most sound recordists say that a cable is more reliable, as it is less prone to interference. This is when the famous clapper board, which has come to symbolise film itself, comes into its own. It is used to begin each shot with a smart thwack, which provides an identifiable point where the image can be precisely matched with the sound. (A handclap will serve the purpose – but you mustn't forget to do it!) Another option is to link picture and sound by synchronising the timecode.

'Natural' sound that is unwanted for the meaning of the scene

One of the aims of sound recording is 'noise' reduction, that is, the minimising of inappropriate background sound, including noisy events that are invisible to the audience because they take place beyond the frame. Much valuable filming time has been wasted waiting for an aeroplane to pass overhead or the truck, which upset Mary Beard so much, to rumble beyond the range of the microphone. In today's mechanised world it is virtually impossible to find a location free from unwanted sounds. There is invariably a pneumatic drill digging up an adjacent street, a police siren or heavy traffic. An interview may take place in a leafy park, but if there's a busy road behind the camera the traffic noise will not make sense and will confuse the audience. Part of the sound recordist's job is to persuade the director to choose a quieter location, or to film the traffic so that the sound can be accounted for. A sound recordist is on constant watch for unwanted noise – will those traffic lights go green just as the interview starts?

Background sounds can pose real problems at the editing stage. A speaker finishes what they have to say and the director calls 'cut', but an aeroplane is passing overhead. The audience will expect the sound of the plane to continue to fade away, not to stop abruptly. The editor may be helped to solve this problem by providing a covering track of a passing plane which can be used to bridge between the shots (see Chapter 14).

Especially in countryside locations, the wind can pose a problem for sound recordists. It is important to include wind protection in the microphone kit. This will include mesh or furry wind gags for larger mics, and coverings for personal mics. In addition a 'pop filter' provides an essential protection when recording speech. It softens what one website describes as the 'dreaded hissing and lisping sounds that come when pronouncing the letter "s", and the explosion of air that follows "b" and "p"'.

Non-synchronised sound recorded on location

Usually some additional sounds are recorded on location for use at the sound editing stage to enrich the final tracks. They include:

Buzz track: a recording of the ambient noise – the background atmosphere, without speech or any other prominent sound. This provides a neutral track for the sound editor to use to bridge over any awkward gaps. 'Neutral' backgrounds differ to a remarkable extent from location to location, depending on weather conditions, traffic, central heating systems and a multitude of other factors.

Wild tracks: these are recordings of a wide range of interesting sounds made separately from the filming. They may include gentle noises, such as birdsong and lapping water for a rural scene, or an urban cacophony – construction sites, traffic noise or the bustle of a busy high street. The aim is to get the clearest possible recording of each separate sound, so that they may be reassembled for best effect at the sound editing stage.

Covering tracks: wild tracks that will enable the editor to bridge over awkward cuts.

Of course there will be occasions, especially when filming for news items, when there is no time for these extra touches nor for the editor to make use of them. Nevertheless they are an important part of a well-constructed audio space.

Non-synchronised sound recorded elsewhere

This may include:

Commentary or other 'voice-over' tracks, recorded in a special commentary studio or in a suitably quiet place with minimal background noise.

Specially recorded sound effects. A cat meows, a victim screams, a chair scrapes on the floor as someone stands up – all can be recorded quite independently, wherever the sound recordist can set up the suitable conditions. A wide range of effects gives the audio designer a great deal of freedom when composing the sound track at the post-production stage.

Library sound effects of various types. Sound libraries store recordings of innumerable sounds – different makes of car revving up, changing gear, ticking over and so on; crowds shouting or murmuring in many different languages; weather effects; animal noises; children playing. Despite the vast range of pre-recorded effects available, it is remarkably difficult to find exactly the one you want, hence the advisability of recording extra sound effects on location.

Music and other sound effects will be created and added at the sound editing stage.

The combination and orchestration of these different types of audio is discussed in Chapter 14, on sound editing.

FIGURE 11.1

Sound recordist Gisela Kraus and cinematographer Guenther Benze filming the Queen's visit to Malta, November 2015, for the German broadcaster ARD. Beyond this apparently peaceful scene the microphone is picking up a cacophony of background sounds, including hip hip hooray, a 21-gun salute and church bells ringing

Photograph: Jörg Ellmers

SOUND QUALITY

Important points include:

Perspective

The perspective of the sound must match that of the image, or credibility is threatened. An intimate, close-up voice coming from a distant figure in the frame may be used as a creative, non-naturalistic device, but on the whole the audience will expect to hear closer speakers sounding closer and distant speakers sounding as if they are far away. Obtaining this effect is helped by the fact that, in a close shot, the sound recordist can position the microphone so that it is near to a speaker but outside the frame. However, if the speaker is wearing a radio mic, the sense of perspective may be difficult to maintain as the microphone will always be close to their voice. A scene in which the wearer of the radio mic is in the middle of a crowd can cause confusion as it may be difficult to work out who is speaking.

The acoustics of a room

Sound is not only direct, but multiply reflected from the surfaces of a room. This needs to be taken into account in choosing locations:

Reverberant rooms have hard reflective surfaces. They tend to be 'live' and echoey, reflecting back both wanted and unwanted sounds, such as footsteps, ventilation noise or scenery movement.

'Dead' rooms, such as television studios, have highly absorbent surfaces. Soft furnishings, carpets, curtains or special sound-absorbing materials attached to the walls can muffle the sound.

A *sound studio*, especially designed for sound recording, will have a mixture of surfaces for different effects.

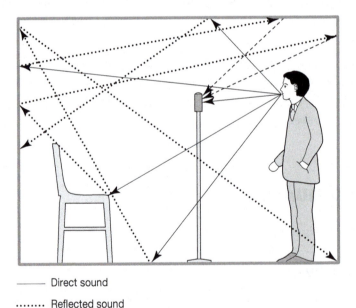

——— Direct sound

········ Reflected sound

As sound strikes it may be absorbed or reinforced by structural resonance. The reflected sound, now modified, adds to the original, augmenting or partially masking it.

FIGURE 11.2
The acoustics of a room

Sound presence

As a speaker moves closer, the sound of their voice changes in value and quality as well as in volume, becoming fuller and richer. This is described as sound presence. It is a function of the ratio between direct and indirect sound waves picked up by the microphone and depends on many factors, including the type of microphone used, the acoustics of the room or other location, and the volume of the sound source.

Wurtzel and Rosenbaum give an American example of the effect of sound presence on audience perception, from NBC's *The Tonight Show*.

> From the show's beginning in 1954, its hosts – from Steve Allen and Jack Paar to Johnny Carson and Jay Leno – have used ribbon mics placed on the desks in front of them. The guests have been covered by a boom microphone suspended overhead. The ribbon mic produces a richer, warmer, fuller sound than the boom mic. The result of the hosts using a ribbon microphone positioned

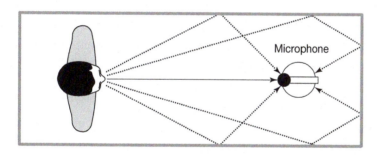

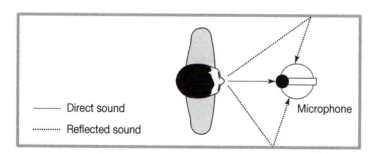

Sound presence increases as the subject-to-mic distance decreases because the microphone receives more direct sound waves and fewer reflected waves.

FIGURE 11.3
Sound presence

nearby is that they have sounded 'closer' to the audience than the guests and seemed dominant among the performers on the show.

(Wurtzel and Rosenbaum 1995: 47)

Microphone selection

There are basic factors to be taken into account when setting out to record sound for a particular scene:

- The selection of the best microphone for the job
- The placement of the microphone

In *selecting* a microphone, several aspects need to be taken into account. The aesthetic effect needs to be balanced against a consideration of the frequency response needed, the appropriate pick-up pattern and whether the microphone is rugged enough to withstand the packing, unpacking and constant handling of location shoots. Here we shall be concentrating on their use and referring to the technical factors as they become relevant.

Examples include: the full frequency range of a condenser microphone is best for music; a highly directional mic may be chosen for an observational documentary in which the subjects are to be followed as they walk through a crowd; miniature radio mics can be clipped to a lapel and the transmitter slipped into a pocket. These are convenient when the subject is out of range of the more traditional microphones.

Factors that should be taken into account when selecting a microphone include:

Physical features – shape, size, robustness, portability and so on.

Sensitivity to a range of sound – this is a microphone's 'frequency response'.

Audio quality – the nature of the sound recorded, its fidelity and accuracy.

Installation suitability – what mountings are available: can the microphone be concealed from vision? Radio mics are convenient because they use a miniature radio transmitter, so they can be attached to characters or participants who are at some distance from the recorder.

Directionality

An omnidirectional microphone is sensitive in all directions. It will pick up sounds equally from all sides, with a 360 degree sensitivity range. This can limit its usefulness, as it will pick up unwanted sounds from the direction of the film crew as well as from the subjects being filmed.

Unidirectional microphones (with a cardioid, or a heart-shaped, pick-up pattern) are designed to suppress sounds that come from the non-sensitive parts of the mic.

The use of a parabolic reflector, a metal or fibreglass dish about 3–4 feet in diameter with the microphone mounted at its centre, increases the directionality.

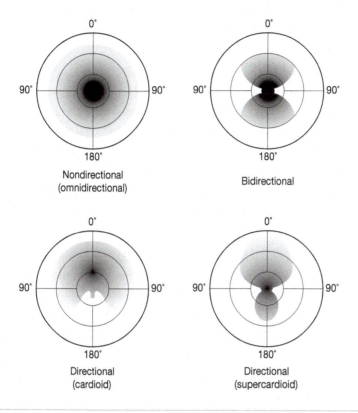

FIGURE 11.4
Polar diagram

Highly directional microphones (super-cardioid) are designed to pick up sound within a very narrow angle of acceptance. Mounted on a long tube, they are described as 'gun mics' because of their appearance. They can be used at greater distances from the subject and may isolate the speech of an individual from that of a crowd.

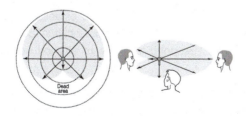

FIGURE 11.5
A cardioid pick-up pattern, which is a broad heart shape, is insensitive on its rear side

Usually encased in a wind shield, they are often hand-held for observational filming, recording natural conversations in real situations and excluding many unwanted sounds. The problem is that they must be pointed very precisely at the sound source or a weak or muffled sound will result.

Personal radio microphones

Radio mics come with a small transmitter pack which sends a signal to the receiver attached to the audio mixer or the camera. Personal mics can be clipped onto a lapel, or arranged in other ways so that they are close to the source of the sound, usually the speaker's voice. They are small enough to be inconspicuous and convenient because they do not inhibit movement. Directors and camera people like them because it gives them more freedom to frame their shots and they are a useful tool for video journalists (VJs) who are operating camera and sound at the same time as conducting an interview.

Radio mics are an indispensable part of the sound recordist's kit. However, recordists point out that their quality is less predictable than other microphones, and they do not always give the right character of sound as they do not allow for flexibility in perspective (see above). In addition, some people wear noisy clothing and its rustling is easily picked up by the mic. Recordists report that they are often expected to put radio mics on everyone, but that it's important to recognise that they are not the solution to every problem.

There are a number of other issues with radio mics. They transmit on the radio spectrum, on which terrestrial television is broadcast. Since the coming of digital, which takes up less space than analogue television, frequencies on the spectrum have increasingly been put up for sale to the mobile phone companies. This has caused considerable consternation among sound recordists, as it means that the frequencies that are reserved for other purposes – such as the emergency services and the microphones used in meetings and lectures, as well as the radio mics used by television crews – are increasingly squeezed.

The available frequencies are licensed and closely monitored by the communications regulator, Ofcom. Some are licence-exempt, but access to the most reliable and interference-free VHF and UHF frequencies requires a licence. Studios and large drama productions filming on location will have established designated frequencies, but for documentary crews, who move from location to location, and especially for news crews who must respond to an event at short notice, there are bigger problems.

Many news or documentary sound recordists carry a licence for Channel 38, which is a shared channel covering a range of frequencies anywhere in the United Kingdom. In addition, 'Coordinated Frequencies' are licensed at a specific site for short- or long-term. Ofcom advises that 'they provide the best protection against interference from other licensees and are planned to avoid interference from television transmissions' http://licensing.ofcom.org.uk/radiocommunication-licences/pmse/equipment/mics-monitors/.

Within the coordinated spectrum, the recordist may be able to scan to see what space is available to avoid interference (rather like scanning a domestic radio tuner across the channels). Many, but not all, radio mics have the ability to scan. However, for a breaking news story, as many as fifty teams may converge on a location. The big organisations – such as the BBC and ITV – get priority. That means that, for the smaller crews, there is a real danger of interference from other radio mics at the same location.

The regulations on the use of radio mics are detailed and complex, but a sound recordist must be aware of them, especially as Ofcom carries out spot checks to ensure that users are licensed (refer to www.canford.co.uk/Technical/Article/UK LegalRadioMicFrequencies).

Most freelance sound recordists own a kit of licensed radio mics. In fact, sound kits are getting bigger, as radio mics are so popular that it's necessary to carry ever more of them.

Microphone placement

Some basic principles:

- Place the microphone as close to the desired sound source as is practically possible so as not to pick up unwanted or reflected noise.
- Avoid feedback, that high-pitched screech that comes if a microphone faces the audio monitors or speakers in the studio.
- Avoid picking up unwanted ambient sound (see above): turn off a radio playing in the background. It may even be possible to turn off air conditioning. Background music in a shop or restaurant poses a particular problem, as snatches of music in the background of separate shots make them difficult to edit together.

Microphones may either be *visible* in shot or *invisible*, kept beyond the edge of the frame.

In-shot, visible microphones

Miniature radio microphones – these may not be visible, but if they are, it tends to be taken for granted.

Hand microphones – designed to be held by the presenter or reporter. It must be rugged, omnidirectional and have a windshield to protect it. A hand microphone will either be cabled or will transmit a radio signal.

Stand microphones – placed on a desk or table or in front of performers such as stand-up comics or singers.

An in-vision microphone may be *'practical'*, playing a role within the scene as in the radio station in *Northern Exposure*.

Out-of-shot, invisible microphones

Even when invisible to the camera, the microphone must be as close to the source of the sound as possible. That may mean that it is concealed behind a vase of flowers or a piece of furniture or, usually, that it hovers just beyond the edge of frame. Invisible microphones may be:

- Hand-held by the sound recordist, as with the gun mic, which is provided with a hand grip.
- Fixed around the set or location, or invisibly attached to the participants. Fixed-rig productions, such as *One Born Every Minute* and *Educating Cardiff,* combine an input from twenty radio mics and fifty to sixty strategically placed 'effects mics' www.rts.org.uk/magazine/article/how-fixed-rig-has-transformed-factual.
- Slung or suspended over the performance area.
- Held in position by the recordist or a 'boom swinger', usually the sound assistant, on a fishpole boom. This needs steady arms and strong muscles to keep the boom aloft while adjusting the microphone to follow the source of the sound. Nevertheless, the best effect is often achieved through skilled boom swinging.
- In a studio the microphone may be mounted on a large boom fixed to a wheeled platform with a long, telescopic arm, which may be extended and retracted (see Chapter 12 for studio work).
- Journalists and directors who are doing their own filming usually use a camcorder, either with a built-in microphone, which can be set to automatic, or with a mount in which a directional mic may be fixed.

Audio control

As well as managing the microphones, the sound engineer's job includes using a sound mixer to balance the input from the various microphones as it is recorded. A wide range of equipment is available and is constantly being upgraded, so that sometimes the sound kit is bigger than the camera. A large, sophisticated audio mixer can deal with twelve or more microphone inputs, but for location work something more portable is needed. For news and documentary work, the various inputs tend to be mixed on location so that a single, mixed track is recorded on the camera or the separate recording device. For a drama the editor may be provided with a number of separate tracks produced by the different microphones.

The recordist must:

- Monitor the sound levels, as displayed on the meters on the mixer. The meters display the intensity of the sound measured in decibels and in percentage of modulation. The levels should be adequate, even and not distorting. A signal that is too low or too high will result in a muddy or distorted recording.
- Assess the quality of the sound through their headphones.
- Ensure that the desired sound, most usually the speaking voice, is separated from the background or ambient sound.
- Provide suitable wild tracks and buzz tracks of the ambient sound.
- Ensure that the desired sound is free from interference (see above). It is up to the sound recordist to listen out for those things that the director, concentrating on the content of the scene, may overlook – such as a passing aeroplane which may obscure the dialogue, or a contributor making a strange noise by scratching his chin. Another problem is posed by speech overlaps, when one contributor begins to speak before the other has finished. These can make a scene difficult to edit. Sudden bangs, such as closing a desk lid in a classroom scene or the clash of knives and forks during a meal, can sound unnaturally loud and distracting in the context of a recorded scene.

Overall, the sound recordist contributes to the 'audio design' and the 'audio space' of a scene. 'The sound recordist is part of a team, and 50 per cent of the job is to contribute to the team effort. You need to know about the pictures as well as the sound, and understand how the jobs fit together', said one experienced recordist.

But ultimately, location work is always unpredictable. Decisions must be pragmatic, and based on experience. The final result may well be a compromise between the various problems that need to be solved.

KEY TEXTS

Rumsey, F. and McCormick, T. (2009) *Sound and Recording*, 6th edn, Oxford: Focal Press.
Wurtzel, A. and Rosenbaum, J. (1995) *Television Production*, 4th edn, New York: McGraw-Hill.

CHAPTER 12

Studios and studio work

'LIVE' AND 'AS LIVE'

In the early days the studio *was* television. It was a guarantor of distance vision (the literal meaning of 'tele-vision'), and of the extraordinary fact that those people on that tiny black and white screen were actually speaking these very words at this very moment, from many miles away. The 'On Air' warning light above the studio door signalled something special.

'Live' studio work is still what distinguishes broadcast television from other moving-image media, such as cinema and online. The word 'live' is in inverted commas because we are including programmes that are pre-recorded as if they were live. These are transmitted later, sometimes following editing, sometimes not. Many programmes are recorded 'as live' in advance of transmission, to give the opportunity to correct mistakes, eliminate unwanted expletives and ensure that the programme is the right length for its slot. The panel comedy programme, *Have I Got News for You*, which depends on spontaneous responses from its participants, will record 90 minutes so that only the best jokes will be used in both the main 29 minutes programme, and the various other versions transmitted across the week. 'The high quality depends on the heavy editing down', its producer Richard Wilson told Jeremy Tunstall (2015: 285). Other 'live' programmes, including *Strictly Come Dancing*, include many pre-recorded sections. On *Strictly* they are inserted between the live dances that are part of the competition, and the Sunday night results programme is recorded on Saturday after the main broadcast.

Meanwhile, for the audience at home the excitement and suspense of watching events as they actually unfold remains. (How will the panellists react to that spontaneous joke? Which competitor will be sent home after the audience votes are counted?) And performers and crew respond to the adrenalin and challenge of a live transmission, often in front of an appreciative but critical studio audience. Studio work, with its direct address to the audience and its impression of intimacy and spontaneity, remains at the heart of the television experience, ranging from election coverage, to celebrity chat on the sofa, to audience sitcoms, and game shows of all sorts, from *Pointless* to *The Million Pound Drop*.

Now that live broadcasts are a relatively small part of the television output, schedulers are constantly seeking formats which will draw in an audience for a simultaneously shared experience. The liveness of contests which depend on immediate audience involvement through voting – *Big Brother, Britain's Got Talent* and the rest – is precisely their attraction. A completely live programme still carries the tension and expectations which characterised the early days of the medium. Hence the buzz around the week of live *EastEnders* episodes, which marked the thirtieth anniversary of the popular soap in February 2015.

Many 'live' programmes make the most of their studio setting by including the studio audience and sometimes the production crew, too. Studio-based sitcoms draw energy from the response of their audience, especially those that break the 'fourth wall' and reveal their studio context. Brendan O'Carroll, as Mrs Brown in *Mrs Brown's Boys*, mutters asides to 'those people out there', while the cast frequently get entangled with the crew, falling over cables, bumping into cameras and causing much hilarity on all sides. *Ant and Dec's Saturday Night Take-away* whips up a noisy and ecstatic audience response, offers substantial prizes and draws individual audience members into the performance. Meanwhile glimpses behind the scenes, introducing wardrobe, make-up and other members of the usually invisible crew, feature in the spin-off programmes that back up block-busters such as *Strictly Come Dancing* and *The X-Factor*.

WORKING IN THE STUDIO

The studio spaces

In a television studio, the work of 'production' is carried out in the *studio space*, which may or may not be adapted to hold an audience; while the work of 'post-production' is carried out in the *studio gallery* or control room. These two processes, normally separated for 'filmed' programmes or segments, are, for a 'live' studio broadcast, carried out simultaneously.

The *studio space* is a sound-proofed area, with a flat floor, a high ceiling and an array of lights attached to a grid in the ceiling. Extra facilities may include permanent but adaptable sets, which, in the case of QVC, may be conveniently transformed from an elegant bedroom to a fully functioning kitchen. A big studio may be equipped with three to five cameras, some with their own operators, others controlled remotely from the gallery. In addition there may be 'sky cameras' mounted in the ceiling of the studio. Some studios have permanent facilities for a studio audience; for others, ranks of audience seating can be rolled into place. There will be large doors for scenery to be moved in and out, usually from an adjacent store.

In contrast to the sound-proofed studio, all the major news broadcasts transmit from an open-plan work space, so that effectively the whole area becomes part of the 'studio'. At Sky News, the presenters, organised in a rota over the 24 hours of transmission, sit on a rostrum against a backdrop, while researchers, script writers, production managers and news editors – including the editor of the day – are busy at their computers, checking stories as they come in, booking guests, preparing scripts. People are coming and going, exchanging information, preparing the guests for the next item, researching items. The bustle of a busy workplace continues around the edges of the shots. Presenters and guests are at the centre of this activity. When necessary the presenter can move to another part of the studio, in front of a green screen, where relevant background images can be fed in by the vision mixer in the gallery (see Chapter 17 for more on news).

The *control room*, or *gallery*, is a separate space. It may be behind sound-proof glass panels through which the studio can be seen, but all contact with studio floor is through personal microphones. The gallery personnel sit in front of a bank of monitors that preview the input from the cameras on the floor, alongside numerous other sources. This is where the 'editing' process is carried out simultaneously with the action, as a selection is made between the shots on offer. For a news broadcast there are feeds from reporters based in locations around the world, together with the output of other news channels and material offered by the international agencies such as Reuters and Associated Press. In addition, screens display the preparations by the studio crew – off-shot cameras moving into position, graphics being set up, lighting adjustments and images shuttling through at speed.

Some studios, like those for some local television stations, are very small, and the director may be alone in the gallery, vision mixing the output from fixed cameras. In others, such as QVC, idents, trailers and advertisements will be previewed in the gallery ready to be inserted, and a range of 'stings', promos and trailers are to be kept in reserve in case they are needed to fill an awkward gap. Studios that are part of a national network like ITV will broadcast their own regional 'opt-out' material, including local news and local advertisements, but feed their networked programmes to a *master control room* where the linking material is provided.

> TX. Presentation. Playout. Whatever you call it, they're the people responsible for taking the programmes, promos, adverts and continuity, packaging it all up, and making sure you have something to watch on your television . . . with the absolute bare minimum of breakdown captions

writes John Hoare, in a vivid account of his work for Channel 5 as a TX controller in a master control room www.dirtyfeed.org/2015/08/24-hours-in-channel-5-tx/.

Near to the main studio gallery will be a *sound control suite*, where the sound engineer monitors and balances the live inputs and adds any necessary extra sounds from other sources.

The *studio complex* will also contain make-up rooms, dressing rooms and a green room where guests can be entertained. In addition, there are usually editing facilities and video graphics facilities near by – especially in the case of news or a topical show which will need facilities to prepare last-minute 'filmed' sequences and effects to be inserted in the show.

The studio personnel and gallery personnel may vary between different studios and different productions; below we list the key roles:

Studio personnel

Set designer and scenery team

The overall appearance of a show is planned by the set designer in consultation with the producer. The designer will then supervise the building of the sets ready for transmission. The scenery team includes both those who build the sets and the scene shifters whose job it is to move them into position as needed during the studio day. Very often the designer will monitor the show from the gallery.

For a regular show the sets may be either permanent or easily rolled into place. For shows in which a celebrity host greets a number of guests, the static set-up of a two- or three-way conversation may be introduced by a dramatic entrance: the host bursts in through a double door or arrives down an impressive staircase. For the interviews it's important to have a background that is interesting, relevant, but not too busy, as it may dominate the speakers. This is a trap that some studio set-ups which enjoy complex background projections frequently fall into.

Make-up and costume

Specialists in make-up and the wardrobe department will have fully equipped make-up rooms and dressing rooms to help prepare presenters and guests.

Floor managers

Prior to a broadcast, together with their assistants, the floor managers ensure that the studio set is prepared, that the necessary props are in place, and that the cast, whether actors or presenters and guests, is ready. *Assistant floor managers* will be in charge of meeting and greeting the guests and dealing with any necessary jobs. During the broadcast the floor manager orchestrates the action on the floor, liaising with the director in the gallery through talk-back. It is their job to ensure that the next item is ready, that the guests are prepared and that the camera operators have the correct running order. They must also keep everyone up-to-date with changes to the planned schedule. The role of the floor manager and assistants (at QVC they may include students on work experience, see below) is crucial here, as they ensure the smooth running of the show. 'If things are not in the right place at the right time', floor manager Mark told viewers of *The Xtra Factor*, 'it's my fault' (29 November 2015).

Camera crew

A television studio is equipped with its own specialised cameras, usually mounted on a pedestal or a jimmy jib. These send their signals directly to the mixing desk in the studio gallery. Those cameras that are live on the floor are controlled by camera operators who have two-way contact with the gallery and respond to instructions – for example, to zoom in on a particular performer or to pan to reveal a prop. Bigger productions will include several operators, and there will be one or more 'cable clearers' (usually called 'cable bashers') whose job it is to control the camera's cables to ensure that they do not get tangled up or cause an obstruction. In addition, a camera supervisor advises on difficult shots and the technical aspects. The camera operators line up their shots before they are needed so that they can be previewed in the gallery, enabling the director to select the appropriate moment to cut to the next shot. Each camera has a light that comes on, to indicate which one is live on air.

FIGURE 12.1
Filming with a studio camera mounted on a pedestal with an autocue screen attached

Photograph: Neil Goridge

Sound crew

Currently a mixture of personal mics, radio mics and microphones suspended from fishpoles are used to record sound from the individual contributors. These have tended to replace the boom operator, who stands on a trolley to move a microphone into place, above the heads of the speakers. On a larger production, where a boom is used, the microphone is in a cradle at the end of the arm, and can be swivelled in multiple directions through an elaborate system of belts and pulleys. This cumbersome but flexible studio device needs two people to operate it, including a 'grip' who pushes the trolley into position when necessary.

Lighting personnel (sparks)

The sparks will move and adjust the studio lighting, following instructions from the lighting supervisor.

Autocue operator

The autocue displays the script for the presenter to read, or may give guidance when the presenter is improvising. Autocue monitors are attached to the cameras, or may be strategically placed where the presenter can read them. The operator moves the script along, varying the speed when necessary, and ensures that the correct text is being shown.

Gallery personnel

Director

The director is in charge of the gallery and of the studio. He or she plans the camera script in advance of the studio day, supervises the rehearsals, then, during transmission, calls the shots and drives the programme along. When the director says 'we're going in five', everyone springs into action. The countdown begins. . . . 'Ready studio. Five four three two . . .' The floor manager raises his arm to cue the performers, the camera operators line up their shots. What the director says goes, but a good director will see themselves as a facilitator and allow the crew to collaborate. For example a camera operator may offer a shot the director had not thought of. That way it is clear that everyone's contribution is valued.

Production assistant

Prior to the studio day the production assistant prepares the camera script, running order and other documentation, liaising with the production manager over contributors' contracts, copyright agreements and other necessary paperwork. The PA is also in charge of booking the contributors.

On the studio day, the PA keeps an eye on continuity, and during the broadcast PAs are in charge of timings. They have to cue the title sequence, count down to the advertising breaks and make sure the director always knows how much time is left, as well as checking the exact duration of each item. Production assistant Vicky Andrews says: 'I run four electronic stopwatches throughout the show to keep an eye on all timings' (Orlebar 2011: 254). Like so many television personnel, most studio PAs are now freelancers on short contracts.

Technical manager

As their name suggests, the technical manager oversees the technical facilities of the studio, including the source inputs, dealing with the inevitable technical problems.

He or she is also in charge of transmission, and ensuring the correct format for transmission.

Technical director

Controls the cameras, balancing the input and operating the robotic cameras.

Vision mixer

Operates the vision mixing panel that creates the cuts, dissolves or wipes from one shot to the next as the director calls the shots. Present-day mixing panels can be extremely complex, offering a range of refinements, and it is up to the vision mixer to ensure that the basic transitions from one shot to the next run smoothly. A second vision mixer may set up and control the video effects.

Lighting director

The lighting director liaises with the set designer to plan the positions of the studio lights in advance of the studio day. During the studio day their job is to monitor the lighting, control lighting changes and liaise with the lighting team on the floor.

Frequently the producer and sometimes the set designer will also be present in the gallery.

Sound supervisor and assistants

These usually work in a separate control room, apart from the studio gallery. Here the audio control engineer (who may be described as a sound mixer or sound supervisor) selects and blends the various programme sound sources through an audio control console (also known as the board or mixer panel). It is the sound supervisor's job to:

- Keep the volume indicator within system limits by using the faders (also called amplifier gains), which increase or decrease the volume of each input.

- Monitor the programme sound and communicate with the director in the gallery when necessary.

- Check audio quality.

- Watch the picture monitors showing live and preview shots, checking sound perspective and warning against microphones coming into shot and boom shadows.

- Select and control the outputs of the various audio sources (microphones, discs, tapes etc.).

The person in charge of inputting these extra sources is often called a 'grams operator' – a term first used when music and many effects were all inputted from gramophone records.

The studio day

A great deal of preparation is needed in the run up to a studio day, and the quality of the output largely depends on the accuracy of this preparatory work. Scripts must be prepared, guests booked, contracts drawn up, copyright checked, archive material and music tracked down. These and other tasks are the responsibility of the producer and the production manager (see Chapter 8).

Prior to the studio day the production team draws up a floor plan, showing the positions of the sets and of the cameras, indicating what shots will be required. They also prepare a shot-by-shot breakdown of the show. Every camera operator will have a copy of this shot list, as will the director and vision mixer in the gallery. But, of course, things can change – and usually do in an unpredictable live show.

A studio day is rarely less than ten hours. The sets and lighting must be prepared before rehearsals can start. For some programmes there is only time for a quick run-through before transmission time: 'marking' positions and checking that the planned shots will work. For others, time is scheduled for more detailed rehearsals. In this case, performances can be worked on and any necessary adjustments can be made.

For many shows the presenters are key and they liaise closely with the director during rehearsals and transmission. Presenters use an earpiece that allows contact with production staff in the gallery. One presenter explained: 'While I'm conducting my on-screen dialogue with the participants, I expect a second dialogue through my earpiece, offering advice on questions and giving prompts about how the interview might go.'

Behind the scenes a large number of people is involved in a mounting a studio show. *The One Show* needs a crew of about thirty to prepare the set and lighting and to get it on air. The smooth running of a live show depends on everyone performing their job accurately to the last detail. One small slip – a missed cue, a prop in the wrong place, a cut to the wrong camera – can spoil the overall effect. Everyone involved needs to understand how all the different processes fit together.

STUDIOS

The big television organisations have their own studios; in 2013, the BBC moved from the Television Centre in White City to the ultra-modern New Broadcasting House in Central London. In addition, its sports and children's departments have their studios in the shiny new Media City complex in Salford. ITV also has studios at Media City, as well as on the South Bank in London and in many of the cities where the independent ITV companies were based. In addition the company has production centres around the world. Sky has a complex of offices and studios

FIGURE 12.2
Director/vision mixer and graphics operator in the studio gallery at QVC

Photograph: Vanessa Ridley. Courtesy: QVCUK

near Isleworth in West London, while the shopping channel QVC has its purpose-built studios in Chiswick (see below). In addition, a number of fully equipped studios around the country are available for hire by independent companies.

To a certain extent studios are becoming more specialised. The studio arrangement for news broadcasts tends to be very different from that of a comedy show. *Strictly Come Dancing* has its own specially adapted studio at Elstree, and, of course, *Big Brother* has its house, subject to 24-hour surveillance. *The One Show* has a small studio with multicoloured glass windows that look out onto the courtyard in New Broadcasting House. Sometimes passers-by can be seen beyond the windows and the programme itself often moves outside. Soap operas such as *EastEnders* and *Coronation Street*, and long-running dramas such as Casualty, combine the practices of 'filmed' and 'live' programmes. They are produced in permanent sets specially constructed with cameras in place and facilities organised so that, effectively, there is a great deal in common with a studio set-up. *EastEnders*, for example, is filmed in short sections. These are edited 'live', then the final programme is assembled in the editing suite.

As with all areas of production, technologies are changing rapidly, and the distinction between 'filmed' and 'live' programmes is becoming less clear. Nevertheless the basic principles of careful planning, scripting, attention to detail and collaboration throughout the process remain.

QVC: THE SHOPPING CHANNEL

What is QVC?

QVC is the one channel where live studio television is the norm. QVC (the initials stand for Quality, Value, Convenience, but this is rarely referred to) is housed in a spectacular new business development in Chiswick Park, London. Postmodern office blocks are arranged around an artificial lake inhabited by geese and swans (which occasionally invade the buildings). Many international media companies, including Discovery and Disney, have facilities here, and QVC has purpose-built studios and technical facilities. QVC UK has five channels and its main channel runs for 24 hours – live from 9am to 1am. It can be found on the EPG, tucked between Film4 and Really. However, it has a different brief from the channels that surround it. 'This is a shop as much as a television channel', says studio manager Vanessa Ridley.

The company employs teams of expert buyers, researching and ordering products which range from jewellery to bedding, from kitchenware to foot cream. The only purpose of the continuous live broadcasts is to promote and sell the products. Viewers/shoppers buy while live on air by telephone, 'tap the app', or via the internet. Giant warehouses in Liverpool stock thousands of items which can be instantly dispatched. The proceeds from the sales fund the television output.

So does a shop have a place in a book that discusses UK television from the point of view of practitioners and new entrants to the industry? Those who work at QVC, from directors to student interns, think it does.

Although the line between promotion and entertainment is becoming increasingly blurred, marketing through entertainment is not new. In the early days of ITV, a number of advertising magazines (known as 'admags') filled a late-night slot. The most famous was *Jim's Inn*, set in a pub where cheery landlord Jim promoted a range of products. The admags disappeared when it was ruled that there must be a clear separation between programmes and advertising.

But although QVC is clearly a shop, it offers more than just shopping. Its flow of live television uses an entertaining chat-show format, with charismatic hosts and expert guests. Producing the live output demands the careful planning, competence, fast reactions, skill and alertness which characterise all studio production.

The studios

The two live television studios are equipped with three or four adaptable sets that can be quickly made ready for use. A spacious Mediterranean house, with pale, off-white walls and elegant pillared windows, can be rapidly transformed into a working kitchen or a bedroom with patterned wallpaper. Each studio is used for an hour of transmission, while the other is set up for the following hour. In addition there's a 'rehearsal' studio where material is recorded for transmission on the other QVC channels and for the web, and a stills studio where pack shots of products are prepared, ready to be used in the live broadcast or edited into the pre-recorded promos. Sometimes pictures of the models who will be demonstrating clothes and beauty products are taken for a 'before and after' sequence. This is how she looked before she used this particular hair product – just look at her now!

The production team

The production teams require the range of skills and capabilities of any live studio broadcast. Teams work in two shifts, from 7.30am to 4.30pm, and from 4pm to 1am. The daily schedule is prepared six weeks ahead by the planners, and each shift starts with a production meeting when the producer confirms the tasks of directors, floor managers and performers. Each shift has two *producers*, working one hour on, one hour off.

Before transmission a *category producer* liaises with the set designers and arranges the overall presentation, coordinating between the brands and the production teams.

A product activities list (PAL) is produced for each show a day in advance. This lists items with their lengths (average nine to ten minutes), and includes a product description ('*Confessions of a beauty addict*' is promoting 'Illuminating body butter in toasted coconut') together with a forecast of sales. These may range from 5,000 to as many as 15,000.

During their shift, everyone wears a head set, a microphone and a talk-back unit so that team members can communicate with each other at any point.

On the studio floor

There are four *studio managers* at QVC, who keep track of the activity throughout the day, preparing detailed lists and schedules, and generally keeping things moving. They work with a team of *floor managers* who alternate between a one hour live show and an hour of 'prep'. Lunch breaks have to be fitted in wherever possible. Following their individual schedules, everyone knows where they should be at what time.

During transmission, all floor managers do the same basic work, liaising with the *set dresser*, cueing the performers, and relaying the information from the gallery. In a QVC show, the props/products for sale are of key importance, and one of the floor managers' main tasks is to ensure that they are available and correctly placed. ('That clothes rail's not in the right place', says the director down the ear piece, 'I don't like it there.' 'But that's where we marked it . . .' protests the floor manager. 'I don't care. It's not right. Move it when you can.' The floor manager checks which cameras are live, then slides between them to push the rail to its new position.)

FIGURE 12.3
Floor manager Georgia Dunstone and assistant sorting the product for SBC skincare show

Photograph: Vanessa Ridley. Courtesy QVCUK

When I visited QVC, a third-year BA television student, Georgia Dunstone, was employed on a three-month contract, and her day was scheduled along with the other floor managers. ('Whether they're on work experience or employed, we expect them to do the job', says Vanessa Ridley). Floor managers Dave and Max both said how much they enjoyed the work. There was the excitement of a live show, and there was also job security. 'This is one of the only jobs in television where they give you a full-time contract. That's very rare today . . .'

The studios are equipped with four cameras, but usually only one camera operator is on the floor. The other cameras are controlled remotely from the gallery.

In the gallery

In the two galleries, two teams control alternate hours of the continuous live broadcast.

During the show a *line producer* passes relevant information to the crew and monitors sales. Information is fed back from the Liverpool depot and a screen displays a constantly updated list. Another graph monitors the phone activity, showing how quickly a product is moving. The producer prompts the presenters and generally oversees the hour.

There are two *producers' assistants* (PAs). One greets the participants as they arrive – usually at least one hour ahead of their scheduled time because of the frequent changes to the running order – and generally prepares them for their slot, while the other works in the gallery with the producer. They must monitor the information about the products displayed on the broadcast image, and check the stings, promos and other material that comes between the live items. They also deal with phone calls. There are regular invitations to viewers to call in, either to take part in competitions or simply to comment on the programme, and frequently comments are put on air. Viewers can also send in pictures, and their tweets are put up on screen.

In the gallery the *director* calls the shots and also does the vision mixing, while a *broadcast technical operator* controls two or three remote cameras, a task which, as one commented, requires a great deal of concentration. The gallery team also includes the *graphics playout operator* and a *sound supervisor.*

In a big open plan office adjacent to the studio, a team of *editors* and *video effects designers* prepare edited packages; the promotional material and the tops and tails, which occur every ten minutes or so.

On the set the *presenters* wear their own earpieces and are accustomed to continuous prompts from the gallery. 'Buy now! There are only ten left. And don't forget you can buy online or by phone.' As the producer prompts, his words are picked up by the presenter almost before he's finished speaking.

A day at QVC

A day at QVC involves a 7.30am meeting for the first shift. The master control room transmits recorded material until the channel goes live from Studio A at 9am.

The space between the two studios is filled with boxes, rails of clothing and other products. There are floor managers, brand representatives, presenters and guests coming and going, preparing their items. Everyone checks their schedules and keeps up-to-date through their headsets as transmission alternates between the two studios.

Changes to the schedule are frequent. Item 1 is replaced by item 6. In the gallery the director rearranges the running order and calls up a reserve promo to cover the delay. A PA runs to fetch the new set of guests, while the producer goes through the floor positions, and decides where the clothes rail will be and how the props and performers will move in and out of the set when the shots allow.

There's a new lunch-time show that involves lots of cheerful chatter between experts and presenters trying out each other's products – with varying degrees of competence. The 'beauty tip of the month' is a product for the feet. A male presenter takes off his shoes to try it out, accompanied by jokes from the other contributors (and from the gallery over the earpiece). Throughout the show there are constant prompts from the gallery. 'We've sold over 10,000 this month, and there's been 100 orders today so far.' Despite the careful planning, the running order changes again – which means more work for the floor manager, and more promos to be found to cover the gap. There is an item on coloured nails, and another on floaty summer garments. Finally 'Roll promos. Clear studio'. And transmission moves to Studio B.

At 4pm there is a production meeting for the late shift. Once more the hour-by-hour schedule is carefully planned. The early shift teams prepare to go home and the new teams take over.

Working at QVC

Many QVC producers and directors have worked elsewhere in the industry. Although many have degrees (not all in media studies), one director began in the post room and worked his way up. Senior floor manager Vanessa graduated from Stafford University. She began as a floor assistant, worked as a runner for Jools Holland and has been with QVC for seventeen years. She says that television students make good interns, working as PAs or floor managers, and are frequently given short paid contracts.

With thanks to Vanessa Ridley for help and advice with this chapter, and for taking the pictures.

KEY TEXTS

BBC Academy College of Production's Guide to a TV Studio, www.bbc.co.uk/academy/production/article/art20130702112135564.

Brown, L. and Duthie, L. (2016) *The TV Studio Production Handbook*, London: I. B. Tauris.

Singleton-Turner, R. (2011) *Cue and Cut: A Practical Approach to Working in Multi-camera Studios*, Manchester, UK: Manchester University Press.

CHAPTER 13

Post-production processes: editing

EDITING AND POST-PRODUCTION

Editing is television's great invisible process. Whether it is carried out in high-tech facilities attached to a major broadcaster or on a personal computer at home, the task is to create a coherent whole from the flow of images and sound captured at the production stage. The editorial team, working with the director and producer, or, for some productions, an 'edit producer' (or 'preditor'), must now give the final shape to a programme. The intensity of the process can give rise to creative tension, inspiring those involved, or to ferocious differences of opinion. Nevertheless, together the team must ensure that the result will inform, amuse, intrigue or enthral its audience.

As technologies have developed, the work of post-production has become increasingly important to the television output, and the separation between the production and post-production stages is being reduced. News crews can now edit their reports on location, and for many major productions, the editing stage begins in parallel with the filming. Fixed-rig documentaries, which can produce 6,000 hours of material for a one-hour programme, pose special problems for post-production. Owen Tyler, operations director at the post-production company Evolutions, writes:

> Originally people would come to us with tapes [e.g. for *One Born Every Minute*]. That meant 6,000 hours of material, which we would have had to ingest at a massive cost . . . We now go to the location and capture it straight on to our servers . . . We're working more closely with the production, which is fundamentally different for us.
> www.rts.org.uk/magazine/article/how-fixed-rig-has-transformed-factual.

And constructing a programme is now rarely confined to material from the shoot, since dozens of different facilities are available in contemporary editing and graphics software. Visual effects and CGI contribute to the density and texture of the image and bring their own visual impact. These may be the responsibility of an in-house graphics department, or they may be created in a separate facilities house. Either way they make a major contribution to the television experience. In particular they are responsible for creating the title sequences, trailers, advertisements, channel idents and other material which are both part of, and supplement, the programmes (see Chapter 14).

Current editing practices are constantly responding to the challenges posed by developing technologies. However, despite innovations and new approaches, the basic principles remain. In the early days of cinema, the work involved physically handling the celluloid film: selecting shots, snipping out the relevant sections, then gluing them together in the desired order. The editor was a 'cutter' working in a 'cutting room'. (A memory of this technique is preserved in the image of the 'trim bin' on the Avid editing programme, showing long strips of celluloid film waiting to be used.) Today's 'edit suite' has rather grander connotations, but the skills of an editor remain rooted in the long history of the craft.

Editing creates the structure and texture of the television output, from high-quality drama to the multitude of innovative factual formats. In this chapter, we will discuss the principles that underlie the practice of constructing a programme, and will give some relevant examples.

Shot, sequence and structure

The editing process is based on the transition between shots, and is basic to the construction of every programme, from an early morning chat show to a major international drama. It may be carried out in the studio as the action unfolds, such as a live programme such as *The X-Factor*, but is at its most powerful with those documentaries and dramas which are filmed shot by shot and then, at the editing stage, patiently built into a coherent whole. This is the creative stage of editing: the stage where the *shots*, however disorganised, are reassembled to form the *sequences* that create the overall *structure*, balancing the visual and the aural, the graphic and the verbal. The editing decisions guide the audience through the movement of sound and images which makes up the television output.

The aim is to create a rich but seamless flow. However, every time there is a transition from one shot to another there is literally a jump in space or time – from one point of view to another, or from one point in time to a different one. Theorists of the 1970s who analysed the basic structures of cinema described the transition as a rupture, a gash, which must be smoothed over – shots must be 'sutured' together as a surgeon sutures a wound. Every time a transition is created, a decision must be made on whether the change will be smooth and imperceptible to the audience, or whether it will be used to jolt them into attention or add to the visual impact of the scene.

Types of transition

The cut is the simplest and by far the most frequently used transition between shots. It is the fundamental transition, in which one shot is instantaneously replaced by the next.

The dissolve ('mix' or 'cross fade') involves the outgoing shot gradually disappearing, giving way to the incoming shot, which eventually takes over.

The fade out is the gradual darkening of the shot until the image disappears, leaving a black screen. This is a slow transition, frequently used to mark the end of a sequence, and usually followed by a *fade in* on the next shot. A fade out indicating the end of the day may be followed by a fade in suggesting the following morning.

The wipe is a device whereby the incoming and outgoing shots are both at full intensity, but the incoming image chases the outgoing one off the screen. The wipe was very popular in black and white movies from the 1940s, and made a comeback on 1980s television, when the arrival of computerised technology began to make visual effects easier to achieve. It may employ a variety of different shapes, from the folding venetian blinds so popular with early film noir, to star bursts and images that fold, swirl or collapse into fragments.

Visual effects. Digital technology has made a huge range of effects available to an editor. These are effects that can play with the relationship between shots rather than creating simple transitions. Current software packages, such as Avid Media Composer and Final Cut Pro, can flip pictures, slow down or speed up an image, create superimpositions and split screen sequences, and can insert graphics and text into live action. More complex sequences are created by specialised graphic designers who produce the visual panache of the title sequences and channel idents which characterise contemporary television (see Chapter 14 for visual effects).

Creating meanings

Editing conventions vary between genres and can be grouped loosely into those in which the logic of the programme is carried by action and dialogue, such as a drama or an observational documentary, and those in which it is carried by the flow of voice-over narrative. In this case, there may be no relation between the images apart from the words that they are illustrating. Each style carries conviction in its own way and has its own form of naturalism (see Chapter 15 for a discussion of realism and the realist 'effect'). However, televisual naturalism is a fragile construction, always in danger of being broken by unexpected juxtapositions and new ways of addressing the audience. The debate about editing between Dziga Vertov and Sergei Eisenstein in the Soviet Union of the 1920s has its reverberations today.

Vertov argued that completely new meanings may be constructed through the rhythms of the editing and the juxtaposition of shots, which are in themselves relatively meaningless. Filmmakers should manipulate the raw material for their own creative ends. They should challenge rather than reinforce the audience's sense of reality. His documentary masterpiece *Man with a Movie Camera* is a joyful cacophony of cinematic devices and dizzying high-speed sequences – and all this in 1929. Eisenstein's response, from the point of view of a narrative filmmaker, was that the flow of the shots must be determined by the demands of the plot and its emotional effect on the audience. Eisenstein and Vertov were debating silent cinema. By contrast in contemporary television, the spoken word has come to dominate and the narrative-based view has tended to win hands down. However, supporters of a more deconstructive style continue to argue that other approaches are also needed and that more attention should be paid to images and the way they work together and react with each other (see Chapter 15). Although Eisenstein was in the narrative camp, he was ultimately less interested in smooth continuity than in impact. He wrote extensively about the different forms of juxtaposition and sequence construction possible for maximum audience effect, proposing a 'montage of attractions', in which every shot would have its own special 'attraction', or intensity, which will either be contrasted with, or linked to, the next (Eisenstein 2016). Today, computer-generated graphics contribute to an increasing use of intricate visual sequences – especially as titles, flashbacks or eye-catching interludes.

THE WORK OF EDITING

Technologies and contexts

Although the effect may be similar, television editing takes place in some very different contexts:

Real-time vision mixing

When a programme originates from a studio or from an outside broadcast or fixed-rig set-up using a number of 'live' cameras, the editing is carried out in a studio gallery or a special facility provided with the equipment for switching between the various inputs. Rather than 'editing', this is known as 'vision mixing'. The director may cue the cuts from a pre-prepared script, or, in the case of chat shows and other programmes where the action is unpredictable, must make spontaneous, on the hoof, decisions (see Chapter 12).

Fixed-rig documentaries can have up to a hundred cameras in place – but only three or four will be recording at any one time. A rough assembly from these will be put together in the control room, and the remainder of the editing carried out in an editing suite.

Linear and non-linear editing

In the early days of cinema, editing became a skilled and highly respected craft, as editors manipulated 35mm and sometimes 16mm film, and dealt with the evolving technologies for adding recorded sound – first through optical devices, then magnetic tape. At first the role of a film editor working for television was to prepare filmed inserts for studio-based programmes and to edit location documentaries. As time went on and cameras became more portable, drama directors saw location filming as giving greater realism, and these too began to be shot on location and to be edited on film, rather than being created in the studio.

The increasing use of magnetic tape, from around the mid-1970s, meant that film editors must become tape editors, and 'linear editing' became the norm. Editing on tape meant that the selected shots must be transferred, or 'dubbed', from the rushes tapes on to a new tape in the desired order. No physical cutting was involved and the task of assembling the programme was 'linear'. To make a change in the order or length of shots, the editor must start from the beginning each time. Digital tape-based recording and linear editing is still occasionally used.

The 1990s saw a slow transition to digital, and editing came full circle back to its non-linear days. At first rushes were 'digitised' from analogue sources, but now rushes from a digital camera are directly 'ingested' into a computer where the material is stored as a digital file on a hard disc. The images and sound tracks are displayed on the screen so that it is possible to select any shot or part of a shot. The sound track can also be edited, manipulating several inputs in relation to the picture. This means that sequences can be speedily constructed and reconstructed. The system brings together video, audio and graphics, together with a wide range of visual and aural effects.

As the material is computer-based, some productions do not need specialised editing suites or even specialised editors. Experienced independent current affairs programme-makers can do their own editing, while portable, lightweight units enable journalists reporting for news programmes to edit on location.

Most recently, the new Avid Everywhere initiative promises cloud-enabled 'real time connectivity', so that editors may 'ingest, edit, and move media fluidly between the story site and production facility from everywhere'. The cloud-based process means that the filmed material is not downloaded to any specific computer and so is instantly available in several locations, making simultaneous editing – assembled on location and fine cut back at base – increasingly possible. 'Now there's no time for a tea break', complains editor Karl Rawstrone.

The work of editing

The work of editing begins when the completed rushes, the material shot during the production period, are viewed and assessed for their own value. This should be done in what Michael Rabiger describes as 'a state of innocence' – by which he means putting aside any knowledge of the sweat and tears that went into the filming, as well as of the effect that was *hoped for*, in order to see the rushes *as they are*: raw material for building a programme (Rabiger 2015). The editor has a certain responsibility to the material, aiming to draw out its potential. And the possibilities vary for different genres. In a comedy, always aware of the audience, timing is all: a well-placed reaction shot or surprise juxtaposition will prompt laughter. For a drama the editing work can enhance both script and acting. Careful selection and juxtaposition of takes can enable a good performance to come through and can sometimes 'cut round' a poor one. By contrast, a documentary rarely has a written script to follow, and is more likely to be built into its final shape in the edit itself. This is the time when the all-important *structure* of a programme is worked out and built up, from *shot* to *sequence*, from the original material.

There is an important genre of programmes which comes out of library/archive research rather than location filming. Archive programmes, such as the BBC series *Timewatch*, are *created* at the editing stage. Some draw on material from the distant past, while others reassess more recent events and supplement the archive shots with interviews with participants and commentators, as in recent programmes commemorating the First and Second World Wars. Once again, it was one of that group of creative filmmakers working in Moscow in the 1920s who is credited with inventing the compilation form. At that time, as so often since, it was easier for women to become editors than cinematographers or directors. Esfir Shub, who with Elizaveta Svilova, the editor of Vertov's *Man with a Movie Camera*, was one of the great editors of the time, put together *The Fall of the Romanov Dynasty* (1927) from carefully researched and rescued footage. Her inventive irony gave it a just reputation as the first compilation film in which a new narrative is constructed from old material (Cook 1985: 206).

Today it is the job of a specialist 'film researcher' to identify relevant material, preserved in film libraries and archives, like those held by the television companies and by the BFI National Film Archive, as well as tracking down private collectors and more obscure sources. It is a job that is complicated by the numerous changes in format which have characterised film and television programme-making since the early days of the moving image. Researchers liaise closely with archivists and technicians who specialise in preserving and converting earlier formats, as well as with the editor and director of a compilation programme. Recent initiatives to put archive material online, such as the BFI Player, have made research easier.

The time and conditions available for editing vary enormously. At one end of the scale, a major documentary or drama may have six to eight weeks to edit, during which time editor and director will usually work closely together. At the other, a topical current affairs programme may be put together at high speed, with the editor working throughout the night to meet the transmission deadline. With developing technology, a topical item may be transmitted only minutes after editing. In such cases there is little time for refinement or second thoughts. This is one reason why editing can be discussed in the same breath as a major art form and as the most routine of technical tasks. It remains both.

EDITING PROCESSES

The best-edited programmes are rarely simply strung together, one shot after the next – although shortness of time available, say for some news reports, does occasionally make this necessary. For most documentary and drama programmes, considerable time and thought will go into deciding the final shot order, cutting points and cutting rhythm, as well as working with the sound track. The programme may be structured and restructured several times before it is ready for transmission. Broadly, these are the processes that must be followed:

Dealing with the rushes

Preparing the material to be used in the programme, including the specially shot rushes and any archive or other bought-in material: a digital imaging technician (DIT), or 'data wrangler', carries out these tasks, which would previously have been done by an assistant editor. Material is shot on different standards, so the job of the DIT is to take the card that contains the rushes from the camera and ensure that a high-resolution copy is made and that the material is converted into a low resolution copy – a proxy – suitable for editing. The original material may be a 'raw file' (equivalent to unprocessed film) and not directly viewable. The use of file-based data has brought a need for more sophisticated 'wrangling'.

Syncing and logging: the DIT then synchronises the sound with the picture and logs the length of the shots and the relevant timecodes on a standard metadata form.

Preparing transcripts if required: typed-up transcripts should be made of interviews and dialogue.

The initial processes

Paper edit: an editor or director may prefer to do a 'paper edit', in which the structure of a programme is worked out in advance. This is a useful way of trying out different segments from the transcripts of interviews.

Building up the sequences, creating the units that will form the structure of a programme.

Making a first assembly, in which the whole programme is loosely strung together to give a suggested overall shape.

Making a rough cut and trying out various options. The rough cut will be longer than the required programme length in order to give some flexibility when paring it down to produce the fine cut. Television programmes have to fit their available slot exactly, so must be timed to the second.

Editing decisions

Editing depends on an important series of decisions. These include:

Selection of shots for inclusion in the final programme from the mass of original material. People who do not understand the process, and even some who should know better, speak of a shot or sequence being cut 'out' of a television programme. Since shooting ratios vary from three to one (three minutes shot for every one used), which is extremely efficient, to fifteen to one or more, it would be more accurate to speak of cutting material 'in'. A drama, and many documentaries, will offer several 'takes' of the same shot. Often the director will have pre-selected which take is to be used; sometimes it is up to the editor to decide, or they may work together. As documentary shooting is looser and less predictable, there are different types of choices to be made. Extracts from an interview, for example, must be carefully selected as they may form the spine of a programme and carry its argument. In the case of observational filming, the editor must select from a mass of unstructured material those sections that will create coherent sequences that appear to flow naturally. Fixed-rig multicamera set-ups usually employ an 'edit-producer' who is present during the filming, and makes a preliminary selection from many hours of material.

The order of shots: the order in which the chosen shots will be arranged must be decided, and how each will follow the next.

The speed and rhythm within each sequence and between the sequences. This involves decisions about the duration of each shot and the precise moment at which one shot will end and the next begin. There are occasions when a quick-cutting series of short shots may be more effective than one or two slow ones. The rhythm may be varied throughout a programme.

The overall structure of the programme: a drama will have been filmed to a script, which already has a narrative structure, but a documentary must frequently be constructed in the cutting room. Various devices may be used to hold the structure together. Some possibilities are:

- *A presenter controls the narrative* – addressing the audience and directing their attention. It may be Brian Cox on the solar system or Mary Beard on ancient history. The editing prioritises the presenter.

- *A time sequence*, for example, following a single event over a period of time – a day in the life of a hospital ward, a month in a tropical jungle, a year on a housing estate.

- *An argument made by an interviewee*, around which sequences may be constructed – say a doctor putting a controversial case for a new cancer cure.

- *A series of interweaving themes* – an oral history programme about the 1950s may cover youth culture, the arrival of commercial television, women's fashion and so on.

- *A narrative structure built around a moment of crisis* – a meeting of long-lost relatives, a trial, a competition. This is a common structure for formatted programmes, 'constructed reality' and other factual genres, which depend heavily on editing for their impact (see Chapter 16).

- *A journalist's report carried by commentary* – this is the most usual way of linking a current affairs programme.

Although such structuring devices are usually worked out before filming begins, they are surprisingly often developed at the editing stage. The addition of a commentary or captions in the final stages of editing can strengthen the structure (see Chapters 15 and 16 for more on narrative and structure).

STYLES OF EDITING

Over the history of the moving image – cinema, television and online media – there have been intense debates over the nature of editing and its possibilities. As we have demonstrated, the work of editing controls the pace and flow, as well as much of the emotional impact, of a programme, so it will be worth concluding this chapter by exploring different styles of editing more closely.

Continuity editing

Successful continuity editing is the invisible art. It erases the evidence of its own operations by maintaining an illusion of continuous movement within a sequence, and making the transitions from one shot to the next as smooth as possible. In practice it follows a number of well-established conventions that achieve an illusion of reality. If the conventions are broken, the viewer will experience a jolt in perception and the illusion may be broken. Continuity is based on the cut, since the instantaneous transition from one shot to the next draws minimal attention to itself, while devices such as fades, wipes and mixes break the flow and usually mark the end of a sequence (see p. 200 below for further discussion of the naturalist conventions implicit in maintaining continuity).

An impression of continuity depends partly on the imagination and expectations of the viewer. Walter Murch writes of 'emotional continuity' (Murch 2001). If the editing indicates a continuous action, that is what the viewer will tend to perceive, even if the original shots are completely discontinuous. For example, a man climbs the steps to the front door of a house and enters. We cut to an interior as he comes into the hallway. These shots may be, and in many cases are, shots of two totally different houses, or of a location exterior and studio interior. Even so, the viewer 'reads' it as the same house and as a continuous action.

As well as temporal continuity, editing links action and reaction. In a comedy, the editing can prompt a laugh by cutting to reaction shots. The juxtaposition of two different shots leads the viewer to assume a relationship between them. In the early 1920s the Russian filmmaker and teacher, Lev Kuleshov, conducted a series of editing experiments. The same shot of the actor, Mosjoukin, was juxtaposed, 'now with a plate of soup, now with a prison gate, now with images suggesting an erotic situation' (in Schnitzer *et al.* 1973: 70). The viewers commented on the subtlety of the acting, perceiving a change of expression when none existed in what became known as the 'third effect'. The active work of the audience in interpreting a sequence of images can be played upon by the filmmaker's skill.

Whether it depends on dialogue, commentary or effects, the sound track helps to carry the audience's attention across the cuts. In a drama the dialogue will dominate the audience's interest; in a commentary-led programme the voice will provide the thread that the audience follows, so that the images are perceived as an illustration of the words. At its worst this can be seen as 'moving wallpaper', at its best the interrelation between words and image can be witty or illuminating (see Chapter 14 for sound editing).

Continuity conventions

The various devices that are used in composing the shots for a continuity sequence are described above (see p. 105), and these need to be maintained during the editing process:

- Avoid 'crossing the line' as it gives the illusion of a complete change of direction, thus:

  - If editing together shots of two people walking in the same direction, or one person chasing another, the two should consistently move either from right to left or vice versa, unless a bridging shot or a cut-away breaks the sequencing.

  - In a conversation cutting between, say, a news presenter and their interviewee: if A is facing right, B must be facing left, or else they may appear to be looking in the same direction rather than facing each other.

—   In a dialogue with both A and B in the same shot, a change of camera angle must maintain A on right of frame and B on left (or vice versa). If the director has inadvertently changed the position of the characters in this way, the editor must find a transition shot to enable the audience to readjust.

• Maintain visual continuity in all details of a shot. Cutting away from a speaker wearing glasses, then back to the same speaker without glasses will feel discontinuous, unless there is a shot of the glasses being removed. The editor must search the frame for other such changes between shots, including jackets that had been done up suddenly becoming open, objects and people appearing or disappearing, vases of flowers apparently jumping to different positions on a table.

• Maintain the impression of continuous movement from shot to shot by cutting on movement. The movement or gesture which 'motivates' a cut 'sutures' over the gap between one shot and the next.

    Cutting on movement is normally planned when shooting a sequence. A movement filmed in a wide shot, say when an actor sits in a chair, will be repeated in the close-up, giving the editor a variety of 'cutting points' to choose from during the movement. When editing verité-style shooting, which does not have formal shots and does not provide the editor with pre-planned cutting points, the constant motion of the camera nevertheless gives plenty of moments where a transition can be seamlessly created.

• When editing several shots of the same person together, cutting between shots of a different size avoids confusion. A clear cut from medium shot to close-up reads more naturally than one that goes from medium to slightly closer; a cut from a right-hand profile to a left-hand one of the same person can be disorienting and not easily recognised, unless of course it is done deliberately to achieve a particular effect.

• Consistency should be maintained when cross-cutting between shots of two different people. Their heads should be a similar size within the frame. Cutting between A in big close up and B in medium shot would look very strange. If an interview has been shot using a single camera, the director will usually have filmed the interviewer separately, asking the questions and nodding in response to an imagined answer. For the editor the 'noddy' provides a helpful cut-away to bridge a deleted section in the interviewee's speech or to smooth over awkward changes in shot size (see p. 219 for interview techniques).

Relational editing

This is the form of editing that builds up the rhythm of a programme through parallels and comparisons; for example, constructing an alternation between two or more narratives for dramatic effect.

Analytic editing

This is the form of editing in which the sequence of images is constructed to follow an argument rather than a narrative. Sometimes the flow of the images matches the flow of a narrating voice on the sound track, and makes no sense if seen alone. Sometimes the images can create a visual dynamic of their own.

Montage editing

Although the word 'montage' can mean editing in general, it is most often used to describe a sequence that is built up through the juxtaposition and rhythm of images and sounds. This may be independent of narrative or argument, as in some avant-garde film and video making, or it may act to illuminate or punctuate the narrative or argument.

New genres, new styles: reflexivity

As with all aspects of programme-making, the 'rules' of editing are never hard and fast. As conventions change and new genres evolve, the rules tend to be revised and rewritten. In many long-established styles, it is not considered acceptable to draw attention to the filmmaking process by including 'unmotivated' camera movement or a direct recognition of the camera/audience by a member of the cast or a participant in an observational documentary. When hand-held cameras and observational filming first evolved in the 1960s, new ways of editing had to be worked out to deal with the vagaries of 'wobblyscope' – such as the occasional loss of focus, the sudden pans and readjustments of the frame – but this had to be achieved without acknowledging the presence of the filmmaker (Jaffe 1965). Of course, 'avant-garde' and experimental styles have long been reflexive in this way, drawing particular attention to the filmmaking process (*Man With a Movie Camera* was an early example – the cinematographer was seen everywhere – even rising up from a glass of beer), and one aspect of cinema verité in the 1960s was to acknowledge the truth (verité) of the filmmaking process (see Jean Rouch's *Chronicle of a Summer* (1961) for a classic example).

Many recent styles have embraced reflexivity with enthusiasm. From the docusoaps which became popular in the 1990s, through to the 'constructed reality' genres of the 20teens, it has become a standard practice for those observed to talk back to the camera and for the filmmaker to intervene explaining their intentions and engaging with the action. In these genres, disguising mistakes and avoiding unwanted glances no longer poses a problem for the editor. Most filmed material, including the unexpected and unplanned, is now available for use. Now that digital technology has given greater control over the image, the use of glitches and judders, which would have been mistakes with analogue technology, can now be a nostalgic reference to an older style. As always creativity and understanding must go together with technical skill and know-how.

THE FINAL STAGES

- *Recording and placing commentary* where appropriate.

- *Fine cut.* Producing a fine cut at the correct length with the audio in place. Incorporating the work of the visual effects designer, including title sequences visual effects, graphics and end credits (see Chapter 14).

- *Preparing the sound tracks* ready for the dub when they will be combined for the final version. There may be several versions, especially if the programme is to be sold overseas and foreign language versions are needed. This means relating the sound to the visuals and preparing sync dialogue, commentary, music and sound effects on separate audio tracks. The next chapter will present a more detailed discussion of the sound editing process.

- *Approval.* The producer, executive producer and sometimes a channel controller must view and approve a programme.

- *Finishing process.* The programme may then go to a facilities house for the finishing processes (this is sometimes called an 'online edit'). An edit decision list (EDL) is produced, through the appropriate software, and this enables the online editors to match the offline version. At this stage extra effects can be added, images can be 'tidied up' to eliminate unwanted content or to blur the faces of people who should not be identified.

- *Grading.* Colour correction is part of the finishing process. The shots are graded by a 'colourist' so that their quality is consistent throughout. If there is no time for quality control during the shoot, or if the film is shot by a self-shooting director who is not experienced in camera work, corrections can be made in the grading suite.

    Recently the easy availability of grading programmes such as Da Vinci has meant that some professional grading suites have gone out of business. However, a professional 'colourist' has a special skill www.youtube.com/watch?v=LFmyh-cKjQQ.

- *A broadcast master copy* is created at this stage, bearing in mind that different broadcasters have different requirements. Some news and low-budget programmes can be transmitted directly from a desktop.

- *Technical delivery standards*. At every stage a programme is checked for quality. Standards are laid down by the Digital Production Partnership (DPP), a company founded by ITV, the BBC and C4, with reference to the International Telecommunications Union (ITU) and European Broadcast Union (EBU) technical standards. The editor must carry out a technical review to ensure that standards are met. Programmes are accompanied by an XML (Extensible Markup Language) data file known as Programme Metadata. This digital format allows a wide range of information about the programme to be recorded, including title, duration and even details such as locations used. And it contains relevant technical information, including the timecode and file integrity information, which cues the file for broadcast. The Metadata format is far more easily searchable than paper-based systems, which is of great benefit to archivists and researchers (Chapter 14 gives more information on compliance and other post-production issues, p. 179) www.digitalproductionpartnership.co.uk/.

The editor is a technical expert, but he or she is neither a technician nor a broadcast engineer. The editors' technical fluency allows them to communicate effectively with, and meet the standards required by, the people with ultimate responsibility for the technical quality of broadcasts. 'It's up to the editor to make sure it doesn't come back from the broadcaster because it's not up to standard . . . being on top of the technical aspects gives greater creative capacity', says editor Karl Rawstrone.

With thanks to VT editor Karl Rawstrone, Programme Leader MA Post-Production Editing, Bournemouth University.

KEY TEXTS

Eisenstein, S. (2016) *Towards a Theory of Montage,* Volume 2 of Selected Works (ed. Richard Taylor, trans. Michael Glenny), London: I. B. Tauris; see also: www.youtube.com/watch?v=MzXFSBlQOe4.
Murch, W. (2001) *In the Blink of an Eye: A Perspective on Film Editing*, Los Angeles, CA: Silman-James Press.
Weynand, D. and Piccin, V. (2015) *How Video Works: From Broadcast to the Cloud*, Oxford: Focal Press.

CHAPTER 14

Sound, visual effects and preparing for broadcast

THE AURAL DIMENSION: CREATING THE AUDIO SPACE

As we saw in Chapter 11, sound is both a separate dimension of the television experience and an inseparable part of its total communication.

The editing process adds to the image track a number of sound tracks that may be combined in various ways. On television this 'audio space' is usually dominated by the human voice, as commentary or dialogue. That means that an initial task at the sound editing stage is to make sure that the voices, which carry so much of the meaning, are clear, audible and well placed (the BBC's 2015 production of *Jamaica Inn* was severely criticised in the press and on social media for 'mumbling' actors and inaudible dialogue). At the same time, the introduction of layers of sound from many different sources creates a rich and varied audio dimension. On feature films and large productions, a supervising sound designer with a team of assistants work on the sound tracks, while on some television productions such as news broadcasts, it may be necessary for a single editor to put together both picture and sound. Occasionally, in the high-speed near-panic conditions that characterise some topical television work, sound editing may be reduced to some hasty 'track laying' a few hours before the dub.

The bigger the overall budget, the more time can be given to the sound design, and, as more facilities become available, the role of the sound designer has become more important. The title 'sound designer' was invented for Walter Murch who worked on the film *Apocalypse Now*, remembered for its audio impact, particularly the ominous, rhythmic sound of the American helicopter approaching Vietnam (1979). (For video games the person in charge of sound is referred to as the 'audio designer'.) The celebrated director David Lynch is quoted as saying 'sound is at least 50 per cent of the image if not more'. As with cinema, careful attention to sound can transform a television programme.

The power of sound is often overlooked in writing about television, and, indeed, may be overlooked by some television producers. But an innovative use of sound has a long history. Back in the 1930s, before location shooting with synchronised speech was easy to achieve, documentary-makers constructed richly textured sound tracks, using music, poetry and voices (for example, *Night Mail* 1936). In the 1950s and early 1960s innovative documentaries were developed on radio by Charles Parker, Peggy Seeger and Ewan McColl who created the celebrated *Radio Ballads* (1957–63) by interweaving the rhythms of everyday conversation with music and recitation. The great television documentarist Denis Mitchell came out of that tradition. His early television films, including *Morning in the Streets* (BBC 1959), contained sync dialogue, but were to a large extent made up of impressionistic silent filming accompanied by evocative sound effects and a rich montage of voices, including snatches of conversation and regional inflections which he captured with an unobtrusive tape recorder. As time went on, the tyranny of sync made that sort of audio exploration less fashionable. *Blue* (C4: 1993) was an exception. Dying of AIDS, the avant-garde filmmaker Derek Jarman was losing his sight. Commissioned by Channel Four, the image track for his last film was simply the intense and unvarying colour blue, but on the sound track a complex mixture of voices, music and commentary reflected on the tragedy of AIDS and Jarman's own mortality. Dramas are increasingly aware of the role of sound. Stephen Poliakoff's *Shooting the Past* (1999) used an overlapping montage of voices on the sound track to evoke memories and emotions.

Focus on sound has changed considerably in the last few years, especially in prestige television drama, which aspires to feature film quality. The contrast between the 1971 film of L. P. Hartley's novel *The Go Between* and the BBC's 2015 adaptation is striking. The story, set in 1900, includes a cricketing scene. In the film the sound track included the thwack of bat on ball, some polite applause from the well-bred spectators and the occasional whispered comment. The 2015 version of the same scene, although made for television, has greater depth and intensity. The audio track enhances the action with a range of sound from many perspectives: heavy breathing and grunts from the exertions of the cricketers, robust applause and shouts from the spectators, significant details such as feet shuffling in front of the wicket, the bat carefully placed on the crease and the hardly perceptible but significant 'ssh' as the bowler polishes the ball against his trousers.

Synthetic sounds and effects which can be enhanced to create a mood, such as echoes and creaking doors, have long been part of the repertoire of television's audio space. The new *Dr Who* still uses the eerie title music based on the track created by the BBC's radiophonic workshop back in 1963. The workshop had been set up in 1958 especially to produce atmospheric sounds and electronically manipulated music.

With advances in technology, natural sounds can be heightened and treated in many ways. Walter Murch described his work on those helicopter blades back in 1979:

> We took those realistic sounds and deconstructed them on synthesisers . . . the helicopter provides you with the sound equivalent of shining a white light through a prism – you get the hidden colours of the rainbow.
>
> http://designingsound.org/2009/10/walter-murch-special-apocalypse-now/

Non-naturalistic sound has become a regular feature of the television output. Many documentaries, such as nature docs, are not recorded sync and the sounds – some recorded on location, some constructed – are added later. 'All film, including the sound track, is a matter of construction', argues editor Maike Helmers.

Beyond the programmes themselves, the attention-grabbing 'stings', fanfares and sound effects that accompany programme logos and title sequences are an important feature of the television experience. The image of the broadcasting mast with its circulating waves, which introduced the first television news broadcasts in 1946, came with its own jaunty tune. The famous *News at Ten* flourish, which ends with the 'bongs' of Big Ben, between which the headlines are read, remains a relished landmark in British television despite some recent revisions. Equally, producers of commercials pay a great deal of attention to their sound tracks, not least in their use of music.

Of all the sounds that enhance the television image, music is the most direct in its emotional effect. Many programmes – from *Later with Jools Holland* to *The X-Factor* and the *BBC Proms* are music-based. And across the output, music makes an essential contribution to the audio space of most dramas and many documentaries. It has become an expected part of a programme. However, some argue that it tends to be overused, especially when it runs continuously in the background of a drama, or heightens the mood of a documentary where it may not be appropriate. Nevertheless, well-chosen and well-placed music can set a mood and pace a programme, as well as adding its own ironic or foreboding commentary. Music introduces and closes most programmes, acts as a signature tune or familiar marker for well-known performers and series. It can transform a solemn moment into a light-hearted one and vice versa. The selection, placing and prominence of the music are essential to the feeling of the programme as a whole.

SOUND EDITING

Types of sound

At the *sound editing* and *track laying* stages, different types of sound will be placed on separate tracks, so that the quality of each of them can be monitored and adapted. In addition, they can be moved around in relation to the image and to each other.

At the *dubbing* stage the separate tracks will be combined and balanced to produce the final tracks that will accompany the broadcast image. There may be several different versions if, for example, a stereo track is required or foreign language versions are needed for overseas sales.

Sound sources include:

Synchronised sound (sync)

Most television programmes are shot with synchronised sound which arrives in the editing suite together with the picture from the location or studio. If the programme is recorded and edited 'as live', the sound from the different microphone sources will have been balanced by a sound engineer as the recording goes along. If a programme is filmed with individual, pre-planned shots, the editor's first job is to ensure that when the shots are cut together, the synchronised sound flows evenly from one to the next and remains in sync with the image. We do not always want to look at the person who is speaking, so sound overlaps may be used. In a conversation, the sound of a character's voice may precede the cut to their face or it may continue during a shot of the person listening to them. This way the impression of flow is enhanced and a sense of interaction between the characters is created.

For the editor, if the sync sound is disengaged from its image, it becomes possible to use it to complement as well as to accompany the action. Whether in an interview or scripted dialogue, strategically placed reaction shots of the listener add to our understanding of the scene. They also offer the opportunity for the editor to make a cut in the spoken track without breaking the flow of the sound.

ADR (automatic dialogue replacement)

Sometimes creating the desired effect may involve removing the sounds recorded on location – that scream may not be very convincing or a period piece may have been spoilt by traffic background – and replacing them with one created separately – a more bloodcurdling scream or a suitably period track of clopping horses and twittering birds. If the sync sound is not appropriate it may be necessary for actors to be recalled to revoice a sequence: perhaps the dialogue is not clear because of background noise, or perhaps the director wants an actor to adapt their performance. Depending on the actors' availability this can take place months after filming. This type of post-sync replacement is known as automatic dialogue replacement (ADR).

In big feature films it is not uncommon for the whole film to be revoiced. *Lord of the Rings*, whose New Zealand location is near a noisy airport, is an example of this. In this case, the location sync is used as a guide track as the actors match the movement of their lips to their image filmed on location. Some actors use headphones, and it is the editor's job to mark the picture with cue lines to indicate to the ADR artist when to begin speaking. This technique is also used when films are dubbed into other languages. There are actors who specialise in this sort of post-sync work. Some have become famous as the Spanish or German 'voice' of well-known Hollywood actors.

Other voice sources

These will be separately recorded, sometimes before the editing begins, sometimes as part of the post-production process.

The commentary or voice-over for documentary programmes is the most important of these. It must be 'laid' so that the spoken words are juxtaposed with the picture in an appropriate way: it would be confusing to discuss the nesting habits of the blue tit if the image on the screen shows an eagle in flight. Juxtapositions can be very precise. The exact moment at which a word is placed can emphasise a cut or a camera movement, or can create an impression that may be witty and or emphatic. Words and image work together as a single, specifically televisual experience.

Other sound effects (sfx)

These may be specially recorded on location, or they may be acquired from a sound library. They may be created live as a 'spot effect' at the dubbing stage, or they may be created in a special studio, known as a Foley studio, named after an early Hollywood sound pioneer, Jack Foley. This is provided with equipment of various sorts, ranging from bells, hammers and creaking doors, to different types of ground surfaces for footsteps. Sand, gravel, parquet flooring, paving stones: to the practised ear they all sound different to the non-practised ear something indefinable seems wrong if the sounds are incorrect. For example, a footstep artist will own a variety of shoes and can tiptoe or stamp as required. Speaking on Radio 4's *The Film Programme* (26 May 2015) foley artist Barnaby Smyth demonstrated the use of dishwasher salt to create the sound of walking on frozen grass, then added a layer of meringue nests to give the impression of ice. Effects may be manipulated in the sound studio, but many sound designers argue that these 'natural' sounds are more convincing than ones that are created electronically. At the sound editing stage each of the effects is placed on a special track, positioned so that it will have the greatest effect in relation to the picture.

For the sound editor, ordering ADR and Foley, or arranging a post-sync session in a dubbing theatre, is one of the final stages before assembling the tracks ready for the dub.

Music

Music for television programmes is particularly important. The choice of title music and theme tunes can mark a series for decades – think of *Dr Who* or *EastEnders*. Many series keep variations on their familiar themes available for the sound editor to call on. Otherwise music may be either specially composed or acquired from a music library that specialises in 'background' music. Sound libraries can provide sample sounds – for example, the website of the Vienna Symphonic Library describes a range of 'bundles' including its 'Appassionata Strings bundle'. 'If you are looking for that larger-than-life Hollywood sound, the Appassionata Strings are the perfect answer.' Its website notes: 'You're going to be fooled by them for years on movie soundtracks, commercials, games, and pop tunes.' www.vsl.co.at/en/Strings_Complete/Appassionata_Strings_Bundle#!Reviews.

In addition libraries such as the Vienna offer a modular system that can be customised by a composer using a keyboard, rather like a piano keyboard, to call up the different inputs. Rather than employing an orchestra, composers may now work from their home computers www.youtube.com/watch?v=GB_QueMQ7kI. However, major series will still use specially composed and recorded music. For the BBC's *The Hunt*, the score, by composer Stephen Price, was performed by the 65-piece BBC concert orchestra.

Of course, music may also be selected from published recordings and the copyright purchased for reuse. This is a complex and expensive process involving clearance from many different individuals and companies, including composers, performers, the Performing Rights Society and the recording company among others.

Sometimes the music for a sequence is chosen before the pictures are edited. In this case, the editor may compose a visual sequence that matches its moods and rhythms. But if the music is specially commissioned, it will be created with the edited programme in mind and timed to fit the action. In this case it may either be recorded together with the film, projected in a special studio, or prepared independently then laid into position by the editor.

Dubbing

The final stage in the preparation of a programme's sound is when the prepared tracks are brought into a dubbing suite, where the dubbing mixer combines and balances them according to the editor's pre-planned instructions.

For news programmes and other programmes that are very current, for example, *Panorama* whose brief is to react to the events of the week, the track laying and dubbing processes may happen in a tremendous rush, sometimes in the middle of the night or just before transmission. For dramas and documentaries with a longer editing schedule, the conditions may be more like those for feature films, with the work on the audio taking several weeks. Either way, sound designers are always under pressure, as all the processes must be gone through. They are always fighting for more time, as pictures tend to take priority and, as transmission day approaches, every process becomes speeded up.

At the dub:

- The tracks carrying the different types of sound – speech, music, effects and even background nothingness – known as a buzz track (see Chapter 11) – are checked for quality and combined.

- The tracks are balanced against each other: for example, holding the music in the background when it is intended to back up the dialogue, then swelling it to a crescendo where needed; making sure that important speech is not drowned out by effects or unimportant sounds.

- Some sounds may be manipulated to create a special effect, such as adding echo. 'Spot' sound effects may be added.

- Extra tracks are created where needed. If a programme is to be dubbed into another language, a music-and-effects track (known as an 'M and E') will be created without commentary or other voice elements.

Some high-end television series, such as *Breaking Bad* and *Game of Thrones*, both with extremely complex sound tracks, will be in a form of 'Surround Sound' known as 5.1. In other words, separate tracks are prepared for five speakers, which can be distributed around a cinema or even a living room, together with a 'subwoofer', which carries the extra low frequencies, placed below the screen.

In this case the audio designer, together with the dubbing mixer, can arrange the tracks for depth and perspective – allowing the action to move not only from left to right, but around the room, to create what the promotion describes as a 'surround sound home theatre experience'. In this as in many other ways, the experience of television and of cinema are beginning to overlap.

Sign zone

An extra note on sound: there is a significant proportion of the population who are deaf or hard of hearing, for whom the full television experience requires a translation. The BBC has a 'sign zone' that is transmitted on BBC2 late at night, when popular programmes are repeated with a sign translation superimposed. Alternatively, subtitles are available for all channels, sometimes prepared in advance, sometimes generated by voice recognition software, but frequently produced simultaneously by highly skilled palantypists www.bbc.co.uk/ouch/opinion/bring_on_the_palantypist. shtml.

With thanks to editor Maike Helmers, senior lecturer in sound design, Bournemouth University.

GRAPHICS AND VISUAL EFFECTS

Visual fireworks

Contemporary television is changing the way it looks, largely due to the influence of CGI and visual effects. By the second decade of the twenty-first century, it could be argued that the televisual experience, in its various manifestations, is based on graphic as much as photographic media, on design as much as representation.

CGI and digital effects have greatly expanded television's visual range. They can modify and enhance the image produced by the camera, expanding the impression of realism as well as creating fantasy and spectacle. Visual effects structure the title sequences that begin the programmes and the graphic elements that contribute to them. In particular the interstitials – the material that comes *between* the programmes, the advertisements, trailers and channel identifications (idents) – are the work of visual effects teams who combine the skills of the graphic artist and of digital design.

Animation is an important part of the graphic designer's repertoire. Genres which for many years created their effects using models, animatronics (robotic devices), puppetry and stop-frame animation now call on the visual effects team to create strange monsters, time travel and magic events. When the drama series *Call the Midwife* dealt with the effects of the drug thalidomide, they used animatronics and CGI to create realistic babies suffering from the dreadful deformities caused by the drug.

At the same time, many of the older animation techniques have been revisited. Even in the feature industry, techniques such as miniature models and motion control cameras are still used, due to their cinematic visual quality. On UK television the children's series *The Clangers*, first broadcast between 1969 and 1972, was reprised in 2015, with its knitted puppets and lunar landscapes filmed in stop-frame animation. However, work on animated programmes –from the all-American two-dimensional *Simpsons*, to the puppets and plasticine of classic children's series such as *Magic Roundabout* – is a specialism in itself and is, unfortunately, beyond the scope of this book. In this section, we will be discussing the role played by the video effects team in television production.

Cinema films, with their frame-by-frame photographic structure, had experimented with visual styles from the earliest days of the moving image. Already in the 1890s, filmmakers such as Georges Méliès were using animated sequences, multiple exposures, composite images and optical effects of many sorts. But unlike the richness of the cinematic image, live broadcast television did not lend itself to this sort of manipulation. In the early days of the medium, graphics meant black and white caption cards placed on music stands in front of a studio camera and changed by hand.

However, the television organisations had their own graphics departments and were increasingly using film to create animated sequences and innovative channel identifications. When ITV was launched in 1955, for the first time advertisements appeared, both between the programmes and at 'natural breaks' within them. The ads were made on film and a great deal of expense as well as creative design went into their production. With their inventiveness and graphic resources, advertisements posed a visual challenge to the programmes that surrounded them. As technology developed over the years, specialist companies began to experiment with electronic effects and a wider range of imagery, resulting in the stylish polish of the colourful 1980s.

Television in the 1980s indulged in high-tech gloss and sparkle, and set out to celebrate the new techniques. These were the days of *Max Headroom*, the jerky computer-generated interviewer with a metallic voice. Commercials and pop videos exploited the new technologies, and these in turn influenced the expanding area of youth programming, energetically promoted by Janet Street-Porter, first at Channel Four, then the BBC. Her *Network Seven* and *Def II* broke all the rules and pioneered a path towards the sparky and the outrageous. The programmes exploited early computer graphics for all they were worth, with simultaneous multiple imagery and text, strange colours, floating figures and superimpositions all prefiguring the mythical worlds of the high-tech electronic future, which utopian writers of the time were claiming would revolutionise consciousness itself.

Effects designers gained a new prestige. In 1982 Channel Four was launched, and its landmark multicoloured logo, created by designer Martin Lambie-Nairn, was based on children's bricks flying through three-dimensional space. As channels proliferated, their brand identification became more important and channel idents became television gems in their own right (Johnson 2012). In 1992, Lambie-Nairn went on to design BBC2's witty and predatory 2s that came alive, puffed themselves up and transformed themselves into unpredictable materials from the harshly metallic to the furry or the squiggly plastic. Some planed their way round the floorboards with an alarming disregard for the realities of space and time. These were the forerunners of the complex title sequences of the 20teens, such as Channel Four's exploration of landscapes – rocky coastlines, dock-side cranes, council estates – which miraculously configured themselves into the figure 4.

Producers in all genres began to realise that even serious interviews needed no longer be presented as straightforward talking heads. A speaker could be super-imposed on archive material, or the image could be enlivened with mottled backgrounds or glowing colours. Heads could be separated from their bodies, moved around the frame or combined with text or graphics in surreal fashion. Science documentaries, arts and history programmes, current affairs – all genres began to use such devices, exploited, for example, in Channel Four's *Essential Guide* to the war in Bosnia, made in 1993.

Now, in the 20teens, digital effects are central to the television repertoire. The informational graphics that had begun life as flat caption cards have developed into complex multidimensional events, spectacular or entertaining in their own right. They are an essential part of the language of contemporary programme-making, in which 'explainer' graphics need to be as attractive as those presented for pleasurable effect. And, beyond the specifically informational, increasingly sophisticated digital techniques, which had been developing in the feature film industry since the 1990s, have found their way into television programmes. Now it is taken for granted that television drama, especially in the science fiction and fantasy genres such as *Game of Thrones* and *Dr Who*, will amaze their audience with their fantastic and other-worldly effects.

The arrival of 'photo-real' computer graphics in the late 1980s and early 1990s meant that creatures such as dinosaurs and robots could be created virtually, and animated for insertion into filmed footage. In 1999, the BBC's *Walking with Dinosaurs* was celebrated for its use of CGI together with animatronics. In 2015, in a ground-breaking advertisement for Galaxy Chocolate, the visual effects company Framestore 'resurrected' the actress Audrey Hepburn. Using computer graphics they spent five months re-creating her face, with a startlingly realistic effect www.theguardian.com/media-network/media-network-blog/2014/oct/08/how-we-made-audrey-hepburn-galaxy-ad. Today's interactive and convergent media have no option but to be graphics-based.

Just as graphics lead the surfer through the complexities of the web, multichannel, multiplatform television needs similar signposts and markers. 'These days, a television channel is just another product on an increasingly crowded television supermarket shelf', the designer of those flying 4s and unpredictable 2s is quoted as saying. The concept of 'branding', which served both a commercial and a creative purpose for advertisers throughout the twentieth century, is now part of the strategic thinking of television executives as well as of television design. This is one important influence behind the numerous trailers and eye-catching station idents which characterise the contemporary television experience (Johnson 2012).

Many cinema-orientated companies, such as Framestore, now have a commercials division. More 'boutique' companies, such as Realise Studio or Glassworks, focus solely on television adverts and music videos. At the same time, some television organisations, including the BBC, have their own in-house visual effects departments.

The language of computer graphics and digital effects is now fully established, and while new tools and technologies continue to emerge, they are based on the same technological foundation and principles. This means that the ABCs of the industry now exist, and, as a result, offer something very concrete for those new to this area. Although new techniques and processes are constantly developing, their informational and promotional functions remain. In some cases simplicity is more important than spectacle.

Below we look first at some of the uses of graphic elements and text, where their informational role predominates, and then at the work of the visual effects artist and the ways in which visual effects are now an intrinsic part of programme-making.

Informational graphics and text

As titles for the beginning of programmes and as end credits. Most programmes have a specially designed title sequence, which combines informational text with complex visual creations and vibrant music. Some, like the swirling, vertiginous tilts for the revised *Dr Who*, have become celebrated in their own right (on the role of the title sequence, see Gray 2010). End credits, those all-important lists that name the skilled technicians whose creativity and hard work have actually got the programme on air, have, nevertheless, tended to lose their pride of place in the frame. The need to win audiences means that the list of names is frequently squeezed to one side to make space for channel idents and the promotion of future programmes.

As written information on the screen. This includes the 'strap titles' at the bottom of the frame, which name interviewees and participants, and the subtitles that translate foreign language programmes. Here the imperative is clarity and legibility. The rule of thumb is to leave lettering on the screen long enough to be read aloud twice, so that even slow readers can assimilate it.

Pictorial graphics such as paintings or still photographs. They may be used as an illustration or as an essential contribution to a programme such as *Who Do You Think You Are?* in which photographs of ancestors play an important role. An effect of movement is often created by 'exploring' the picture, picking out details, panning across its surface or animating elements within the image, creating a 'two and a half dimensional' photographic effect – multilayered, but each layer is flat.

Statistical graphics such as graphs and bar charts. The point of these is to convey factual information. They include simple graphs used to illustrate opinion polls and other numerical data, particularly at times like elections, when voting trends and exit polls are scrutinised and measured. Sometimes they involve complex three-dimensional effects taking over the whole studio. During the 2015 election, the *Newsnight* presenter summoned up three-dimensional bar charts from the floor, which appeared to rise under his hands. The 1994 comedy series *The Day Today* had anticipated this use of bombastic statistical graphics in its knowing satire on the news.

The principles of visual, special and digital effects

Continuities with the past

Digital effects follow similar principles to the optical effects that characterised cinema from its early days. These include back projection, superimpositions, composite images, stop frame and, of course, drawn animation. However, digital effects now combine elements from different images in a more seamless and naturalistic way than the techniques used by celluloid film.

Digital compositing

This is the use of a 'matte' in the camera to block out part of the frame, so that it can be replaced with another image. For example, a car interior may be shot in the studio and a moving landscape inserted by an optical process as if through the car window.

This technique was used in the ground-breaking police series *Z-Cars* back in the 1960s. With today's digital technology this has become a computerised post-production technique known as *'digital compositing'*. It is often used to place figures in impossible settings, and was heavily relied on in films such as *Avatar* (2009) and *Star Wars* Episode 3 (2005).

Digital assets

A digital asset is a digital object or event which can be used again and again (a creature, a robot, an explosion, a water effect etc.). It is possible to create a library of digital assets available to be reused when needed. Libraries of assets are provided by the software, but the digital effects companies involved in research and development develop their own, higher level assets. An illusion of 3D can be created, as the effects are calculated in 3D space, but ultimately they are presented to the viewer as fast-moving, still-frame 2D images.

Special effects (SFX)

Special effects are real-world assets, such as models and puppets, developed to create a certain effect or shot. They are very often used in addition to digital effects. Some films, such as *Jurassic Park* (1993), used a combination of computer graphics and animatronics-based puppets.

Digital effects (DFX) created by camera/computer

These include motion control, which allows identical camera moves to be repeated. The shots can then be combined for a particular effect. For example, the same actor can appear on screen at the same time in different positions. This effect was used in Kylie Minogue's *Come Into My World* video www.youtube.com/watch?v= 6Fe1Scu5fdw.

Tracking and motion capture

Tracking software analyses the pixel detail and contrast information of a shot, enabling the precise insertion of an object or other digital asset www.thepixelfarm. co.uk/products/PFTrack.

Motion capture is the use of tracking sensors, markers or points on actors to record their movement in three-dimensional space. This generates data so that their actions can be exactly reproduced by a digital creature – say an ape, as in *Dawn of the Planet of the Apes* (2014) www.youtube.com/watch?v=IezfSn09n5g.

Computer-based digital effects

Digital effects are computer-based processes developed to create a certain effect or shot. They include digital make-up, which can simulate wounds or blemishes when needed. Alternatively, they may erase blemishes to give the impression of perfect skin. Head replacement enables a digital head of a character to be replaced on a stuntman's body. And simulations range from adding hair to an actor or digital creature, to blowing up a planet. A drag-and-drop 'explosion tool' is available. Digital effects also enable the creation of digital creatures – from dinosaurs to robots. Often entire shots are fully computer-generated.

Television is increasingly moving to near-cinema standard effects on programmes such as *Dr Who* and the ABC series *Once Upon a Time*, which updates well-known stories with a visual panache that attracts adults as well as children.

Visual effects across the production processes

Pre-production

A production will generally employ a visual effects supervisor and a number of visual effects artists. As with all aspects of production, the work of pre-production is crucial. This is when the visual effects supervisors will work with the director and the team to plan a sequence in detail. First they will create a sense of the *appearance* of the effect by producing images known as *concept art*, which will give an impression of the shot to be produced. They will then plan the role of the effect within the sequence, and lay it out on a *storyboard*. Finally they will create a moving image sequence, known as the *animatic*. This is a pre-visualisation of the final sequence and will help the director plan the shots carefully before production begins. At pre-production every aspect of the effect should be planned and developed. For the film *Gravity* (2013), in which the protagonists were suspended in space, the entire film was visualised in this way before the principal photography began.

Production

It is important for the location crew to provide the effects artists with a 'background plate' for a sequence, which will be enhanced at the post-production stage. It should be an image of the shot without actors or events, but carefully composed and lit. This is referred to as the *cinematography* of the image, and the effects created will take place against this background. It may be difficult to compose because the effects to be created cannot be seen (for example a hoard of rhinos will come charging through the background of the neat little house in *Jumanji* 1995) www.imdb.com/title/tt0113497/. However, the crew can provide the designers with shots which have in place 'survey references', such as markers and measuring sticks, to give a clear idea of the dimensions of a scene. They should also provide a 'clean plate', which is a second take of a shot without the foreground action, to provide additional information for compositing tricks.

Usually other data will be collected at the time of shooting, including lighting information, based on the way that light from the environment falls onto a grey or chrome
sphere. Visual effects supervisors and artists are frequently present on location or
film sets to collect such data and advise the production crews.

For the effects to appear realistic, the effects artist must pay attention to:

- *Matching the light*: a chrome ball can be photographed from a number of
  angles to record the light at a scene. This makes it possible for virtual
  backgrounds to be matched.

- *Matching the material:* software can be used to create familiar surfaces,
  ranging from highly reflective steel to the complex texture of knitted wool
  and even invented surfaces.

- *Camera matching*: recreating on the computer the characteristics of the
  camera that filmed the original shots.

Together these principles can create a seamless photo-realism.

Increasingly technologies are developing which enable an initial impression of a
effect to be created while the filming is in process. For example, an actor may be
able to view the sort of landscape that will eventually replace the green screen
behind them. This, of course, helps them develop their performance. The full details
of the landscape will be created at the post-production stage.

Post-production

The 'composite' is where all the production assets are brought together for compilation into the final sequence within the digital effects facility. This is when the work
of the effects team is completed.

And finally

Across the whole of the production and post-production period, liaison with the
rest of the team is crucial. Video effects designers must pay attention to what is
referred to as the 'directability' of their processes. They must be aware of the
demands and practicalities of deadlines and producers' requirements. Designs
must be fluid so that they can easily respond to the director's requests for changes,
while speed and efficiency are all important – there's no point in creating the
most impressive effect if it will take a month to make and the deadline is next
week. And there should be an awareness of the level of detail needed – an object
which is at a distance does not need as much detailed work as one that is in the
foreground.

In a situation where technology is constantly updating and improving, the ultimate
aim is to create digital effects that will enhance the image in various ways. Digital
effects can create images that are more exciting than the real world. There is a

fine line between representing reality and creating a convincing and seductive image that viewers would not believe is computer-generated.

With thanks to Phil Spicer, Programme Leader MA Digital Effects, Bournemouth University.

KEY TEXTS

Allen, D. (2007) *Encyclopedia of Visual Effects*, San Francisco, CA: Prachpit Press.
Glintenkamp, P. (2011) *Industrial Light and Magic: The Art of Innovation*, New York: Abrams.
Murch, W. (2001) *In the Blink of an Eye: A Perspective on Sound Editing*, Los Angeles, CA: Silman-James Press.
Rickitt, R. (2006) *Special Effects: The History and Technique*, London: Aurum Press.

POST-PRODUCTION: PREPARING FOR BROADCAST AND DISTRIBUTION

Before a programme can be broadcast it must be reviewed to ensure that it meets certain standards – some technical, some concerned with content – ensuring that it will be neither offensive nor unlawful in any way. For programmes transmitted within the United Kingdom, this means compliance with Ofcom's Broadcasting Code, which outlines legal obligations and principles such as respecting the 9pm watershed. Children's programmes, in particular, must comply with stringent regulations. Most programmes are carefully monitored, and often 'lawyered', throughout the production and post-production stages.

When programmes are to be transmitted overseas, it is also necessary to check that the content complies with the legal and cultural requirements of the territory where it will be shown. Some territories are stricter than others, with compliance requirements relating to language, violence, nudity and sexuality. There is a range of specific requirements pertaining to each of the territories. Checking for these requirements is the job of a compliance officer, who must note what changes are needed and ensure that they are carried out.

In addition, there needs to be a quality control (QC) check at every stage. For technical standards we have seen that it is up to the programme editors to QC material before broadcast. They must carry out a review to ensure that standards laid down by the Digital Production Partnership (DPP), are met and must submit an XML (Extensible Markup Language) data file known as Programme Metadata to the broadcaster. This contains all the relevant details about the programme, including the timecode and the file integrity information, which cues the file for broadcast (see p. 163 for Editing: final stages).

Additional post-production work, including compliance and quality control, may either take place in-house, or in a specialised post-production company. For example, BBC programmes that have been transmitted in the United Kingdom and are now to be broadcast overseas by BBC Worldwide come to the post-production company TVT (Television Versioning and Translation). TVT is an international company with its headquarters in a complex of media organisations in Chiswick, West London – postmodern offices and studios arranged around an artificial lake (see also QVC p. 145). The company's high-tech facilities take a programme through the necessary processes, including broadcast compliance, quality checking and other preparations such as subtitling or dubbing into the relevant language, and finally distribution and media archiving. Many highly skilled technicians work in these less visible areas of post-production, and it is worth considering how important these jobs are to the television output.

In a post-production facility such as TVT, which describes itself as a 'digital media lab', the technician's first job is to ingest the material – usually the programme to be prepared for overseas broadcast – as it arrives at the facility. Low-resolution files can then be prepared for the compliance viewers and the subtitlers. The next job is QC. The material must be quality controlled for any errors that may have occurred in the ingestion process or elsewhere. There may be picture or sound issues: for example, breaks in the visuals or the audio, sudden peaks or drops in the sound, colour saturation or timecode loss. The programme then goes to an editor who indicates where the advertisements will come (unlike the other BBC channels, BBC Worldwide is a commercial enterprise) and makes any compliance changes. If the destination time-slot is shorter than the original, the programme must be edited for time.

Finally it comes back to the machine room where the technicians work. 'The machine room is the beating heart of TVT', says the company's website. But the all-important servers must be kept at a very low temperature, which means that the technicians who work there are always cold. 'I always wear my woolly hat, even in summer', says VT technician Luke Sothinathan.

PROFILE

Luke Sothinathan: VT technician

'After graduating, my first jobs were as a freelancer working for a tiny production company – just a couple of people – Little Fish Films, based in Deptford, South London. We were making short films for charities. It was one of those companies where everyone does everything. I had a go at most jobs, including boom swinging, which was very difficult because you've got to keep your arms really steady.

I then did a trial interview as a runner at a major London post-production house, Envy www.envypost.co.uk/. The company offers the whole range of post-production work and describes itself as concerned with 'design, branding and commercials'. But as a runner it turned out that I would be mostly working in the kitchen, making tea for everyone . . . so I wasn't happy with that.

Eventually I moved to TVT where I began as a video checker. The job involves checking all outgoing material against the compliance form; making sure the media works by spot checking each programme from beginning to end; and inputting timecode and other data into the XML file. Initially this work had been done by the coordinators, but due to the volume of material coming in and the fact that a proper procedure had not yet been established for the new file-based formats, the position of checker was established. Sometimes we found lots of mistakes, but it was certainly better than working in the kitchen.

I did various jobs in the company. For a while I was a media manager, dealing with the assets on the servers. The media manager's job is to follow the progress of programmes from when they come into the facility to when they leave. That meant that once the material was ingested I had to create any low-resolution copies that were needed, and to make sure the material was available for the editors, subtitlers and others. I also had to move stuff around as needed, and finally to transcode and compress the material to create an MXF broadcast-quality file. This is a file that is compressed but at the same time of very high quality. Each media manager covered three channels – for example, Scandinavia, Prime Europe and Poland – and the most important thing was to ensure that everything was ready for the transmission date. It was very competitive because everyone was focused on their own transmission date regardless of the others. *Top Gear* was a particularly pressured programme to deal with because it sold so widely. It was transmitted in the United Kingdom on a Thursday then had to be instantly turned around for overseas sales. It was hard work but I learnt a lot.

I was also involved in archiving as well as doing some compliance editing, but then I became a VT technician. This involved less multitasking and more dealing with the job in front of you.

PROFILE

PROFILE

After a few years at TVT I went freelance. There are a number of intermediaries who act as agents for freelancers and employers, and they contact us when we're needed. I've had a variety of freelance jobs. I did some stuff for BT when they were starting up a channel, and I've worked for various different companies. The money's better than for a full-time job, but you usually work very long hours – 12-hour days – or night shifts.

Next I'd like to train to do EVS editing for live sports'.

Note: For major sporting events each camera has an EVS facility that can create overlays and insertions as the live action continues. This is a facility also used for creating the slow motion 'virtual advertisements' which appear during the action.

For more on a VT technician's job, see: www.inputyouth.co.uk/jobguides/job-vtoperator.html

Part 3

Programmes and genres

CHAPTER 15

Drama and television narrative

THINKING ABOUT NARRATIVE

Storytelling and narrative structure are at the heart of the television experience. 'The narratives of the world are numberless', wrote the French critic and theorist Roland Barthes:

> Able to be carried by articulated language, spoken or written, fixed or moving images, gestures, and the ordered mixture of all these substances . . . caring nothing for the division between good and bad literature, narrative is international, transhistorical, transcultural: it is simply there, like life itself.
>
> (Barthes 1977: 79)

In his survey of television theory, *Television Culture* (1987), John Fiske began his chapter on 'Narrative' with the above quotation from Barthes, and a similar conviction of the all-pervasiveness of narrative has carried the day with many writers about television. All television programmes have depended on a relationship between the visual image and the flow through time, and the narrative structure is a powerful way of organising that flow, even in the age of multiplatform and increasing interactivity. After all, Barthes noted the 'ordered mixture' of many forms of communication. The nature of narrative, asking what makes narrative work, has fascinated practitioners and critics since Aristotle first analysed the powerful dramas of Sophocles and Euripides in the fifth-century BCE. In the intervening centuries numerous writers have pondered on the structure, shape and characteristics of the narrative form, while storytellers have experimented with ever-evolving media. The television medium has itself produced a positive explosion of theoretical exploration to match the abundance of narratives on offer.

Theorising about narrative has tended to refer to fiction, and to assume a tightly structured linear form, with a beginning, middle and end usually one after the other. (It was Jean-Luc Goddard who remarked that yes, his films did have a beginning, middle and end, but not necessarily in that order.) In the era of multiplatform, simultaneous narratives, of narratives that move between media and spill out beyond the limits of the screen, narratives that depend on interactivity and audience participation, many accepted narrative theories are being questioned – or at least modified. However, in television fiction, it remains important to sustain the attention of an easily distracted audience with a shaped and structured, time-based form. For this reason, concepts based on narrative are regularly applied to other genres. 'Constructed factual' and similar non-fiction formats seek out a sense of 'jeopardy' – a risk, a danger, an unresolved problem – that will create tension, structure their stories and keep the audience hanging on (see Chapter 16 for more on factual programmes and formats).

In this chapter, we will first look at drama and fictional narratives within the contemporary television landscape and say something about the ways in which they are produced, then will go on to discuss some of the theoretical ideas that have underpinned the idea of 'narrative' itself. It is notable that much theoretical discussion of narrative has concerned audiences and the ways in which audiences actively make sense of the texts they encounter. As this book focuses on production, we will consider these perspectives as they have influenced those who make and commission television programmes.

FICTIONAL NARRATIVES: DRAMA

Fictional programmes on television range from feature films to soap opera, from block-buster international series that run over many years to popular sitcoms. Drama is a prestigious part of the television output and a staple of everyday viewing.

Easy access to multiple channels has broadened the scope. And American dramas such as *Breaking Bad* and *The Wire* – often hyperbolically described as the best television dramas ever – have a long life on on-demand channels and DVDs.

At the same time, the major UK broadcasters set much store by their drama output. Mainstream series with a genuinely popular touch, such as *Downton Abbey* (ITV 2010–15) alternate with series that push at the boundaries, such as Jane Campion's *Top of the Lake* (BBC 2013). Dramas have marked the high points of UK television: memorable dramas include *Cathy Come Home* (BBC 1966) with its heart-rending documentary-style realism; *The Singing Detective* (BBC 1986), which challenges the narrative form as it interweaves flashback, hallucination, musical interludes and B-movie detective fiction; *The Jewel in the Crown* (Granada/ITV 1984), a gripping period serial with superb acting and exotic settings; *Boys from the Blackstuff* with its comic commentary on its times and unforgettable characters (BBC 1980–82). There are many more (see Lez Cooke's *British Television Drama: A History* 2003).

Meanwhile, what one writer described as the 'endless disruption and deferral' of the long-running, ever-popular soap operas continues to explore characters, plots and everyday life (Allen 1992). Today drama is one of the genres that Jeremy Tunstall has described as being in 'rude health' (2015: Chapter 4).

Drama productions tend to be classified as one-offs, series, serials and soaps, each with their different approaches and rhythms of work and a different distribution of responsibilities between writers, producers and directors.

One-off dramas

In an angry address to the Edinburgh International Television Festival in 1993, television playwright Dennis Potter deplored the demise of the single play on television. The strategy of grouping plays under a regular title and transmitting them at the same time every week had been an innovation of the 1950s and 1960s. It was a format that gave priority to creative writers. For the BBC's celebrated strand, *The Wednesday Play* (1964–70), Sydney Newman, the innovative Head of Drama, encouraged new writers 'to throw away the rule books of hitherto accepted drama conventions and . . . to look at life with a new awareness'. Newman had come to the BBC after establishing the pioneering *Armchair Theatre* (referred to by its detractors as 'armpit theatre' because of its gritty realism) at ABC Television from 1956. Series like these enabled a specifically televisual form to be evolved and two decades of truly remarkable single dramas followed, seen as the creative work of a new generation of writers. 'You can forget the Old Vic', said producer Tony Garnett, 'television is the National Theatre without a question' (Garnett 1970). In the view of critic Sean Day-Lewis, the plays of the early 1970s 'continue to linger in the mind more than the imitation theatre that went before and the imitation cinema that has developed since' (Day-Lewis 1992). It was a format that writer Jimmy McGovern briefly revived in 2007–8 with *The Street,* which linked separate stories of people living on the same street.

Serials

Both serials and series may come from many different subgenres, each with its own conventions and audience expectations, ranging from adaptations of classic novels, to science fiction, crime, police procedurals, political thrillers or comedy drama. In a serial, the plot develops over several episodes, usually between three and six, and comes to a conclusion in which the plot lines are (usually) resolved. Like *The Missing* (BBC 2014) and *Happy Valley* (BBC 2016), they are written by a single writer, directed by a single director and in many ways are an expansion of the creative coherence of the single play. These are the novels of the air, and are often adaptations from classic novels. Granada's serials *Brideshead Revisited* (ITV 1981) and *The Jewel in the Crown* (ITV 1984) are remembered as high points of television history. There has been a recent tendency to end a serial leaving some plot points unresolved, allowing for the possibility of a return. In this way serials are coming closer to today's dominant dramatic form, the drama series.

Drama series

In a long-running series there are many interweaving narratives, but there is no final resolution at the end of a run, so that the threads can be taken up again when the series returns. Series tend to transmit around 15 episodes per year and run on average from three to five years, building on what John Fiske described as television's 'routine repetition' (Fiske 1987). They are more predictable for the schedulers than the shorter serials and offer reassuring signposts to audiences, since the same characters and settings recur over many years. The audience gets to know a group of individuals, frequently with a charismatic but flawed central figure – a doctor, a judge, a detective – who may be professionally brilliant but is grappling with personal demons. Series may sometimes be structured so that it is possible to appreciate a single, relatively self-contained episode; for example, in *Death in Paradise*, detective Humphrey Goodman solves a new murder each week. Other series, such as *Lost*, develop complex, apparently insoluble, never-ending storylines which can run for years.

Series are collaborative productions, using rotating teams of writers and directors working within the basic formula. They report to an executive producer, who may also be the main writer and is often referred to as the 'showrunner'. For *Dr Who* Stephen Moffat is both producer and oversees the writing team (see Tunstall 2015: 111 note 24 for the extensive academic literature on *Dr Who*, which has 'attracted more books than any other TV series').

The early success of police series such as *Dixon of Dock Green* (BBC 1955–76), and medical dramas such as *Emergency Ward 10* (ITV 1957–67) have been followed up by many long-running serial dramas in which institutions including hospitals, police forces and law courts have figured large. From the gritty realism of the Liverpool-based *Z-Cars* (BBC 1962–78), which emphatically broke with PC Dixon's cosy image, through Thames Television's *The Sweeney* (1975–78), which came in for criticism for showing the brutality of plain-clothes police work, up to *Lewis* and *Luther*, the police have been an endless source of dramatic interest, including char-acterful women asserting themselves in a man's world in series such as *The Gentle Touch* (ITV 1980–84) and *Prime Suspect* (1991–2006). By 2016, the longest-running UK crime drama series was *Silent Witness*, which began in 1996, closely followed by the nineteen years of *Midsomer Murders,* which began the following year.

In contrast to the realism of police/detective dramas, the subgenre of fantasy/ science fiction/thriller has been able to exploit to the full the developing possibilities of special effects. *Dr Who*, which ran from 1963 to 1989, and then was revived in 2005, is the prime example. Very long-running series have attained 'semi-soap status' with permanent sets and a substantial team of producers, writers, directors and actors. In 2010 *Casualty* made the *Guinness Book of Records* for the longest-running hospital series when it clocked up 700 episodes. In 2012 it moved to a new permanent set near Cardiff. From the outset the production has employed professional advisors and conducted thorough background research into the medical emergencies that are featured (see Holland 2013: 169–77 for an account of its early days). Working on these long-running series, writers, directors and actors have the opportunity to hone their skills over many years.

Recently the distinction between series and serials has become less clear. Writers and schedulers now think in terms of 'returning' drama series. Serials, such as Jimmy McGovern's *The Lakes*, are written with ambiguous endings, keeping open the possibility of another run. The ongoing nature of television and a contemporary rejection of conventional forms of finality make another series of any drama an ever-present possibility. Jason Mittell has noted the *'narrative complexity'* of American series such as *Lost* and the *X-Files* as 'an alternative to the conventional episodic and serial forms'. For Mittell this marks a 'new form of storytelling' (Mittel 2006). With series like these the notions of 'quality' and 'popular' are no longer seen as in opposition to each other. Many of the most popular series on contemporary television, such as *Breaking Bad* and *Game of Thrones*, come from the American cable network HBO, which prides itself on its 'quality drama'.

All series have their accompanying websites and many have extensive fan sites, which add material to the narrative as it overflows the television screen. In this way a narrative becomes more than a linear construction. 'Viewers take an active role in consuming narratively complex television and helping it to thrive', writes Jason Mittell (2015: 12–15). Indeed, *Dr Who* was kept alive by the activities of its fans from 1989, when it was cancelled, until its return in 2005.

Soaps

Finally, of course, there are the well-loved soaps whose devoted audiences can reach ten million and above. Yet when Granada launched *Coronation Street* in 1960 the *Daily Mirror* critic described it as 'doomed from the outset with its dreary signature tune and grim scene of a row of smoking chimneys' (Day-Lewis 1992: 10). Soaps are never-ending serials which continue on and on, just like life. Key families are at the heart of the plot lines, and the stories unfold in real time, with the characters ageing as their actors age. The priggish student Ken Barlow, who, in the first episode of *Coronation Street*, berated his working-class parents for their lack of education and bad table manners, was still living in the street 55 years, several marriages and many affairs later.

Each new British soap has been created with its own special qualities and production values. The London-based *EastEnders*, launched in 1985, is busy and visually cluttered, with its market and pub scenes, its multiracial cast and its unhesitating use of contemporary social problems to fuel its plots. It celebrated its thirtieth anniversary in 2015 with a week of live programmes. *Brookside*, which ran from 1982 to 2003, was conceived within an austere social realism, and kept close to its roots in Merseyside. *Emmerdale* began as *Emmerdale Farm* in 1972. The name was changed in 1989 to widen its appeal to an urban population. *Hollyoaks* was launched by *Brookside* producer Phil Redmond in 1995 to cater for a younger audience.

The long-running development of character, and the interweaving of multiple story-lines, which can never be resolved since the end is never in sight, are the defining characteristics of soap operas. Even characters who are thought to have died can return years later – in a recent example, Kathy Beale, thought to have been killed in a car accident, returned to her family in *EastEnders*. The characters develop like 'normal people', like friends to the viewers, which means the participants accept a special responsibility to their audience. Sue Johnstone, who played Sheila Grant in *Brookside*, spoke of the incident in which Sheila was raped. 'It was more than just acting a role. I worked with rape crisis groups and responded to many letters' (*Soap Weekend* C4 1995). *EastEnders*, in particular, has featured a number of serious medical and social problems, each thoroughly researched in liaison with specialists in the field, and each with substantial online back-up. Recently when Phil Mitchell was diagnosed with cirrhosis of the liver, the *EastEnders* team worked closely with the British Liver Trust, checking details from the earliest stage of script development. There was advice and back-up material on the programme's website.

Feminist critics have argued that the soap opera style, with its open narrative, has more 'feminine' qualities than other dramatic formats. It is more suited to the rhythms of women's days, and closer to the low-key emotional texture of everyday experience than the heroic drive of the classic narrative structure (Geraghty 1991; Brunsdon 2000). However, in recent years, all the British soaps have become more sensational in their plot lines. Abuse, villainy, madness and murder have become everyday occurrences. However, the strength of the soap opera form lies in the ability to keep a plot line running, as *Brookside's* celebrated 'body under the patio' showed. The *Brookside* team took a deliberate decision that, when the despicable Trevor Jordache was killed by the wife and daughters he had terrorised, his body would not be discovered for at least two years.

Soap opera is not identified with a particular writer or producer. However, soap is where many new directors and writers get their first opportunities. Teams of writers, directors and technicians overlap with each other. It is a demanding job, working under production-line conditions with very tight shooting schedules and deadlines.

At the time of writing *Coronation Street* broadcasts five episodes a week, *EastEnders*, four. They both have permanent sets, *Coronation Street* in Salford, *EastEnders* at Elstree. In 2015 *Coronation Street* had seventeen full-time writers who met regu-larly. An executive producer and writers' group met four times a year to plan ahead for longer storylines. Each director controlled a block of five shows, which were completed in six weeks. Usually two crews will be working simultaneously. The executive producer oversees all stages of production, from script through to post-production. He or she can have 100 episodes under review at any one time (Tunstall 2015: 119). In the words of Phil Redmond, 'you're constantly doubling back' (Redmond 2000: 204).

From 2008 soaps began appointing 'digital producers' for their online material. This includes games: 'Test your knowledge of all things *EastEnders*'; behind-the-scenes information on how sequences were filmed; comments from the actors; and back-up and support for the various medical or social problems that have been featured. When appropriate, an episode will conclude with a link to a back-up helpline to call 'if you have been affected by any of the issues portrayed in this programme'.

Sitcoms

Situation comedies, are located in the entertainment rather than the drama departments of television organisations. Nevertheless they are fictional narrative series in which each week an impossible and insoluble situation reveals new comic possibilities. Although the comedy may be resolved in each episode, the situation never is. In the best of them, hilarity comes close to tragedy, as in *Steptoe and Son* (BBC 1962–74) with its poignant relationship between a not too bright but aspirant son, and his nagging, wickedly idiosyncratic but ultimately dependent father. Classic British sitcoms have pushed the unacceptable close to the bone, with the racist Alf Garnett in *Till Death Us Do Part* (BBC 1965–75) and the lovable hustler Del Boy in *Only Fools and Horses* (BBC 1981–2003). Sitcoms have been able to relish social and psychological fissures, from *Dad's Army* (BBC 1968–77), through to *Miranda* (BBC 2009–15), and to put their finger on the culture and politics of the moment, as with *Yes, Minister* (BBC 1980–84), *The Thick of it* (BBC 2005–12), and *W1A* (BBC 2014–15). Writers such as John Sullivan and writing teams such as Ray Galton and Alan Simpson, Lawrence Marks and Maurice Gran, Dawn French and Jennifer Saunders have made a glorious contribution to British television.

Sitcoms are frequently studio-produced in front of an audience, whose laughter is heard, although they are not always seen. This breaks the realist code of straight drama which does not admit to the presence of an audience. But in *Miranda*, Miranda Hart frequently confides in the audience, while in *Mrs Brown's Boys* the cast fall over cameras, get tangled up with cables and generally admit that this is only a show, and the audience and production crew are very much part of it.

Hybrid genres

Drama sometimes works with and influences other genres. Many documentaries and other factual formats include reconstructed sequences, while an important strand of narrative-based programme-making has been the drama-documentary. Here factual information is put over in a dramatic form, scripted and performed by actors, but nevertheless true to real events. Perhaps the most powerful historical example of this is *Who Bombed Birmingham?*, made in 1990 by the current affairs team at *World in Action* (Granada/ITV), dramatising their own investigation into the miscarriage of justice when the wrong men were convicted of a terrorist attack on a Birmingham pub in 1974. The men were released in 1991.

The writer/director Peter Kosminsky has evolved a style of his own, making a number of programmes based on factual events, including *The Government Inspector* (C4 2005) about the weapons expert found dead at the time of the Iraq War. Derek Paget has looked in detail at drama-documentary and docu-drama in his book *No Other Way To Tell It* (1998).

We will be considering documentary and other factual formats in the next chapter, but it is worth noting here that many 'constructed factual' programmes are effectively fictional situations. In programmes that range from *The Only Way is Essex* to *First Date*, although they are performing as themselves, the participants are, to a greater or lesser extent, presenting a persona that will fit with the narrative structure of the programme. In addition the introduction of 'jeopardy' into a situation creates a narrative shape. In a formatted programme, the narrative is set up as the characters are faced with a challenge. The question is posed: how will they cope? The theme runs from *Don't Drop the Baby* through the notorious *I'm a Celebrity: Get Me Out of Here.* (For more on formatted programmes, see Chapter 16.)

The narrative principle is a powerful one. The next section will consider narrative theory.

NARRATIVE THEORY

Theorising narrative

Nowhere has the gap between practitioners and theorists gaped so widely as over the tortuous complexities of some narrative theory, versus the pragmatic common sense of writers, directors and producers. Even so, many of their concerns are similar. Narrative theory has a *confirmatory*, a *critical* and a *utilitarian* mode. On the one hand it may be written as pure *analysis*, 'reading' a completed programme to reveal and confirm its structural bones; or it may be a *critique*, in which narrative structures are chided for their ideological nature and for putting a straightjacket on possible artistic freedoms; or it may be presented as *instrumental advice* for practitioners, based on the premise that there are clear-cut narrative techniques, which can be studied and put into practice. We know that this *works*, goes the argument, and that's all we need to know. The charismatic writer and lecturer Robert McKee has been a foremost exponent of such advice, as have various handbooks, notably those by veteran writer Syd Field. There *are* rules, they assert. These are immutable and they underlie all dramatic constructions. Despite the multitude of actual stories with which the world is filled, there are, they argue, very few narrative structures.

Ever since Aristotle's *Poetics*, theorists have been anxious to discover the 'rules' by which fictions work, and practitioners have been more or less inclined to take such analysis as pragmatic advice. In the 1920s, formalist theorists in the Soviet Union developed a method by which the different elements of narrative could be isolated and labelled, so that the *form* and *structure* of a literary or cinematic work could be revealed. This *structuralist* approach was taken up by a number of French cultural critics in the 1960s, including Roland Barthes, notably in *S/Z*, his forensic analysis of a short story by Balzac (Barthes 1974). In the 1970s and 1980s structuralism developed into *post-structuralism*, which brought together the complex and heady disciplines of *semiotics*, which analysed the structure of 'signs' in language and imagery; *marxism*, which launched a head-on critique of the power-structures of society; and *psychoanalysis*, which explored the unconscious mind. This led to an extensive literature. In France Christian Metz, and in Britain, Peter Wollen, Laura Mulvey and the writers around the journal *Screen* explored the structure of the cinematic narrative using these approaches. This became known as *Screen*, theory which also sought ways in which a narrative might escape its formal shackles. *Deconstruction* was as important as *construction*. More recently *postmodern* theorists have argued that, in a world full of *texts*, a single, formal structure is no longer necessary. Narratives are about other narratives. They can be multiple, ironic and interact with a knowing audience.

A narrative may now be dispersed across many media, but, nevertheless, in the words of Henry Jenkins, *transmedia storytelling* may still create 'a unified and co-ordinated entertainment experience ... each medium makes its own unique contribution to the unfolding of the story' http://henryjenkins.org/2011/08/defining_transmedia_further_re.html.

The theoretical literature is wide-ranging and complex. Below we will summarise some concepts that are relevant to understanding and creating narrative.

For more details of the terms used in this and other chapters, see the Glossary p. 285. For a more extensive discussion of relevant terms, see Calvert *et al*. (2007) *Television Studies: The Key Concepts*, London: Routledge Key Guides.

Analysis of the narrative form: structuralist theories

Theories of narrative based on structure have proved more useful to practitioners than those, like that of David Bordwell (1995) based on audience cognition, or that elaborated by Roger Silverstone (1981) based on narrative and myth. Structuralist theories look for those elements that *construct* a narrative, in order to put the finger on precisely what it is that turns a flow of images and words into a story. After all, even a three-year-old who demands 'tell me a story' knows what *counts* as a story and what does not.

Structuralist theories have concerned themselves with definitions and distinctions. Below is an account of some of them. The terms described here are those that are most helpful in understanding how narratives work. The books to which I refer give a more detailed teasing out of the various analyses, often introducing a much more complex set of subcategories and technical terms than I have chosen to use below. Some words are put in inverted commas because they are used here in a special sense.

Story and plot

A narrative has two modes, labelled by the linguist Tzevan Todorov as *'story'* (*fabula*) and *'plot'* (*syuzhet*). The 'story' is what actually happens, the material of the tale, while the 'plot' is the way a narrative is organised (Todorov 1977). 'What actually happens' is always rich and diverse. In a writer's original concept there will be a number of characters all engaged in different actions, possibly simultaneously in different places. There is no way of ordering such diversity into a linear time-based flow without using a range of plot devices. Even in soap opera, narrative time cannot be the same as actual time. The 'story' has many dimensions, but the 'plot' must be linear. If I tell the 'story' of *The Singing Detective* to someone who missed it on transmission, my telling may well be different from the way the series put its 'plot' together. In the case of Dennis Potter's celebrated drama dealing with sickness, murder and a fascination with B-movie detective fiction, the realisation of the 'plot' is made up of a complex of flashbacks, fantasy sequences and musical interludes. To make sense of the 'story', the audience must be prepared to decode the 'plot'. This distinction between 'story' and 'plot' helps us understand how the material a writer begins with may be organised in a multitude of different ways.

Contemporary 'postmodern' dramas such as *Dr Who* have embraced the complexity pioneered by Dennis Potter, as the plot moves alarmingly back and forth through time, with little reference to the 'story'. However, the ability to pause the programme, or to accompany the viewing with extra material on a second screen – whether a laptop, a tablet or a mobile phone – means it no longer needs to be seen as solely linear. Viewers can check out the latest news, rate the programmes and debate the plot developments and characters.

Story and discourse

A narrative/programme has two aspects, identified by Christian Metz in 1977. He pointed to a distinction between its *'story'* (*histoire*) or its *'discourse'* (*discours*). The 'story' is simply what happens in the narrative, with no indication of who is telling it or to whom. The normal conventions of television drama – as followed in *Downton Abbey*, to take one example from thousands – makes no recognition of a watching audience, nor are we aware of any particular individual apparently 'telling' the story. It just unfolds, as if we were peeping in on 'life'.

By contrast Frances Urquhart in *House of Cards* winks at the camera/audience and lets them in on his dastardly plans for climbing the political ladder. This device is part of the programme's 'discourse'. Its 'discourse' is the *way* in which the programme-makers have decided that the story should be told. Every programme has its own distinctive approach to camerawork, style of acting, visual effects and many other aspects. It inevitably carries traces of the work of its scriptwriter, director, producer and others, and demonstrates their distinctive voice and other influences on the programme. Avid fans and tele-literate members of the audience may relish hunting down hints and indications of authorial style.

Arguably, the rise of the digi-sphere, with its increasing penumbra of online inform-ation, Twitter debates and fan sites, has created a more visible layer of discourse and given a new meaning to this long-established distinction. For many 'cult' series there is a knowing interaction between fans and producers, which may not be visible to casual viewers. For example, fans claim that the producers of *Sherlock* deliberately plant clues – say the exact position of a chair – which are only recognisable by dedicated followers.

Narrator's image and the viewer's image

The 'discourse' of a narrative tells us something about the *narrator's image* and the *viewer's image* (sometimes referred to as the 'reader in the text'). This refers to the ways in which the text itself conveys the relationship between 'viewer' and 'narrator'. These are in inverted commas here because they do not refer to the *actual* narrator/programme-maker or any particular real-life viewer. But looking for discursive signs within a drama, we learn something about the fictional 'narrator': about the fact that there *is* a narrator who is communicating with us. And we also discover something about the sort of viewer the narrator has in mind. *Magic Roundabout* clearly 'expects' an audience made up of children, just as *Have I Got News For You* 'expects' an audience who are up to date with the items the programme satirises. This question of who the audience are, how much they are expected to know, and what sort of demands are to be made on them is crucial to the pitching of much television drama. ' "I" and "you", the sender and receiver of the utterance, always appear together', writes Seymour Chatman in his discussion of narrative theory (Chatman 1995: 482).

In this way, the 'narrator' has a relationship with the audience, but they also have a variety of different relationships with the characters in the drama. Of course, the *real* narrator, the writer, knows everything about them, because he or she has invented and manipulated them. But within the plot the 'narrator' may take various positions:

In *the view from behind*, the 'narrator' knows *more* than the characters. They can 'see through the wall of a house as well as through the hero's skull'.

In *the view with*, the 'narrator' knows *as much as* a specific character. The audience follows the clues together with Miss Marple, instead of being shown who the murderer is before she finds out.

In *the view from outside*, the 'narrator' knows *less than* any of the characters, and does not have access to anyone's consciousness. In this case, actions may appear mysterious and without explanation (Todorov 1977: 29).

This understanding of the role of the narrator and their relationship to the viewer underlies much critical writing devoted to teasing out the intentions and messages of a programme.

The documentary *Dockers Writing the Wrongs* (1999), which followed the writer Jimmy McGovern as he worked with a group of sacked Liverpool dockers to create a dramatic reconstruction of their experiences, gave a fascinating insight into the actual construction of these rather abstract concepts. C4 commissioning editor Gub Neal wanted the dialogue to incorporate a certain amount of background information for the benefit of the audience. From the point of view of the writers – who, in this case, were actually part of the events they were portraying – this made it seem unnatural. These were things they were ignorant of at the time, so how could they talk about them? Jimmy McGovern explained the dramatist's dilemma as a question of 'exposition and want'. 'Gub wants our characters to say things, but we've got to find a way of our *characters* wanting to say this.'

Open and closed narratives

A narrative may be *'open'* or *'closed'*. A 'closed' narrative is neatly rounded off. All the loose ends are tied up and the audience easily recognises that it has reached the final moment. Ending devices are many, ranging from the revelation of who committed the murder in an episode of *Death on Paradise*, to the death of the main protagonist, as in *The Final Cut*. 'Open' narratives are less final, leaving problems unresolved or allowing audiences to draw their own conclusions. On television the serial form means that there must be cliffhangers at the end of each episode to encourage the audience to watch the next, whereas a series may round off each episode, while keeping the main basis of the problem open. There's always another *Casualty* to be rushed into Holby General, another unsolved case to be reopened by the team in *New Tricks*. One example of an 'open' narrative is the never-ending soap. Soap operas run multiple plots in parallel and, as long as the characters remain in the series, none of the plots is ever finally resolved. A character will continue to have effects on the others even after their death. 'In soap opera narrative time is the metaphorical equivalent of real time, and audiences are constantly engaged in remembering the past, enjoying the present, and predicting the future', wrote John Fiske (1987: 145).

A different example is the rise of what Jason Mittel describes as the open-ended 'narrative complexity' that characterises long-running American series such as *Lost*. Unlike soaps these are driven by plot points rather than character (Mittel 2006).

He argues that a deliberate use of unexpected and disorientating events – sometimes reversing the whole trajectory of a plot 'intensifies viewer engagement'. It 'rewards viewers who have mastered each programme's internal conventions of complex narration'.

Constructing narratives

Despite the argument that narratives must now be complex and interactive, some classic formalist accounts of how to construct self-contained narratives are still frequently referred to. Some of these are outlined below, but I will begin with some blunt advice from a Hollywood professional . . .

Syd Field's paradigm

Syd Field, whose numerous books are based on his Hollywood experience as scriptwriter, script reader and screenwriting teacher, offers concrete advice in a hard-boiled staccato prose. He makes clear his emphatic commitment to a basic underlying narrative structure, and offers a model which he calls the paradigm of dramatic structure:

'What is a screenplay?

A screenplay is a STORY TOLD WITH PICTURES.

It is like a *noun* – about a person or persons, in a place or places, doing his or her "thing". All screenplays execute this basic premise. A motion picture is a visual medium that dramatises a basic story line. And like all stories, there is a definite *beginning*, *middle* and *end.*' (Field 2005)

In this spirit of bluff pragmatism, Field usefully asserts that the standard screenplay is 120 pages long, or two hours.

> It is measured at one page per minute. It does not matter whether your script is all dialogue, all action or both. The rule holds firm – one page of screenplay equals one minute of screen time.
>
> (pp. 7–8)

Syd Field's paradigm is very precise and takes the form of a diagram:

Beginning	Middle	End
Act 1	Act 2	Act 3
Set up	Confrontation	Resolution
pp. 1–30	pp. 30–90	pp. 90–120
	Plot point 1	Plot point 2
	pp. 25–27	pp. 85–90

(In fact the script for the 90-minute drama of marginal existence, drugs and comic survival, *Trainspotting* (1996), was 245 pages long, according to its screenwriter, John Hodge.)

For Syd Field 'the basis of all drama is conflict' and the movement through the plot, from the setting up of characters and situation through the confrontation to the final resolution, can be neatly measured out in minutes and pages.

> Don't take my word for it. Utilize it as a tool, question it, examine it, think about it . . . If you don't believe the paradigm, check it out. Prove me wrong. Go to a movie – go see several movies – see whether it fits the paradigm or not . . . The *paradigm* works. It is the *foundation* of a good screenplay.
>
> (Field 2005)

Formalist structure: actions

In more analytic language, the formalist theorist Tzevan Todorov offers a model narrative structure that is remarkably similar: 'An equilibrium is disrupted, usually by a villain. The disruption is worked out and another equilibrium is established, similar to the first but never identical' (Fiske 1987: 138). Todorov describes the beginning of a narrative as expressing an 'enigma', a complex of circumstances just crying out to be unravelled.

Formalist theories claim that, however unlike each other different narratives may seem, their form is constituted by a sequence of *actions* (functions) which come out of the relationships between the *characters*. The arrangement of the 'functions' obeys a logic, which employs certain recognised devices that underlie *all* narratives.

Vladimir Propp, who analysed 100 Russian fairy stories in 1928, found thirty-two narrative *'functions'* common to them all. He divided them into six sections.

David Bordwell described a similar 'canonical format' (Propp 1995: Bordwell 1995):

> Propp: Preparation
> Bordwell: Introduction of setting and characters
>
> P: Complication
> B: Explanation of the state of affairs
>
> P: Transference
> B: Complicating action
>
> P: Struggle
> B: Ensuing events
>
> P: Return
> B: Outcome
>
> P: Recognition
> B: Ending

The stage of 'complication' is an essential one to the maintenance of the narrative structure. This is where the device of *retardation* comes into play. The Russian formalist critic Viktor Shklovsky spoke of a 'stairstep construction', with each step offering a hope that is then dashed. Alfred Hitchcock spoke of 'frustration'. In Hitchcock's films false trails are laid that retard the development of the plot. These are his famous 'McGuffins'. In *Rear Window* there are two: First, is the dead Mrs Thorwald in the trunk? On investigation it's only her clothes. Second, what is the connection between the little dog's interest in the flowers and its death? Lisa and Stella dig up the flowers but find nothing. Both these narrative threads run over a number of scenes before they are discarded.

> More often than we are usually aware, narratives invoke expectations only to defeat them . . . Narrative art ruthlessly exploits the tentative, probabilistic nature of mental activity.
>
> (Bordwell 1995)

The viewer is invited to make hypotheses, build up expectations and arrive at conclusions as the narrator tempts and teases by laying false trails, dealing in exceptions and upsetting assumptions.

Formalist structure: characters

In formalist theory, characters are important to the narrative because of what they *do*, rather than what they *are*. The same role may be split between more than one character, and the same character may fulfil different roles.

In his analysis of traditional fairy tales, Propp described eight characters in seven spheres of action:

The dispatcher: sends the hero on a quest or mission

The hero: departs on a search, reacts to a donor, attempts difficult tasks, including marriage

Donor (provider): gives the hero a magical agent or helper

Helper: makes good a lack, rescues the hero from pursuit, solves difficult tasks, transforms the hero

Villain: involved in villainy, fighting and action

The princess and her father: a sought-after person who assigns difficult tasks, exposes, recognises and punishes

The false hero: has unfounded claims to the hero's sphere of action

Roger Silverstone has used a Proppian structure to analyse various television programmes (1981). John Fiske applied the model to an episode of *The Bionic Woman*
and found that it corresponded very closely. Speaking of American television in
the 1980s, he wrote: 'the structure underlies the typical TV narrative with remark
able consistency' (Fiske 1987: 138). Despite the contemporary move to narrative
complexity, these principles still underpin many television dramas.

NARRATIVE REALISM AND OTHER REALISMS

Most narrative theories hinge on the creation of a coherent and convincing fictional
world sustained by certain codes of realism. Realism 'constitutes perhaps the basic
demand that our society makes of its film and television representations, apart from
a very few, limited exceptions', writes John Ellis. Forms of realism operate at many
levels, not just sustained by an easy equivalence to the real world. A principle of
consistency applies even to fantasy genres through 'a complex network of conventions of portrayal, and conventions of audience expectation alike' (Ellis 1982: 9).

Codes of realism

The 'codes of realism' include:

- The fictional world should be *governed by spatial and temporal verisimilitude*
  (see visual grammar p. 91 and continuity editing p. 159).

- A drama should *obey the laws of cause and effect* and explain itself
  adequately to its audience. At the mundane level of visible motivation, if a
  character is walking down the street with an open umbrella, it should be
  raining or the fact should be otherwise explained – perhaps the character
  suffers from Alzheimer's disease or perhaps they think it's raining. The
  principle also applies to a more complex level of character motivation within
  the plot.

- A drama should *conform to expectations based on psychology and
  character*, so that the characters remain consistent even when 'weird' and
  'unnatural' events take place. The search for the motive is the underlying
  thread in many a detective drama.

- A plot should not stray too far from what we expect to happen. This means
  that it should *obey the laws of physical and natural science*, unless it is
  dealing in the supernatural, as with horror or science fiction. Someone who falls from a high building will crash to the ground unless rescued
  by Superman. But even fantasy should be consistent in order to be
  convincing.

- A television drama should have a surface accuracy or consistency within
  its own world. That means a consistency of costume, setting and props.

In a contemporary drama, a police officer's uniform should be a real police officer's uniform or one level of credibility is lost.

Expectations can also operate at the ideological level. John Ellis describes this as 'perhaps the most conservative' of realist requirements, because it 'represents the spectator's desire that a representation should conform to common sense and taken-for-granted notions of events', which may include questionable expectations about the relations between the sexes, for example, or stereotypical notions about racial characteristics (1982: 7) (see p. 227 on representation).

All of the above contribute to an internal coherence which, according to John Fiske,

> requires that the diegetic world appear self sufficient and unbroken. Everything that we need to know in order to understand it must be included, and everything that contradicts or disturbs the understanding must be excised.
>
> (Fiske 1987: 131)

Realism and genre

Generic realism means conforming to the conventions of the genre, rather than the realities of the world. Each narrative genre has its own set of established conventions and audience expectations which apply across narrative types, and each genre brings its own permitted deviations from realist representation. A comedy writer can take liberties denied to someone working on a naturalist soap; Dr Who's tardis can be bigger on the inside; a police series can abbreviate much material concerned with police procedure because it is familiar to the audience from other dramas in the genre; a psychological drama can play tricks with external reality to convey the inner life of the characters – we accept that we can see Sherlock's thought processes, a perception invisible to those around him. Although the conventions are not hard and fast – new genres arise and old ones change with the work of creative writers and directors – anyone writing a script will need to know what *kind* of a drama they are aiming for and where it will fit in.

At one extreme of the realist continuum are the conventions of the naturalist genre. They include an unemphatic acting style; the use of real locations; stories and characters drawn from ordinary life; and camerawork and editing that do not draw attention to themselves. On British television the naturalist style has a long and important history, beginning with series such as *Z Cars* and the *Wednesday Play*, which pioneered a new level of biting social comment. Some argued that its naturalistic style tricked viewers by giving the impression that dramas such as *Cathy Come Home* or *Up the Junction* – with all their heart-wrenching emotions – were really documentaries, observations of real life. In a 1969 interview, Ken Loach, director of *Cathy Come Home*, explained: 'We wanted people to stop thinking of films as fiction, but to think of them as having a factual point.' He spoke of 'that enervating atmosphere of show business that we hate' (Levin 1972).

The works of directors such as Mike Leigh and Peter Kosminsky have reinterpreted naturalist conventions, each in their own way.

Unlike fictions, which use a naturalistic style similar to documentary, docudrama is a genre that derives its realism from the actual events it represents. The approach had a resurgence in the 1990s and is recognised as a powerful genre in its own right (Paget 1998). Programmes such as *Who Bombed Birmingham?*, *Hillsborough*, *The Murder of Stephen Lawrence* and *The Government Inspector* are based on scripts that are sometimes verbatim and sometimes imaginative, to give a clear and committed view of high-profile public events. They can draw attention to personal emotion and injustice in a way that would be difficult in a factual genre. Treading a fine line between fiction and reality, docudrama is constantly redrawing its own boundaries.

'Down with the scented veil': the 'classic realist text' and critical narrative theories

In the 1970s, the rediscovery of the 1920s formalist theories (see above) was part of an energetic, committed, exciting, if highly theoretical, development of critical work, which had a big influence on practice. There was a sense that a new spirit was abroad, and that forms of radicalism were possible which would draw together politics, the arts and popular culture. Abstract theory was carried along on a tide of enthusiasm created by the events of May 1968 in Paris and London, as well as the radical students' action in the United States and the Prague Spring in Czechoslovakia. A demand for a politicised and committed practice energised writers, filmmakers and critics alike. The new marxism was strongly culturalist and an analysis based on the concept of ideology was central. As the rediscovery of formalist theories led to an emphasis on the *constructed* nature of cultural forms, there was a recognition that they are put together according to well-worn formulae. It became a cause for outrage that such forms are presented as if they are *natural*. They *conceal* those all-important processes of construction.

The 'classic realist text', as Colin McCabe called the conventional narrative structure, is a prime example of such naturalisation (McCabe 1974). A 'classic realist text' has everything neatly sewn up. Every plot element falls into place in a way that is so convincing that the audience are swept along without question. A 'realist' narrative of this sort is constructed around a hierarchy of voices in which the voice of the real author is concealed. The social and political assumptions on which the narrative is based seem completely natural. The flow of the story is perceived as a 'metalanguage which tells the truth' and 'appears to emanate from no identifiable speaker' (Bordwell 1995). Critics argue that, because the structure is so seamless and so convincing, it closes off the possibility of alternative views or different perspectives. The flow of a drama, even when it does not adopt a mimetic naturalist style, is a continuous illusion, rather like the realism of a dream.

Writers such as Laura Mulvey used psychoanalytic theory to demonstrate the dream-like nature of the cinematic experience (Mulvey 1989). Cinematic realism cannot reflect the real world, they argued. Its formal coherence and its ability to bypass reason allows it to go straight for the dream world of the human unconscious. This makes it an *ideological* form. It is designed to lull the audience into assent, to pacify them by pulling the wool over their eyes, so that they are blind to social injustice and the harsh realities of everyday existence.

An *ideological text* conceals the underlying intentions and purposes of those who produce it. If those who produce it are not part of the ruling class themselves, it is argued that they are always in their pay. Louis Althusser gave a structuralist twist to this twentieth-century version of Marx's nineteenth-century critique. He divided the far more complex society of the 1970s into separate 'levels' – ideological, political, legal and economic – of which, he argued, the economic level finally, 'in the last instance', determines the shape of the others. Ultimately cultural forms follow economic requirements. However, cultural products such as films and television programmes could be seen as 'relatively autonomous' from their economic base. They can be radicalised in their own right, without waiting for a transformation of society to generate cultural change. The argument was that radical filmmaking should reject realism. It should be unconventional and challenging.

Writers and filmmakers, notably Jean Luc Godard in France, took up the challenge. They went back to the ideas of documentarist Dziga Vertov and dramatist Bertolt Brecht to find ways of breaking the conventional narrative form. Both had rejected a naturalist style in favour of making visible the means of production and making reality *strange* rather than cosy and familiar. Tactics like actors stepping out of character to discuss the action, direct address to the audience and interruption of the narrative with captions or photographic stills were designed to demystify. The idea was to get the audience to *think* rather than becoming caught up in the emotional flow of the story. 'Long live the consciousness of the pure who can see and hear! Down with the scented veil of kisses, murders, doves and conjuring tricks!', wrote Dziga Vertov in 1924 (Schnitzer *et al.* 1973: 83).

During the 1980s and 1990s, a far wider range of dramatic forms became familiar on television, not always inspired by the political motives of a Godard or a Brecht. Writers such as Denis Potter expanded the television language. The development of computer technology meant that graphics, video effects and non-naturalistic sequences became part of the dramatic repertoire. Advertisements became more experimental and this had an effect on television styles. John Hodge, writer of *Trainspotting*, with its celebrated fantasy of an addict swimming down a lavatory bowl in search of his lost drugs, expressed the view of many writers when he said: 'I am always looking for ways out of conventional realism' (National Film Theatre talk, March 1996).

Theories of *postmodernity*, which embrace irony, fragmented narratives, disruption and an awareness of technology, have come to represent contemporary consciousness more accurately, if less politically, than the concept of ideology. The idea that a 'mass' audience is taken in by the media does not seem relevant to today's multimedia world. The arrival of multiplatform and the availability of many layers of information mean that reflexivity and debates about production processes have become normal. *Intertextuality*, with cross-references and a knowing awareness of other texts, is a feature of today's multitextual world. In many genres it is now acceptable for a programme to reflect on the nature of the medium, and to acknowledge the presence of an author and an audience. Some writers have regretted that this new form of disruption and its questioning of the codes of realism no longer has a critical political edge (Page 2015: 68).

IDENTITY AND NARRATION

The arrival of Channel Four in 1982 made space for experimental and critical work, and, in particular, widened the range of identities whose narratives could be told on UK television screens. Set up partly as a result of campaigning by black and Asian, gay and feminist filmmakers, the early Channel Four, under its first chief executive, Jeremy Isaacs, aimed for diversity. The channel made a difference, with series such as *Black on Black*, *Eastern Eye* and *In the Pink*. *My Beautiful Launderette* was a Film4 cinema release with a gay, multiethnic theme. However, thirty-five years later, there still remain issues with the representation of diverse identities within the narratives on our screens. Recently, the celebrated black actor Lenny Henry argued: 'If you have one set of people deciding what stories get told, you will always end up getting the same kinds of stories' (BAFTA Television lecture, 18 March 2014). (See Chapter 19 for more on diversity.)

Theorists have argued that the structure of narrative itself can influence the ways in which identities are portrayed. In particular, feminist studies refer back to Laura Mulvey's classic article, 'Visual pleasure and narrative cinema', written in 1975 (Mulvey 1989). Mulvey's work was part of that 1970s mood which drew together radical filmmaking, political campaigning and high theory in a powerful conjunction. She argued that it was necessary to understand why women have been so visible on the screen and yet at such a disadvantage behind the camera. It was not enough to change the content of the programmes; the organisation of the media must also be transformed.

Her argument was that classic Hollywood cinema is constructed around a masculine gaze. The conventional structure of the narrative tended to place the male central character as the one who carries the action, and the female lead as the object of his fascination and curiosity. On screen the hero gazes at the woman, and in doing so relays the gaze of the audience, who look through his eyes to treat the woman as a form of spectacle. In psychoanalytic terms she becomes a fetishised object. The requirements of the 'classic realist text', frequently driven by investigation and enquiry, reinforce this structure. This gives rise to considerable problems and confusions on the part of female spectators who find that the plot expects them, too, to identify with the male hero.

Taking up this argument in her article 'Women's Genres', Annette Kuhn contrasted the experience of cinema – in which there is a sense of powerlessness as you sit in a darkened theatre, perhaps next to a stranger, looking up at a brilliantly illuminated screen – with the experience of television, seen in a domestic environment, actively watched or half-watched by a small group of family members or a single person. The structure of television, with its low-key, open narratives, depends less on exploiting the spectacular image of a woman, and these naratives are more woman-centred in their construction. Soap opera, in particular, deals with everyday life in a way that is close to most women's experience (Kuhn 1987).

Laura Mulvey's conclusion was that, for women filmmakers, the only escape from this dilemma was to abandon conventional narrative and to turn to avant-garde work, which *deconstructs* conventional genres. Her own filmmaking has been in this style, and many women film- and video-makers have followed her advice. There is a large and interesting body of feminist deconstructive work. The approach was taken up by black filmmakers such as the Black Audio Film Collective, whose innovative *Handsworth Songs* was commissioned by Channel Four's *Eleventh Hour*.

An increasing number of women writers have created television narratives which follow a conventional narrative form, but have women as a powerful centre. Deborah Jermyn has argued that Lynda la Plante's *Prime Suspect*, broadcast in 1991, 'constitutes a transitional text in the history of TV crime drama'. In the series, Helen Mirren plays Detective Chief Superintendent Jane Tennison, who is in charge of a body of policemen who are not all overtly sexist, but are suspicious of her position of power. Bearing in mind Mulvey's argument that the way a programme is filmed conveys unconscious attitudes, Jermyn points out that its 'camerawork is structured around a gendered dichotomy and there is an explicit concern in the text with who "looks", and at whom' (Jermyn 2010).

Many women writers, including Paula Milne, Sally Wainwright, Debbie Horsfield and others, have, in recent years, created a wide range of women characters on UK television who inhabit positions of authority without denying their femininity. This is not just a question of presenting women in traditional masculine roles. Catherine Cawood, in Sally Wainwright's *Happy Valley*, is an effective police officer and also a grandmother bringing up her eight-year-old grandson. The change has led to a reevaluation of masculinity as well as of femininity, and a greater willingness to explore emotion and vulnerability. The scope, for both men and women writers, has become wider. Across the genres, dramas are now able to deal with issues of sexuality, exploring gay and lesbian themes as well as a more nuanced reflection of the relations between the sexes (Warhol and Lanser 2016).

Vigorous campaigning, together with equal opportunities legislation, diversity commitments and changing social expectations, have led to more women and people from BAME communities working in television as directors, producers and executives. However, there is still a substantial imbalance. We explore the issues further in Chapter 19 below.

KEY TEXTS

Cooke, L. (2003) *British Television Drama: A History*, London: BFI.
Creeber, G. (ed.) (2015) *The Television Genre Book*, 3rd edn, London: BFI.
Thomas, B. (2016) *Narrative: The Basics*, London: Routledge.

From documentary to factual entertainment

CONTEMPORARY FACTUAL PROGRAMMING

To illustrate the scope of factual programming in the mid 20teens, I picked a single evening schedule at random. Between 6pm and midnight on Tuesday 18 August 2015, across the five terrestrial channels, factual programmes dealt with no fewer than 14 different topics:

History: *Who Do You Think You Are?* BBC1

Cookery: *Hairy Bikers Bakeation* BBC2; *Great British Menu* BBC2; *Couples Come Dine With Me* Channel Four

Housing/property: *The House That £100k Built* BBC2: *How To Get a Council House* Channel Four

Scrapyard: *Scrappers, Back in the Yard* BBC2

Countryside: *The Dales* ITV

Gardening: *Love Your Wild Garden* ITV

Schooling: *Are Our Kids Tough Enough? Chinese School* BBC2; *School Swap, The Class Divide* ITV

Parenting: *Three Day Nanny* Channel Four

Disaster: *Terror on Everest: Surviving the Nepal Earthquake* Channel Four

Sex/issues: *Revenge Porn* Channel Four

Policing: *Police Interceptors* C5

Domestic animals: *The Dog Rescuers with Alan Davies* C5

Poverty/benefits: *Benefit Life: Jailbird Boys Going Straight* C5; *The Benefits Estate* C5

Medical: *Joined at the Head: Twin Life* C5

The following evening three more categories were added: the natural world (wild animals), ancient history and shopping. And there were more during the night and on the digital channels.

The range of content is indicative of the scope of the contemporary factual television output. The list includes many topics that have long been staples of the documentary genre: poverty, education, crime and policing, medical issues; as well as a range of what are usually referred to as consumer topics: holidays, gardening and shopping. However, the *styles* and approaches of this randomly sampled list range well beyond the traditional documentary, with formats, genres and subgenres which make use of factual material but bear different relations to the everyday world. Strikingly, the majority of the programmes listed here are constructed around devices designed to add interest and entertainment value to their topic. In *Who Do You Think You Are?* a personal, frequently emotional, dimension leads the audience through an account of social history, as we follow public figures investigating their ancestry. *Are Our Kids Tough Enough?* explores teaching styles through the device of introducing Chinese teaching methods and Chinese teachers into a British secondary school. In *Three Day Nanny* a charismatic child psychologist is given just three days to sort out the behaviour of a difficult child. Most of these programmes deal with common, everyday experiences. One, *Joined at the Head*, is part of a medical subgenre, which treads a fine line between imparting helpful information and presenting shocking and arguably voyeuristic material. Only one programme, *Terror on Everest*, employs a classic documentary style, drawing on the techniques of observational filming, interviews, archive footage, reconstructions and an informative commentary.

The range of topics and styles which characterise factual and 'reality' programming has expanded over the 2000s. This chapter will map out the territory, and will note the blurring of boundaries between long-established genres and the newer, more entertaining approaches. In the 20teens, commissioners and programme-makers need to decide where their programme will be placed along a continuum of styles which blur traditional boundaries and frequently overlap with entertainment formats. Indeed Sky 1 has changed its commissioning categories so that 'factual' and 'entertainment' are merged, simply described as 'non-scripted' (see Commissioning Chapter 21). Meanwhile, at the other end of the continuum, long-established documentary styles continue to thrive.

In this chapter, we will review some important innovations, including the use of new techniques such as fixed-rig set-ups and the use of surveillance camera and mobile phone footage, and we will consider the development of 'formats' to structure factual content. We will then go on to look at practical questions of research and interview techniques, and finally will discuss some of the ethical issues faced by factual filmmakers, bearing in mind that, for those who are new to television, making a documentary-style film with your own camera may be one of the most accessible ways to begin. But first we will outline a brief history of the documentary genre and its developing place within the television landscape.

BRIEF HISTORY OF UK DOCUMENTARY: 'THE CREATIVE TREATMENT OF ACTUALITY'

When John Grierson founded the British documentary film movement in the late 1920s, he described his approach as 'the creative treatment of actuality'. The pioneer documentarists of the 1930s and 1940s saw themselves as innovative artists as well as observers of the world around them. They developed their craft through the years of the Second World War, recording the actuality of the conflict in creative and often poetic styles. However, from the 1950s, it was on television that the documentary vision had its greatest flowering in the United Kingdom. Grierson's broad definition came to embrace genres and styles as widely disparate as observational filmmaking, interview-based programmes, reporter-led current affairs, expositions of art and science, dramatised documentary and experimental, avant-garde image-making. Some of these emphasise the 'actuality' of the definition, others the 'creativity'. And the 'treatment' has varied over the decades according to fashion, technological development, the personal style of the programme-maker and the requirements of the programme strand. Nevertheless, all factual formats bear some relation to what documentary theorist Bill Nichols characterised as the 'historical world'. Nichols defined documentary as *representing* reality' since the act of 'representing' covers a whole complex of relationships between filmmaker and subject, including reporting on, engaging in dialogue with, investigating, observing, interpreting and reflecting on. All factual forms stand in some sort of relation to the reality which is their subject matter, and bear some sort of responsibility towards it (Nichols 1991).

The first Documentary Department at the BBC attempted to *recreate* 'real life' in the studio, adapting to the special qualities of live television. But directors were keen to take their film cameras out on to the bleak streets of urban post-war Britain. At ITV's Granada Television, where early episodes of *Coronation Street* began with the documentary feel of kids playing skipping games on the cobbles, Denis Mitchell developed a personal style that drew on the innovative work developed by radio documentarists. His dense, interwoven sound tracks, made up of snatches of conversation, local sound effects and overheard music, were laid over a visual montage of faces and glimpses of street scenes (Corner 1991).

Although there was very little sync shooting in programmes such as Denis Mitchell's *Morning in the Streets* (1959) the quintessential device for factual television rapidly established itself as the 'talking head'. Many documentaries are built around a charismatic presenter, while as interviewees, ordinary people and experts, those with a story to tell and those with an achievement to celebrate, have made up the millions who have taken part in factual programmes (see p. 219 below for a discussion of interview techniques). Together with the commentary, it is the flow of narrative speech that leads the audience through a programme.

In the 1970s, a strict *observational* style was introduced. Pioneered by the 'direct cinema' filmmakers in the United States, it was argued that filmmakers should be a mere 'fly on the wall': no interviews, no presenters, just straightforward observation of life as it is lived. As so often, the style was driven by a technological innovation, in this case the development of portable lightweight cameras linked to sync sound. The style was taken up by series such as Roger Graef's *Space Between Words*, and, although it is rarely used in its purest form, rapidly became part of the documentarists' repertoire.

From its early days UK television developed a range of specialist series in its factual slots. Series on science and the arts have thrived on both the BBC and ITV in strands which ran for many years: *Horizon* for science, *Omnibus* and *The South Bank Show* for the arts. Current-affairs documentaries such as *Dispatches* and *Unreported World* specialise in investigative journalism. For many years ITV's *This Week* and *World in Action*, with their teams of dedicated journalists, vied with the BBC's *Panorama* (see below p. 212 for documentary subgenres).

The scope of documentary on UK television expanded with the launch of Channel Four in 1982. The channel had a brief to make space for voices not represented elsewhere on the airwaves, and to commission a range of styles. *The Eleventh Hour* showed films such as Black Audio's *Handsworth Songs* on the 1984 riots in Birmingham, while series such as *Channels of Resistance* made space for filmmaking by under-represented minorities around the world. In addition, the BBC's Community Programme Unit, established in 1972, enabled campaigning groups and others to make their own factual programmes. In the 1990s the unit launched a Disability Programme Unit and developed the *Video Diary* and *Video Nation* strands in which members of the public used domestic camcorders to document their lives. From a dedicated football fan to an ex-prisoner, it introduced a new way of making factual programmes and a new televisual 'look'. Low-tech, with a less polished appearance, the video diary technique seemed to bring the audience even closer to the realities portrayed. Before long, the approach was taken up across the television output.

At the same time, substantial documentaries continued to deal with the major events of the century. Across the 1990s, both Channel Four and BBC2 scheduled 'seasons', which featured a range of different films on topics including Channel Four's *Soviet Spring* and *Bloody Bosnia*, and the BBC's *African Summer*. And substantial documentary-making need not sweep across a global canvas. In 1995 the BBC launched *Modern Times*, which showcases films documenting life in contemporary Britain.

Bill Nichols described documentary as a 'discourse of sobriety', and in this sober spirit, factual genres, in all their wide variety, have aimed to lead rather than follow audience taste. In many ways that is still the aim, but by the 20teens, the range of the factual output has undergone a transformation. The new genres of the 2000s can be traced back to concerns about the future of 'serious' programming which began in the more commercial, multichannel environment of the 1990s. The search was on for documentary styles that would be more immediately engaging. As producer Stephen Lambert, one of the pioneers of the new developments, put it: 'it's where the pressure to be entertaining and popular is as great as the pressure to capture something about the way the world is' (Chalaby 2015: 137).

We can point to three important developments in which factual programming drew inspiration from other parts of the schedule: first there was an expansion of consumer programming – travel, home improvement, antiques, gardening, cookery and similar topics, which combined educational material with information and entertainment. Jeremy Tunstall described this as an 'edinfotainment maelstrom' (Tunstall 1993). Many of these strands were developed from what had previously been low-prestige 'daytime' genres. Broadcast in the off-peak hours, these had been confidently evolving a light and informal style which would come to exert its influence across the factual output.

A second innovation was the 'docu-soap'. In *Airport* and *Driving School*, just like a fictional soap opera, the audience followed the fortunes of a group of characters chosen for their quirkiness and entertainment value. The style remains popular and has further developed into the 'constructed factual' of *The Only Way is Essex* and *Made in Chelsea*.

The third influential innovation was the 'reality' genre, which evolved forms of 'social experiment', placing ordinary people in extraordinary situations. This approach was not entirely new. The great documentarist Jean Rouch had used reconstructions and performances in his ethnographic works back in the 1960s. He stated: 'I do not film life as it is, but life *as it is provoked*' (Ten Brink 2008). However, the arrival of *Big Brother* brought a competitive element. This was reality *entertainment*. The contestants in that first *Big Brother* house sat around singing 'it's only a game show'. With its 24-hour observation and disparate contestants, *Big Brother* became the landmark programme of 2000.

Most of the prominent factual genres of the 20teens are constructed around a 'format' that can be codified and marketed (see p. 52 above for the role of formats in the global television landscape). In his detailed study of *The Format Age*, Jean Chalaby points out that a 'formatted show' is not a genre, as several genres, including drama, are adapting themselves to its marketing needs. Following numerous interviews with their creators, Chalaby has identified three factual formats: *reality competitions, factual entertainment* and *constructed reality*. Today the schedules are bursting with programmes that hover on the boundary between informing and entertaining their audience. The BBC now has a 'factual entertainment' commissioning area, while BAFTA offers an award for 'reality and constructed factual' programmes. The situation is fluid. Descriptions of the subgenres are not fixed ('reality entertainment' may be described as 'constructed factual', for example), boundaries are no longer clear-cut, and the range of topics and styles is ever-expanding.

DOCUMENTARY AND CONTEMPORARY SUBGENRES

Presenter-led

Many documentary subgenres employ charismatic presenters who guide the audience through a programme on topics that range from natural history to science and the arts. Presenters such as Mary Beard on ancient history, Tony Robinson on the archaeology of our landscape, Brian Cox on the physics of outer space, Lucy Worsley trying out the costumes of earlier centuries, and, of course, David Attenborough, who has been the audience's guide through more than sixty years of natural history programmes, are all much-loved television figures. Celebrity presenters, referred to in the industry as 'the talent', remain an important ingredient of documentary as well as entertainment programming.

Fixed-rig

In series such as *Educating Yorkshire, 24 Hours in A&E* and *One Born Every Minute*, the daily life in a chosen location can be recorded by up to seventy cameras fixed in strategic positions and operated remotely from a temporary control room/gallery. The approach gives unprecedented coverage of the daily life in an institution, while programmes tend to centre on specific individuals, often at moments of crisis. The relationship between Musharraf, who suffered from a stutter, and his teacher, who helped him overcome it, was a driving narrative of *Educating Yorkshire*.

The Channel Four commissioning website notes: 'The big changes in the last two or three years are that an increasing number of programmes are mixing rig and single camera material – *Royal Marines, 24 Hours in Custody* – and that new companies are embracing the rig technology and taking it into different worlds or spaces' www.channel4.com/info/commissioning/4producers/documentaries.

'Access' shows

This is when cameras get 'access' to an institution, such as a high street store (*Greggs*; *Harrods*) or an elite school (*Harrow: A Very British School*). These series may use a range of techniques, including some fixed cameras and some observational filming as well as extensive interviews. The institutions 'have to be big, and have to fit in to that sense of enjoying life', says Siobhan Mulholland, Sky commissioning editor. (The term 'access' has also been used to refer to programmes where non-professionals and marginalised voices get access to programme-making. See Community Programme Unit pp. 106 and 208).

Captured footage

Numerous series depend on footage captured by mobile phone or CCTV cameras. The use of CCTV was pioneered by *Crimewatch*, which appealed to the public to help the police identify criminals, and is now used extensively for programmes compiled from dramatic or humorous moments, often supplemented by mobile phone footage sent in by viewers. Many of these 'caught on camera' series have titles such as *Britain Sees Red: Caught On Camera* and *The Nightmare Neighbour Next Door*.

Similar formats include undercover journalists employing surreptitious filming (see Gio Ulleri p. 245), and series in which participants in an event wear personal cameras. For *Our War*, which documented the fighting in Afghanistan, the action was recorded by the soldiers themselves wearing helmet cameras. The footage was edited into to create two series on BBC3 with accompanying websites.

Current affairs

Documentary journalism, or 'current affairs', for example, in the *Dispatches* and *Panorama* slots, falls between news and documentary. Current affairs aims to address the news agenda in greater depth and to *explain* as well as report what is going on, providing a 'window on the world'. Programmes may deal with international events, conduct an investigation into wrongdoing, focus on a little-known issue (as in *Unreported World*) and make use of the full range of documentary techniques.

Current affairs can never compete for the largest audiences. For many years the genre was protected by the television regulator, but now Jeremy Tunstall has identified it as a 'genre in jeopardy' (Tunstall 2015: 181–201) However, documentary journalism is also commissioned by online channels such as Vice, Discovery and international channels including National Geographic (see Gio Ulleri p. 245).

Authored documentaries

Although UK television has become more timid, there is still some space for documentary-makers with a distinctive personal voice. Substantial documentaries, co-funded by television organisations, may also be shown in cinemas, at documentary festivals and online. The BBC placed *Bitter Lake* by Adam Curtis, who uses archive footage to create personal political essays, first on the iPlayer. Many documentary directors still see their programmes as forms of creativity, and documentarists such as Brian Hill, Sue Bourne and Kim Longinotto continue to evolve their own personal styles.

Formatted 'reality' genres

As we have seen, the biggest innovation of the 20teens is the rise of 'formatted' genres, which we will consider here in greater detail. Jean Chalaby describes a 'format' as a set of rules and principles which structure a programme and enable it to be remade within different cultures and different contexts. He argues that this global adaptability, part of the 'de-territorialisation' of television, is its main characteristic.

Discussion of formats has evolved its own vocabulary: each format is set in a *precinct*; it has a *recipe* for remaking the programme; an *engine* that constructs its narrative, and specific *'format points'* that generate *trigger moments*. This ensures that something entertaining will happen and that a narrative will unfold, leading to the transformation of the protagonists. 'The TV industry has learned to tell a story without a script', writes Chalaby (2015: 131).

Each programme's format is documented in a *bible,* which covers every aspect, from budgets to casting. The bible is backed up by *flying producers* who act as consultants when a series is remade. Together the formulae, backed up by advice and expertise, enable a format to cross cultural boundaries. *The Great British Bake-Off* has become *The Great Australian Bake-Off* and around twenty others. Each territory respects *Bake-Off*'s basic format points: the competition, the stately house, the tent, the engaging celebrity judges and presenters.

Chalaby describes three types of 'reality' formats: *'reality competitions'* are the furthest from 'reality' and the most constructed (2015: 143–7). They are tightly structured, with a strong competitive element and an elimination process. *Big Brother* launched the genre, and its engine has inspired others, such as *I'm a Celebrity: Get Me Out of Here.* The setting is specially constructed and the cast carefully selected, whether made up of 'ordinary people' or celebrities.

By contrast, *factual entertainment* is more lightly structured. Chalaby summarises: 'A precinct sets a solo character or a group on a journey structured by format points' (2015: 143). Stephen Lambert, who originated many of the docu-soaps of the 1990s (*Clampers*; *Airport*), developed the mode with programmes such as *Wife Swap*, in which wives from very different households move in with each other's family. The receiving household must write a manual to describe how their household works. But the families have been selected because of their incompatibility, and the production team ensures that the manual 'is like a red rag to the incoming wife'. Stephen Lambert also devised what became known as the 'fish out of water formats', including *Secret Millionaire* and *Undercover Boss.* 'The whole set up is designed to push people to their edges – to their limits – and that's where you hope the drama comes', an ITV producer told Chalaby (2015: 147).

Third, the *constructed reality* format, which features *'real* people in *managed* situations' (Chalaby 2015: 181), blurs the boundary between documentary and drama. Although, at least in the United Kingdom, the lines are not scripted, the groups of friends followed by *The Only Way is Essex (TOWIE)* and *Made in Chelsea* are performers. They perform themselves as they respond to situations devised by the programme-makers. In *TOWIE*, which celebrated its 200th episode in March 2016, narratives are based around the romantic attachments of a group of young people, in the context of their business interests and their obsession with fashion and lifestyle.

All series overflow into numerous paratexts. Programmes such as *TOWIE* are incomplete without the blogs, fan-sites, marketing and allied media that accompany them – including tourist trips to Brentwood, where the series is set. In fact, most popular factual formats are accompanied by 'companion shows' which 'go behind the scenes to root out all the latest gossip and reveal all the latest goings on with the participants', according to the blurb for *Take Me Out: The Gossip* (*Radio Times* 20 February 2016). Participants make appearances on chat shows and news items, while informative websites expand on the educational aspects (offering advice on weight loss or medical conditions, publishing the recipes from *Come Dine With Me*). It can be argued that these contribute a great deal of information and educational material as well as entertainment value.

RESEARCH FOR FACTUAL PROGRAMMES

Research is the motor of factual programme-making across its genres. It is research that generates programme ideas and ensures that those ideas are well worked out and that a programme achieves its aims.

The chief skill of a researcher is to know how to find out. Television research involves a great deal of poking around: telephoning contacts, following up press items, searching the internet, visiting locations, identifying possible participants and getting to know them, observing activities and checking facts. It also means building a network of useful contacts and developing a good understanding of industry requirements. Researchers must also be aware of, and work within, relevant legislation and regulations, such as copyright, data protection and public liability.

Some researchers are experienced generalists who can move with ease from one topic to another. Others are experts in a particular area, say, medicine, finance or the arts. BBC researcher Kathy Chater, in her useful guide to media research, makes some rather depressing, but realistic, comments about the researcher's job within a big organisation. If a programme is a success, she writes, the producer and director will accept the accolades. If it is a failure, they will say 'the research wasn't very good' (Chater 2002). Nevertheless, especially in smaller companies, research is very often a collaborative effort between writer, researcher, producer and director. Either way liaison across the team is essential, as researchers present their findings to the decision-makers.

Depending on the programme, types of research may include:

Factual research

This is concerned with verifiable information and accuracy. Factual research may involve consulting:

- Experts and others working in the relevant area: nurses as well as doctors, class teachers as well as head teachers.

- The specialist press and online sources in the areas being researched.

- Press sources, either through the newspapers' own websites or the British Newspaper Archive, which is an initiative by the British Library to digitise material from the Library's vast collection www.britishnewspaperarchive. co.uk/help/about.

- Government departments and press offices.

- The press and public relations offices of other relevant bodies: from commercial companies to pressure groups, most organisations have websites which describe their work and a system for responding to press enquiries; it may be useful to build up some personal contacts here.

- Research agencies: sometimes a programme will finance some specialised research or conduct their own poll to compare with official figures.

Many programmes depend on establishing accurate factual information. Current affairs, in particular, follows the news agenda and often conducts its own painstaking investigations.

Even presenters who are experts in their field need to be backed up by extra research effort. Professor Mary Beard told of some important artefacts, well known to scholars, which she had intended to film but which 'had quite simply disappeared or were no longer where they were supposed to be. Our concerted efforts did run some of them to ground – but each one took several days of technical, antiquarian work. So much for "dumbing down"!' (*The Guardian* 13 July 2015: 13).

Whatever the subject matter and whatever the budget, in seeking out the facts of the case, a researcher should compare several sources, treating any one of them with a healthy scepticism.

People research

This includes recruiting and supporting:

- *'Experts'*: people with standing in the field whom the researcher can consult to check the accuracy and the relative importance of information they discover from other sources. 'Experts' may also be needed as interviewees, either to give weight to an argument or simply to offer authoritative factual information. It has been said that a researcher needs to be an 'expert at finding experts'.

For many years it has been pointed out that programmes, especially news and current affairs, are dominated by men, and several recent initiatives have been designed to ensure that the names of women experts are put forward. A 2015 study by City University found that there has indeed been a change in some areas, with a 37 per cent rise in the number of women interviewed on Channel Four news in the previous year. In November 2015 the ratio stood at 2.6 to one www.city.ac. uk/news/2015/november/research-reveals-success-of-campaign-to-increase-proportion-of-women-experts-in-news.

- *Other interviewees*: these may be people who are prepared to speak of personal experiences that illustrate the theme of a programme; people who were witnesses to an event; people speaking of their memories. Suitable interviewees may be found through social media, through support networks and pressure groups, or through professionals working with the relevant group, say, single parents or tenants in poor housing. The researcher will have preliminary conversations, then, depending on the nature of the participation, will keep in touch in the run-up to the filming.

- *Participants* in an observational documentary: this includes all who may be filmed in the hospital ward, police station or any of the other institutions that have opened their doors to the television cameras. Written permission must be gained from everyone who may appear, and it is usually up to the researcher to build up a relationship with the 'characters' who stand out and are likely to be featured on screen.

- *Subjects* who will feature in formatted or constructed factual programmes.

Researchers may contact potential participants through social media or other networks. In addition, broadcasters invite applications for numerous shows on websites such as *Be on Screen.* At the time of writing, examples include: 'Do you have a medical or physical condition which you feel can make dating tricky?' and 'Has something driven you apart from someone you once loved? Do you think it's time to forgive and forget? Or maybe you are hoping to be forgiven?' www.beonscreen. com/uk/tv-shows.

Those who take part in these programmes must be fully aware of the nature of the programme and of their role. Senior researchers will assist producers in the processes of selection, ensuring that those selected are fully informed, can cope with the inevitable stress which will be created by the programme, and are supported throughout (see ethics p. 223 below).

- *Specific individuals*: as the history of television itself becomes longer, many programmes have attempted to follow the fortunes of those who appeared in earlier shows: How are they faring five years after their heart operation? Do they remember singing in that choir when they were a child? For such programmes researchers need to track down specific individuals. The revealing Granada programme *Seven Up*, made in 1964, showed a sample of seven-year-olds from different class backgrounds. The audience was amazed by the differences in their manner and attitudes. Seven years later the team tracked them down again, then took on the task of keeping in regular contact. The most recent programme, *56 Up*, was broadcast in 2012 (Bruzzi 2007).

- *Celebrities*: normally celebrities have agents who will negotiate their fee and the conditions under which they appear.

Location research: setting up the shoot

Sometimes an expert location manager is part of a team; sometimes the location, or 'precinct', is intrinsic to the subject – as with an 'access' programme about an institution or a fixed-rig production in a hospital or school. If not, finding appropriate locations often falls to the researcher, working together with the production manager. This includes:

- *Finding suitable locations* within easy reach of the production base; getting the relevant permissions from owners and others affected, and planning where the filming will take place. Relevant factors are the expense, the appearance and the suitability of the location for recording sound (see p. 122). An elegant garden will pose problems if it is next to a car breaker's yard. A recce includes checking out practicalities, including finding available parking space, arranging where to have lunch and working out how long the journey will take to and from the location.

- *Overseas filming*: this involves arranging visas and permissions through Embassies and High Commissions; checking out what jabs are needed, and checking local regulations on such issues as alcohol consumption and dress codes. It is inappropriate to travel around the world assuming that Western European practices are universally acceptable.

Archive research

This can be a specialist area. Identifying and acquiring suitable filmed material which may be needed, for example, to illustrate a reference in a documentary requires a knowledge of relevant film libraries and archives. These range from major collections such as the BFI National Film Archive to smaller regional or company archives and even private collectors. Series that depend on explorations of the past, such *as London on Film* and *The Secret History of Our Streets*, draw on a wide range of sources. The programmes list around ten different archive sources and credit an archive producer and archive researchers. (Confusingly an archive researcher is often referred to simply as a 'film researcher'.) Many of the films which have been commemorating the centenary of the First World War were made in close collaboration with archivists at the Imperial War Museum.

For less specialist productions it may fall to the researcher, in liaison with the editor or edit producer, to track down a news item or a sequence to illustrate a particular point. Major collections such as British Pathé and the BFI Archive have easily searchable catalogues, and have made a great deal of material available to view online. It is sometimes possible to download low-resolution clips for use in offline edits. All the websites have information on how to license material for broadcast or other use, and what the charges are. Both Film Archives UK, which represents all public sector film and television archives, and the British Universities Film and Video Council run courses on issues such as copyright clearance, negotiation skills and archive sources for film researchers.

The use of material from personal collections, home movies or mobile phone footage must be negotiated with their copyright holders.

Useful references for archives

http://filmarchives.org.uk/

www.filmarchives-online.eu/

www.bfi.org.uk/archive-collections/searching-access-collections/archive-resources-online

bufvc.ac.uk/archives/

www.iwm.org.uk/global-tags/film-and-video-archive

www.britishpathe.com/

Final note

Many of the areas of work in which researchers are involved, including contracts and copyright, have legal implications. All production companies take legal advice when necessary, and the larger organisations employ teams of lawyers.

INTERVIEW TECHNIQUES

The ability to secure successful talking-head interviews should be at the forefront of any documentary-maker's arsenal, argues Brian Hill, discussing his documentary *The Confessions of Thomas Quick* (2015). However,

> it's a skill that doesn't get taught in film school. Some documentary makers don't turn up to an interview with a list of questions, they turn up with a list of answers. I want [my subjects] to explain what happened in their own words, and, as I'm listening to their responses I'm processing how it will work in terms

of the film. You have to give people a lot of time, particularly with a story as complicated as this. I never take notes, I just sit and talk to people; if you make it more discursive, more conversational, you can get into areas that you never thought of www.bfi.org.uk/news-opinion/news-bfi/interviews/confessions-thomas-quick-he-ultimate-unreliable-narrator.

There are many types of documentary interview. The intimate, self-revelatory style described by Hill is at the heart of the penetrating, thoughtful approach preferred by many of today's key documentarists. In *Directing the Documentary*, Michael Rabiger describes the technique when dealing with participants as 'a search for naturalness' (Rabiger 2015). With very few exceptions this is the case. Visually interviewees may be presented in many different ways, but as speakers they must remain relaxed and convincing.

However, it is important to distinguish between the different reasons for conducting an interview. What is needed from an interviewee will be determined to a large extent by the genre of programme. Clear factual information will be all important for a science based series such as *Horizon*. A current affairs investigation may be challenging and antagonistic. By contrast, in a travel programme the interviewees need to be engaging and entertaining.

But whatever the style of interview, three aspects need to be taken into account; the *initial briefing*, the *manner* in which the interview is conducted, and the way in which what is said is *incorporated* into the final programme.

Questions may be

- Requests for information
- Follow-up or supplementary questions, and requests for examples
- Leading questions that expect particular answers
- A challenge to the interviewee's position
- A carefully judged moment when the interviewer says nothing, allowing the interviewee space to expand on their thoughts.

Topics

Interviews may be designed to elicit various different types of material, including:

- *Factual or expert information*; in which case there will be a need to assess the weight of information given, partly by judging the reputation and standing of the interviewee, partly by research into other sources.
- *Expert opinion*; in which case there will be a need to draw out the opinion by putting alternative views, bearing in mind the question of balance.

- *Personal, non-expert, opinion.*

- *Witness accounts*; in which case it will be important to ensure that the interviewee is, indeed, a competent and genuine witness. If the interview may put the interviewee in danger, it is possible to conceal their identity by blurring their face and replacing their voice with that of an actor.

- *Anecdote*; in which case the interviewee should be a good raconteur or have a good camera presence.

- *Emotion*: the growth of the various 'constructed factual' genres means that interviewees/participants have come to expect that their discomfiture will be visible.

Tears on screen have become more acceptable. However, the interviewer should always be aware of the distress that may follow in the aftermath of such an interview, especially if they are a vulnerable person. Where possible they should be offered relevant support (see ethics p. 223).

Strategies

Interviewers may adopt different strategies, partly depending on whether the interviewer themselves is a personality who is featured in the programme, or whether the questions will be edited out.

Strategies include:

- *Eliciting information or opinion*: in this case the interviewer will be as self-effacing as possible.

- *Challenging* the interviewee, for example, in a political interview. This involves putting contrary opinions with provocative emphasis. The abrasive manner of Jeremy Paxman on *Newsnight* became notorious. BBC Director General John Birt himself once criticised aggressive interviewers who are 'sneering, overbearing and disdainful' so that the 'policy difference behind the disputes go unexplored' (*The Guardian* 17 July 1995). Birt himself, as editor of *Weekend World* in the 1970s, became known for what he described as the 'mission to explain', the need for television to clarify complex political issues, sometimes in the face of politicians' desire to obfuscate. Nevertheless, even the toughest interviewer must give those challenged a space to reply to their critics.

- *The conversational interview*: this takes the form of an interviewer and interviewee chat, whether comfortably seated on a sofa in a daytime show, or some other context, such as strolling informally through a park.

- *The intimate interview*: in *Face to Face*, first evolved by John Freeman in the 1960s, then revived by Jeremy Isaacs in the 1990s, well-known personalities, agreed to respond to extended probing, filmed in big close-up.

- *The emotional interview*: this was the approach first developed by *Man Alive*, (BBC 1965–81) in which interviewees are selected because of the personal and emotional nature of the stories they have to tell. The interviewer's job is to encourage that story to come out, often merely through sympathetic nodding.

'If somebody was in a poor way and the tears were rising', said Angela Huth, reviewing her time as an interviewer on *Man Alive*, 'and you did a bit of nodding and didn't say anything, then they felt that they had to help *you* out, so they'd come out with much more of the ghastliness, whatever it was, the tragic story. We all got quite good at knowing how to deal with them when they began to glitter.'

(*Can I ask you a personal question? – The 'Man Alive' story* BBC2 30 August 1993)

Practical points

There are some practical points that should be taken into account for most types of interview:

- Decide whether the interviewer's questions will be included in the programme or edited out. This will change the way in which the questions are asked. If the questions are to be edited out, responses like 'Yes, I agree' are inappropriate. All the information must be included in the answer.

- Prepare a list of questions before the interview. Make them precise and designed to elicit the type of answer needed. But remember that it is important to maintain eye contact with the interviewee, rather than constantly consulting prepared notes.

- Decide on the best place for the interview. An interviewee is likely to be more relaxed in their own home in familiar surroundings. Or the interview may take place in a location relevant to the programme – for example, while gardening, or at work – explaining these activities to the viewers.

- Decide on the relationship between interviewer and interviewee: is this, for example, a single formal encounter or a relationship built up across the programme.

- If dealing with an inexperienced interviewee, it is important to explain the procedures to them. For example, if you will need to play devil's advocate and challenge their views, then they should understand that this is to clarify the issues for the audience and they should not take it personally or get annoyed (unless, of course, this is the interviewer's intention!)

- Interviewees who are speaking of difficult or sensitive topics may ask to have their identity disguised. This is appropriate in many cases – for example, victims of rape, ex-terrorists speaking of their experiences, and others who feel that exposure may put them in danger. They can be filmed from behind, in silhouette, or in some other way that does not reveal any identification. Alternatively their faces can be blurred and voices distorted at the editing stage.

DOCUMENTARY AND FACTUAL ETHICS

Working on documentaries and factual programmes can be a demanding experience and in the excitement it is all too easy to overlook the ethical dimension which comes into play when real people and real events are represented on the screen. Some of the most heated debates over the television output have concerned the ethics of the genre. Whether making a substantial documentary or a popular formatted series, a factual programme involves a tension between those two aspects identified by John Grierson a century ago: *'actuality'*, in all its subtlety and diversity, and its *'creative treatment'* by the filmmaker. Balancing the two is always an ethical challenge, especially in the context of pressures from budgets and schedules.

There are no easy answers, but the issues can be divided into two main areas. The first concerns the programme-makers' relationship with their viewers; the second, their relationship with those who appear in their films. Both the BBC and the broadcasting regulator, Ofcom, publish rules and codes of practice which address these issues and they offer useful guidelines for programme-makers to follow (Ofcom 2015b). The rules apply to UK broadcasters and have been drawn up with reference to relevant legislation. Those who feel that they have been misrepresented, that broadcasters have overstepped the mark, or that factual mistakes have been made, can complain to Ofcom. Below we give an account of the most important issues, referring to the regulator's guidelines and to some of the debates that continue to surround factual programme-making.

Relations with viewers

Objectivity, impartiality and factual truth

Genres establish a compact between programme-makers and viewers. When a programme is labelled 'drama', 'factual' or 'entertainment', viewers understand what to expect and what its characteristics will be. Documentary and factual genres are expected to present a picture which the viewer can accept as a credible representation of 'actuality'. Ofcom's Rule 2.2 states that 'factual programmes or items, or portrayals of factual matters, must not materially mislead the audience'. But all documentary-makers know how much they must control their work. Forms of artifice are integral to the documentary toolbox. Every change of camera angle carries its own implications; creating the structure and rhythm of a film is inevitably selective (see Part 2 for more on these activities). The possibility of absolute documentary 'truth' has long been questioned.

Over the years, dedicated documentarists have tried to develop technologies that would bring filmmakers closer to capturing 'actuality' as it unfolds in the real world. The fixed rig is a recent example (RTS 2015). Back in the 1960s, the proponents of 'direct cinema' made cameras less obtrusive and insisted that interviews, commentary and background music should not be used, since these were not part of the original scene. For them the filmmaking process should be invisible, allowing a direct insight into life as it is lived. But others have argued that making the filming invisible is, in itself, a deception. Since all films are constructions, it is more honest for filmmakers to let the audience see the process of construction for themselves. This was Dziga Vertov's view when he made the seminal *Man with a Movie Camera* back in 1929. The documentary follows the cameraman as he films a day in the life of the busy city, and observes the editor as she selects the shots and builds up the sequences.

As we have seen, across today's television output there is a wide range of factual subgenres constructed according to different principles and creating different audience expectations. At one extreme is current affairs journalism, which is expected to be truthful and accurate, and at the other, the 'factual entertainment' style. Here the links with 'actuality' are more tenuous and programme-makers need to make the audience aware of their constructed nature. The opening caption of *The Only Way is Essex* states: 'The tans you see might be fake but the people are all real although some of what they do has been set up purely for your entertainment.' A variety of documentary approaches and formatted set-ups fall between the two extremes. Questions of 'truthfulness' and 'actuality' become more difficult to negotiate as the boundaries between real life and performance, between 'factual' and 'entertainment', are increasingly blurred.

At the current affairs end of the spectrum the rules are clear. Current affairs documentaries must abide by the regulations that apply to news: they should be 'reported with due accuracy and presented with due impartiality' (Clause 5.1). One of the principles of public service broadcasting is that viewers have the right to receive unbiased information, and to hear all sides of a story. This means that, unlike newspapers, the journalists who represent the broadcasters may not express a political commitment or an editorial opinion. An 'authored' programme putting a controversial argument must be balanced by another arguing the opposing view.

Arguing a case, seeking to persuade

The expectation of balance in factual programming has meant that broadcasters have come in for a great deal of criticism over the years. Many have argued that, despite the impartiality rule, *their* viewpoint is excluded, or that the language used implies a subtle bias one way or other. A great deal of scholarship has been devoted to analysing issues such as the coverage of elections and of overseas conflicts. One of the policies of Channel Four in its early days was to respond to such criticisms by making space for programmes which could argue a case and widen the spectrum of debate. The journalist John Pilger has become well-known for his polemical documentaries. However, in recent years the activist documentary has only had a marginal place on our television screens. Documentary-makers who want to use their skills to promote a political position or make a point tend to turn to the internet as an outlet for their work, or they may submit their films to one of the many documentary festivals, or become part of a network like the Radical Film Network.

Nevertheless an address to an audience as engaged actors, rather than as individuals passively seeking entertainment or relaxation, remains an important impetus behind much factual programming. Such an approach is in direct line from John Grierson's vision of the documentary as part of the social democratic project, providing insight for an informed citizenry.

Commercial messages

A completely different example of seeking to persuade involves questions of patronage and sponsorship, which may affect the content of a film. Ofcom requires that there should always be a clear distinction between editorial content and advertising, and 'unsuitable' sponsorship is not allowed. As we have seen, many factual programmes on ITV and Channels 4 and 5 are sponsored ('Misubushi Mirage, changing perceptions with documentaries on 4'; 'Sofology at Sofa Works sponsors *Gogglebox*'; and 'The weather, sponsored by Qatar Airways' on Sky News).

But Ofcom rules that the sponsor must not influence the content or the scheduling of the programme (Clause 9.11). Surreptitious advertising is prohibited, products, services and trademarks must not be promoted. Product placement (i.e., payment from the advertisers for including a particular product as part of the action) is specifically prohibited in current affairs and consumer advice programmes (see p. 42 on branding). The overall requirement is that editorial independence should be maintained and the audience should not be deceived.

Harm and offence

Other aspects of programme-makers' relations with viewers include a duty not to cause harm or offence. This involves being aware of a diverse audience with a range of different beliefs and attitudes (see representation p. 227 below). It also means that content which may be deemed offensive – say in a programme that comments on different religions, or contains bad language – must be clearly labelled. Material that is unsuitable for children and young people under 16, such as overt sexual content or excessive violence, must not be broadcast before the 9pm watershed. This means that programme-makers should ensure that their programme is suitable for its scheduled slot, even though this regulation is more difficult to impose with the growth of on-demand viewing (Part 2).

Relations with the people filmed: support and informed consent

The second major ethical concern is around programme-makers' relations with their subjects. Unlike drama, which features trained performers, the people who appear in factual programmes are non-professionals, 'ordinary people' with no experience of the publicity and exposure that appearing in a television programme may bring. Their experiences vary, as participants may be featured in a number of different ways, partly depending on where the programme sits on the spectrum of subgenres. At the investigatory current affairs end of the spectrum, programme-makers may film unwilling subjects, perhaps using concealed cameras to expose an official who has been accused of corruption. Otherwise factual programme-makers are expected to obtain the consent of their subjects. Under the heading of 'Fairness' Ofcom insists that simply signing a contract is not enough. 'Consent' should always mean *'informed consent'*, and programme-makers should always 'give a clear explanation of the nature and purpose of the programme and the nature of their contribution' (Clause 7.3).

For an authored documentary, filmmakers may select the style of their films and find ways to establish a close relationship with their subjects, building their trust and allowing them to express themselves. For *Malcolm and Barbara: A Love Story* Paul Watson filmed over eleven years to record Malcolm Pointon's slow deterioration with Alzheimer's disease and his wife Barbara's ways of coping and caring. Brian Hill has collaborated with poet Simon Armitage to enable participants to express their circumstances and their trauma through poetry and song. Subjects range from *Feltham Sings* (2002) with inmates in a young offender's institution, to *The Not-Dead* (2007) featuring soldiers dealing with the aftermath of war.

Beyond the authored documentary, contemporary formats pose their own ethical dilemmas. For the fixed-rig *Educating* series, the production company Twofour must gain the consent of staff and students who will be under constant observation, and also from the students' parents or guardians. The team spend time in a school for many months before filming begins, and ten key members get to know the staff. The producers are careful not to include students who may be at risk, and they make it clear that anyone may opt not to participate. A number of support structures are in place during the filming and throughout transmission. A psychologist is part of the team and speaks with the main students every day. Director and Executive Producer David Clews says that the staff were quite wary when they were preparing for the first series, *Educating Essex*. However, for the second, *Educating Yorkshire* (2013), there were fewer objections. 'If I hadn't watched *Essex* I would probably have said no', said *Yorkshire*'s Headmaster Jonny Mitchell. 'It was emotionally intelligent rather than sensationalist' (talking at the *Radio Times* Festival 2015).

The experience of *Benefits Street* (Channel Four 2014) was rather different. Love Productions described it as a 'fair and balanced observational documentary' about a Birmingham street where the majority of the residents were drawing benefit. Although filming took place over a year, many of those portrayed were angry when they saw the programme. 'They told us they wanted to capture the community spirit of James Turner Street and show the positive of that', said resident Anna Korzen, 'but all they have done is show the negative' (BBC News 8 January 2014). The participants were not told what the title would be, and were not aware that the focus would be on benefits. Media theorist John Ellis pointed to the wider context of the broadcast: 'The problem is that the characters have to bear the weight of the current social debate about benefits, and are unprepared for that' (blog 2014).

Following transmission, participants in both *Benefits Street* and the *Educating* series were subjected to abuse on Twitter – something they were also unprepared for.

There is a significant difference between the observational mode, which films subjects in a familiar situation, and a formatted factual programme that depends on placing participants in *unfamiliar* circumstances and deliberately putting them under pressure. Formatted programmes are structured around a preconceived 'narrative', and the participants must expect to play their part, even if it is emotionally demanding. They must be warned that they will need to respond to difficult and often unexpected situations, whether surviving on a remote island (for *The Island with Bear Grylls*, viewers are invited to 'watch them struggle' – *Radio Times* 26 March 2016), or coping with unfamiliar demands. Such programmes are treading a fine line between representation and exploitation. In every case, programme-makers must follow accepted codes of practice as they build a relationship with the participants, respecting their dignity and their rights. But ultimately the production is in the hands of the broadcaster. 'You may feel intrusive while you are filming, but in the edit suite everything shifts', said one director (see also Anne Parisio p. 229 on directing a formatted programme).

Representation and stereotyping

Factual programmes involve turning the lives of others into forms of entertainment. The ethics of *representation* affect relations both with the participants and with the audience. It is a question both of how the participants are represented, and of how the audience will perceive them – which may be different from the intentions of the filmmaker.

Participants may serve various functions within a film. They may appear because they represent many others in the same situation, or because, like White Dee in *Benefits Street*, they are a 'character' who will appeal to the audience. But the danger of stereotyping is ever-present. Stereotypes strip participants of their individuality in order to play up their common characteristics. Familiar stereotypes – the sexualised woman, the Asian shopkeeper, the lazy benefits claimant – are usually exaggerated and frequently carry negative connotations. And stereotypes are perceived within particular social circumstances. As John Ellis pointed out, the stereotype of the irresponsible work-shy claimant was current in the wider media when *Benefits Street* was broadcast. As they circulate, stereotypes reinforce a particular image.

For many years, feminists, lesbian, gay, bisexual and transgender (LGBT) groups and campaigners from BAME, disability and other disadvantaged minorities have argued against the ways in which they have been stereotyped across the media, and real changes have been achieved. Contemporary factual programmes represent a wide diversity of individuals. However, there is a danger that the assertion that we have moved beyond stereotypes in order to present, for example, *Britain's Fattest Man* or *The Undateables* on what appear to be their own terms may easily become an excuse for voyeurism and intrusion.

Relations with the people filmed: forms of collaboration

Brian Winston has argued that, however conscientious the programme-makers, there is a degree of voyeurism inherent in the medium itself (Winston 1995). Factual television always involves exposure as the audience, cosy in their familiar homes, observes the activities of people they have not met. Those on the television screen are always deprived of their living presence. They are *being* presented, not presenting themselves. Winston argues that this exploitative relationship can only be broken by documentary styles which give some control to those who appear in them, and which draw attention to the distortions brought about by the act of filming itself.

Over the history of UK television a number of spaces have been made for what were called 'access' programmes, when control was handed over to the contributors. In 1972, when a group of workers in a Guinness factory canteen complained to a visiting film crew about being misrepresented, the BBC responded by setting up the Community Programme Unit. In the words of the opening titles to the unit's initial series, *Open Door*, its aim was to allow participants to 'have your own say in your own way'. Over its thirty-year history, the unit enabled non-professionals, campaigning groups and 'ordinary people' to make their own television programmes, retaining editorial control at every stage of the production. Many of the programmes had a campaigning edge – against hospital closures, criticising stereotypes in the media and so on. In the 1990s, the unit originated the innovative *Video Diaries* and *Video Nation* in which cameras were given to members of the public who were invited to make films about their lives. Channel Four, which was set up to provide programmes not available on the other channels, also enabled a more collaborative type of programme-making, as it funded regional and other community-based 'workshops'. For many years the ITV companies were also required to provide 'access' slots. In the more commercialised television atmosphere of the 20teens these slots have disappeared.

Today, a great deal of collaborative documentary-making is online. Mandy Rose, the co-founder and producer of *Video Nation* (1994–2000), has created a number of collaborative projects and has curated a collection of films on the MIT Open Documentary Lab's 'docubase'. This website is given over to documentary work which is both collaborative and interactive. It includes curatorial selections, offers advice and invites participation http://opendoclab.mit.edu/comeindoc-documentary-series-launch-on-open-doclabs-website.

NOTE

In the United States, where there is no equivalent to the BBC and Ofcom's codes of practice, the Independent Documentary Association, which represents most of the notable documentarists in the United States, has argued that there is a need for a code. In 2009 it produced a report, *Honest Truths*, which was based on extensive interviews with practising documentarists discussing the ethical challenges they have faced. The report recognises the difficulty of producing hard and fast rules, but is based on three principles: 'do no harm, protect the vulnerable, and honor the viewer's trust': www.cmsimpact.org/sites/default/files/Honest_Truths_Documentary_Filmmakers_on_Ethical_Challenges_in_Their_Work.pdf.

PROFILE

Anne Parisio: Parisio Productions

Anne Parisio is an experienced camera/director who has been filming and directing documentaries for television for over 20 years and has won a number of awards. Here she discusses her experience of working on the formatted series Don't Drop the Baby, *for BBC3. Originally called* Don't Just Stand There I'm Having Your Baby *it is described as the 'series in which the midwives are called in to rescue young and clueless dads-to-be'.*

'I filmed and directed two episodes of this series in 2014, using a XF305 hand-held camera. Filming for the show usually starts eight to six weeks before the birth. A number of couples are 'cast' and two producers follow two couples each. The series producers decide which couple will be linked with which and each episode features two of the couples. For the earlier sequences we film conversations between the partners and with the midwife. The production team works with and prepares one of their couples while filming with the other.

The BBC has a watertight protocol. All potential contributors must be interviewed by psychiatrists and prepared for the filming. The series producer also negotiates with the hospitals and the midwives. They make it clear that either the hospital or the contributors can ask us to leave or stop filming at any time. Also everyone on the ward must give permission. All of this must be done well in advance because we don't know exactly when the birth will happen. We don't know which doctors will be on duty, so we have to discuss it with all the possible ones. Of course, in my experience, this is exactly what we would do for any respectful observational documentary.

The entertainment 'format' of the show is created first by a 'bromance': a meeting set up between the two fathers. They are taken to a cinema to see films of women giving birth. Then there are challenging situations to make the fathers confront their fears. Everyone in the crew thinks up ideas for this, including the midwife. It can be quite surreal. You have to create humour, put it in their context, and think up situations that will be unique to the people involved. For example, one father was a security guard: strong, muscly, did lots of exercise – but felt faint at the sight of blood and didn't want to be involved with the birth. Going to the hospital made him feel ill. His partner wanted a water birth, so we arranged to film in a bathroom in the hospital. The midwife provided a pile of bottles with red, blood-like water and asked him how much blood he thought she would lose. When she poured it into the bath it was much less than he'd thought. Another father was a farmer near Liverpool. The midwife had the idea of showing him a placenta. I was following him with the camera and showed him gradually edging away from it.

When it comes to filming the birth itself, that's pure observational filming.

As a filming director I'm always thinking about the editing as I shoot. But sometimes the producers wanted a two camera set-up, so that there would be more options. As the filming largely depended on cooking up ideas, that left the subjects in the hands of the edit producer. I really regretted the split between location producers and edit producers, because, as a director, I'm accustomed to following a programme through to the final edit. I'm used to being in contact with the subjects from the beginning to the end of the process, so they build their trust in you.

It's always important to get permission. For example, I followed the emergency team for a series on social workers for BBC Scotland. They were called to a young woman with small children who was drinking and wanted respite care. As she opened the door, I immediately asked if I could film, and she agreed.

Another series, *Sudden Death*, was a *Cutting Edge* programme that followed the stories of people who died alone in mysterious circumstances. We uncovered their stories through following the work of local council funeral officers whose job it was to look for relatives and organise pauper funerals if none were found. I was shooting on film in close consultation with relatives.

PROFILE

If they said no at any point, I would continue shooting but not process the rushes. I put it in the fridge, so I could go back to it if they agreed later.

I recently had an interview for a Channel 5 series. When I brought up these ethical issues, they said: 'Oh we don't do *that*. You're not suitable for Channel 5. You should work for BBC2.'

KEY TEXTS

Chalaby, J. (2015) *The Format Age: Television's Entertainment Revolution*, London: Polity.
Chater, C. (2002) *Research for Media Production*, London: Taylor and Francis.
Emm, A. (2014) *Researching for the Media: Television, Radio and Journalism*, London: Routledge.
Nichols, B. (1991) *Representing Reality*, Bloomington, IN: Indiana University Press.
Rabiger, M. (2015) *Directing the Documentary*, 6th edn, Oxford: Focal Press.

CHAPTER 17

News, politics and television as information

Lisette Johnston

Dr Lisette Johnston is a senior broadcast journalist working with BBC World News TV in London. She has been a journalist for thirteen years, the last six with the BBC, where she has also worked with the BBC News Channel and internal communications.

News is essentially the portrayal of current events. Television is just one of many different media through which journalists tell their audiences about what is happening in the world around them, from a local, national and international perspective. This chapter looks at the processes through which news programming is created for television, the jobs of different people working in news, as well as different types of programmes which incorporate journalism in them. In particular it will focus on the specifics of producing news for television and online broadcast in the United Kingdom today. In some places I will refer to specific events and examples based on my own experience.

HISTORY

The BBC produced the UK's first television news bulletin in January 1948, eighteen months after the end of the Second World War. Until then, those wanting to watch news events had to do so at the cinema, so the *Television Newsreel* was based on that experience. It was broadcast from London's Alexandra Palace rather than the news department at Broadcasting House, and at first was seen as 'soft news' compared to the topics and debates heard on BBC Radio. However, the television news format as we know it was established six years later, when *BBC News and*

Newsreel aired on 5 July 1954, presented by Richard Baker. The bulletin saw Baker reading the news accompanied by a series of photographs, maps, stills and one film. Within a year things had evolved and the amount of airtime devoted to television news on the BBC had doubled.

Commercial television appeared in that same year and Independant Television News (ITN) launched on 22 September 1955. When Channel Four arrived in 1982, for the first time there was an hour-long news programme, also provided by ITN. Today there are many news providers available in the United Kingdom. The main 'terrestrial' channels are BBC, ITV, Channel Four and Channel 5, while Sky News is also available on Freeview. The BBC produces thirty-six daytime and evening news bulletins, including those at 1pm, 6pm and 10pm on BBC One, and both the BBC and Sky have rolling twenty-four-hour news channels. ITN also produces ITV national news and 5 News. Both the BBC and regional parts of ITV produce bulletins with geographically specific content about 'news in your area'.

The terrestrial television channels are regulated by Ofcom to whom the public can complain about issues such as harm and offence and unbalanced or inaccurate content (Ofcom 2015B Section 5). Further, BBC news is guided by the Corporation's editorial guidelines, set out in the BBC Charter.

Thanks to satellite and digital technology, there are many other international news products that are available to viewers, such as Russia Today, France TV, CNN and Al Jazeera English, all of which have bases in the United Kingdom and broadcast globally.

It is important to note that, as viewing behaviour and media consumption have changed, so has delivery of news. This means that 'television news' is now available not just on television sets but online, via live streaming on news websites, and also on-demand via online players such as BBC iPlayer. Live news programmes from dedicated news channels or mainstream channels can also be accessed via mobile phones, while news is also disseminated through social media networks such as Facebook and Twitter. Here items allow viewers to 'click' to be referred back to the site, as well as 'sharing' them with followers. There are many ways to watch television news and, when they select what to include in programmes, journalists must bear in mind that they may be watched on laptops, mobiles and tablets as well as large television sets.

TYPES OF NEWS AND CURRENT AFFAIRS

Television journalists work on many different types of news programmes, and this section outlines some of them. One thing to mention is that in some organisations news and current affairs are seen as separate departments. 'Current affairs' in general refers to 'long-form' journalism, which can include investigative reports, political documentaries, long interviews and so on. Programmes such as *Dispatches,*

HARDtalk and *This Week* all fit into the category of current affairs. At the BBC different journalists work on *Panorama* and the News Channel and the teams don't usually mix, although there can be some crossover.

Rolling news

This refers to twenty-four-hour news channels which bring headlines each hour but contain both short- and long-form journalism. In the United Kingdom there are many different channels available, from the BBC News Channel to Sky News, CNN International and Al-Jazeera English.

Bulletins

These are usually short programmes, read by a presenter, which offer updates on the news of the day. They can include news packages, live reporting and short video clips shown with the presenter out of vision – these are known as 'oovs'.

Built programmes

These include longer news programmes, such as the BBC's *News at Ten* and *Channel Four News*, which give a round-up of the news of the day. They might include a mixture of long and short news reports, live interviews with correspondents and sometimes guests. There might be special reports or stand-alone features. On *Channel Four News*, these are delivered in more of a 'magazine' style.

Magazine

These programmes might cover 'on-the-day' news stories, but often include subject matter that relates to political affairs or is topical but not necessarily linked to a particular event. These include programmes such as *Newsnight,* and magazine-style discussion programmes such as *This Week*.

Live programming

These are programmes that go out 'live' and can span a variety of different themes. The BBC's morning news programme, *Breakfast*, from Salford in North West England, goes head-to-head with ITV's *Good Morning Britain*. Both have an informal style and include a news round-up as well as films, guests and other items on light-hearted and entertaining topics designed for early morning viewing.

The BBC's *Victoria Derbyshire* goes out mid-morning and contains a mixture of news, films and non-time-sensitive topics discussed by a panel. Other programmes have a particular slant. Sky's *Murnaghan* and the BBC's *Andrew Marr Show* are political programmes that go out live on a Sunday morning and include high-profile politicians as well as films and reports relating to political events and policy.

Long-form programming/current affairs

This refers to pre-recorded programmes in strands such as *Panorama* and *Dispatches*, and documentaries linked to topical subjects rather than day-to-day news. Examples include Dan Reed's documentary *Three Days of Terror: The Charlie Hebdo Attacks*, which aired on BBC 2, and *Jihadis Next Door*, a Channel Four documentary featuring interviews with Abu Rumaysah, named by some as the masked man in an IS (Daesh) video in early 2016.

Investigative

These often fit into the category of long-form programming and current affairs. They set out to look at a particular topic or reveal previously unknown information, including controversial or sensitive topics. Investigative programmes might be planned over weeks and months and do not relate to on-the-day news. However, they might be tied to certain events such as court cases or anniversaries. These programmes sometimes use undercover reporters and undercover filming, but this would only be sanctioned if there was no other way to get the information. Some topics reported for BBC's *Panorama* and Channel Four's *Dispatches* fit into this category (see also Gio Ulleri p. 245).

TELEVISION NEWS TEAMS

Any news operation, whether it be a pre-recorded programme or a 'rolling' twenty-four-hour news channel, requires a team of people to work together to produce its content. News is very much journalist-led, and any team would usually include staff who are journalists but have different roles, including editors, producers, presenters, correspondents and so on. There is also a number of other production staff, including camera people, floor managers, engineers, directors and technical staff. News programmes and/or channels usually have an overall editor who will drive the news agenda and take the lead in terms of what stories are covered on the day. The editor usually works with at least one senior producer, more on a twenty-four-hour channel. Between them they shape the look and feel of the programmes.

This section looks at some of the main roles involved in creating news programmes – although individual organisations and departments might arrange and describe their staff differently, and distribute tasks and responsibilities in different ways.

News editor

Usually a senior journalist, they have overall editorial control over the programme being produced, and make major decisions about how each of the stories is treated and what content should be shown on air.

FIGURE 17.1
Richard Murrell directing for BBC World News from an outside broadcast control room
at the World Debate in Dhaka, Bangladesh

Courtesy: Richard Murrell

Deputy editor

Deputy editors work with the editor to ensure the programme is produced. They often
assign tasks and manage the editorial team, which includes producers, researchers
and staff working in graphics and editing.

Director

A live television news programme goes on air and is controlled through a studio gallery.
For live programming the director takes charge of technical aspects and is responsible
for what the audience sees on air. They might work with an assistant director or vision
mixer to choose which cameras are used, cue presenters and work with the editor
and output producer to ensure that the programmes look good. The gallery has audio
and visual links to the studio, where a presenter will read a script via autocue. The
studio may have multiple cameras or only one. These might be manual or automatic,
controlled from the gallery (see Chapter 12 for more on studio production).

Producers

Depending on the size and scope of a news organisation, from a major broadcaster to an independent company producing individual programmes, producers
might have very general or very specific responsibilities; this section outlines just
a few of them:

Responsibilities involve:

- *Processes*: writing scripts, headlines and briefs about guests. These will often be done by different story producers but will be overseen by a news presenter or anchor who puts them into their own style. Other staff work as producers assisting correspondents by arranging interviews, filming and supporting the rest of the crew. Producers will also sort out logistics and organise pictures and story straps that appear on screen.

- *Packaging*: producers may work with correspondents, looking out the best pieces of footage or pictures for a news report, while the correspondent writes a track or voice-over to be laid over the pictures. This can be a team effort, either in the newsroom or filed from out in the field with a cameraperson, producer and presenter working together. Smaller organisations or regional bureaus might use multimedia journalists working as a one-man band, shooting, editing and fronting a package entirely by themselves.

- *Outputting*: usually the editor or senior producer will work with a director, co-director or vision mixer and sound person in the gallery, using an electronic running order as a guide for the template of the programme.

Specific producer tasks:

- *Output or senior producer*: responsible for ensuring that live news programmes go on air. While a live programme is on air, they will make decisions on issues such as how long certain sections should last, what order news stories go in and when 'breaking news' and other live elements, such as press conferences, should be introduced.

- *Story producer*: updates scripts and ensures that the most up-to-date information about a news event is available to the editor and presenter. If it is a 'breaking' news event, such as the terrorist attacks in Paris in November 2015, all the producers in a team might work on the story. Otherwise, each producer might be given one story or one 'segment' of a news programme to focus on.

- *Graphics producer*: works with other producers to create the graphics which can be added to the news packages or brought up on screen to explain complex topics.

- *Text producer*: takes responsibility for the story straps that appear on screen. They must be up-to-date and relevant to the stories that are being covered.

- *Other producer roles*: there may also be producers who are dedicated to researching stories (known as researchers); interview producers whose main role is finding contributors for certain stories or on-air items; and chief writers who double-check scripts and stories before they go on air.

- *Planning producers*: focus on future events such as the Olympics, the G20 or major diplomatic meetings, and commission relevant content in relation to these. Planning staff might work days, weeks or even months ahead of transmission.

Reporter/correspondent

Part of a journalist's job might be to report a story. This can involve doing research, filing packages and often doing live 'two ways' with a presenter in the studio. Many journalists do not work in a big newsroom, but 'in the field' on location. Alex Crawford from Sky News and Ian Pannell from the BBC are two such correspondents. Field producers might travel overseas to different places, or be based in a specific region. News reporters might cut a package with their team for the nightly television news, record a radio dispatch and write an analysis piece for a news website.

Video/multimedia journalist

These journalists film sequences, edit packages with correspondents and make their own reports, which may be used online and on social media platforms as well as on television. Often this will also involve writing articles. BBC *Pop-Up* is filmed by video journalists, including Matt Danzico and Benjamin Zand, working as 'one-man bands'.

Social media editor

Tasks for the social media editor might include monitoring social media platforms such as Facebook and Twitter for breaking news, and posting content from their organisation onto different platforms such as YouTube, in order to reach a wider audience and to increase audience engagement with their brand.

Presenter

This is usually a seasoned journalist who may have worked as a correspondent previously. They must be able to write scripts, have a good interview technique with guests, and be able to read from an autocue while listening to both the director and the output producer speaking to them through their earpiece while they are on air.

Video editor

In a big news production there are usually dedicated editing staff who work with producers and correspondents to create individual news reports, known as packages, as well as longer pre-recorded programmes. Sometimes they work in the field, as well as from editing suites at head offices and bureaus.

Other staff

Over and above this list there will be many other staff, including those in 'news-gathering' who manage correspondents and deployments, chiefs who run foreign and regional offices, and people who work in technical teams to ensure that the audience gets to see programmes and news reports. In most cases, at least some of these people will be journalists, which is one way in which television news is different from other types of television production.

Specialisms

Some people come into journalism and television news having studied media production or journalism either at college or university. Some may undertake one of the varieties of journalism traineeships which are available across the industry – both ITV and the BBC offer a graduate scheme. Faisal Islam, Political Editor of Sky News, gained a postgraduate Diploma in Newspaper Journalism from City University in London. He moved to Sky having worked in print media, then for *Channel Four News* for ten years. Others may work in local radio and then move to television. For example, the BBC's Matthew Price started out as a trainee local radio reporter. He worked at BBC Radio Lincolnshire, the BBC in Newcastle, and *Newsround*, the long-running current affairs show for children. He then became a foreign correspondent for BBC Television, based in New York, Jerusalem, Belgrade and most recently, Brussels. By contrast, some people come into journalism from other industries, or having studied subjects such as science, business or finance. The BBC's business editor Simon Jack worked in the City for ten years, including as an economist, before joining the BBC in 2003. Even if you haven't studied a particular subject, there is scope to specialise in areas as diverse as sport, war reporting, politics and economics. Over their careers, journalists may rotate between teams and roles, moving from reporter to anchor, producer to editor, or researcher to production staff. Increasingly, staff are also learning to work in a 'multimedia way' and to create content not just for television but also for online and/or radio. They will also know how to write news articles for websites and social media, and how to edit videos that will work on mobile devices and digital platforms.

The rhythms of news

Regardless of the organisation, a working 'news day' usually involves an editorial meeting at the beginning of a shift. For daily programming or a twenty-four-hour news channel, that involves establishing what the 'story of the day' is. Often journalists will look at what the ratings are saying or what stories are doing well online, using analytical software to mark how popular certain topics have been. They might also find out what content has been made available from the planning team, investigate which correspondents are deployed 'in the field', and discuss how certain stories should be treated. Editorial decisions made in the morning meeting or later meetings throughout the day relate to content and tasks for staff: Do producers need to get a reporter in the field to come up and do a 'live'? Would the story be told better with a guest or would a news package be the best way to inform the audience about what is happening?

In advance of a meeting, the editor might also ask producers to determine what resources are available. This includes looking at content coming in from news agencies such as Reuters, Agence France Press (AFP) and Associated Press (AP). Other tasks undertaken before and after the editorial meeting might include looking at what stories people are sharing on social media sites such as Twitter and Facebook. Producers might also search for good eyewitness content being uploaded from breaking news or hard-to-reach events onto video-sharing platforms such as YouTube. Meetings will continue throughout the day and will determine what correspondents are working on that day and who will be filing content and reports. To determine which stories are interesting and worthy of coverage, journalists refer to news values.

THE NEWS AGENDA

News has an important role in informing people about events and allowing them to construct their own version of reality. Journalists make decisions about what news events should be covered and the stories their audiences should know about. This informs their decisions about who to interview and what 'lines', viewpoints or information to include in a news report or programme segment. Certain stories are considered to have a higher impact or news value, for example, the Tunisia beach attacks in 2015. This was seen as a big news event for a number of reasons. First, it was sudden and involved a large amount of people. Second, pictures were available from agencies shortly afterwards, so it was timely. Third, it also involved a large number of British people. The proximity of a story to a news programme's audience can determine whether it has a high 'news value'. News values may vary over time, but some of the main factors that might influence whether editors and journalists cover certain events and turn them into news stories were identified by two researchers in a classic article in 1965. They include:

Timeliness

Proximity

Prominence

Negativity

Conflict

Human Interest

(Galtung and Ruge 1965)

Key issues affecting the news agenda include:

Ratings and audience feedback

Journalists pay attention to what their audiences like to watch and can, at times, tailor their content accordingly, especially if they get audience feedback. Successful ratings are always welcome, and news organisations can spend a lot of time and resources focusing on audience needs. Ratings are not usually calculated by journalists themselves but by data and analytical teams in areas such as research or publicity. Software is available to help organisations keep track of what their audiences spend time watching. Understanding audience needs and getting their opinions is much easier now, in the age of social media, when correspondents are expected to have a presence on Twitter and actively engage with viewers.

Primary definers

It is through consuming news that audiences find out about important issues, such as the workings of their country's government, politicians, wider society and the economy. In many cases, information about these people and these stories comes from 'élite sources', including politicians, high-profile business people and other powerful individuals in modern society. Such people are known as 'primary definers'. When Mark Zuckerberg, CEO of Facebook, makes an announcement, it is big news because of who he is, even though he does not hold office and is not directly involved in politics. However, journalists also have access to information coming through from wire services and a range of other sources which can also shape what appears in news programming (see below).

Public relations

There is increasing pressure on journalists to work in a multimedia way, at a time when there are more platforms to work on, but fewer resources. This means PR companies that have 'ready-made' content may be more successful at getting that content used by media organisations, including on television news. PR companies can provide guests or footage of events. For public service broadcasters, using this content can be problematic, as news channels and programmes are required to be independent and free from interference or bias.

Government interference and spin

This usually refers to the work of political PR staff and government media managers. These individuals have attempted to manipulate journalists, making content available to media organisations so as to get a favourable outcome for their party. They were known as spin doctors, and for many years went 'unseen'. This changed in the late 1990s and early 2000s, with more high-profile media campaigns and deals over coverage, particularly in the press that is not regulated in the same way as television. Alastair Campbell, who was Prime Minister Tony Blair's Director of Communications and Strategy, is one of the best-known 'spin doctors'. Pippa Norris (2000) warned at the time: 'It may become harder to trust political messages and political messengers if everything in politics is designed for popular appeal.' News management continues to change and journalists are aware of many of the tactics employed by political parties in order to get favourable coverage. However, the relationship between journalists and spin doctors can be complicated as the parties retain big PR machines. Complete objectivity and balanced coverage is harder to achieve than it might initially seem.

The requirement for balance

News in general should strive to be accurate, balanced and impartial, particularly when covering elections and politics (BBC Editorial Guidelines: Ofcom Broadcasting Code Section 5). In the United Kingdom, there is a legal requirement that equal time needs to be given to candidates standing for office. This prompted much discussion in the 2015 General Election about how televised debates should be carried out, since there were many different parties, some of which were devolved. A study carried out by the University of Leeds concluded that having these debates was important, as they performed a valuable civic role in informing the public about the election and main parties (Coleman *et al*. 2015).

Assumptions embedded in language

The language used in news broadcasts can convey a certain message, even when the news programme or channel tries to be balanced. Examples include terms such as 'migrants' vs 'refugees', 'execution' vs 'killing', 'terrorist' vs 'freedom fighter'. A journalist must be mindful of how certain terms may be interpreted by the audience and media critics, even if that is not what is intended.

PRODUCING THE NEWS

Sources

Agencies

Correspondents

The competition

Other news media

Social media

Activists and eyewitnesses

PR sources

Governments

Technologies

Running orders

Wire services

Email

Satellite

BGAN (Broadband Global Area Network) – a global satellite internet network using portable terminals when satellite links and trucks are not possible.

Skype – using a broadband connection and a webcam in a portable studio. The quality of the line is affected by the strength of broadband.

Live streaming – this can be done using applications such as Periscope on a mobile phone.

Chat Apps – these can be used not only for newsgathering but also for dissemination. For example, the BBC used WhatsApp to provide coverage and alerts about Ebola in Africa. CNN is currently using Snapchat Discover as a platform to provide magazine-style content.

Social media platforms – platforms such as Facebook, Twitter and Instagram are used not only to disseminate news but also for social media newsgathering. It is as a way to monitor what people are saying about news and live events, and also to track eyewitnesses or user-generated content (UGC).

Changes and challenges

News consumption

A key challenge for many television news organisations is to remain relevant in a digital world where more people have access to news via mobile. The *Reuters Institute Digital News Report 2015* states that the proportion of audiences who accessed news from smartphones increased from 37 per cent in 2014 to 46 per cent in 2015 across the eighteen countries included in the study. The move away from television news is most pronounced among the under 35s, and only 46 per cent of United Kingdom under 45s now watch a scheduled television bulletin, compared with 56 per cent in 2013 (Newman *et al.* 2015: 9)

Internationalisation

Today audiences have more choice than ten or even five years ago. There are also many more international channels, such as Al Jazeera English, TRT TV (Turkey) and CCTV English (China), which give viewers the opportunity to see news stories covered by different outlets and from a number of different perspectives. Russia Today's coverage of the downing of the MH17 flight in 2014 was very different from the treatment by CNN International, with different sources and points of view put forward.

Digital changes

Television news is competing with social media, and the sharing nature of these platforms is important for the dissemination of news. Results of a 2014 study by the Reuters Institute showed that: 'Around half of Facebook (57 per cent) and Twitter users (50 per cent) say they find, share, or discuss a news story in a given week, but news is considerably less important in other networks' (2014: 70). Stories may also break on social media before they are picked up by news organisations. A pertinent example was the US Airways plane that crashed in the Hudson River and was tweeted by an eyewitness back in January 2009.

More sources and the need for verification

Sources also include the rise of citizen journalists. During the Arab Spring, from 2011, local people captured content from the protests on their smartphones and recorded events in places journalists could not reach. This eyewitnesses' record is referred to as user generated content (UGC). It has value, but there are also risks associated with its use.

As sources proliferate, there is a need for journalists to check the authenticity of UGC and other content they find on social media sites. It is not just a question of identifying *who* has filmed it, but *where* it is alleged to have been filmed and *what* it shows. This is easier to do in some cases than others. For example, journalists who found footage from the 2015 Shoreham air show crash were able to track down the person who filmed it and posted it on YouTube and Twitter. However, there are other situations where it may be impossible to find the original picture or video because so many clips are being shared and republished, such as during the 2016 Taiwan earthquake. In the case of video, this is known as 'scraping'. It is not always possible to speak directly to an eyewitness who has uploaded content, although this is preferred. This is particularly a challenge in conflict zones such as Syria, Iraq and parts of Ukraine where the safety of eyewitnesses could be at risk if a journalist from a media organisation contacts them.

The UGC Hub at the BBC employs journalists who are trained in verification to help check content. They might use software such as Google Image Reversal and TinEye, and look at metadata as a way of establishing whether content is what it claims to be. Investigations can be quite complex. The experts analyse details such as people's clothes, their accents, the weather and even flowers in the landscape to establish whether a video is what it says it is. They may become involved in a forensic process of examining data and cataloguing when the material was first found online (like a librarian). However, a good journalist will still ask the common sense questions they would ask wherever the footage came from, such as 'Why is someone sharing this footage?'

Ideally, no matter what the content shows, if it is UGC and you cannot verify its content, it would go 'on air' with a caveat or a label. However, a report from the Columbia Journalism School shows that this doesn't always happen, and unverified content is frequently transmitted (Wardle *et al.* 2014). There remain challenges around labelling UGC when it is used in news programmes, and news organisations run the risk of not informing their audiences enough and not crediting the copyright holder.

KEY TEXTS

BBC *Editorial Guidelines*, www.bbc.co.uk/editorialguidelines/guidelines.
Galtung, J. and Ruge, M. H. (1965) 'The structure of foreign news: the presentation of the Congo, Cuba and Cyprus Crises in four Norwegian newspapers', *Journal of Peace Research*, 2(1), 64–90, www.zurnalistikos-laboratorija.lt/wp-content/uploads/2014/03/Galtung-Ruge-Structure-of-Foreign-News-1965.pdf.
Norris, P. (2000) *A Virtuous Circle: Political Communications in Post-Industrial Societies*, Cambridge: Cambridge University Press.
Ofcom (2015b) *Broadcasting Code*, London: Ofcom.
Schudson, M. (1989) 'The sociology of news production', *Media, Culture and Society*, 11(3), 263–82.
Wardle, C., Dubberley, S. and Brown, P. (2014). *Amateur Footage: A Global Study of User-Generated Content in TV and Online News Output*, Tow Center for Digital Journalism: A Tow/Knight Report, http://towcenter.org/research/amateur-footage-a-global-study-of-user-generated-content/.

PROFILE

Gio Ulleri: journalist/filmmaker

Giovanni Ulleri is an Emmy-nominated investigative television journalist and producer, who now works as a freelance self-shooting producer/director. Here he discusses his career, his work with concealed cameras, and his recent programmes for the National Geographic's series Drugs Inc.

'After my postgraduate City University Journalism course, I began working as a print journalist and then as an investigative producer at BBC Radio 4 *Face the Facts*. I soon moved to television, working on *World in Action* at Granada TV in the 1990s.

Unlike other current affairs programmes, *World in Action* did not employ specialist reporters who fronted the programmes. The producers and assistant producers were the journalists who conducted the investigations and wrote the scripts. The ethos of *World in Action* was to 'comfort the afflicted – and afflict the comfortable'. I worked on around thirty-five programmes for the series. At the time our biggest rival was BBC's *Panorama*, which was a bit academic and reporter-led with a very traditional top-down approach to current affairs. Our approach was more bottom-up – tabloid in the best tradition of popular tabloid journalism and in your face.

At *World in Action* we were given the time to research. We were told: 'However long it takes – make sure you get it right.' For example, the celebrated 'Birmingham Six' investigation, which revealed that the wrong people had been convicted and imprisoned for Irish Republican Army (IRA) pub bombings in Birmingham, ran for many years and led to a drama documentary, *Who Bombed Birmingham?* in 1990. Now you don't get the time to do proper investigations – current affairs has become an extended news item. During the 1990s, Granada TV had new owners and became more business-oriented. After thirty-five years on our screens, in 1998 *World in Action* was axed. It was replaced with a magazine current affairs series, *Tonight With Trevor Macdonald*.

I became involved in undercover filming using hidden cameras. I made a film on child labour in Morocco, allegedly making clothes for a major high street retailer. For *Welcome to Britain* I went undercover and pretended to be an Italian tourist coming to London for a holiday and exposed dangerous hotels, ticket and taxi touts, and sleazy Soho clubs. It was the highest viewed programme of the year with over 11.5 million viewers – unheard of now with so many more channels.

The first hidden cameras we used were simply a camcorder in a bag with a hole. Then we were able to use specialised cameras developed by a former ITN engineer. Now mini-dv cameras can be concealed in virtually any object or article of clothing http://realscreen.com/2002/08/01/tech-20020801/.

I got to train journalists and members of the public in how to film with hidden cameras. For example, you need to work out where to sit in a room. If the subject is in front of a window the image will be in silhouette.

One of the best uses of hidden cameras was in a film called *The Pits* (1995) for the Channel Four series *Undercover Britain*. It focused on safety in a privately

PROFILE

owned drift mine in South Wales, at a time when the deep mines were closing and miners were losing their jobs. This mine was illegal because the miners were paid on piece work while claiming unemployment benefit. The owners had gone back to the old style of mining, with underground coal skips pulled by pit ponies. They cut corners and conditions were extremely dangerous. Pit props are supposed to be metal and 3 feet apart – these were wooden and 6 feet apart; there should be a special thick skin waterproof cable to pump out the water because of danger of flooding, but a cheaper thin cable was used and miners had been electrocuted. I arranged for a member of NACODS (the trade union for miners who are responsible for safety) to go into the mine with a camera concealed in his sandwich tin. The footage he secured deep inside the mine showed a series of dangerous breaches of health and safety that subsequently led to a prosecution and the closure of the mine. The film won a Royal Television Society award.

The use of hidden cameras is tightly regulated. You always have to provide the network with clear reasons, in writing, why using this method of filming is necessary to secure evidence that would stand up in court.

When I left *World in Action*, I became freelance and worked on series such as ITV's *The Big Story*, Channel Four's *Dispatches* and *Cutting Edge,* and *Kenyon Confronts* for the BBC. I also produced the UK sequences for Michael Moore's Oscar-nominated documentary, *Sicko* (2007).

For the last ten years I've filmed my own programmes using my own equipment. I used to film with a Sony PD150, which uses cassette tapes, then I learnt to use a bigger camera, so now I use a Sony PMW 300 k1, recording on memory cards. I use radio mics for the interviewees and there's a top shotgun mic on the camera. The viewfinder also shows the input from the two mics, so I can make adjustments to the balance if necessary. My camerawork has been inspired by watching and working with *World in Action*'s legendary cameraman, George Jesse Turner.

Recently I've been working for the independent production company Wall to Wall – now owned by Warner Brothers – on a series for the National Geographic channel on the illegal drugs trade. *Drugs Inc* has run for eight series and I've made three films for them. Each of the programmes is shot in cities around the United States, focusing on the drug that affects that particular city. For example, my film *The High Wire* was about heroin in Baltimore, famous for the television series *The Wire*.

Drugs Inc is very well known and followed by all sides – police, addicts and the dealers themselves – which helps in building up contacts. As filmmakers we wanted to show how a drug affects the city from every angle. We want to show how the police try to arrest the dealers. In Baltimore we had excellent location producers (fixers), with excellent contacts in the criminal world, who made contact with the dealers. They can go to places where we as white middle-class television producers can't. The police won't go into some of the more dangerous estates in Baltimore (known as the 'projects'), and I was told that a white man shouldn't go. But I was OK because I was accompanied by our fixers who had gained the trust of the dealers. I filmed one crew cutting up a large two-kilo bag of heroin into small packages ready to sell.

The location producers had identified a derelict building which overlooked a particular corner well known for deals, and we followed the activity on that corner. Drug dealing is a young guy's business. Each of the gangs controls its own corner, and the dealers see themselves as businessmen. They're very wary but once we gained their trust they spoke freely about their enterprise – although we disguised their identities. They argued that heroin is good business because users, called 'fiends', get hooked, so come back for more. One shocking thing they told me was that they were unconcerned if someone died of an overdose. In fact, they said it was 'good for business' as it showed that their batch was stronger than the competition, and that brought more 'fiends'. The law enforcement officers know about the gangs but the problem is so large that when one gang's corner is closed down, another one opens up.

After completing *The High Wire* I went on to make a film about MDMA (methylenedioxymethamphetamine; 'ecstasy') in Miami and another about marijuana dealing in Boston, home of Harvard and MIT, where we interviewed college student drug dealers paying their student fees through dealing.

I love my work; in what other job would you meet drug dealers one minute and world leaders the next?'

PROFILE

Part 4

Training and industry contexts

Training, education and getting into the industry

TRAINING AND GETTING INTO THE INDUSTRY

There are many routes to working in the media industries. A single individual can purchase the necessary equipment to create online content or offer their services at low cost to charities or campaigning groups. At the other extreme, high-end television production draws on complex technology, employs large crews and requires a wide range of sophisticated skills and specialist know-how. And there are many different set-ups in-between.

Within this fluid landscape, the days are long gone when young people could begin from scratch and simply learn on the job, gradually building up experience over time. Permanent jobs, with the opportunity of on-the-job training and the prospect of moving up the employment ladder, are increasingly rare. For those starting out, some apprenticeships and traineeships are available (at the BBC 'apprenticeships' are for those without a degree, while 'traineeships' are for graduates, covering expert areas including business and legal). Independent companies can claim tax credits to support apprentices, but most find it difficult to find the funds, which means that not many are available. 'It's a casualised, freelance world', said one producer, 'it doesn't suit if you want a stable life.' Consequently, most jobs advertised on websites such as 'The Unit List' or the BBC's 'Vacancy Search' expect some prior training and experience.

Today, it is universities and colleges that play a major role in training television practitioners and providing their first experience of professional work. Job placements are an important component of every course. Most television and media courses have close links to the industry, and many experienced professionals take up university posts.

FIGURE 18.1
Filming with Solent Productions at the Glastonbury Music Festival 2015

Courtesy: Solent Productions

At the same time, there has been a huge expansion in less formal training opportunities for those just starting out, as well as those who want to upgrade their skills.
This is also the age of the self-taught. Online tutorials abound, some created by
equipment manufacturers such as Avid whose editing systems are used across
the industry, others by organisations such as the BBC Academy, which offer learning
resources that can be easily accessed. An online search will find masterclasses by
top scriptwriters, talks by designers and costume experts, advice from experienced
cinematographers and much more. In addition, it is possible to enrol on short
courses where established professionals share their skills. These are run by
organisations such as the British Academy for Film and Televsion Arts (BAFTA) and
many others around the United Kingdom, including Creative England and Creative
Wales which promote training and jobs in the nations and regions. In addition, a
number of independent training projects run longer courses to professional standards
(see list below).

In 1992, Skillset was launched as the industry training organisation (ITO) for the broadcasting, film and video industries. It was managed and funded by representatives of
the independent producers, advertisers, broadcasters and trade unions. Now it has
become Creative Skillset, with a much broader remit across the creative industries,
but it remains the key organisation in the promotion of television training provision,

pointing out that in-work training is increasingly necessary. Many media companies are reporting a shortage of skills in specialist areas, partly because technological developments follow each other so rapidly. 'The pace of change in jobs out-paces education to catch up', Creative Skillset's Chief Executive, Dinah Caine, has pointed out (in a talk to the Westminster Media Forum 2016). The organisation carries out regular research into training needs and provision, and builds links between the industry and training providers, including colleges and universities. It has also published 'best practice' models for internships and apprenticeships http://creativeskillset.org/assets/0000/6234/Guidelines_for_employers_offering_work_placements_in_the_Creative_Industries.pdf.

This section will explore in greater detail the relationship between training, education and getting into the industry. We give some case studies, with examples of the transition between training and employment, and on p. 226 we list some relevant contacts and organisations which provide training.

The weakening of the boundaries between educational institutions and the industry has significant advantages, as many universities and colleges have become involved in production to a professional standard. Some of these arrangements may be formal, like the agreement between Southampton Solent and the BBC regarding the Glastonbury Festival (see below). Others may be made on an ad hoc basis. A university may take on a commission to make public service or corporate videos, which they may partly fund themselves or which may be wholly paid for by their sponsors. There may be opportunities for students to back up or augment professional crews when the event is very large, or spread over a considerable space. In 2012, the Olympic Broadcasting Association put out a call for student volunteers to work on the filming of the London Olympics. It set up a training day and selected a thousand suitable candidates from a number of universities.

In these different ways many students find themselves working on broadcast or online professional material while still at university. Many find that, through contacts built up by their university, including with ex-students who have now become commissioners or run independent companies, they can take the first steps towards a job that may lead to the career they are seeking. At the very least, valuable contacts can be made, and students have access to facilities to produce a showreel of their work that will be useful in their hunt for jobs.

Despite the availability of training to professional standards, many professionals regret the fact that access to the industry still depends heavily on 'who you know'. There are still major issues concerning diversity, and a need to broaden the basis of recruitment (see Chapter 19). However, as we will demonstrate, there are more opportunities than ever before to *get to know* the right people. In today's shifting landscape, while employment is less secure, there is space to make your own opportunities. Below, our case studies illustrate some of these links between education, training and the industry.

REDBALLOON AND SOLENT PRODUCTIONS

A number of UK universities have evolved schemes to form a bridge between the academic and professional worlds, with initiatives such as Fuse TV, a YouTube channel run by Manchester University's Students' Union. Southampton Solent University and Bournemouth University have both set up production units through which students can work on professional commissions. At Bournemouth's RedBalloon Productions students work alongside professional freelancers (often BU graduates) and an experienced full-time producer. Solent's Solent Productions does not employ outsiders, but gives one-year contracts to ex-students to act as full-time production managers.

Both companies pay the students who work on their commissions, and both serve local and regional clients. Under its producer, Stephanie Farmer, RedBalloon's reputation brings in numerous corporate clients, including Dorset Police, the National Trust, Nuffield Health and many others. Students are involved in every part of the production where possible, including meetings with clients, creative concepts and working to client briefs and budgets.

At Southampton Solent University, Tony Steyger, who had previously been a producer at ITV Meridian and also in the BBC's Community Programme Unit, launched Solent Productions in 2007 to provide students with professional work experience, and to obtain Skillset accreditation. The company set up Solent TV as an online channel serving Southampton www.solenttv.co.uk. The channel screens three new videos a week and is followed by 7,500 people, mostly local viewers. The project can attract funding to try out new developments such as 4K web broadcasting, and it has a commissioning budget. Students pitch to the graduate producers. If accepted, they get £100 to make their videos, and the best are screened. Tony Steyger says that Solent Productions is about work experience, and also about research and innovation. It generates research on how to attract a new audience and how the audience consumes the output.

The company also specialises in outside broadcasts. It owns two fully equipped OB vehicles, and can do multicamera shoots with up to nine camera operators. In particular, students work with the annual Glastonbury Music Festival in partnership with the BBC. The BBC broadcasts the festival live, and Solent records it for the festival archive and for distribution to news feeds around the world. This experience has generated a subject specialism in OBs for television students. Graduates who work at Solent Productions are in a good position to get a job as they are accustomed to working with the latest kit (see Figure 7.2).

RedBalloon continues to engage with outside events. In 2015 the unit was commissioned by the Guardian Edinburgh International Television Festival to provide video recording of all the speaker sessions at the three-day event. This included four or five events a day in each of five venues, creating over sixty-five web videos. In addition, students filmed and live-streamed the prestigious James McTaggart

Lecture, given by Armando Iannucci, as well as the Alternative MacTaggart with Nicola Sturgeon, First Minister of Scotland. Twenty students and seven members of staff worked on this demanding project.

In 2015, the unit worked with Salisbury Cathedral and their design agency Haley Sharpe on a project that celebrates the 800th anniversary of Magna Carta. The Cathedral has one of the four original thirteenth-century documents and commissioned RedBalloon to create all the screen media for its permanent exhibition. This included an animated story of King John, an 'immersive' film, using archive footage and graphic techniques, to illustrate historic struggles for human rights in the spirit of the Charter. They also installed a touchscreen interactive globe, made two more web films and created a mobile phone app for the Cathedral. The commission provided paid work experience for over sixty students and graduates across all the projects. In March 2016, RedBalloon was awarded two Royal Television Society (Southern) Professional Awards for their portfolio of work, for 'Best Non-Broadcast' and 'Best Post-Production'. Over 250,000 visitors a year visit the exhibition.

FIGURE 18.2
Young visitors enjoying the interactive globe at Salisbury Cathedral's Magna Carta exhibition

Courtesy: RedBalloon Productions

RedBalloon's Executive Producer and Director Stephanie Farmer writes:

> Work experience is crucial. I got my first job through my work placement and it's still true today – if not even more important. We know that those students who have engaged with RedBalloon during their time here get interviews. They get a foot in the door, and they have the confidence to say 'I can do that'. That's invaluable to employers. It also develops networking and leads to further opportunities. For our clients it means we can provide exceptionally high-quality professional output. Quality is assured by the exec team and the combination of professional and student input works really well.
>
> Students often come back and thank me for giving them their first professional job and it's been a pleasure to help them on their career paths. Whatever university you are at – make the most of the opportunities on offer.

CHAPTER 19

Opening up the industry: diversity and access

The 2011 British Census showed that over 40 per cent of Londoners are non-white. Yet, the 2012 Employment Census published by Skillset in July 2013 showed that ethnic minority representation across the creative industries has fallen in recent years to just 5.4 per cent of the total workforce. At senior levels the numbers are far lower. The absence of diversity in the creative sector is not only bad for our society but is also bad for business, which thrives on having a diversity of ideas and opinions.

Creative Access, http://creativeaccess.org.uk/about-us/history

DIVERSITY AND ACCESS

Employment in the creative media, including television, has long been dispropor-tionately male, white and middle-class. Women, people from BAME communities, white working-class people and people with disabilities have been in the minority both behind the camera and on the screen. In recent years, changing attitudes, equal opportunities legislation and a greater public awareness mean that television organisations such as the BBC, Channel Four and Sky have declared their commit-ment to changing that situation. For many who are part of those under-represented groups, this is a continuation of a campaign for access and wider representation which has been running for many decades.

In the early years of television, recruiting was through contacts, and by and large training was on the job through forms of informal apprenticeship and patronage. This excluded huge swathes of the population. Even though the companies that made up the ITV network were regionally based and drew on regional talent, the barriers to entry were high, and the television industry seemed impenetrable to outsiders. Although the BBC organised formal training for programme directors and the technical grades, it also ran an exclusive fast-track training scheme for high-flyers. Many of these young graduates, almost all Oxbridge-educated and almost exclusively male and white, would become future Controllers of Programmes and Directors General. Despite increasingly vocal campaigns, there was a huge gender imbalance and almost no ethnic diversity.

The 1970s was a radical decade when this situation began to be challenged. The establishment of 'access' programming meant that ordinary people from a range of backgrounds, with a range of accents, gained a small space on the airwaves. At the BBC, the Community Programme Unit, set up in 1972, facilitated programmes by local groups with a case to argue, and there was a move across the ITV network to schedule 'access slots' to which non-professionals could contribute on their own terms (Dowmunt 2000). Before the days of YouTube and Facebook this was a remarkable innovation, but it did not affect the overall structure of professional employment.

The 1970s saw some vigorous campaigning by members of under-represented groups, including women, BAME communities and those based in the UK regions and nations. The campaigns had some success when Channel Four was set up in 1982, as a non-profit-making, publicly owned channel, funded by a levy on ITV (Brown 2007). Unlike the BBC and ITV, the channel did not make its own programmes, but commissioned independent companies, and it was given a specific remit to represent under-represented groups. The landscape of UK television began to change as new production companies were set up, including many run by women and people from BAME communities, to make programmes for the channel. Jeremy Isaacs, the channel's first chief executive, gave over the main current affairs slot to two women-only companies, and launched magazine programmes for the black and Asian communities (Isaacs 1989). In addition the channel funded a number of independent, locally based 'workshops', many of which organised their own forms of small-scale training. Women filmmakers, in particular, felt there should be training especially for them, where technologically confident men would not dominate. A number of BAME workshops and independent production companies were launched, including Sankofa and Black Audio – many of whose films, such as Black Audio's *Handsworth Songs* (1986), made for *The Eleventh Hour*, have become classics of documentary history.

But in the increasingly commercial environment, Channel Four could not sustain the minority commitments of its early days. When its funding changed in 1996 and it was required to sell its own advertising, the pressure to attract large audiences increased. Many of the independent companies set up in the 1980s collapsed. Others became larger and more mainstream. The channel changed its tone as the extraordinary range of material, which had characterised its early years, began to disappear. At the BBC, the Community Programme Unit became Community and Disability Programmes in the early 1990s but was closed down in 2002. Despite lip-service, the arrival of the multichannel landscape and the competitive atmosphere of the 2000s meant that commitment to minority audiences, diversity and access became less important across the industry.

One of the original aims of Skillset, when it was established in the early 1990s, had been to combat that trend, to support training in the growing independent sector, to widen access to skills and employment, and to 'break the mould of an exclusively white, male orientated industry' (Gates 1995: 52). The organisation has continued to publish regular reports on employment and diversity, and to pressure for changes within the industry, including the shocking census in 2012 which revealed that the number of BAME people working in the UK television industries had actually declined by 30 per cent.

However, by 2015, partly in response to high-profile campaigners such as Lenny Henry, all the UK channels have signed up to a code of practice on diversity. In 2015, Channel Four published a *360° Diversity Charter*, which sets targets for in-house employment for people from BAME backgrounds, people with disabilities, gender equality and people from the LGBT communities. Since the entire channel's programmes are made by independent companies, commissioning is particularly important. The channel has set up a 'diversity database' to source talent and 'start the diversity dialogue at the beginning of the commissioning process not the end' (Channel 4 2015: 3).

In particular, the *Charter* notes the lack of diverse talent in senior leadership roles, and many other commentators have noted that while discussions of diversity tend to focus on new entrants, new entrants need role models. Those in positions of power can act as gatekeepers and can make a significant difference.

A number of organisations promote diversity within the television industry. These include:

> *The Creative Diversity Network* (CDN) which offers awards (see MAMA below) and runs an industry-wide monitoring system, the 'Diamond' project. 'Diamond will allow us to answer the key questions "Who's on TV?" and "Who makes TV?" with greater confidence and precision than ever before.'
>
> http://creativediversitynetwork.com/news/
> diamond-is-coming-are-you-ready/.

> *Creative Access*: a charity which acts as an agency for paid internships for young people of graduate (or equivalent) standard from under-represented black, Asian and other non-white ethnic backgrounds. 'We aim to improve their chances of securing full-time jobs and, in the longer term, increase diversity and address the imbalance in the sector.'
>
> http://creativeaccess.org.uk/

RELEVANT DOCUMENTS

BBC (2016) *Diversity Strategy*
www.bbc.co.uk/diversity

Channel Four (2015) 360° *Diversity Charter*
www.channel4.com/media/documents/corporate/diversitycharter/Channel4360
DiversityCharterFINAL.pdf

Creative Skillset (2012) *Employment Census of the Creative Media Industries*
http://creativeskillset.org/assets/0000/5070/2012_Employment_Census_of_the_
Creative_Media_Industries.pdf

MAMA YOUTH PROJECT

In contrast to the university experience, the MAMA Youth Project is an independent programme that provides training to a professional level for eighteen to twenty-five-year olds from under-represented groups, especially people from BAME backgrounds and others who have had less access to opportunities.

MAMA is a charity part-funded by the industry. Sponsors include Sky, the BBC, Endemol/Shine and Procam, a service company with extensive contacts across the industry. Like the universities, the charity has its own production company, Licklemor Productions, through which trainees produce a youth magazine show on Sky 1. *What's Up TV* is described as a 'culture arts and lifestyle show that is breaking down the negative image and stereotyping of youth culture in the UK'. Six thirty-minute episodes are produced from scratch over the thirteen weeks of the course www.whatsuptv.co.uk/#!about/cee5.

Twice a year twenty-four students are enrolled on a thirteen-week course, mainly funded by the BBC in spring and Sky in the autumn. The courses are strongly oriented to professional production and culminate in the production of *What's Up TV.* The charismatic founder of MAMA Youth, Bob Clarke argues that 'young people, especially people of colour, are part of mainstream society and therefore a show like *What's Up TV* needs to be on a mainstream channel'. For the last two years *What's Up TV* has run on Sky 1 and has been nominated for a Creative Diversity Network award.

Each of the trainees is recruited to a specialism: two on camera, two on sound, three editors, fifteen researchers, one production coordinator and one production manager. After producing *What's Up TV*, trainees go on to work placements at one of the sponsoring organisations. They begin at entry level but, as Bob Clarke points out, this gives them the opportunity to make contacts. They frequently get involved in production work, go out on shoots and generally get to know a work environment. The trainees must apply for their placements, and the project will only recommend those who are up to scratch.

During the preparation for *What's Up TV* the researchers come up with ideas for items. They are organised in four teams: comedy, arts and events, music and current affairs. When an item is green-lit they must then secure the contributors and the locations.

The researchers do all the necessary paperwork, both at the beginning of the production (risk assessments, budgets etc.) and at the end (copyright checks, location agreements etc.). The company employs one full-time producer (currently an ex-trainee) and an associate producer. There is a professional director present during the filming, but the trainee whose idea it is acts as item producer and has full responsibility. They also supervise the editing. 'We don't let up on the pressure', says Clarke. 'They've never worked so hard in their lives.'

FIGURE 19.1
Trainees at MAMA Youth filming for *What's Up* Season 9

Photograph: Lyle Ashun. Courtesy: Licklemor Productions

PROFILE

Bob Clarke: Executive Producer, MAMA Youth Project

Director of the project, Bob Clarke, is its driving force. Here he tells his story:

'At school we were all told we would make nothing of our lives. So when I left school I joined the Army. Eventually I joined the Territorial Army.

My day job was working in the warehouse at a video duplication company, Humphries Video Services (HVS). One day I was asked to take a parcel to the technical area and I saw a dark room all lit up with fairy lights and many monitors and televisions. It was like Santa's grotto! I love Christmas and thought that working there would be like Christmas every day, so I immediately asked for a job. My boss laughed as I had no qualifications but I think he admired my cheek. He said I could work there in the mornings as a trial, and back to the warehouse in the afternoon. Two months later I was offered a full-time position as a video tape (VT) operator, working with one-inch and two-inch tapes. It was a life-changing moment. I was so excited I ran the five-mile journey home like Forrest Gump.

I learnt to be a VT operator and eventually became shift leader. I was put above those with better qualifications because I worked so hard and wanted to take full advantage of the opportunity. After two years I became a shop steward for the trade union, ACTT. At HVS I began to do basic machine-to-machine editing. This directed my thoughts and my goal to become an editor. HVS didn't have edit suites so I applied as a VT operator at Services Sound and Vision Corporation (SSVC). I got the job and became an editor within a year.

In the late 1990s, I bought some Avid non-linear editing equipment and set up an editing company in Soho. As far as I'm aware, I may have been the only black-led independent post-production facility at that or any other time. Then, in 2005, after twenty years in the business, a colleague commented that there were not enough black people in the industry. It really made me think, as someone had said the same thing on the day I'd started twenty years earlier. I wanted to help address this lack of inclusion. After all, I'd managed to maintain a successful career without qualifications and no network at the beginning. By then I'd sold the editing business and set up MAMA Productions (unofficially MAMA stands for Me And My Avid), so I thought if I get young people from the same background as me and help them to make a programme to the disciplines of broadcasting, this will give them real practical experience. They would be an immediate asset as a new entrant to a company. I also included young people from the white working-class, because they were under-represented too.

So I advertised and recruited sixteen young people. I funded the production of two one-hour DVDs of *What's Up London*, a magazine show produced to the disciplines of broadcast television. I paid for thousands of DVDs to be

duplicated and distributed. On completion of the DVD productions, fourteen out of the sixteen trainees got jobs. That's when I realised I could make a difference to young lives and help change the face of our industry. I'd decided to produce a DVD rather than try to get the show commissioned by a broadcaster because I knew it would be seen as 'niche', with a large number of young people and people of colour in front of the camera.

In 2009, the Community Channel asked to screen the show and I gave it to them free as this saved me the cost of duplication and distribution. But I continued to be the main funder of the charity, which meant remortgaging my house twice and maxing out on all my credit cards. This personal cost to me and my family was now running at over £300,000. I was continuing to work night shifts editing, and was at the charity during the day. I was surviving on four hours sleep a night!

Then, in 2010, Sophie Turner Long, MD of Sky News and Entertainment, saw *What's Up* at an awareness event at BAFTA and was very impressed. She had already been supporting the charity through Sky, with some financial and pro bono support, because of her strong belief in diverse talent. But after seeing the high production value of what the young people were producing, she asked to acquire the show for Sky 3 (which later became Pick TV). It did so well it's now in its fourth season on Sky 1.

In 2009, MAMA Youth was recognised by the Council of Europe as a top company for diversity – on a level with the BBC and Channel Four. And the Creative Diversity Network (CDN) gave me a special recognition award. This recognition meant a lot to me as I felt sure it would bring financial support for the charity and relieve me of that burden. Unfortunately, I was wrong. I still continued to work nights editing, while training young people during the day with no pay or expenses. But in 2011, Sophie Turner Long arranged for Sky to sign a three-year contract with the charity to fund one training course per year, and in 2013 she helped the BBC to come on board to fund the second course. At last, I could receive a salary and be at the charity full-time – although I knew I would never see a return on the £350,000 I'd put into it. I've got my family into great debt, from which I am still suffering – as well as developing high blood pressure. But at least I could now stop working night and day. This was a major goal in my personal ambition for the MAMA Youth Project.

It has been quite a journey and is still continuing. MAMA Youth has a reputation within the television industry because of our unique style of training. Currently 99 per cent of our trainees get their first paid placement, and 82 per cent are still employed. Now we have over ten years' worth of alumni, so by the end of 2016, we will create the MAMA Youth Talent Pool, which will be made up of selected talent trained by MAMA Youth since 2005.

MAMA Youth trainees are competing for jobs against others who have networks and contacts. My aim is to level the playing field.'

PROFILE

GETTING INTO THE INDUSTRY

Jonny Yapi is a graduate of the MAMA Youth Project. Here he tells his story: how he got established in the industry through work experience and training projects.

PROFILE

Jonny Yapi – my story

'I was raised in Walthamstow, a rough area in East London, where I grew up in a council flat on an estate. My time in secondary school was not the greatest. I was always the joker in the class and the prankster, and I had a very short temper, so I always got myself into trouble. At Rushcroft School I got into a lot of fights, so they didn't want me in their school. I then attended Norlington School for boys, which was notorious for bad behaviour. My parents moved away from the area so I stayed with my sister who was still living in Walthamstow. By then I was well behaved in school and tried to avoid trouble. But outside school I had a confrontation with a pupil from a different school while still in my school uniform. He was pushing me for a reaction because he knew my reputation. I reacted and was permanently excluded. So I ended up leaving school before I had the chance to do my GCSEs.

Since I was chucked out I had to attend a Pupil Referral Unit where all the naughty kids go. I didn't know anyone and there were kids who were more badly behaved than me. When I finished my time there, the company Connections recommended me to a place called First Rung where I gained the qualifications I did not receive in school. I got Employability, Customer Service, Maths, English and Information and Communications Technology (ICT). The course included one month work experience and I was offered a place at a recycling company. That was when I realised my life really needed to change. I knew I was not destined for that sort of life – with all due respect to people who work in recycling. I had ambitions, and working in recycling was not one of them. One of my tutors, Pat Leacock, had been in the entertainment industry and had won a MOBO award for best jazz album. He knew where my passion lay and introduced me to a man called Bob Clarke who ran the MAMA Youth Project.

I was accepted by the MAMA project and knew I was never going to look back. I had nothing to lose and was never going to let this opportunity go. We worked on a show called *What's Up*, an urban youth culture magazine show that came on the channel PickTV (formerly Sky 3). I was the youngest in the group, just turned seventeen at the time. Others had university degrees and other

PROFILE

experiences, but I had literally no experience of work. But I didn't feel threatened because they were doing the same job as me. My role was junior researcher and I organised three shoots. I did the call sheets for them, contacted every location we needed, and sorted out the contributors. This experience was priceless for me. I was noticed because I was young and got invited to events such as the CDN Awards. I was interviewed by the BBC about my experiences and parts of my interview were shown on VT at the ceremony. It was amazing. Then I was sponsored by Sky. Sky is an important partner with MAMA Youth in their objective of helping people like me. My mentors, Tamara Kaye and Eleanor Bailey, helped me get six weeks' work experience at a company called Magnum Media where I worked on *Duck Quacks Don't Echo*. While I was there I did some secret work for Freshwater Films as they were in the same building. It paid off. Freshwater offered me two weeks' work experience with them, on *Ross Kemp: Extreme World Series 3*. I had a great time because I'd always watched the shows. Then they offered me a contract for four months. I was credited for three episodes as a junior researcher. The executive producer, Matt Bennett, then suggested I get experience as a runner at a post-production house. In all honesty I didn't enjoy my time there. I didn't want to be an editor so it was purely for experience. Then my mentor from Sky asked me to do the casting for their new Sky Ride advert. It was the first time I had ever done anything like that, so it was an exciting experience. When I finished I wanted to stay at Sky, so I used my contacts and got work experience for a couple of weeks on *Soccer AM*, a Saturday morning live football show on Sky 1. I was hungry for more experience and once again used my powerful contacts in Sky to get a job as a runner at the Isle of Wight festival with CC-Lab. I had one of the best times of my life and got to work very hard but play harder!

When I came home I got odd day jobs here and there, but needed some stability. I was struggling for money and wondering whether I needed to leave the industry. Not working for a few months really knocked my confidence and I was suffering from a minor case of depression. So I turned to my roots at the MAMA Youth Project and they referred me to a scheme called The Hatch at the Shine Group. I was accepted, which was a blessing for me. Part of The Hatch was to complete BBC Academy training, alongside the youth marketing agency Livity. I was working on briefs for Google and Cancer Research, and pitching to both companies. Finally I went back to *What's Up*, which was also part of that contract. I already knew the process and how to go about sorting out shoots, and I got to do a lot of self-shooting. One of my colleagues referred me to a company who were covering the MOBO awards, because they were looking for someone to help the female celebrities up and down the stairs. As you can imagine I was very excited by this. Part of the scheme was to get work experience, so I went to Woodcut Media, based in Eastleigh, Hampshire.

PROFILE

The Shine Group said commuting from London cost too much, but Derren Lawford, Creative Director of Woodcut, urged me to sign up to Creative Access because Woodcut Media wanted me to apply for an internship role. I was accepted and moved to Southampton for the job, initially for six months. I am enjoying my time here very much and have had countless work and life experiences because I'd never moved away from home before.

While I've been at Woodcut Media, Sky contacted me again to be interviewed as part of the Sky Academy campaign. I represented the television sector in the advertisements and newspapers. This has been brilliant exposure for me as I keep going forward in my career. My long-term aim is to be a development producer as I'm good at developing ideas and would love to see an idea I had developed all the way through to being broadcast.'

TRAINING AND OPPORTUNITIES: A LIST OF USEFUL REFERENCES

Online tutorials

Avid
The manufacturer of editing systems offers a range of online tutorials.
www.avid.com/education/training-resources

BAFTA Guru
From the British Academy for Film and Television Arts (BAFTA), BAFTA Guru contains advice from top professionals across the industry.
guru.bafta.org/welcome-to-bafta-guru

BBC Academy
The BBC's online training covers a wide range of topics on every aspect of production, from commissioning through to delivery.
www.bbc.co.uk/academy

The Royal Television Society (RTS)
RTS organises masterclasses with industry professionals, which are available online.
rts.org.uk/education-training/rts-masterclasses

Short courses

BAFTA Guru Pro
Short courses for those with six months to two years' paid professional experience.
guru.bafta.org/live/pros

Frontline Club, London.
Regular training workshops on all aspects of production, especially in relation to journalism.
www.frontlineclub.com/tag/training-2/

Open City Docs
A two-week Easter film school related to documentary filmmaking. This is linked to an annual documentary festival, for which films produced on the course may be selected.
http://opencitylondon.com/courses#current-courses

Royal Television Society (RTS)
The RTS's website includes useful links to entry-level training opportunities.
https://rts.org.uk/education-training/entry-level-training

Soho Editors
This post-production agency runs short courses with advanced professional training in all aspects of post-production and makes free tutorials available online.
https://sohoeditors.com/search/training
https://sohoeditors.com/training-pages/free-final-cut-pro-x-davinci-resolve-12-tutorials

CHAPTER 20

Hannah's diary

To give an example of the experience of transition from university to employment in the television industry, Hannah Mellows kept a diary of her experiences.

Hannah studied for a foundation degree (FDA) in Digital Media Practice at the BRIT School in London, then graduated in Global Media Practice from Bournemouth University in 2015.

HANNAH'S DIARY: APRIL–NOVEMBER 2015

April 2015: Tinderflint Productions

I got my first proper paid job while I was still at university, working as a runner for Tinderflint Productions, who needed extra help for a video they were making. The founders of the company had both studied at BU, and had given a talk at a BU event.

Tinderflint had a commission to produce an online video for a company which create live promotional events. This one was to launch a new Adidas brand of multicoloured trainers. The location was Hackney Reservoir – a big venue used for all kinds of events: boating clubs, weddings, as well as film locations. The Adidas event was a spectacular light show, with a DJ, installations, digital advertising screens and 'shoe art' – shoes hanging from fixtures, a rainbow of shoes on a table, clothing floating on buoys on the reservoir, smoke machines and drones. There was lots of footage, including material from the drones – all for a 1.5-minute video www. youtube.com/watch?v=25yU0VktpXA. I acted as camera assistant, following the two cinematographers with lenses, batteries and cards.

We all had to wear black – no sports attire from other brands! We were given free shoes from Adidas, but most of us arrived in rival sports brands and had to take them off and walk around in our socks before getting shoes from the Adidas people. We had to keep the clients happy!

The event finished at 10pm and the deadline for the video was 9am the following morning. That meant an overnight edit. My job was of utmost importance. It involved keeping track of SD cards and getting data to the editor working on site. It was a small crew: director/producer, production coordinator, two cinematographers, an editor and a runner. Although this was online content, not for TV, the production values were very much the same as TV commercials. It was very high quality.

This was my first proper paid running job. But I'd had lots of experience doing similar work during my time as a student.

Summer 2015: Jurassica – ongoing

Jurassica is an attraction theme park/museum built in a former quarry on the Isle of Portland, on Dorset's Jurassic coast. I became involved with a voluntary project to create online documentary content about it, working for project coordinator Alison Smith, an ex-BU student I'd met while at uni. I filmed promotional events: the Annual Jurassic Coast meet-up, Meet the Sea Monsters event, the BU Festival of learning. Producing my own stuff, doing the filming and editing, has been great to keep up technical skills: keeping the creative juices flowing and meeting interesting people. It's nice to give back to the community. My family is from this part of the country and fossil hunting was a big part of my childhood, so it's really great to revisit it and get involved.

But balancing voluntary with paid work can get tough. I didn't expect to be lucky enough to land a full-time job so soon after finishing university, so I haven't been able to dedicate as much time to Jurassica as I would have hoped. But I'm very committed to it and passionate about the progress of the project.

July 2015: Woodcut Media

In July I got a two-week placement with Woodcut Media, based in Eastleigh. I'd met the CEO of the company at a BU event. This was unpaid, but I was reimbursed for travel expenses.

My work included tracking down archive footage, location hunting, researching stories and contacting interviewees – including Lord Alf Dubs for *Combat Trains* on the History Channel. In addition I did some transcribing and logging of footage. It was a great atmosphere: always very busy but chilled. Everyone was lovely and hardworking. The whole team stayed late on a Friday night to sort out loads of paperwork before a well-deserved evening out to celebrate a birthday, the completion of a job and my last day!

August to October 2015: Chalkboard TV

I met Jonny Yapi at Woodcut, who had previously worked at Chalkboard TV. Chalkboard is an independent production company that has made some substantial factual entertainment programmes: *The Office Christmas Party* for ITV and *Troll Hunters* for BBC3, as well as developing new game show formats.

Jonny received a message from Chalkboard's production manager about a two-day production assistant job coming up, so Jonny recommended me. I sent my CV through. Two days later I received a call from the director of the programme to explain about the shoot, and we met in a coffee shop in Dalston for an interview, which was fairly relaxed. The programme was called *Sex Toy Secrets*, a series of short docs for Channel Four Shorts Online, following an online retailer called Bondara www.channel4.com/programmes/sex-toy-secrets/episode-guide.

The initial shoot was a two-day trip to Amsterdam (we nearly missed the plane!) where we followed the MD of Bondara on his quest to find the most exciting new sex toys. It was all very ridiculous. Similar to my previous work, it was a small crew (just me and the director) so I was really able to get stuck in and learn lots. I shot some footage on a Canon C300, and got to pick the director's brain about his experience in television. It was tricky subject matter – hard not to laugh. I didn't expect one of my first jobs in television to be filming dildos, but it was surprising how quickly I became desensitised to it all. Everyone was very open-minded and relaxed about it, and the end product was light-hearted and fun – kind of like *The Office* in its comedic style. But it also opened up lots of questions about our attitude towards things like this. It was an exhausting two days of filming and travelling, but extremely worthwhile and a great start to my time at Chalkboard, plus I was lucky enough to see a new city and stay in a really nice hotel!

The director told me about a sensitive long-term production that Chalkboard were producing for Sky 1 dealing with issues around death and dying. He mentioned that they could do with an extra hand, so after contacting the production manager, they had me in for a few weeks to transcribe some interviews and log some actuality footage. I also assisted with sourcing potential contributors, setting up shoots, and carried out general running duties in the office – admin, sourcing props and so on. This subject matter was of course completely different from *Sex Toy Secrets*, though both were similarly eye-opening, and dealt with real people and taboo topics – opening up discussions that people generally shy away from.

Working on this could be hard at times because of the sensitive subject matter, so it was nice to get out of the office on occasion and work on other Chalkboard productions. I assisted the development team to pitch some new game show formats and factual entertainment series ideas. The two pitches I worked on weirdly involved skintight bodysuits for different reasons. The job involved keeping contributors, contestants and the crew happy and caffeinated by supplying food and drink, as well as emergency batteries and props. Once I was sent out on a quest to acquire a strange assortment of props – a tiara, a toilet brush, a picture frame, champagne glasses and a feather duster. I also took care of paperwork, including release forms and scheduling; booking transport for cast and crew; helping with setting up the studio; and generally helping to make sure the day ran smoothly. On one occasion I had to stand in for one of the contestants and take part, which was a fun experience!

Working on such a range of productions has been a fantastic experience, and I've been very fortunate to work here for three months as a freelancer. I've learnt that just being enthusiastic and offering help with bits and bobs makes you an asset to a company. And being willing to try out tasks associated with a number of roles (runner, logger, transcriber, camera assistant, casting researcher, production coordinator, production assistant etc.) really does allow you to learn quickly and improve on your skills! I didn't expect a two-day job to turn into almost three months, and I learnt so much about the industry and working in factual entertainment, getting the chance to work on some very exciting and inspiring programmes – with some inspiring people too!

October 2015: job hunt

Time is up at Chalkboard. Essentially I'm a freelancer. No contract. There isn't enough work to warrant an extra person on the team. Began job hunting for something more secure.

If you are a freelance runner/logger it's recommended you work for a few companies, but that can be difficult at first as you're still making connections and getting to know companies and how the industry works. Very useful to freelance after university though, as it allows time to settle into working life. It's flexible – some weeks working Monday to Friday, some weeks only for one day. But there may be periods of time when there is no work – it's unpredictable, so there are potential financial issues. I'm lucky to live in my family home in London, so I've got the freedom to work freelance and not pay a ridiculous amount in rent/bills, and I've got time on other projects (Jurassica: assisting a wedding photographer). It's a question of finding your feet in the industry and making connections. You have to build a CV including your television work, voluntary work and other useful things.

There's a television runners Facebook group, which is a useful place to search for jobs – companies advertise there with mostly entry-level jobs: production runner, drivers, post-production runner, office runner, production assistant, logger, transcriber, researcher, admin, receptionist vacancies. Often there are last-minute calls for day runners, as well as more permanent jobs. Also there are lots of tips on how to get into the industry from top industry professionals. You can post your CV there and get feedback from people. Helpful articles, blogs and videos are posted. Events are advertised. There are opportunities for networking.

While I was at Chalkboard I applied for two jobs – Dragonfly TV and the BBC. Now I've applied for four jobs: three office-based runner/admin roles (Angst Productions, CC-Lab, WhizzKid) and a one-day runner job for *The X Factor* (Talkback Thames). Most of these were advertised on the Unit List and/or Facebook. They get lots of applicants and you don't always hear back if you were unsuccessful.

I didn't hear back from WhizzKid or *The X Factor* but got interviews for Angst and CC-Lab.

Tuesday 27 October 2015

Had to rush back from Dorset for my interview with Angst. They make comedy: *Mock the Week, Whose Line Is It Anyway?, Fast and Loose*.

The interview was with Sarah and Jenny – the production management team. They both made me feel at ease, and I met the founder of the company, Dan Patterson, briefly, who quizzed me on my CV. The job had been advertised as not suitable for recent graduates without experience. I'd had a bit of experience during uni and after, but wasn't sure if this was enough ... hopefully they'd be impressed that I'd managed to get something despite only being out of education for a couple of months. They went through what would be expected of me (able to use Macs, experience in admin, dealing with petty cash, tea-making skills etc.). I was lucky to have had the time at Chalkboard to talk about, as the job role was similar. I'd be working closely with them – which was good as I'd like to go into production management. I'd also be working closely with Dan, 'keeping him happy' and generally helping with his workload: anything from making tea and getting his lunch, to booking haircuts and dinners, ordering books, typing up emails, scanning and photocopying. Essentially like a PA. Came out of the interview feeling like it went really well, but also feeling as if my lack of experience may let me down – not sure if Dan was as confident in me as S and J were.

Wednesday 28 October 2015

Next day woke up feeling prepped for CC-Lab interview, which I was told would be very short as they had lots of applicants and wanted to do a shortlist for second interviews. CC-Lab's office was just around the corner from Angst, so I had scoped it out on my way home last night to escape the stress of getting lost around Soho. I always tend to get to interviews way too early and kill time wandering around ...

At CC-Lab, I was greeted by Megan (freelance production coordinator) and Fran (production manager), both very lovely and easy to talk to. Offices were really lovely with an open fire and a homely feel. Interview was very quick – only five to ten minutes (Angst was half an hour); discussed my CV and the job role and why I was interested in this job. CC-Lab do music television – festivals, sessions, branding. Went out feeling like it went well, but was difficult to tell because it was over so quickly.

Thursday 29 October 2015

Out for a massage with my mum, received a call from CC-Lab asking me to come for a second interview on Friday. Out shopping with mum, received an email from Angst offering me the job! In two minds as to what to do. Felt happy at both companies – but felt as if Angst would be a more sensible career move as it's more related to what I want to do. It has lots of well-established people who have been in the industry for a long time. Accepted the job after holding out for a few hours (and watching James Bond *Spectre*) – still not sure whether to go to the CC-Lab interview. Would be a good experience to have another interview, but worried that I might be in the position of being offered two jobs. Not sure who I would want to go with, didn't want to mess either company about. Asked people's advice and most thought it would be best to cancel the CC-Lab interview.

Friday 30 October 2015

Emailed CC-Lab first thing in the morning, then got a call from Fran – basically saying they wanted to offer me the job – persuading me to rethink! They were looking at offering a better wage, seeing whether I'd consider coming in anyway for a chat. In two minds; but thought it would be a waste of their time if I came in, because I was pretty sure I'd go through with the Angst job anyway. A shame because I'd really liked it at CC-Lab. Didn't expect to get one job, let alone almost two! So I signed my contract at Angst later that day! Stressful morning . . .

Wednesday 11 and Thursday 12 November 2015

After a week and a bit of lounging around and enjoying my last free week for a while, I came into Angst for a two-day handover with their current office runner, Lizzie.

My responsibilities were opening and closing the office; stocking the kitchen, cleaning products and stationery; making tea; sorting out Dan's breakfast and lunch; petty cash, admin, being the first point of contact for guests, dealing with phone calls (people calling the office with programme ideas and sales calls), emails, extra pair of hands coordinating things when shoots are happening, prep for production, postal stuff, contact with post-production house, contact with IT company, accountant and so on.

November 2015–May 2016

Angst is based in Soho, the heart of television in London. Their two most popular shows are *Mock the Week* (BBC 2) and *Whose Line Is It Anyway?* (now on the CW Network in the United States). *Mock the Week* (*MTW*) runs in two blocks during the summer of every year (June–July, September–October), and *Whose Line Is It Anyway?* is filmed in the United States over two blocks in January and March/April. During my month's trial, everyone was prepping for the first block of *Whose Line is it Anyway?* as well as developing some new programme ideas for game shows.

It turns out that if people get busy, they pass on bits of work to you which is good, as it means learning different job roles as you go along. I got to help out with game show trials (and take part as a contestant and embarrass myself by trying to eat as many cream crackers as possible in a minute); lent a hand with pre-production for *Whose Line . . .?*, and cut some games footage from the show's archives. Christmas was also on its way, so I helped to organise the Angst Xmas do too! After passing my trial period, my contract was extended until the end of May, before the start of *Mock the Week.*

January 9 crew off to LA. Just myself and Sarah, line producer, in the office. It's a huge change from a busy office buzzing with creativity and big personalities. It was nice to get some peace and quiet though and get some office maintenance bits done and out of the way before things get busy for *Mock the Week* – window cleaning, IT checks, new fridge, carpet cleaning, touch-up painting, lighting changing and so on. I've been responsible for tracking the drives from LA to the post-production house, Suite TV, in Soho, then sending the finished cut-off to the United States. This has been tricky considering the time difference! Angst also has a stage show of *Whose Line Is It Anyway?* on at the Palladium in June, so I've been helping Jenny (production manager) with some travel documents too.

Working on *Whose Line . . .?* has been really interesting – I've learnt a bit about job roles I didn't know much about before: script supervisor, post-production supervisor, commissioning editor and so on. Learning a lot more about how the industry works – how it all ties in together. More options than I thought, a lot to learn. Angst has a handful of permanent staff, and uses freelancers during production. For example, on *Whose Line . . .?* we had the script supervisor and editor come in before heading off to LA. Interesting talking to them about their careers and they quizzed me on how I feel university prepared me for industry, and how I'm finding it so far – lots of helpful advice. When *MTW* starts it'll be an office full of people, and hectic studio days with lots of people to meet and lots to learn!

I'm very lucky. I've had a lot of trust and responsibility. In bigger companies runners just make tea and buy people lunch. I do that too, but a lot more. You absorb a lot from being in that environment. The people here are very good at what they do. I find it inspiring; I'm learning a lot. If I stay on at Angst until summer, it will be good to get some studio experience on *Mock the Week* – learning more about how it all comes together in a production environment, meeting new people – networking. I'll be settled in then and will know everyone. I'll be more comfortable to try new things and put myself forward, and ask lots of questions.

CONTACTS FOR ENTRY-LEVEL JOBS

The BBC has a production trainee scheme, open to all, and a production apprentice-ship specifically for non-graduates:
www.bbc.co.uk/getin. www.bbc.co.uk/careers
It also offers work experience placements:
www.bbc.co.uk/careers/work-experience
and a number of relevant job profiles:
www.bbc.co.uk/academy/work-in-broadcast/getting-a-job

Creative Access promotes opportunities for under-represented BAME groups:
http://creativeaccess.org.uk/opportunities

Creative Skillset lists the range of entry-level jobs:
http://creativeskillset.org/job_roles/entry-level_roles

The Unit List
www.theunitlist.com/jobs/

and there are numerous informal websites and Facebook links including:
Film-Runner.com
'The website dedicated to helping you break into the film, TV and commercials industry.'

CHAPTER 21

Making programmes: pitching and commissioning

TURNING AN IDEA INTO A COMMISSION

Those who aspire to work in television tend to be driven by something more than a search for employment. Many are drawn to the medium because they see it as a challenge and a form of self-expression. They would like to create material of their own devising and under their own control: produce works that express their creativity, argue for a cause they care about, or achieve an aesthetic effect. But a glance at the realities of the television world shows that the bulk of the output is driven by other priorities. Those in charge of scheduling and commissioning must balance their appreciation of creative programming with a concern for audience appeal and, often, the need to attract advertisers. Processes are increasingly formalised and commissioners are understandably cautious, preferring to rely on producers and companies with a proven track record. Creativity must find uneasy bedfellows in accounting, law and business practices. To get a programme commissioned you must demonstrate not only that the idea you have is an attractive and viable one, but that it fits with the channel's requirements and that you are competent to produce it. This is why many television courses now include units on business practices and the paraphernalia of running a company (see Kate Beal p. 32). Effective budgeting and working to deadlines are necessary components of the practice of programme-making.

Although it usually takes many years of experience to become an established producer or director with control over your own output, changing technologies and the expansion of the internet have brought more outlets for original work than ever before. But between the extremes of creating a prestigious series for a major broadcaster and uploading some mobile phone footage onto YouTube, there are many ways of getting ideas onto the screen. As we have seen educational and training institutions make it possible for students and trainees to create their own work, whether for a local internet channel (Southampton Solent), a commission for a broadcaster (MAMA) or a voluntary project (Jurassica) (see Chapters 18, 19 and 20). Those with access to equipment may make films for charities and local activist groups. Some have used their initiative to set up their own internet channels. In addition, there are opportunities to gain a commission from a number of more formal outlets.

All the major broadcasters have teams of commissioners. These are the people who set the trends, but must also follow the trends. Channel 5 has a team of seven who consult together, but usually commissioners specialise in genres, especially drama, factual and comedy. Commissioning is related to scheduling, and to the need to reinforce a channel's identity and to build its 'brand'. 'You must do what feels right for your brand. ITV does not often take risks', says Satmohan Panesar, Factual Commissioner for ITV. All commissioners monitor audience figures closely and have a clear idea of which genres and styles attract viewers and advertisers.

What the broadcasters say

All the major UK broadcasters are required to commission programmes from independent production companies. Ever since Channel Four was set up in 1982 to be a 'publisher' rather than a producer of programmes, building a working relationship with commissioning editors has been central to the activities of the indies. In seeking commissions, newer, smaller companies are inevitably competing with those who are well established. The BBC, for example, has a registered list of suppliers who must be able to demonstrate a track record. Nevertheless most broadcasters state that they remain open to innovative ideas. 'Sometimes the best ideas come from a one-man band', says Siobhan Mulholland, who commissions factual programmes for several Sky channels. But 'if an untried person approaches us with a proposal we like, we usually put them in touch with one of our regular companies' (BVE 2015).

Although individual programme-makers would be advised to approach an independent company with their idea rather than going directly to a broadcaster, information about the broadcasters' thinking is public and easily accessible. They all have informative websites where potential programme-makers can learn who the commissioners are, what genres they cover and details of their priorities, as well as how to submit ideas. *Broadcast* magazine and other trade papers monitor developments in the industry and publish regular interviews with commissioners and controllers. In addition there are numerous meetings and events around the country when programme-makers can quiz the industry bosses. Commissioners visit colleges and universities, give talks at organisations such as BAFTA and at industry events such as the Edinburgh International Television Festival and BVE (see list on p. 283).

When commissioners specify their needs, they are anxious to point to the particular qualities of the channel they represent. For example, Sky, as a broadcaster chiefly funded by subscription, is more concerned about their audience than about their advertisers. 'Our subscribers pay for the service. They need value for their money, so we should be different from the others', says Adam MacDonald, Controller of Sky 1. As well as audience ratings Sky carries out 'value' surveys to find out what viewers like about the programmes they watch. 'More than anywhere else I've worked we're obsessed with our "customers". We call them "customers" because they pay.'

As Channel 5 is the smallest of the terrestrial channels, it has a smaller budget than other broadcasters. That means decision-making tends to depend on how much money a programme will make. 'We need ideas that will buy viewers', says Factual Commissioning Editor Greg Barnett.

Although the other channels are commissioning an increasing proportion of programmes from UK independent companies, Channel Four was set up as a publisher-broadcaster and commissions its entire output. The channel is a non-profit-making, publicly owned organisation which remains aware of its special remit to innovate, to provide programmes the other channels do not, and to promote diversity. 'It is the job of Channel Four to reflect the contemporary world to British television audiences, and one of the most important ways we do this is through our substantial and multi-award-winning documentary output', states its commissioning website. There is some doubt as to whether the channel would be able to continue this commitment if it were to be privatised.

Although each broadcaster has its particular qualities, and each has its 'family' of channels with different specialisms, popular trends tend to apply across the output. All are interested in a returnable format that can be marketed across territories, and all are looking for new approaches to well-established subjects, just as fixed rig brought a different way of doing to programmes about hospitals and schools. Many of them feel that a risky subject may be mitigated by using a well-known presenter, and celebrity is important. A celebrity can create 'a halo effect' through tweeting and appearing across the schedule. And all commissioners confirm a shift towards entertainment and 'feel-good' factors. Adam MacDonald of Sky 1 declares: 'There's a lot of serious telly out there. We want stuff with a twinkle in its eye . . . our key words are "joy" and "energy".' The channel has established a tradition of 'funny factual' at 9pm. For commissioning purposes, 'factual' and 'entertainment' have been merged, and described as 'non-scripted'. Now the broadcaster has three commissioning teams: entertainment (non-scripted), drama and comedy.

Despite the popularity of catch-up and online viewing, all broadcasters are aware of the linear schedule. Breakfast time and daytime have their own particular qualities, and all channels have specific requirements for evening and peak viewing. And they all keep an eye on what the other channels are doing: the success of *The One Show* depended on researching what viewers wanted at 7pm; 8pm is the time for the ever-popular soaps; and at 9pm 'you are most exposed'.

Pitching an idea

Researching a programme idea and writing a proposal can be a committed and time-consuming business. Many production companies employ a development team, with a number of researchers who work on developing ideas, while experienced producers stress that the most important aspect of their job is their relationship with the commissioning editors. Ideas are often developed in collaboration with commissioners, who tend to trust producers they know and have worked with. 'If they don't know who you are then they don't know if you can make the programme', said one. Filmmakers who are not employed by an organisation, but are dedicated to a particular project or simply determined to get a commission, are at a disadvantage. They must be prepared to make an extra effort and use a variety of tactics to get their idea accepted.

Most commissioners agree on the principles of pitching. The following advice is taken from talks given by commissioners for factual programmes from the main channels. All agree that potential programme-makers should research the channel they're targeting ('It annoys me when they haven't watched other stuff we've done', said one). They should be aware of the target audience (e.g. *All 4 shorts* are aimed at sixteen to thirty-four-year olds), and of a target time slot (early evening, late night). They should also be aware of the genres and approaches which fit the mood of the moment – but should not simply send in imitations of the current hit. 'When *Gogglebox* became a success, the following week I got 15 similar ideas', complained one commissioner.

There are no rules, but a proposal usually begins with an e-mail, accompanied by an outline detailing the subject matter of the programme, its scope, its content and the style in which it will be produced. This should not take up more than one page. A catchy subject heading is a good start. If the proposal depends on particular characters or participants, some video footage is needed. A written description or a still photograph is not enough. 'If you have a great character, I need to see them', said one commissioner. 'A mobile phone video is OK. Just upload it and send it in.'

So the first approach is brief and to the point, but a number of other documents and visual materials should be available:

- CVs of the producer, director and others involved in the production with examples of their previous work.
- Background information on the 'talent': celebrities or featured presenters with examples of their previous work.
- Information on the programme style: will it be studio-based or filmed on location? Will it be observational shooting or will it involve actors? Will it aim for a glossy HD format or a low-tech video diary style and so on?
- What crew will be required? How many of these are already on board?

- A projected budget.
- If appropriate, a pilot video – sometimes referred to as a '*sizzle reel*'.

Experienced producer Liz McLeod of True North, an independent production company based in Leeds, who has produced programmes for all the main UK broadcasters, argues that a suitable programme idea must have three 'T's: an engaging *title*, a *twist* – something specific to that idea – and *talent*. 'It's important that the presenter/performers should be charismatic and able to carry the programme.'

Commissioning editors encourage applicants to be persistent. 'Above all, you should pitch with conviction. You've really got to believe in your idea – and have done your homework.'

A large number of proposals are of necessity turned down, and even the bigger independent companies are prepared for a high proportion of refusals. They may put in twenty proposals for every one accepted. Rejection does not mean that the idea was in itself a bad one: sometimes it is just that the timing is wrong. What would have been acceptable yesterday is not today and vice versa. Applicants must be able to bear rejection even if it is sometimes unkind, and should keep trying.

Quotations from commissioners in this chapter are taken from public talks and private conversations.

KEY TEXT

Lees, N. (2010) *Greenlit: Developing Factual/Reality TV Ideas from Concept to Pitch*, London: Methuen.

Commissioning contacts:

BBC
www.bbc.co.uk/commissioning/tv/articles/who-we-are-how-we-commission
Currently the BBC operates a quota for outside commissions, and companies must register in order to pitch.

Channel 5
about.channel5.com/commissioners

Channel Four
www.channel4.com/info/commissioning/4producers

ITV
www.itv.com/commissioning

Sky
corporate.sky.com/about-sky/other-information/commissioning-and-ideas-submission/
ideas-submission

PACT
The independent producers' trade association: provides advice and information.
www.pact.co.uk/member-services/resourcelibrary.html

OPPORTUNITIES AND FUNDS

As well as the high-profile, prestigious outlets, a range of organisations, including some of the major broadcasters, offer opportunities to independent filmmakers and have created a space for more personal programmes, both broadcast and online.

The Community Channel

The Community Channel has a slogan: 'We believe that everyone should have a voice and the opportunity to be heard.' The channel, which celebrated its fifteenth birthday in 2015, was set up by the Media Trust, a charity supported by all UK broadcasters and most of the press, specifically to 'represent the unrepresented and tell untold stories to the nation'. The channel transmits throughout the day on a number of free-to-air HD channels as well as online, including on the BBC iPlayer. As well as producing in-house with its small team of filmmakers, it recently started co-producing with small independent companies. It will also commission items from individuals for slots such as *UK360*, a magazine show 'designed to give a voice to communities and enable people to share their local news and stories with the nation by sending in films, documentaries and reports'. Its website includes helpful 'Production Packs' to advise on how to go about it. It will also transmit suitable films that have already been made: www.communitychannel.org/london 360/news-details/1957/teach-me-how-to-pitch-for-tv/; www.communitychannel.org/local360/about/

The Guardian

The Guardian newspaper has set up a Documentary Unit that commissions short (up to twenty minutes) international stories, which are placed on its website. Head of Documentaries Charlie Phillips describes them as being 'at the intersection of documentary and online journalism' and has curated a range of work by both established and new filmmakers www.theguardian.com/news/series/the-guardian-documentary

Channel Four

In the days when the independent sector was in its infancy, the special character of Channel Four was created with a remit to search for a diversity of suppliers, and despite the threat of privatisation, it has continued with that commitment. For example, Channel Four has changed its on-demand service, previously called 4od, to All 4, a service that commissions new material as well as providing reruns. Its 'online shorts' are provocative three-minute items designed to be viewed on laptops, phones and tablets. Around 40 per cent of All 4's commissioned programmes come from small companies new to the channel www.channel4.com/info/commissioning/4producers/online/shortform.

On Channel Four's main channel, *First Cut* is a strand designed to launch the careers of new factual directors. It is open to anyone who has not directed a sixty-minute film for broadcast on a terrestrial channel or BBC3. The channel's website states: 'We look for up and coming directors we feel have the potential to make prime time programmes for the Channel, and subjects which give them an appropriate opportunity to show their flair and vision.' Most commissions go to people within the industry who have not yet directed their own documentary, but recent film school graduates are considered. In the spirit of its remit, the channel has an innovation fund to help companies in their early stages, and to help them grow www.channel4.com/media/documents/commissioning/Firstcutbrief.pdf.

Online channels

Commissioning for online is different from commissioning for broadcast, partly because, unlike the broadcast schedule, there are no fixed lengths. For online channels such as Vice and BBC3, films can be long form or short form and do not have to conform to audience expectations for a particular time of day. 'Online we don't have to think about "9pm Wednesday"', says All 4's Commissioning Editor Adam Gee. Commissioners are aware that, for the viewers, the experience of browsing the internet and sampling interesting content is quite different from settling down in front of a television set and selecting a programme. This means that the audience is less predictable. Many companies use software that monitors viewing practices and records the points at which viewers turn off. The conclusion is that the first fifteen seconds of an online film are particularly important to involve a viewer's attention. Consequently *Guardian* commissioner Charlie Phillips states that the films he selects must be fast-paced and must work on YouTube, Facebook and Vimeo. Online is 'a different language from TV'.

Funding, distribution and awards

Independent programme-makers need to become adept at tracking down sources of funding. Obtaining even a small grant can mean that a piece of work can get made and shown, even when not commissioned by a broadcasting organisation. Local arts organisations or other schemes offer support for broadcast and non-broadcast work. These include bodies such as the National Lottery, the Arts Council and the British Council, which offers a travel grant for filmmakers to show their work at international film festivals. In addition, there are a number of awards to which filmmakers can submit their films, for example, through the Royal Television Society student awards and the Limelight film awards, a short film competition for emerging filmmakers sponsored by a number of media companies (see below).

In addition, a number of independent filmmakers, especially those with a campaigning edge, have made their films with the help of crowdfunding. The Radical Film Network provides links between radical filmmakers who are after something different from the mainstream. Members organise screenings and make links with festivals such as the Bristol Radical Film Festival where filmmakers can show their work.

Here we list some relevant contacts:

Arts Council
www.artscouncil.org.uk/funding

BAFTA Awards scholarships 'to support talented people at all stages of their career in film, television and games'.
www.bafta.org/initiatives/supporting-talent/scholarships/uk-programme

British Council (film)
film.britishcouncil.org/our-projects/on-going-projects/shorts-support-scheme

British Film Institute Film Fund
www.bfi.org.uk/supporting-uk-film/film-fund

BVE
An annual London exhibition and event for the industry, dealing with broadcast, production and technology.
www.bvexpo.com

Creative England Production Fund
Supports 'projects from regionally-based talent – both first/second time feature directors and more established directors looking to experiment with new approaches'.
creativeengland.co.uk/film/production-funding#creative-england-production-fund

From the Heart
A US-based organisation, but its website gives some helpful tips on crowdfunding.
fromtheheartproductions.com/indiegogo/

Grierson Trust
The Trust makes an annual award for the best student-made documentary.
Sponsored by Sky Atlantic.
www.griersontrust.org/about-us/

Limelight film awards
An annual short film competition
limelightawards.com/index-1.html

Small Axe
Short film award from the Tolpuddle Radical Film Festival.
www.tolpuddleradicalfilm.org.uk/small-axe/submissions

Organisations and festivals

It is possible for new filmmakers to joining organisations such as:

Documentary Film Group

Radical Film Network

Women in Film and TV Network

And to submit work to festivals including:

Bristol Radical Film festival

Open City Documentary Festival

Sheffield International Documentary Festival

Straight-jacket Guerrilla Film Festival (online).

Glossary

See also the Index for page references to these terms.

Access programmes:

a. 'Access' programmes are those where a production company is allowed 'access' to an organisation or an institution, and allowed to film its daily activities.

b. Spaces in the television schedule which allow access to the airwaves by members of the public and non-professionals.

ADR (automatic dialogue replacement): Removing the dialogue recorded on location and replacing it with dialogue created at the post-production stage. See Chapter 14.

Ambient noise: The background sound of a location such as traffic noise or air conditioning.

Animatic: A pre-visualisation of a sequence which will be created by the visual effects team. See Chapter 14.

Animation: A style of filming which creates movement from inanimate objects, including art work and puppets.

Animatronics: Puppets, models and other robotic devices for use in creating visual effects. See Chapter 14.

Audience Appreciation Index (AI): A survey of viewers' opinions about the programmes they have seen, giving 'appreciation ratings' as a score out of 100.

Audio space: The combination of elements – dialogue, music, sound effects and so on – which create the sound track of a programme.

Auteur: The 'auteur theory' argued that a director is an 'author', responsible for creating every aspect of a film. Promoted by writers around the French journal *Cahiers du Cinema* in the 1950s.

Autocue: A screen attached to the front of a camera which displays a presenter's script. The presenter may then read the script while looking directly at the camera.

Avid: The brand name of a standard computer editing system.

Background plate or 'clean plate': A sequence or shot without actors or events, for use by video effects artists at the post-production stage. This is referred to as the *cinematography* of the image. See Chapter 14.

BARB (Broadcasters' Audience Research Board): A specialised research organisation, which produces regular television viewing figures. Its methods include monitoring the switching on of television sets and conducting polls among the public.

Barn doors: Side flaps fitted to studio and portable lights, used to blank off part of a light source and control its spread and direction. See Chapter 10.

BECTU Broadcasting, Entertainment, Cinematograph and Theatre Union: The trade union representing employees in the film, television and theatre industries. In 2016 BECTU merged with the engineers, managers and scientists' union, Prospect.

BGAN (Broadband Global Area Network): A global satellite internet network using portable terminals.

Blog: Abbreviated from 'weblog': a website that is regularly updated with personal, informal content.

Boom: An adjustable telescopic pole, from which a microphone can be suspended in a shockproof cradle. It may be a portable fishpole boom or it may be mounted on a movable base with adjustable extensions.

Boom swinger: The sound assistant who holds the fishpole boom aloft while adjusting the microphone to follow the source of the sound. See Chapter 11.

Brand: A product marketed under a recognisable name or symbol. See Chapter 5 for an account of branding and promotional material on television. See also Johnson, C. (2012) *Branding Television*, London: Routledge.

Broadcaster: The organisation that commissions and transmits television or radio programmes. In the United Kingdom, the BBC, ITV and Channels 4 and 5 are licensed to broadcast over the 'radio spectrum' (see below).

Buzz track: A recording of the ambient noise which is the background atmosphere of a scene. Sometimes referred to as an 'atmosphere' track or simply 'atmos'. See Chapter 11.

CAA (Civil Aviation Authority): The organisation responsible for non-military aviation in the United Kingdom. Its regulations control the use of drones.

Camcorder: A camera with the ability to record picture and sound.

Cardioid microphone: A directional microphone with a heart-shaped pick-up pattern. See Chapter 11.

CGI (computer-generated imaging): The creation of images by programming computers.

Channel: A broadcast channel is an organised sequence of programmes. The main UK 'broadcasters' control several 'channels', each with its own identity. See Chapter 3.

Chroma key: A process by which two images are combined. Used for filming a presenter or a sequence against a 'green screen'. This can be replaced with a different background.

Cinema verité (or cine-verité): Literally 'cinema-truth'. The use of the term has evolved and changed since it was first used by Jean Rouch to describe his documentary *Chronicle of a Summer* in 1960. Although the original meaning referred to the director being part of the film and explaining his intentions, it is now usually used to describe 'fly-on-the-wall'-style observational filming. See Chapter 16.

Cinematography of the image: See above, 'background plate'.

Citizen journalism: See UGC below.

Clapper board: The clapper board identifies each take and provides a point from which the image and sound track can be synchronised. See Chapter 11.

Clapper/loader: The assistant on the camera crew who is in charge of the clapper board. The description 'loader' is a residue of the days when the job also entailed loading the camera magazines with film.

Classic realist text: A narrative that appears 'real' because it does not draw attention to the artifice which goes into producing it. See Chapter 15.

Cloud: A network of remote servers that can be used to store, manage and process internet data. Cloud computing provides shared resources and data on demand.

Codec: The 'file wrapper' system to code and decode the images and other information in a digital camera. See Chapter 10.

Colourist: See 'grading' below.

Colour temperature: A method of describing the colour characteristics of a light, usually either warm (yellowish) or cool (bluish). See Chapter 10.

Commissioning/commissioner: The process by which an idea for a programme is selected to go into production. See Chapter 21.

Compliance: At the post-production stage the editor or a compliance officer must ensure that a programme complies with Ofcom's Broadcasting Code for broadcast in the United Kingdom, and then with the specific requirements of other territories if it will be shown overseas. See Chapter 14.

Concept art: The first stage in creating a visual effects sequence, creating an impression of the appearance of the effect. See Chapter 14.

Continuity: When referring to film and television, 'continuity' implies a smooth flow between the shots in a sequence. There should be no inconsistencies, even if they are filmed at separate times and in different places. See Chapter 9.

Continuity editing: A style of editing which prioritises smooth continuity. See Chapter 13.

Convergence: The process by which previously separate media technologies merge together.

Coordinated frequencies: Available frequencies on the radio spectrum which are licensed by Ofcom at a specific site for short- or long-term. They may be used for radio mics. See Chapter 11.

Copyright: The legal right of ownership of written, visual or aural material, including the prohibition on copying material without prior permission from its owner.

Crane: Counterweighted long metal arm with a flexible camera mounting so that the camera can be raised and lowered.

Data wrangler: See DIT below.

Deco-doc: Documentaries which use a wide range of techniques rather than observational filming.

Deconstruction: A way of analysing texts to understand how they are constructed, and a way of creating a text so that its methods of construction are revealed. See Chapter 15.

DFX (digital effects): Effects which are computer-based, produced by a visual effects team. See Chapter 14.

Diegetic: The information contained within the world of a narrative. Added music, for example, will be 'extra-diegetic'.

Diffusers: Flame-proof 'spun' fibre glass sheets fixed over a lamp, or some material such as 'scrim', a heat-proof opaque paper which will diffuse the light and reduce its intensity.

Digital compositing: The use of a 'matte' in the camera to block out part of the frame, so that it can be replaced with another image. See Chapter 14.

Digital assets: A digital object or event which can be used again and again (e.g., a creature, an explosion or a water effect). It is possible to create a library of digital assets available to be reused when needed. See Chapter 14.

Direct cinema: The term originates with the work of Robert Drew, Richard Leacock and the Maysles brothers in the United States in the 1960s. Now sometimes used interchangeably with cine-verité to describe 'fly-on-the-wall'-style observational shooting, with minimal interference from the filmmakers. See Chapter 16; see 'cine-verité' above.

Discourse (discours): See 'story' below.

DIT: The digital imaging technician, also known as a 'data wrangler', who will be in charge of the memory cards for the camera and will liaise between cinematographer and editor. See Chapter 9.

Dolly: A mobile mounting for a camera. A motorised dolly may be controlled by an operator from the rear platform, or the dolly may be gently moved by a member of the camera crew known as a 'grip'.

DOP (director of photography): The chief cinematographer on a production – in charge of the lighting and camera work, and creating the visual identity of the programme.

Drone: These remotely controlled 'unmanned aerial vehicles' (UAVs) may be provided with special mountings for cameras. See Chapter 9.

Dub: The process of combining and balancing the sound tracks. This is one of the last stages of editing, known as the dubbing stage or the 'dub'. See Chapter 14.

EDL (Edit decision list): A list of timecode numbers showing the beginning and ending of each shot in an edited sequence can be produced through the appropriate software. This enables the online editors to match the offline version.

ENG (electronic news gathering): The use of lightweight cameras and digital technology to record and transmit news pictures and sound.

Enigma: A term used by theorist Tzevan Todorov to describe the opening of a narrative – usually a complex of circumstances which will be unravelled within the plot.

EPG (electronic programme guide): The on-screen guide that lists available channels in the multichannel environment.

EVS: Brand name for a facility which can create overlays and insertions into live action broadcasts.

Film researcher: A specialist in finding suitable archive film.

Fine cut: The final edited version of a programme.

Fishpole boom: A pole from which a microphone is suspended in a shock-proof cradle at one end, with the cable connector box at the other end. It is light enough to be held aloft by a sound recordist, or a sound assistant known as a boom swinger.

Fixed-rig: A method of observational programme-making which involves up to seventy cameras fixed in strategic positions and operated remotely from a temporary control room/gallery. See Chapter 16.

Fixer: A location producer, or local person, who can provide local facilities for a film crew working overseas. See Chapter 17.

Flood: A light source which gives a wide beam, in contrast to a spot that is an intense, narrow-angled beam. See Chapter 10.

Flow: In linear television, programmes and interstitials follow each other in unbroken sequence. This was considered a major characteristic of the medium, until the arrival of multiple screens. Commentators now speak of 'overflow'. See Chapter 15.

Focal length: A characteristic of a camera lens. The longer the focal length of the lens, the narrower the angle of vision and the less there will be in the picture. See Chapter 10.

Focus puller: The member of the camera crew who adjusts the focus as the camera moves and a shot develops. See Chapter 9.

Foley: Named after Hollywood sound pioneer, Jack Foley, a Foley studio is provided with equipment to create sound effects. A Foley artist specialises in creating appropriate effects, including footsteps on various surfaces. See Chapter 14.

Formatted programmes: Programmes constructed according to a set of rules and principles which enable it to be remade within different cultures and different contexts.

Free-to-air: Available channels for which viewers do not pay directly. However, they pay indirectly through advertising and the BBC licence fee.

Fresnel: A lens used in some light sources which enables a light spread to be adjusted between a wider or narrower beam.

FX: Abbreviation for 'effects' as in *sound effects* – the extra sounds that are added to the natural sounds of a scene. See Chapter 14.

Gallery: The studio control room where the director, vision mixer and the sound and video technicians work. They control the input from the studio cameras, seen on a bank of monitors, and give instructions to those working on the studio floor using talkback systems. See Chapter 12.

Gels: Coloured gelatine sheets that may be placed in front of the lights to create different intensities of reds, yellows and blues. They may also be used to alter the colour of the daylight coming in through the windows. See Chapter 10.

Genre: A way of referring to different types and styles of programme, each of which has its own style, its own norms, its own grammar of programme-making and its own history and culture. See Chapter 5.

Gimbal: A pivoted camera mounting that enables the camera to remain steady. See Chapter 9.

Globalisation: The process whereby ownership of television institutions in different nations and regions is concentrated in the hands of international corporations. See Chapter 4.

Grading: The process whereby the shots in a programme are matched for colour and quality by the post-production technicians, known as graders or colourists. See Chapter 13.

Green screen: A background screen that enables an image to be overlaid from another source. See 'chroma key' above.

Grip: A member of the camera crew who sets up the camera dolly, lays the tracks for it to run on, then controls its movement to ensure the shot will be smooth. See Chapter 9.

Gun mic: A highly directional microphone, described as super-cardioid, designed to pick up sound within a very narrow angle of acceptance. Mounted on a long tube, it is described as a 'gun mic' because of its appearance. See Chapter 11.

HD (high-definition television): A high-quality digital system with a wide screen picture. See 'K' below.

'History' (histoire): See 'story' below.

HMI (Hydrargyrum Medium Arc Iodide): This is a large intense lamp, balanced for daylight, with a high light to heat ratio. See Chapter 10.

Hot head: Supports a camera mounted on a jib, enabling it to be controlled remotely. See Chapter 10.

Ident (identification): Symbols representing broadcasters and channels, often made up of graphics or animation.

Ideology: A set of beliefs, attitudes and assumptions. Marxist interpretations imply that ideologies emanate from the ruling class and mislead the rest of the population. See Chapter 6.

Independents (indies): Production companies that are independent of the broadcasters. They make programmes commissioned by broadcasting organisations and other funders or investors. See Chapter 3.

Ingestion: The process of importing and processing digital data for later use.

Interactivity: Giving viewers the opportunity to respond to a programme by sending signals back to the broadcaster, for example, by voting or tweeting.

Interstitials: The material that comes between the programmes, including trailers, advertisements and promotional material. See Chapter 5.

Intertextuality: The interrelationship between different texts. This refers both to the way that programmes are made – many programmes include references to other programmes and other media – and the ways in which viewers interpret them. See Chapter 5.

IPTV (internet protocol television): Services delivered over the internet instead of the usual terrestrial, cable or satellite delivery systems. This enables material to be streamed and viewed at any point. Streamed video is 'video on demand' (VOD).

Jimmy jib: A flexible camera mounting with a long extension arm. The camera s suspended at one end, with a monitor and camera controls at the other. See Chapter 9.

K (as in 2K, 4K): 'K' refers to the number of 'finished picture pixels' in one complete horizontal scan of an electronically scanned image. An explanation of relevant terms can be found at 'Understanding K Resolution' www.fotokem.com/resources/download/student/understanding_k_resolution.pdf.

Key light: The main light source that provides the 'key' to a scene's appearance. A scene may be 'high key', with low contrast between light and shade, or 'low key', with high contrast. See Chapter 10.

LED (light-emitting diode): A low-energy light source that can cover both daylight and tungsten (interior lighting). See Chapter 10.

Licence fee: Annual payment by owners of radio and television sets which is the main source of income for the BBC. It gives the right to view anything on the free-to-air channels at any time at no extra cost. See Chapter 3.

Linear:

a. 'Linear broadcasting' follows a time-based schedule, as opposed to 'video on demand'. See 'IPTV' above.

b. Editing on video tape is 'linear' as selected shots must be transferred from the rushes tapes to a new tape in the final order. Digital editing and editing on film are both 'non-linear'. Shots may be assembled and reassembled in any order.

Location filming: Filming outside a studio, in the environment as it exists, whether in someone's home or on the streets, without specially built sets.

Logging: Listing the content of the shots, using the timecode or other reference.

M&E (music and effects): A sound track with no dialogue or commentary, for use when dubbing into other languages. See Chapter 14.

Marxism: The theories of Karl Marx (1818–83) who analysed the capitalist power structures in society and argued that power was based on the exploitation of working people. See Chapter 6.

Matte: See 'digital compositing' above.

Mise-en-scene: Literally 'put into the scene'. Used to describe the characteristic 'look' of a film or programme, including set design, lighting, costume and other factors.

Montage: Although the word 'montage' can mean editing in general, it is most often used to describe a sequence which is built up through the juxtaposition and rhythm of images and sounds. See Chapter 13.

Motion capture: Motion capture for use in visual effects is the use of tracking sensors: markers or points on actors which record their movement in three-dimensional space, so that they can be digitally recreated. See Chapter 14.

Motivated/unmotivated: A camera movement is described as 'motivated' when it follows an action or is prompted by an event within the scene. A camera movement or a cut which follows no logic but its own is described as 'unmotivated'. See Chapter 9.

MoVI: A portable frame with two handles which allows the camera to be balanced on a giro-controlled gimbal mounting. See Chapter 9.

MXF (material exchange format): A compressed, broadcast-quality format. See Chapter 14.

Narrative 'functions': Elements which some theorists have argued underlie all narratives. See Chapter 15.

Niche: A term from advertising which identifies a small but highly specific target group. Broadcasters also refer to 'niche programming'.

Noise: Used to mean unwanted background sound or visual interference.

OB (outside broadcast): A broadcast made from a mobile complex which may control five or more cameras as well as editing and broadcasting facilities. Used for sports, live theatre performances and other public events.

Observational filming: The style of documentary filming which follows events rather than reconstructing them or using other filmic devices.

Ofcom (Office of Communications): The independent regulator for UK communications industries. See Chapter 3. www.ofcom.org.uk/about/.

oovs: Short video clips shown with the presenter 'out of vision'. See Chapter 17.

Overnights: Viewing figures for the previous night's programming which are available the following morning. See Chapter 5.

Packages: Brief, edited news reports, usually fronted by a reporter. Various types of input make up the 'package', such as visuals, interviews and commentary.

Palantypist (also known as STTR, 'speech to text reporter'): A shorthand keyboard enables a palantypist to input dialogue as it is spoken. It is simultaneously converted into text by a computer and forms the captions that enable a deaf viewer to follow a programme.

Paratexts: Materials that supplement a television programme, including websites, Twitter feeds, magazine articles, spin-off programmes and products which can be marketed, such as DVDs, games and toys. See Chapter 5.

Pitch: A proposal for a programme prepared for a commissioning editor. See Chapter 21.

Pixels: Individual elements that create a digital image. See 'K' above.

Platform: Television and other moving image material may be viewed on many platforms, including television sets, computer screens, tablets and mobile phones. The interrelation between these is described as 'cross-platform'. See Chapter 5.

Pop filter: Protects personal microphones from unwanted sounds when recording speech (such as the explosion of air that follows 'b' and 'p'). See Chapter 11.

Postmodernity: Theories of 'postmodernity' embrace irony, fragmented narratives, disruption and an awareness of technology. See Chapter 15.

Post-structuralism: This theoretical approach drew on 'semiotics', which analyses the structure of 'signs' in language and imagery; 'marxism', which critiques the capitalist power structures in society; and 'psychoanalysis', which explores the unconscious mind. This is often referred to as *Screen* Theory, as it was taken up in the United Kingdom by the journal, *Screen* in the 1970s. See Chapter 15.

Precinct: The word used to describe the setting for a formatted programme. See Chapter 16.

Pro-filmic event: This is the scene that the camera will film.

Promo: Promotional material, such as a trailer for a forthcoming programme. See 'paratext' above.

Proxy: A low-resolution copy of filmed material, suitable for editing. See Chapter 13.

PSB (public service broadcasting): The system under which UK television has evolved, in which certain obligations to the public are legally protected both from government interference and market forces. The principles were first enunciated by Sir John Reith, the first Director General of the BBC. See Chapter 3.

PSC (portable single camera): Usually used by a self-shooting director working alone, often for news material.

Psychoanalysis: A theory and therapeutic method based on the work of Sigmund Freud (1856–1939), who analysed the unconscious and its influence on daily lives.

Quality control (QC): Quality control is necessary at the post-production stage to comply with the technical standards laid down by the Digital Production Partnership (DPP). See Chapters 13 and 14. www.digitalproductionpartnership.co.uk/.

Radio microphone: Personal radio mics come with a small transmitter pack which sends a signal over the radio spectrum to a receiver attached to the audio mixer or the camera. See Chapter 11.

Radio spectrum: The 'airwaves' that carry broadcast signals, including radio, television, mobile phones, the emergency services and other users. Their use is licensed by Ofcom. See Chapter 11.

Ratings: The number of viewers estimated to have watched programmes (see 'BARB' and 'overnights' above). Consolidated ratings, including 'catch-up' viewing, are published once a week.

Raw file: Describes original material from the camera which may not be directly viewable.

Reality TV: Programmes where the unscripted behaviour of 'ordinary people' is the focus of interest. See Chapter 16.

Recce: To recce a location is to check it out both for suitability of content and for practical considerations such as availability of parking. See Chapter 8.

Red button: An interactive service that provides background information to a television programme.

Redhead: 800-watt lens-less spotlight of the 'external reflector' type. They can be mounted on stands or clipped onto a shelf or other object in the location. So called because of the red colour of the head of the lamp. See Chapter 10.

Regulation: Control of television institutions by laws, codes of practice and guidelines. See Ofcom above and Chapter 3.

Representation: The word may be used in two senses that may overlap: the ways in which people are *portrayed* in the media, and the degree to which different groupings are represented among those who *create* and *control* the media. There have been significant campaigns around the representation of women, LGBT and BAME groups. See Chapters 15, 16 and 19.

Resolution: Describes the amount of detail an image holds. Usually measured in pixels. See 'K' above.

Rough cut: The first, provisional edited version of a programme.

Runner: A general assistant in a production team. Usually an entry-level job. See Chapter 20.

Rushes: All the material which has been shot during the production period, including bad takes and other unwanted material. The rushes are the raw material for the editor.

Satellite broadcasting: Television broadcasting in which the programmes are beamed off a telecommunications satellite. Each broadcasts to its 'footprint' and the signal can be relayed by cable networks. Satellite channels transcend national boundaries. Communications satellites are also used for news gathering.

Schedule: The arrangement and sequencing of programmes during the day and over the weeks and months. See Chapter 5.

Scrim: See 'diffusers' above.

Semiotics: A method by which language and imagery can be analysed by identifying the 'signs' from which they are constructed – for example, a word, a gesture, a hair style – each of which carries a meaning. First developed by the Swiss linguist Ferdinand de Saussure (1857–1913). See Chapter 6.

Sensor: The device in a camera that converts the optical image to an electric signal.

Sequence: An element of a finished programme built up of a number of interrelated shots, usually linked by continuity: for example, 'the sequence in the park'; 'the chase sequence'.

SFX: This may be an abbreviation for 'special effects' or for 'sound effects'.

Shot: A single shot runs from the point when the camera is turned on to when it is turned off. During filming the same action may be repeated several times, in which case it is considered to be the same 'shot' with a number of 'takes'.

Showreel: A compilation put together by a filmmaker to demonstrate their work.

Showrunner: The word used to describe the main creative producer behind a drama series, frequently a writer/producer. See Chapter 15.

Sizzle reel: A short pilot video to accompany a pitch to a commissioning editor. See 'pitch' above and Chapter 21.

Skype: IP (internet protocol) telephony, using a broadband connection and a webcam. See Chapter 17.

Social psychology: The academic discipline which studies how people behave in society. Often used in audience research. See Chapter 6.

Sound presence: The quality of a recorded sound, which is a function of the ratio between direct and indirect sound waves picked up by the microphone, and changes as a speaker moves closer to a microphone. See Chapter 11.

Sparks: The electricians who are responsible for the lights on a production. They take their instructions from the lighting supervisor and the DOP (director of photography).

Spectrum: See 'radio spectrum' above.

Sponsorship: The funding of programmes by businesses. Funded programmes may be introduced by sponsors' messages, but Ofcom rules that the sponsor must not influence the content or the scheduling of the programme (Ofcom 9.11). See Chapter 16.

Spot: An intense, narrow-angled beam of light. 'Spotting' is narrowing the beam of light. See also 'flood' above. See Chapter 10.

Spot FX: Specific sound effects, such as a door slam, which are not 'laid' on the track but created 'live', often at the dubbing stage. See Chapter 14.

Spun: See 'diffusers' above.

Steadicam: This mounting straps the camera supports to the body of the operator and incorporates a device that keeps the image steady. See Chapter 9.

Stereotype: A simplified representation of a person, group or a situation, playing up their common characteristics. Stereotypes are usually exaggerated and frequently carry negative connotations. See Chapter 16.

Stills: Non-moving images, for example, photographs or single frames taken from a film or television programme.

Sting: A brief musical or visual insert or punctuation. See 'interstitials' above.

Stop frame: A type of animation that involves shooting one frame at a time, usually using drawings or puppets.

Story: In narrative theory, 'story' is used in two ways:

a. For the linguist Tzevan Todorov, the 'story' (*fabula*) is the material of the tale (it may include many events that happen simultaneously), in contrast to the 'plot' (*syuzhet*), which is the way the narrative is organised. This must be linear.

b. The theorist Christian Metz contrasted the 'story' (*histoire*), a straightforward account of what happens in a narrative, with its 'discourse' (*discours*), the way in which it is presented; in other words its distinctive approach to camerawork, the style of acting, the visual effects and other aspects. See Chapter 15.

Storyboard: A sequence of drawn images showing the shots to be used in a programme.

Strand: A linked series of programmes sharing a common title.

Straps (or 'strap titles'): Lettering that runs across the bottom of the frame, naming interviewees and participants.

Streaming: See IPTV above.

Structuralism: A theoretical approach which seeks to reveal the 'structure' of a work and of social reality. It drew on 'semiotics' (see above) and was taken up by theorists including Roland Barthes (1915–80) in the 1960s and 1970s. It developed into 'post-structuralism' (see above).

Subwoofer: A speaker that carries extra low frequencies.

Sungun: A hand-held light, around 250 watts, which runs from belt batteries and can give an intense beam. Useful on location when other forms of lighting are impossible to set up. See Chapter 10.

Suture: The surgical term for stitching up a wound. Used to describe the way a continuity edit 'stitches up' the gap that existed between the taking of two shots, making them appear continuous. See Chapter 13.

Sync (sometimes spelt synch): An abbreviation for 'synchronised sound', sound that is shot simultaneously with the picture and matches it exactly.

Take: A repetition of the action when filming a scene. Every time a shot is repeated it will have a 'take number' (e.g. 'Shot 6, take 5') for identification during editing. See 'shot' above.

'Talent': The term used to describe presenters and celebrities in factual programmes. See Chapter 21.

Talking heads: The term used for interviews or other head and shoulder shots of people talking to camera.

Technological determinism: The view that technology is the most important factor in creating historical changes.

Telephoto lens: A long lens with a narrow angle of vision.

Telerecording: In the early days of television, live studio programmes were preserved by placing a specifically designed film camera in front of a television screen, described as telerecording.

Terrestrial broadcasting: Broadcasting over the radio spectrum from a ground-based system, as opposed to broadcasting via a satellite.

Text: The content of broadcast and other media. One way in which this has been studied is through 'textual analysis'.

Timecode: An electronic process that gives each frame its own digital identification. This is displayed on the screen as a series of numbers which show hours, minutes, seconds and frames. Timecode allows post-production systems to locate a single frame and provides a reference for running several video and audio machines in sync.

Track:

a. A 'track' or a 'tracking shot' is a camera movement in which the camera is travelling along with the action.

b. The shot takes its name from the 'tracks' laid on the ground to take the wheels of the dolly on which the camera is mounted.

c. The sound of a programme is generally referred to as the 'sound track'.

Track laying: The editing process includes preparing a number of sound tracks in order to place each sound in the desired position. These are called 'dubbing tracks'. See Chapter 14.

Tracking software: This analyses the pixel detail and contrast information of a shot, enabling the precise insertion of an object or other digital asset. Used in the creation of visual effects. See Chapter 14.

Trailer: A short television sequence promoting a forthcoming programme.

Transcript: A written version of spoken content. Very often a filmed interview will be transcribed.

Treatment: A short written outline of a programme.

Tungsten: Lamps with a tungsten filament, used for lighting interiors. See Chapter 10.

Twitter: Social media platform restricted to 140 characters or less.

'Two way': In a news broadcast this is a way of describing a live exchange between a presenter in the studio and a reporter on location.

TX: Abbreviation of 'transmission'; the process of broadcasting a programme to an audience.

TX controller: The job of controlling a channel's overall transmission from a 'master control room', including managing the input from several different sources. See Chapter 12.

UGC (user-generated content): The description of filmed material from eyewitnesses used in news and other programmes. Also referred to as 'citizen journalism'. See Chapter 17.

UHD (ultra-high definition): Images with a very high resolution, known as 4K. See 'K' above.

Unmanned aerial vehicle (UAV): See 'drone' above.

Uplink: The link from a ground station to a satellite. It is then 'downlinked' to one or more ground stations, possibly in a different territory.

Verité: An abbreviation of 'cinema-verité'. See above.

Video checker: The job of checking a programme for compliance and technical problems in a post-production facility. See Chapter 14.

Vision mixing: 'Live' editing in a studio gallery or outside broadcast van by a director or a specialist 'vision mixer'. See Chapter 12.

Visual grammar: The rules that ensure smooth continuity between shots. See Chapter 9.

Vlogger: Someone who creates a video blog. See Chapter 4 and 'blog' above.

VOD (video on demand). See IPTV above.

Voice-over (VO): A voice added to a scene which is not part of its natural sound. It may be the voice of a commentator or of one of the participants.

Vox pops: Brief interviews with random witnesses, often used in news broadcasts. The name comes from the Latin 'vox populi', meaning 'voice of the people'.

VT: Abbreviation for video tape, as in 'VT editor'.

Watershed: The 9pm 'watershed' is designed to help parents supervise their children's viewing and is observed by all terrestrial broadcasters. Ofcom rules that programmes considered unsuitable for children may not be broadcast before that time.

White balance: It is necessary to 'tell' a camera what counts as white in particular lighting conditions by framing on a white surface.

Wild track: Recorded sounds, usually made on location, which are not in synchronisation with the camera. See Chapter 11.

Wind gag: Coverings for microphones which reduce the sound of the wind. See Chapter 11.

Wrangler/wrangling: Dealing with data. See DIT above.

XML (Extensible Markup Language): Data file known as Programme Metadata which contains all the relevant details about the programme.

Zoom lens: A single lens with variable focal lengths. A zoom lens tends to be described by the ratio between its longest and shortest focal length, for example, a 'ten to one' has a zoom ratio of ten. Similarly a 'ten by twenty five' is a zoom whose minimum focal length is 25mm and longest multiplies that by ten, that is, 250mm.

Bibliography

Allen, D. (2007) *Encyclopedia of Visual Effects*, San Francisco, CA: Prachpit Press.

Allen, R. (ed.) (1992) *Channels of Discourse, Reassembled*, 2nd edn, London: Routledge.

Bamford, N. (2012) *Directing Television: A Professional Survival Guide*, London: Bloomsbury.

Barthes, R. (1974) *S/Z*, New York: Hill and Wang.

Barthes, R. (1977) 'Introduction to the structural analysis of narratives' in *Image Music Text*, London: Fontana.

BBC (2016) *Diversity Strategy,* www.bbc.co.uk/diversity.

BBC (2016) *Editorial Guidelines,* www.bbc.co.uk/editorialguidelines/guidelines.

BBC Trust (2015) *The Supply Arrangements for the Production of the BBC's Television Content, Radio Content and Online Content and Services*, http://downloads.bbc.co.uk/bbctrust/assets/files/pdf/our_work/content_supply/2015/content_supply_review.pdf.

Bennett, J. and Strange, N. (2011) *Television as Digital Media,* Durham, NC: Duke University Press.

Bennett, J., Kerr, P., Strange, N. and Medrado, A. (2012) *Multiplatforming Public Service Broadcasting: The Economic and Cultural Role of UK Digital and TV Independents*, http://eprints.bournemouth.ac.uk/21021/1/bennett-strange-kerr-medrado-2012-multiplatforming-psb-industry-report.pdf.

Biressi, A. and Nunn, H. (2007) *Reality TV: Realism and Revelation*, New York: Columbia University Press.

Blumler, J. and Katz, E. (1974) *The Uses of Mass Communications*, Beverly Hills, CA: Sage Publications.

Bonner, F. (2003) *Ordinary Television: Analyzing Popular TV*, London: Sage.

Bordwell, D. (1995) 'Principles of narration' in O. Boyd-Barrett and C. Newbold (eds) *Approaches to Media: A Reader*, London: Edward Arnold.

Born, G. (2005) *Uncertain Vision: Birt, Dyke and the Reinvention of the BBC,* London: Vintage.

Broadcasting Research Unit (1985) *The Public Service Idea in British Broadcasting*, London: Broadcasting Research Unit.

Brown, L. and Duthie, L. (2016) *The TV Studio Production Handbook*, London: I. B. Tauris.

Brown, M. (2007) *A Licence to Be Different: The Story of Channel Four*, London: BFI.

Brunsdon, C. (1998) *The Television Studies Book* (C. Geraghty and D. Lusted, eds), London: Arnold.

Brunsdon, C. (2000) *The Feminist, the Housewife and the Soap Opera*, Oxford: Oxford University Press.

Bruzzi, S. (2007) *Seven Up*, London: BFI TV Classics.

Buscombe, E. (1974) 'Television studies in schools and colleges', *Screen Education* 12 Autumn, London: Society for Education in Film and Television.

Calvert, B., Casey, N., Casey, B., French, L. and Lewis, J. (2007) *Television Studies: The Key Concepts*, London: Routledge.

Chalaby, J. (2015) *The Format Age: Television's Entertainment Revolution*, London: Polity.

Channel Four (2015) *360° Diversity Charter,* www.channel4.com/media/documents/corporate/diversitycharter/Channel4360DiversityCharterFINAL.pdf.

Chater, C. (2002) *Research for Media Production,* London: Taylor and Francis.

Chatman, S. (1995) 'Story and discourse' in O. Boyd-Barrett and C. Newbold (eds) *Approaches to Media: A Reader*, London: Arnold.

Coleman, S., Blumler, J., Moss, G. and Homer, M. (2015) *The 2015 Televised Election Debates: Democracy on Demand?* Leeds, UK: Leeds University Press.

Collet, P. and Lamb, R. (1986) *Watching People Watching Television*, a report presented to the Independent Broadcasting Authority, London.

Cook, P. (ed.) (1985) *The Cinema Book*, London: BFI.

Cooke, L. (2003) *British Television Drama: A History,* London: BFI.

Corner, J. (1991) 'Documentary voices' in J. Corner (ed.) *Popular Television in Britain: Studies in Cultural History*, London: BFI.

Corner, J. (1999) *Critical Ideas in Television Studies*, Oxford: Clarendon Press.

Corner, J. (2011) *Theorising Media: Power, Form and Subjectivity*, Manchester, UK: Manchester University Press.

Creative Skillset (2012) *Employment Census of the Creative Media Industries*, http://creativeskillset.org/assets/0000/5070/2012_Employment_Census_of_the_Creative_Media_Industries.pdf.

Creeber, G. (ed.) (2015) *The Television Genre Book,* 3rd edn, London: BFI.

Crone, T., Alberstat, P., Cassels, C. and Overs, E. (2002) *Law and the Media – An Everyday Guide for Professionals*, Oxford: Focal Press.

Curran, J. and Seaton, J. (2009) *Power Without Responsibility*, 7th edn, London: Routledge.

Dahlgren, P. (1995) *Television and the Public Sphere: Citizenship Democracy and the Media*, London: Sage.

Davies, M. M. (2010) *Children, Media and Culture,* Maidenhead, UK: Open University Press.

Davies, N. (2014) *Hack Attack: How the Truth Caught Up with Rupert Murdoch*, London: Chatto & Windus.

Day-Lewis, S. (1992) *TV Heaven*, London: Broadcasting Support Services.

Dismore, J. (2011) *TV: An Insider's Guide*, Evesham, UK: Hothive Books.

Dowmunt, T. (2000) 'Access: television at the margins' in P. Holland (ed.) *The Television Handbook*, 2nd edn, London: Routledge.

Eisenstein, S. (2016) *Towards a Theory of Montage,* Volume 2 of Selected Works, London: I. B. Tauris.

Ellis, J. (1982) *Visible Fictions: Cinema, Television, Video*, London: Routledge.

Ellis, J. (2000) *Seeing Things*, London: I. B. Tauris.

Emm, A. (2014) *Researching for the Media: Television, Radio and Journalism*, London: Routledge.

Enzenberger, M. (1972) 'Dziga Vertov', *Screen,* 13(3) Winter.

Field, S. (2005) *Screenplay: The Foundations of Screenwriting*, New York: Delta.

Fiske, J. (1987) 'Narrative' in *Television Culture,* London: Routledge.

Freedman, D. (2014) *The Contradictions of Media Power*, London: Bloomsbury.

Galtung, J. and Ruge, M. H. (1965) 'The structure of foreign news: The presentation of the Congo, Cuba and Cyprus Crises in four Norwegian newspapers', *Journal of Peace Research*, 2(1), 64–90, www.zurnalistikos-laboratorija.lt/wp-content/uploads/2014/03/Galtung-Ruge-Structure-of-Foreign-News-1965.pdf.

Garnett, T. (1970) Interview with Tony Garnett. *Afterimage*, 1(1) April, London.

Gates, T. (1995) *How to Get into the Film and TV Business*, London: Alma House.

Geraghty, C. (1991) *Women and Soap Opera: a Study of Prime Time Soaps*, Cambridge: Polity Press.

Gerbner, G. (1998) 'Cultivation analysis: an overview', *Mass Communication and Society*, 1(3–4), 175–94.

Glasgow University Media Group (1976) *Bad News*, London: RKP.

Glintenkamp, P. (2011) *Industrial Light and Magic: The Art of Innovation*, New York: Abrams.

Gray, J. (2010) *Show Sold Separately: Promos, Spoilers, and Other Media Paratexts*, New York: New York University Press.

Hale, N. (2000) 'Cinematographer' in P. Holland (ed.) *The Television Handbook*, 2nd edn, London: Routledge.

Hall, S. (1977) 'Mass communication and the "ideological effect" ' in J. Curran, M. Gurevitch and J. Woollacott (eds) *Mass Communication and Society*, London: Edward Arnold.

Hall, S. (ed.) (1997) *Representation: Cultural Representations and Signifying Practices*, London: Sage.

Hall, S., Hobson, D., Lowe, A. and Willis, P. (eds) (1980) *Culture, Media, Language: Working Papers in Cultural Studies*, London: Hutchinson.

Hardy, J. (2014) *Critical Political Economy of the Media: An Introduction*, London: Routledge.

Hargrave, A. M. (1995) *The Scheduling Game: Audience Attitudes to Broadcast Scheduling* (the Broadcasting Standards Council Annual Review 1995) London: John Libbey.

Higgins, C. (2015) *This New Noise: The Extraordinary Birth and Troubled Life of the BBC,* London: Faber.

Holland, P. (1987) 'When a woman reads the news' in H. Baehr and G. Dyer (eds) *Boxed In: Women and Television*, London: Pandora.

Holland, P. (2006) *The Angry Buzz:* This Week *and Current Affairs Television*, London: I. B. Tauris.

Holland, P. (2013) *Broadcasting and the NHS in the Thatcherite 1980s: The Challenge to Public Service*, London: Palgrave.

Iosifidis, P. (2016) 'Media ownership and concentration in the United Kingdom' in E. Noam (ed.) *Who Owns the World's Media*, Oxford: Oxford University Press.

Isaacs, J. (1989) *Storm Over 4: A Personal Account*, London: Weidenfeld and Nicholson.

Jaffe, P. (1965) 'Editing cinema verité', *Film Comment*, 3(3) Summer.

Jenkins, H. (1992/2012) *Textual Poachers: Television Fans and Participatory Culture*, London: Routledge.

Jenkins, H. (2008) *Convergence Culture: Where Old and New Media Collide,* New York: New York University Press.

Jermyn, D. (2010) *Prime Suspect,* London: BFI TV Classics.

Johnson, C. (2012) *Branding Television,* London: Routledge.

Kael, P. (1971) *The Citizen Kane Book,* London: Secker and Warburg.

Kellison, C. (2009) *Producing for TV and New Media: A Real World Approach for Producers,* Oxford: Focal Press.

Kilborn, R. and Izod, J. (1997) *An Introduction to Television Documentary: Confronting Reality,* Manchester, UK: Manchester University Press.

Kuhn, A. (1987) 'Women's genres: melodrama, soap opera and theory' in C. Gledhill (ed.) *Home Is Where the Heart Is: Studies in Melodrama and the Women's Film*, London: BFI.

Lees, N. (2010) *Greenlit: Developing Factual/Reality TV Ideas from Concept to Pitch*, London: Methuen.

Leman, J. (1987) ' "Programmes for women" in 1950s British television' in H. Baehr and G. Dyer (eds *Boxed In: Women and Television*, London: Pandora RKP.

Levin, G. R. (1972) *Documentary Explorations: 15 Interviews with Filmmakers*, New York: Doubleday.

Livingstone, S. (1998) *Making Sense of Television: The Psychology of Audience Interpretation,* 2nd edn, London: Routledge.

Livingstone, S. and Lunt, P. (1994) *Talk on Television: Audience Participation and Public Debate,* London: Routledge.

McCabe, C. (1974) 'Realism and the cinema: notes on some Brechtian theses', *Screen* 15(2).

Mayer, V., Banks, M. and Caldwell, J. T. (eds) (2009) *Production Studies: Cultural Studies of Media Industries,* New York: Routledge.

Metz, C. (1977) 'Story/Discourse: a note on two kinds of voyeurisms' in *The Imaginary Signifier: Psychoanalysis and the Cinema*, Indiana, IN: Indiana University Press.

Millerson, G. (1990) *The Technique of Television Production,* 12th edn, Oxford: Focal Press.

Mittel, J. (2006) 'Narrative complexity in contemporary American TV', *Velvet Light Trap,* 58: 29–40.

Mittel, J. (2015) 'Genre study beyond the text: *Lost*' in G. Creeber (ed.) *The Television Genre Book,* 3rd edn, London: BFI.

Mulvey, L. (1989) *Visual and Other Pleasures*, London: Macmillan.

Murch, W. (2001) *In the Blink of an Eye: A Perspective on Film Editing*, Los Angeles, CA: Silman-James Press.

Newman, N., Levy, D. and Nielsen, R. (2015) *Reuters Institute Digital News Report 2015.* SSRN Electronic Journal.

Nichols, B. (1991) *Representing Reality,* Bloomington, IN: Indiana University Press.

Norris, P. (2000) *A Virtuous Circle: Political Communications in Post-Industrial Societies*, Cambridge: Cambridge University Press.

Oakley, G. and Lee-Wright, P. (2016) 'Opening doors: the BBC's Community Programme Unit 1973–2002', *History Workshop Journal,* 82 Autumn.

Ofcom (2014) *Public Service Content in a Connected Society: Ofcom's Third Review of Public Service Broadcasting,* London: Ofcom.

Ofcom (2015a) *Public Service Broadcasting in the Internet Age: Ofcom's Third Review of Public Service Broadcasting,* London: Ofcom.

Ofcom (2015b) *Broadcasting Code,* London: Ofcom.

Ofcom (2015c) *A Review of Channel Four,* London: Ofcom.

Orlebar, J. (2011) *The Television Handbook,* 4th edn, London: Routledge.

Owens, J. and Millerson, G. (2012) *Television Production,* 15th edn, Oxford: Focal Press.

Page, A. (2015) 'Postmodern drama' in G. Creeber (ed.) (2015) *The Television Genre Book,* 3rd edn, London: BFI.

Paget, D. (1998*) No Other Way To Tell It: Dramadoc/Docudrama on Television,* Manchester, UK: Manchester University Press.

Propp, V. (1995) 'Morphology of the folktale' in O. Boyd-Barrett and C. Newbold (eds) *Approaches to Media: A Reader,* London: Arnold.

Rabiger, M. (1992/2015) *Directing the Documentary,* 6th edn, Oxford: Focal Press.

Redmond, P. (2000) 'Mersey Television' in P. Holland (ed.) *The Television Handbook,* 2nd edn, London: Routledge.

Reuters Institute for the Study of Journalism (2014) Digital News Report https://reutersinstitute.politics.ox.ac.uk/sites/default/files/Reuters%20Institute%20Digital%20News%20Report%202014.pdf.

Rickitt, R. (2006) *Special Effects: The History and Technique,* London: Aurum Press.

Ritzer, G. (2000) *The Macdonaldisation of Society,* London: Sage.

Roberts, G. (2001) 'The historian and television: a methodological survey' in G. Roberts and P. Taylor (eds) *The Historian, Television and Television History,* Luton: University of Luton Press.

RTS: Royal Television Society (2015) 'How fixed rig has transformed factual', February, www.rts.org.uk/magazine/article/how-fixed-rig-has-transformed-factual.

Rumsey, F. and McCormick, T. (2009) *Sound and Recording,* 6th edn, Oxford: Focal Press.

Schnitzer, L., Schnitzer, J., Martin, M. and Robinson, D. (eds) (1973) *The Cinema in Revolution: The Heroic Era of the Soviet Film,* London: Secker and Warburg.

Schudson, M. (1989) 'The sociology of news production', *Media, Culture and Society* 11(3), 263–82.

Shapley, O. (1996) *Broadcasting a Life,* London: Scarlet Press.

Silverstone, R. (1981) *The Message of Television: Myth and Narrative in Contemporary Culture,* London: Heinemann.

Singleton-Turner, R. (2011) *Cue and Cut: A Practical Approach to Working in Multi-Camera Studios,* Manchester, UK: Manchester University Press.

Small, R. (1999) *Production Safety for Film and Television,* Oxford: Focal Press.

Stump, D. (2014) *Digital Cinematography: Fundamentals, Tools, Techniques and Work-flows*, London: Routledge.

Ten Brink, J. (2008) *Building Bridges: The Cinema of Jean Rouch,* New York: Columbia University Press.

Thomas, B. (2016) *Narrative: The Basics,* London: Routledge.

Todorov, T. (1977) *The Poetics of Prose,* Oxford: Blackwell.

Tunstall, J. (1993) *Television Producers,* London: Routledge.

Tunstall, J. (2015) *The BBC and Television Genres in Jeopardy,* Bern: Peter Lang.

Vertov, Dziga (1984) *Kino-Eye: The Writings of Dziga Vertov,* London: Pluto.

Wardle, C., Dubberley, S. and Brown, P. (2014) *Amateur Footage: A Global Study of User-Generated Content in TV and Online News Output*, Tow Center for Digital Journalism: A Tow/Knight Report, http://towcenter.org/research/amateur-footage-a-global-study-of-user-generated-content/.

Warhol, R. and Lanser, S. (eds) (2016) *Narrative Theory Unbound: Queer and Feminist Interventions,* Columbus, OH: Ohio State University Press.

Weynand, D. and Piccin, V. (2015) *How Video Works: From Broadcast to the Cloud,* Oxford: Focal Press.

Williams, R. (1974) *Television: Technology and Cultural Form,* London: Fontana.

Winston, B. (1995) *Claiming the Real: The Documentary Film Revisited,* London: BFI.

Wurtzel, A. and Rosenbaum, J. (1995) *Television Production,* 4th edn, New York: McGraw-Hill.

JOURNALS

All are available in print and online.

Industry-based publications

Broadcast. Trade magazine of the broadcasting industry. Essential for keeping up-to-date with industry issues. www.broadcastnow.co.uk/

Academic Journals

For important up-to-date research and book reviews:

Adaptation, http://adaptation.oxfordjournals.org/

Critical Studies in Television: The International Journal of Television Studies, http://cst.sagepub.com/

CST also hosts an up-to-date blog on television issues, http://cstonline.tv/bloggers-index

Feminist Media Studies, www.tandfonline.com/loi/rfms20#.Vz8nMa5li6U

Journal of Media Practice, www.tandfonline.com/loi/rjmp20#.Vz8iLq5li6U

Media, Culture and Society, http://mcs.sagepub.com/

Screen, screen.oxfordjournals.org/content/by/year

And two useful journals on media history:

Historical Journal of Film, Radio and Television, www.history.ac.uk/history-online/journal/historical-journal-film-radio-and-television

Media History, www.tandfonline.com/loi/cmeh20#.Vz8mQq5li6U

Programme references

Accused BBC1 2010 (p. 187)
Drama series by Jimmy McGovern following people accused of crimes as each awaits the verdict of their trial.

African Summer BBC August 1985 (p. 210)
BBC themed season of programmes about Africa.

Airport BBC1 1997–2005 (pp. 211, 214)
Docu-soap following life and personalities working at London Heathrow Airport.

An American Love Story PBS USA 1999 (p. 144)
Documentary series about a mixed-race couple, filmed over two years. Directed by Jennifer Fox.

Andrew Marr Show BBC 1 2005– (p. 235)
Sunday morning live political debate.

Ant and Dec's Saturday Night Take-Away ITV 2002 (p. 137)
Saturday night entertainment live from ITV London Studios, with audience involvement.

Apocalypse Now feature film USA 1979 (pp. 165, 167)
Francis Ford Coppola's reinterpretation of the Vietnam War based on Joseph Conrad's novel *Heart of Darkness*.

The Apprentice Talkback Thames with other production companies for BBC 2005– (pp. 7, 30, 38, 44)
Factual entertainment: Successful businessman Lord Alan Sugar gives tasks to potential apprentices/business partners who compete for his favour.

The Apprentice: You're Fired BBC 2006 (p. 7)
Spin-off to *The Apprentice*. Rejected contestants share their thoughts with the audience.

The Ark BBC 1993 (p. 88)
Documentary series about London Zoo, filmed and directed by Molly Dineen.

Armchair Theatre ABC/ITV then Thames/ITV in 1956–74 (p. 187)
Celebrated anthology series of single plays. From 1952 to 1968 it was produced by Sydney Newman.

Benefits Street Love Productions for C4 2014 (pp. 79, 121, 227–8)
Controversial documentary series about James Turner St in Birmingham where a high proportion of residents are unemployed.

Big Brother Endemol for C4 2000–10 Ch 5 2010–
Big Brother's Little Brother
Big Brother's Big Mouth
Celebrity Big Brother (pp. 24, 29, 45–6, 63, 70, 77, 211, 228)
Ground-breaking 'reality' contest. A group of incompatible housemates carry out allocated tasks under twenty-four-hour observation. The progress is discussed and expanded in various spin-offs.

The Big Story Twenty–Twenty Television for Carlton/ITV 1993–98 (p. 247)
Current affairs series.

Bitter Lake Adam Curtis BBC iPlayer 2015 (p. 21)
Documentary essay on contemporary politics and militant Islam.

Bloody Bosnia C4 1993 (p. 201)
A season of programmes concerning the war in Bosnia including *The Essential Guide* which used animation and innovative techniques to give a background to the war.

Blue C4 1993 (p. 166)
Reflections from filmmaker Derek Jarman, made as he was dying from AIDS.

Boys from the Blackstuff BBC Pebble Mill, Birmingham 1980–82 (p. 186)
Classic drama series about low pay and unemployment. Scripted by Alan Bleasdale.

Breaking Bad Netflix USA 2008–13 (pp. 36, 185, 189, 200)
Popular crime drama series filmed in New Mexico.

Brideshead Revisited Granada/ITV 1981 (p. 49)
Classic drama series based on the novel by Evelyn Waugh.

The Bridge BBC4 2012– (p. 113)
'Nordic noir'. Danish/Swedish crime drama series.

Britain's Fattest Man C4 2011 (p. 228)
Documentary about a man who weighed 56 stone. One of many factual programmes about obesity and body image.

Britain's Got Talent Thames for ITV 2007 (p. 137)
Popular talent contest hosted by Simon Cowell.

Brookside Mersey Television for C4 1982–2003 (pp. 77, 102, 121, 190)
Liverpudlian soap opera, created by Phil Redmond.

Call the Midwife Neal Street Productions for BBC 2012– (p. 173)
Thought-provoking drama series about a group of midwives in the 1950s and early 1960s.

Cathy Come Home BBC 1966 (pp. 186, 215)
Ground-breaking drama in a realist style for the *Wednesday Play* series. Directed by Ken Loach.

Can't Pay? We'll Take it Away Brinkworth Films for C5 2014– (p. 24)
Following repossession officers.

Casualty BBC1 1986– (pp. 71, 87, 118, 145, 189)
Long-running hospital drama based in an accident and emergency department.

Caught on Camera ITV 2007– (p. 71)
Occasional series of reality footage filmed by members of the public and containing footage from CCTV cameras. Includes *Britain Sees Red: Caught on Camera* 2015

Channels of Resistance C4 1993 (p. 211)
Documentary series which reported on alternative media from around the world.

Channel Four News 1982– (pp. 234, 239)
The first one-hour long news programme on UK television.

Chronicle of a Summer (Chronique d'un été) France 1961 (p. 162)
Documentary that follows residents of Paris over the summer of 1960 at the time of the Algerian War. Directed by Jean Rouch in a cinema verité style in which the making of the film is part of its content.

Citizen Kane USA 1941 (p. 97)
The life of a newspaper magnate. Celebrated for its striking staging and camera work. Starring and directed by Orson Welles.

Clampers BBC1 1998 (p. 214)
Docu-soap following traffic wardens who clamp cars.

The Clangers BBC1 1969–72. CBeebies 2015 (p. 173)
Children's animated series with knitted puppets. Originally created by Oliver Postgate and Peter Firmin.

Come Dine With Me ITV Studios then Shiver Productions for C4 2005– (p. 215)
Factual entertainment: Competitors take turns at hosting a dinner party.

Come Into My World Video (p. 177)
Music video in which Kylie Minogue apparently appears many times.

Confessions of a Beauty Addict QVC 2016 (p. 146)
Promoting beauty products for 'sale by television'.

The Confessions of Thomas Quick Century Film for Film4 2015 (p. 219)
Interview-based documentary about a man who confessed to multiple murders. Directed by Brian Hill.

Coronation Street Granada/ITV 1960– (pp. 23, 43, 101, 135, 159, 189–91, 209)
Long-running soap opera based in Manchester.

Countryfile BBC1 1988 (p. 89)
Long-running series on rural and environmental issues.

Crimewatch BBC1 1984 (pp. 49, 213)
Studio-based show that invites viewers to help in solving crimes.

The Cruise BBC1 1988 (p. 88)
Docu-soap following life on a cruise liner. Director/camera Chris Terrill.

Cutting Edge C4 1990– (pp. 231, 247)
Strand for strong observational documentaries.

Dad's Army BBC 1968–77 (p. 191)
Classic sitcom about the Home Guard in the Second World War. Produced by David Croft. Frequently reshown.

Dallas Lorrimer Productions USA. Shown on BBC 1978–91 (p. 35)
Popular soap opera based on the lives of the oil-rich Ewing family.

Dawn of the Planet of the Apes USA 2014 (p. 177)
Most recent of the science fiction series of cinema films, beginning with *Planet of the Apes* 1968.

The Day Today BBC2 1994 (p. 175)
Comedy series which parodies current affairs programmes.

Death in Paradise BBC1 2011– (pp. 188, 196)
British/French drama series with regular murders, set on a fictional Caribbean island.

Def II BBC2 1988–92 (p. 173)
Youth series which experimented with visuals and presentation.

Dispatches C4 1987– (pp. 45, 49, 210, 213, 235, 247)
Current affairs strand.

Dixon of Dock Green BBC 1955–76 (p. 188)
Long-running police series featuring Jack Warner as the affable PC Dixon.

Dockers: Writing the Wrongs C4 1999 (p. 196)
Documentary that followed a group of sacked Liverpool dockers and their wives working with the writer Jimmy McGovern to create a dramatic reconstruction of their experiences.

Don't Drop the Baby BBC3 2013– (p. 20)
Formatted factual entertainment about fathers and childbirth.

Don't Tell the Bride BBC3 2007–15; Sky1 2016– (pp. 243–4)
Factual entertainment. A potential bridegroom plans the wedding in secrecy.

Downton Abbey ITV 2010–15 (pp. 23, 30, 87)
Popular drama series. The fortunes of a privileged family and their employees at the turn of the twentieth century.

Dr Who BBC 1963–89; 2005– (pp. 35, 87, 94, 166, 175, 177, 188–9, 194)
Popular time-travelling fantasy, with a regularly reincarnated Doctor.

Driving School BBC1 1997 (p. 212)
Docu-soap featuring terrible driver Maureen and her driving instructor husband.

Drugs Inc National Geographic USA 2010– (pp. 245–6)
Series which looks at the drugs trade across the USA.

Duck Quacks Don't Echo Sky 1 2014– (p. 265)
Comedy panel show.

Dynasty ABC USA 1981–89 (p. 35)
Classic 1980s soap opera about the wealthy Carrington and Colby clans.

EastEnders BBC1 1985– (pp. 70, 71, 137, 145, 170, 189–91)
Long-running soap opera based in the fictional Albert Square in the East End of London

Educating Essex (2011)/Yorkshire (2013)/the East End (2014)/Cardiff (2015)
     TwoFour for C4 (pp. 71, 134, 213, 226–7)
Fixed-rig observation of life in a secondary school.

The Eleventh Hour C4 1982–88 (pp. 205, 210, 259)
Strand for radical and innovative documentaries under its influential commissioning editor, Alan Fountain.

Embarrassing Bodies Maverick for C4 2007– (pp. 25, 46, 61)
Taboo-breaking medical factual series.

Emergency Ward 10 ATV/ITV 1957–67 (p. 189)
Early hospital drama series.

Emmerdale Yorkshire Television/ITV 1972– (p. 190)
Long-running soap based in the Yorkshire dales. Originally *Emmerdale Farm*.

Face to Face BBC 1958–60; 1989–1998 (pp. 93, 222)
Intimate interviews filmed in big close-up. Presented by John Freeman in the 1960s. Revived by Jeremy Isaacs in 1989.

The Fall of the Romanov Dynasty USSR 1927 (p. 157)
Pioneering archive-based compilation film. Directed and edited by Esfir Shub.

The Family BBC 1974 (p. 89)
Pioneering observational documentary series following the fortunes of the Wilkins family in Reading and prefiguring the docu-soap genre. Produced by Paul Watson.

Feltham Sings Century Film for C4 2002 (p. 226)
Documentary in which the inmates of the young offenders' institution express themselves in song. Words by poet Simon Armitage, directed by Brian Hill.

Final Score BBC1 1958– (p. 84)
Football news and results. Long-standing Saturday afternoon live discussion.

Fire Fighters Meridian/ITV 2003 (p. 33)
Factual series on the work of the fire brigade. Produced and directed by Kate Beal.

First Cut C4 2007– (p. 282)
Strand designed to launch the careers of new factual directors.

First Date C4 2013– (p. 192)
Potential couples meet for the first time in a restaurant.

Football Focus BBC1 2009– (p. 85)
Saturday lunchtime discussion about football. From 1974 it had been part of the Grand-stand strand.

Galaxy Chocolate 2015 (p. 174)
Ground-breaking advertisement in which Audrey Hepburn is 're-created' by visual effects technology.

Game of Thrones HBO USA 2011 (pp. 113, 171, 174, 189)
Fantasy drama series. Multiple narratives and rivalries based in fictional territories with a medieval flavour. Filmed in Northern Ireland, among other locations.

The Gentle Touch London Weekend Television/ITV 1980–84 (p. 189)
Drama series about a woman CID officer in London.

The Go Between BBC 2015 (p. 167)
Drama based on the novel by L. P. Hartley. Previously made into a film in 1971.

Gogglebox Studio Lambert for C4 2013– (pp. 38, 52, 225)
BAFTA-winning factual entertainment series featuring enthusiastic viewers watching television, and commenting on it.

Good Morning Britain ITV 2014– (p. 235)
Breakfast time topical discussion and entertainment programme.

The Government Inspector 2005 (pp. 192, 202)
Docu-drama about the unexpected death of Iraq weapons inspector Dr David Kelly. Directed by Peter Kosminsky.

The Great British Bake-Off BBC 2010–2016 (pp. 86, 214)
Baking cakes in a tent. Hugely popular contest series. The format has been sold to many territories.

Handsworth Songs C4 1986 (pp. 205, 210, 259)
Prize-winning documentary about the 1984 riots in Birmingham. Made for the *Eleventh Hour* strand by the Black Audio Collective.

Happy Valley BBC1 2014; 2016 (pp. 187, 205)
Crime drama serial based around a female police officer and her grandson. Written and directed by Sally Wainwright.

HARDtalk BBC World News 1997– (p. 234)
Hard-hitting current affairs interviews.

Have I Got News for You Hat Trick Productions BBC1 1990– (pp. 53, 137)
Entertainment quiz show based on current news topics.

Heidi Fleiss: Hollywood Madam 1995 (p. 123)
Documentary about a notorious brothel owner. Directed by Nick Broomfield.

Hillsborough Granada/ITV 1996 (p. 202)
Drama-documentary retracing the events that led to the deaths of 96 people at Hillsborough football ground in 1989. Written by Jimmy McGovern.

Hollyoaks Mersey Television, then Lime Pictures for C4 1995– (p. 190)
Soap opera that focuses on the lives of young people. Created by Phil Redmond.

Horizon BBC2 1964– (pp. 210, 220)
Long-running science strand.

House of Cards Netflix USA 2013– (p. 208)
Drama series based on the 1990 BBC serial about an unscrupulous politician.

Housing Problems British Commercial Gas Association 1935 (p. 98)
Classic documentary. The earliest use of sync interviews with working-class people.
Directed by Edgar Anstey and Arthur Elton. Interviews by Ruby Grierson.

The Hunt BBC 2015 (pp. 108, 171)
Superbly filmed wildlife series following hunters of all species.

I'm a Celebrity: Get Me Out of Here ITV 2002– (pp. 23, 47, 192, 215)
Contest between celebrities given challenges while stranded in an Australian jungle.

The Island with Bear Grylls Shine for C4 2014– (pp. 51, 228)
Factual entertainment. Groups of 'ordinary people' must survive on a remote island.

Jamaica Inn BBC 2014 (p. 165)
Historical drama serial set in a bleak moorland landscape. Based on the novel by Daphne
du Maurier.

Jeanne Dielman, 23 Quai du Commerce, 1080 Bruxelles 1975 (p. 99)
Belgian feature film by avant-garde director Chantal Akerman.

Jekyll and Hyde ITV 2015 (pp. 21, 61, 77)
Contemporary presentation of the 1886 gothic tale by Robert Louis Stevenson.

The Jewel in the Crown Granada/ITV 1984 (p. 187)
Classic drama series set in India at the end of the British Raj.

Jim's Inn ITV 1955 (p. 146)
An 'admag' (advertising magazine) from the early days of ITV.

Jumanji USA 1995 (p. 178)
Adventure fantasy cinema film.

Jurassic Park 1993 (p. 176)
Science fiction film about recreating dinosaurs. Directed by Stephen Spielberg.

The Lakes BBC 1997–99 (p. 189)
Drama serial based in a Lake District community. Written by Jimmy McGovern.

Later with Jools Holland BBC 1992– (pp. 122, 167)
Live music programme.

The Leader, his Driver and the Driver's Wife 1991 (p. 123)
Documentary that tracks down the leader of the far-right Afrikaaner party in Apartheid
South Africa. Directed by Nick Broomfield.

Lewis ITV 2006–15 (p. 188)
Detective series. Spin-off from the long-running crime drama *Inspector Morse* 1987–2000.

Little Britain BBC3 2003–2004; BBC1 2005–2007 (p. 20)
Comedy sketches featuring Matt Lucas and David Walliams in many guises.

London BFI 1994 (p. 99)
Feature-length documentary in which a voice-over traveller looks at lesser known parts of London. Filmed with long, static takes. Directed by Patrick Keiller.

London on Film BBC4 2012– (p. 218)
Series made up of archive material showing London over the decades.

London Programme London Weekend Television/ITV 1975–2008 (p. 43)
Local news series.

Long Lost Family Wall to Wall for ITV 2011– (p. 79)
Constructed factual series in which family members are tracked down and reunited.

The Lord of the Rings USA 2001, 2002, 2003 (p. 168)
Series of cinema films based on the fantasy series by J. R. R. Tolkein.

Lost ABC USA 2004–10 (pp. 47, 188, 189, 196)
American supernatural drama based on a group of survivors stranded on an island. There are many interweaving plots.

Luther BBC 2010– (p. 188)
Crime drama series with an award-winning performance from Idris Elba as Inspector John Luther.

Mad Men HBO/Netflix 2007–15 (p. 45)
Drama series set in a 1950s American advertising agency.

Made in Chelsea C4 2013– (pp. 38, 215)
Constructed factual: lives and relationships of the Chelsea set.

Magic Roundabout BBC 1965–77; subsequently on several different channels (p. 172)
Children's puppet animation series, originally created in France.

Make it Digital season BBC 2015 (p. 45)
Programmes on digital media across the genres.

Malcolm and Barbara: A Love Story Granada/TV 1999 (pp. 89, 226)
Filmed and directed by Paul Watson over six years, following the progress of Malcolm's dementia.

Man Alive BBC2 1965–81 (pp. 93, 222)
Interview-based series which explored social and emotional problems. Its catchphrase was 'Can I ask you a personal question?' Originally produced by Desmond Wilcox.

Man with a Movie Camera USSR 1929 (pp. 154, 156, 162, 224)
Seminal documentary. Filming a day in a busy city in the Soviet Union.

Mandela, My Dad and Me Woodcut Media 2015 (p. 33)
Documentary in which Idris Elba reflects on the life of Nelson Mandela.

MasterChef BBC1 1990–2001; 2005– (p. 30)
Amateur cooks compete to win the title.

Max Headroom Lakeside for C4 1987 and 1989 (p. 173)
1980s spoof on the digital future.

Midsomer Murders ITV 1997– (p. 188)
Inspector Barnaby solves murders in the fictional village of Midsomer.

Million Pound Drop C4 2010–15 (p. 137)
BAFTA-winning game show where contestants are given a million pounds and must answer questions to keep it.

Miranda BBC 2009–15 (p. 191)
Semi-autobiographical comedy with Miranda Hart.

Miss Marple BBC 1984–92 (p. 195)
Agatha Christie's eccentric sleuth.

The Missing BBC 2014 (p. 187)
Drama serial about a child who goes missing and the parents' search.

Mock the Week Angst Productions for BBC2 2005– (pp. 272–4)
Celebrity panel game with topical themes.

Morning in the Streets BBC 1959 (pp. 166, 209)
Impressionistic documentary of everyday life. Directed by Denis Mitchell.

Mrs Brown's Boys BBC and RTE for BBC1 2011– (pp. 137, 192)
Irish family sitcom with Brendan O'Carroll as Mrs Brown.

The Murder of Stephen Lawrence Granada/ITV 1999 (p. 202)
Docu-drama about the murder of a black teenager, and the bungled police investigation, from the point of view of Stephen's parents. Scripted and directed by Paul Greengrass.

Murnaghan Sky News 2011– (p. 234)
Sunday morning live political debate hosted by Dermot Murnaghan.

Network Seven C4 1987–88 (p. 173)
Youth entertainment programme.

New Tricks BBC 2003–15 (p. 196)
Drama series in which retired police officers solve old crimes.

Newsnight BBC2 1980– (pp. 20, 49, 175, 221, 234)
Late evening news magazine and discussion programme.

Newsround (originally *John Craven's Newsround*) BBC, now on CBBC 1975– (p. 239)
News presented for children.

Night Mail GPO Film Unit 1936 (p. 166)
Classic documentary with innovative soundtrack, using music by Benjamin Britten and poetry by W. H. Auden to celebrate the railway postal service.

The Nightmare Neighbour Next Door C5 2014– (p. 213)
Neighbour disputes filmed with CCTV and personal cameras.

No Child of Mine Meridian/ITV 1997 (p. 33)
Docu-drama directed by Peter Kosminsky dealing with abuse and child prostitution.

The Not-Dead Century Films for C4 2007 (p. 226)
Director Brian Hill and poet Simon Armitage collaborate to explore ex-soldiers' post-traumatic stress.

The Office BBC2 2001–2003 (p. 54)
Sitcom about office life. Starring and written by Ricky Gervais, with co-writer Stephen Merchant.

Omnibus BBC 1967–2003 (p. 210)
Arts strand which was replaced by *Imagine.*

One Born Every Minute C4 2010– (pp. 134, 151, 212)
Fixed-rig show in a maternity ward.

The One Show BBC1 2006– (pp. 144–5, 278)
Early evening topical chat on weekdays.

Only Fools and Horses BBC 1981–96 (p. 191)
London-based sitcom centring on the fortunes of two 'independent traders' of dubious merchandise.

Our War BBC3 seasons: 2011, 2012, 2014 (pp. 33, 213)
Documentary series filmed by soldiers in Afghanistan with their helmet cameras. Accompanied by an informative website.

Panorama BBC1 1953– (pp. 49, 210, 234, 235, 246)
The BBC's main current affairs series.

Pointless Endemol for BBC 2009– (p. 137)
Quiz show where contestants must choose the least obvious answer.

Prime Suspect Granada/ITV 1991–96 (p. 189, 205)
Police drama series following a top female detective. Written by Lynda La Plante.

The Proms: (The Henry Wood Promenade Concerts) BBC 1990– (pp. 70, 122, 167)
Live orchestral music from the Royal Albert Hall where audiences may 'promenade'; that is stand in the arena and gallery as well as sitting in the seats. A major annual event, which began in 1895 and has been broadcast on BBC Radio and increasingly on television.

Question Time BBC1 1979– (pp. 38, 49)
Live audiences pose topical questions to politicians and public figures.

Radio Ballads BBC Radio 1957–64 (p. 166)
Radio documentaries that wove poetry, music and regional voices to celebrate aspects of working life – such as *The Big Hewer* (August 1961) about coal mining. Produced by Charles Parker and musician Ewan McColl. They influenced many television documentarists, including Denis Mitchell.

Rear Window USA 1954 (pp. 115, 199)
Alfred Hitchcock's film about a photographer confined to a wheelchair who observes, and investigates, a murder through his lens.

The Road to Mosul Vice News online 2015 (p. 39)
Documentary that follows Kurdish peshmerger forces as they resist Islamic State (Daesh) in the Iraqi city of Mosul. www.youtube.com/watch?v=KbsesrAMjTw

Ross Kemp: Extreme World Tiger Aspect for Sky 1 2011– (p. 265)
The presenter travels to parts of the world experiencing conflict and hardship.

Sarah Millican Live Chopsy Production for C4 2015 (p. 70)
Live stand-up comedy from theatres around the United Kingdom.

Sarah Palin: You Betcha 2011 (p. 123)
Documentary-maker Nick Broomfield pursues the Republican candidate for the vice-presidency of the United States.

The Secret History of Our Streets BBC 2012– (p. 218)
Series which uses archive film to explore the history of specific urban streets.

The Secret Life of the Four Year Old C4 2015 also ***the Five Year Old and the Six Year Old*** (p. 98)
Series which observes children at play in a nursery/school setting.

Secret Millionaire RDF for C4 2006– (p. 214)
Constructed reality: a millionaire goes undercover to donate money to a worthy cause.

Sex Toy Secrets Chalkboard for Channel 4 Shorts online 2015 (p. 270)
Short films about sex toys.

Sherlock Hartswood for BBC 2010– (pp. 195, 201)
A present-day version of Conan Doyle's classic detective.

Shooting the Past Talkback for BBC2 1999 (p. 166)
Director Stephen Poliakoff's innovative drama about photography and memory.

Sicko USA 2007 (p. 247)
American presenter/documentary-maker Michael Moore explores the provision of health care in the United States.

Silent Witness BBC 1996– (p. 188)
Drama series. Forensic pathologists investigate various crimes.

The Simpsons Fox Global Television Network Sky 1 1989– (p. 172)
Classic cartoon satirising American family life.

The Singing Detective BBC 1986 (pp. 186, 194)
Dennis Potter's seminal drama serial which explored the consciousness of a hospitalised crime writer.

The Sky at Night BBC 1957–2013. 2013– (p. 123)
Long-running series on astronomy. Presented by Patrick Moore from 1957. Since 2013 it has been presented by Maggie Aderin-Pocock.

Sky News 1989– (pp. 29, 138, 226, 233–4, 238–9)
Twenty-four-hour live news on television and online. Sky also delivers a service to commercial UK news channels.

Soccer AM Sky Sports 1995– (p. 265)
Saturday morning football-based comedy talk show.

Soho Stories BBC 1997 (p. 88)
Late-night vignettes on characters from London's most cosmopolitan district. One of the first series to be filmed, by director Chris Terrill, on a small digital camera.

The Sopranos HBO USA 1999–2007 (p. 44)
Crime drama about Italian-American mobster, Tony Soprano, and his personal life.

The South Bank Show LWT/ITV 1978–2010; Sky Arts 2012– (p. 210)
Long-running arts strand presented by Melvyn Bragg.

Soviet Spring C4 1990 (p. 210)
A season of programmes dealing with changes in the final years of the Soviet Union.

Space Between Words KCET USA 1971 and BBC 1971 (p. 210)
Five observational documentaries following the breakdown of relations in various situations.
Directed by Roger Graef.

Sports Personality of the Year (SPOTY) BBC 1954– (p. 84)
Awards ceremony. Each year it is broadcast live from different cities across the United
Kingdom.

Steptoe and Son BBC 1962–65; 1970–74 (p. 191)
Classic sitcom about the misfortunes of father and son rag-and-bone men. Written by
Ray Galton and Alan Simpson.

Storyville BBC 2002– (p. 45)
Strand for international documentaries.

The Street Granada for BBC 2006, 2007, 2009 (p. 187)
Anthology series of single dramas by Jimmy McGovern about people living on the same
street.

Strictly Come Dancing BBC1 2004– (pp. 20, 43–4, 46–7, 49, 71, 114, 136–7, 145)
Celebrities are paired with professional dancers and compete for audience votes.

Sunday Night at the London Palladium ATV/ITV 1955–67; 1973–74 (p. 44)
Live variety show from the popular theatre.

The Sweeney Euston Films for Thames/ITV 1974–78 (p. 189)
Tough cop drama series. Noted for scenes of violence unprecedented on UK television.

Take Me Out: The Gossip 2012–13; 2015– (p. 215)
Spin-off from the dating show *Take Me Out* Thames for ITV 2010–

Teletubbies Ragdoll for CBeebies 1997–2001; 2015– (p. 35)
Series for the very young. An original controversy about using baby language and lack
of educational content gave way to universal acclaim. New, updated episodes were
launched in 2015.

That Was The Week That Was BBC 1962–63 (p. 12)
Ground-breaking late-night satire and political comment.

The Thick of It BBC 2005–12 (p. 191)
Sitcom which satirised the government.

This Week A-R/ITV 1956–68; Thames/ITV 1968–92 (pp. 23, 210, 304)
Reporter-led current affairs series.

This Week BBC 2003– (p. 234)
Late-night political discussion hosted by Andrew Neil.

Three Days of Terror: The Charlie Hebdo Attacks BBC2 2016 (p. 235)
One-off documentary directed by Dan Reed.

Till Death Us Do Part BBC1 1965–75 (p. 191)
Classic family sitcom. Notorious for its prejudiced central character, Alf Garnett, played by Warren Mitchell.

Timewatch BBC 1982– (p. 156)
Strand of historical documentaries, relying heavily on archive material.

Tonight ITV 1999– (pp. 23, 246)
Occasional current affairs series, originally *Tonight With Trevor Macdonald*.

Top Gear BBC 1977–2015 (p. 195)
Global best-selling series about cars and driving. Ended when main presenter Jeremy Clarkson was sacked for attacking a producer. Relaunched in 2016.

Top of the Lake BBC 2013 (p. 186)
Drama serial based in New Zealand, directed by Jane Campion.

Touch of Evil USA 1958 (p. 99)
Cinema thriller directed by Orson Welles.

Tough Young Teachers BBC3 2014 (p. 20)
Documentary series following teachers in their first year in the job and learning to cope.

TOWIE (The Only Way is Essex) Lime Pictures for ITV 2010– (pp. 73, 87, 192, 211, 215, 225)
Constructed reality. Following the lives and relationships of a group of 20-somethings in Brentwood, Essex.

Trainspotting Film4 1996 (pp. 198, 204)
C4-funded feature film on drugs and comic despair among Scottish youth. Directed by Danny Boyle.

Twelve Years a Slave Film4 2013 (p. 24)
Based on the true story of an African-American kidnapped into slavery. Directed by Steve McQueen. Cinema film partially funded by C4.

Twenty-Four Hours in A&E The Garden Productions for C4 2011– (pp. 24 38, 212)
Fixed-rig documentary following an accident and emergency department of a busy hospital. Filmed first at Kings College Hospital, Camberwell, then St George's, Tooting.

Twenty-Four Hours in Police Custody The Garden Productions C4 2014– (p. 71)
Fixed-rig documentary following Bedfordshire police investigating cases in Luton.

The Undateables Betty TV for C4 2012 (p. 228)
People with disfigurements and disabilities meet for a date.

Undercover Boss Studio Lambert for C4 2009 (p. 214)
Senior executives work undercover among employees.

Undercover Britain C4 1994– (p. 246)
Series which aims to expose wrongdoing using covert filming.
The Pits, on lack of safety in a drift mine, won an RTS award (1995).

Unreported World Quicksilver Media for C4 2000– (pp. 210, 213)
Current affairs series dealing with global issues.

Up the Junction BBC 1965 (p. 201)
Young people in South London filmed in a realist style that was considered shocking at the time. Directed by Ken Loach for the *Wednesday Play* series.

Victoria Derbyshire BBC2 2015– (pp. 20, 234)
Mid-morning current affairs and debate programme.

Video Diaries Community Programme Unit for BBC2 1990–2001 (pp. 106, 121, 210, 228)
Members of the public make films of their lives.

Video Nation Community Programme Unit for BBC2 1993–2000 (pp. 106, 210, 228)
Compilations of video notes from a diverse group of 50 people from around the United Kingdom. Two-minute 'shorts' were also broadcast nightly before *Newsnight* on BBC2.

The Voice BBC1 2012–16; ITV 2016– (p. 121)
Singing talent show with celebrity judges. UK version of an international franchise.

W1A BBC2 2014 (pp. 45, 192)
Sitcom satirising the BBC's publicity-driven culture.

Walking with Dinosaurs BBC 1999 (p. 174)
Recreation of the dinosaur era by the BBC's Natural History Unit.

Wednesday Play BBC 1964–70 (pp. 77, 187, 201)
A series of innovative single plays, each with a different author.

Weekend World LWT for ITV 1972–88 (p. 221)
Serious current affairs programme focusing on politics and politicians.

What's Up TV Licklemor Productions for Sky 1 2014– (pp. 105, 260–5)
Youth magazine made by trainees at the MAMA Youth Project.

Who Do You Think You Are? Wall to Wall for BBC1 2004– (pp. 207–8)
Series where celebrities trace their ancestry.

Whose Line Is It Anyway? Hat Trick for C4 1988–99; then Angst for CW network USA 2013– (pp. 272–4)
Comedy games show based on improvisation. June 2016: a live show was mounted at the London Palladium.

Wife Swap RDF Media for C4 2003–9 (p. 214)
Factual entertainment. Wives from incompatible families swap places. The series inspired a number of 'swap' formats.

The Wire HBO USA 2002–8 (pp. 186, 247)
Crime and law enforcement drama series, based in Baltimore, Maryland.

Wolf Hall BBC 2015 (pp. 113, 114)
Serial adaptation of the historical novels by Hilary Mantel about the scheming Thomas Cromwell.

World in Action Granada/ITV 1963–99 (pp. 24, 192, 211, 246–7)
Long-running current affairs series. The docu-drama *Who Bombed Birmingham?* (1990) dramatised the team's investigation into the miscarriage of justice when the wrong men were imprisoned for planting a bomb in a Birmingham pub during the Northern Ireland troubles.

The X-Factor Talkback Thames for ITV 2004– (pp. 23, 43–4, 71, 137, 168)
Popular singing talent series, with spin-off programmes including *The Xtra Factor*. Produced and hosted by Simon Cowell.

X-Files 20th Century Fox USA 1993–95; 1995–2002; 2016 (p. 189)
FBI agents Mulder and Scully investigate paranormal phenomena.

Yes, Minister BBC 1980–82 (p. 191)
Political sitcom. Followed by *Yes, Prime Minister* (1984–88) when the fictional minister was promoted.

Z-Cars BBC 1962–78 (pp. 176, 188)
Classic police series based in Liverpool.

Index

Page numbers in **bold** indicate key references.

180 rule 91

accents 13, 120–1, 258
access to the industry 253, 257–67; *see also* Creative Access
access programmes: 285; about an institution 50, 212–13; community based 32, 121, 229, 303; *see also* Community Programme Unit
ADR (Automatic dialogue replacement) 168–9, 285
advertisements 41–2, 70, 152, 172–3, 183, 204, 291; on Channel Four 13
advertising breaks 181
Al Jazeera 16, 29, 233, 244
Alexandra Palace 11, 119, 232
All 4 38, 280, 282
Althusser, Louis 203
ambient noise 128, 285–6
Angst (production company) 272–4, 317
animation 51, 172, 176, 285, 299, 292, 298, 315
animatic 177, 285
animatronics 172, 174, 176, 286
Annan Committee 14
Ant and Dec 4, 137, 308
apprenticeships 251, 253, 275

archive 20, 42, 106; archive-based programmes 50, 83, 87, 156, 312, 315, 318, 320; archive footage uses of 82, 143, 157, 173, 207, 213, 255; archive research 58, 156, 218–19, 269, 289; *see also* BFI National Film Archive; British Newspaper Archive
Armitage, Simon 228, 313, 317
Arri Alexa 68, 107, 122
Arts Council 283
assistant director (AD) 32, 79, 88
audience: address 13–16, 20, 22–4, 43–4, 48–9, 53, 60–1, 78, 154, 156, 186–91, 202–3, 280; as citizens or consumers 26; to a global/overseas audience 35, 53; in factual programmes 224–5; in narrative 193–6
Audience Appreciation Index (AI) 52, 285
audience participation/interaction 22, 38, 46–7, 70, 77, 174, 189; in the studio 137
audience research 6, 7, 26–7, 36, 52, 56–7, 61–2, 254, 278, 304; *see also* BARB, ratings
audio: design/designer 73, 88, 122, 127, 135, 165, 171; audio engineer 142; *see also* sound; sound recordist

audio space 89, **119–35**, 165–71, 285
'auteur' theory 86, 288
autocue 140–1, 236, 238, 286
Avid 152, 262; Avid Everywhere 155; Avid
    Media Composer 153; Avid tutorials 252

background plate *see* clean plate
BAFTA (British Academy of Film and
    Television Arts) 212, 263, 277; BAFTA
    Guru 266; BAFTA scholarships 283
BAME (Black, Asian and Minority Ethnic)
    communities 6, 205, 228, **258–61**, 275,
    296
BARB (Broadcasters' Audience Research
    Board) 52, 61–2, 286, 295; *see also*
    ratings
barn doors 117, 286
Barnett, Greg 292
Barthes, Roland 185, 193, 298, 301
BBC (British Broadcasting Corporation):
    Board of Governors 11; branding 45,
    173; codes of practice/editorial
    guidelines 224, 230, 242; commissioning
    277, 280–2; Director General (DG) 11,
    12, 20, 30, 38; diversity 315; genres
    51–2: history 10–17, 105, 209; and
    independent companies 31; licence fee
    11, 21, 290, 292; news 20–21, **232–9**;
    and online/cross platform 19, 21, 38, 45,
    72, 283; other channels 28, 45; public
    purposes 19; and public service 19–21,
    25, 294; Royal Charter 10–11, 20–1,
    233; scheduling 43; specialised units 48;
    studies of 57–8; studios 144, 150;
    technical standards 106–7, 118; training
    251–2, 258, 260, 265, 275; working for
    84–5
BBC Academy 150, 252, 265–6
BBC Alba 20
BBC iPlayer 19, 21, 38, 213, 233
BBC Studios (BBC production arm) 21,
    30
BBC Worldwide 19, 180–1
BBC2 13–14, 20, 171, 173, 211
BBC3 19–20, 45, 73, 213, 72, 214, 230
Beal, Kate 32, 313
Beard, Mary 90, 122, 158, 216, 316
BECTU (Broadcasting, Entertainment,
    Cinematograph and Theatre Union) 286
BGAN (Broadband Global Area Network)
    243, 286

'bible' (for a formatted programme) 53,
    214
Birmingham Six 192, 246, 322
Birt, John 221
Black Audio Film Collective 205, 211, 258,
    314
blogs 7, 40, 60, 215, 272, 286, 300, 307
blue screen *see* green screen
Blumler, Jay 62, 301
boom/boom swinger 134, 123, 129, 141,
    143, 181, 286, 289
Bond, Mark 107, 118
Born, Georgina 57, 302
Bourne, Sue 213
Bournemouth University (BU) 8, 118, 164,
    171, 180, 254, 268
brand/branding 5, 22, 41–5, 53, 174, 181,
    277, 286, 304; BBC 45, 173; C4 44–5,
    173; QVC 149; *see also* channel
    identification
Brecht, Bertolt 203, 305
British Council 283
British Film Institute (BFI): BFI Player 156;
    BFI National Film Archive 156, 218–19;
    BFI Film Fund 285
British Library/Newspaper Archive 216
British Universities Film and Video Council
    (BUFVC) 219
Broadcast magazine 7, 52–3, 277, 307
Broadcasting Act 1990 16, 29
Broadcasting Code (Ofcom) 27–8, 77, 87,
    179, 247, 288
Broadsides (production company) 14
Broomfield, Nick 123, 313, 314, 318
BSkyB 15, 28,
budget 7, 77–81, 89, 214, 254, 261, 276,
    280
buzz track 126, 135, 171, 286
Buzzfeed 27, 39
BVE 277, 283–4

CAA *see* Civil Aviation Authority
cable basher 140
cable television 15, 16, 36, 189, 296
cameras 104–9, **107–111**; camcorder 7,
    106, 107, 135, 210, 246, 287;
    concealed cameras 227; digital cameras
    107; helmet 72, 213, 317; High-8
    camcorder 106; mountings **99–102**;
    position/angles/movement **90–104**;
    studio/robotic 140–2, 148–150;

surveillance/CCTV 208–9, 213, 310; 245–6; *see also* Arri Alexa; fixed rig; studio cameras; OB; PSC

Campbell, Alastair 242

cardioid 130–1, 287

Carlton Greene, Hugh 12

CC-Lab (production company) 265, 272–3

CGI (Computer Generated Imagery) 104, 152, 172–9, 287

Chalaby, Jean 211, 213–14, 231

Chalkboard (production company) 270–2, 318

Channel 5 16, 24, 37, 231, 233; commissioning 277–8, 280

Channel Four (C4C Channel Four Corporation) 24–5, 121, 204, 210, 225, 278; branding 44–5, 173; diversity 258–9; and independent companies 29–31, 58, 272; launch 13–16; Shorts Online 270; training 282; *see also* All 4; Film4

channel identification (idents) 22, 41–2, 72, 121, 154, 172–5, 291

Chatman, Seymour 195, 302

chroma key 94, 287, 291; *see also* green screen

cinema verité/ciné verité 106, 176, 287, 289, 304, 311; *see also* direct cinema

cinematographer (DOP) 68, 118; and director **88–103**; and lighting 111–13, 289, 303

cinematography: digital **107–9**, 118; 'cinematography of the image' 177, 286–7

citizen journalism *see* UGC

City University 217, 239, 246

Civil Aviation Authority (CAA) 102, 287

clapper board 89, 100, 123, 125, 287

clapper/loader 89, 138, 287

Clarke, Bob 260–3, 264

classic realist text 202–4, 287

clean plate 94, 95, 178, 286

Clean Up Television Campaign 12

Clews, David 227

cloud (internet) 155, 164, 287

CNN (Cable News Network) 16, 234, 243–4

codec 108, 287

collaborative documentaries 229

colour temperature 113, 117, 287

colourist 163, 291, 287; *see also* grading

commentary 73, 120, 124, 126, 159–60,
163, 165, 169, 171, 211, 224, 292–3; *see also* voice-over

commissioning **276–83**, 288; BBC 277, 280–2; Channel 5 277–8, 280; commissioning editor 80, 212–13, 277; ITV 277, 281; Sky 208, 212, 277–8, 281

Communications Act 2003 17, 22

Community Channel 25, 263, 281

Community Programme Unit (CPU) 40, 106, 210, 228, 259

compliance 83, 179–81, 288, 299

concept art 177, 288

constructed reality programmes 159, 212, 214, 319, 320

continuity 90–1, 115, 139, 142, 200, 288, 298, 300; continuity editing **159–61**, 288

convergence 54, 288, 304

coordinated frequencies 132, 288

co-production 23, 35–6, 53, 281

copyright 82–3, 141, 143, 170, 215, 219, 245, 261, 288

correspondents (news) 242

costume 140, 200, 252; costume dramas 49

Cox, Brian 4, 158, 212

crane 99–100, 288

Creative Access 266, 275

Creative Diversity Network (CDN) 259–60, 263

Creative England Production Fund 283

Creative Skillset 75, 252–3, 257, 259–60, 275, 303

'creative treatment of actuality' 209, 223

Critical Studies in Television (CST) 307

cross-platform *see* platform

cultivation theory 62, 303

current affairs 23, 49, 52, 72, 157, 213, 224, 233–5, 304, 309, 311, 314, 317, 320–2

Curtis, Adam 87, 213, 310

cutaway 90, 91, 95

Da Vinci (grading) 163

data wrangler *see* DIT

deco-doc 113, 288

deconstruction (theory) 193, 205, 288

diegetic 201, 288

diffusers (lighting) 117, 288

digital assets 176, 178, 289

digital compositing 176–7, 288

digital effects (DFX) 176, 288
digital imaging technician *see* DIT
Digital Production Partnership (DPP) 109,
    163, 295
Dineen, Molly 89, 308
direct cinema 100, 106, 224, 289; *see also*
    cinema verité
director 80–3, **86–103**, 239–41, 245–8;
    documentary 213, 231; news 236;
    studio 141–4, 148–9, 154
Disability Programme Unit 48, 259, 210,
    259
discourse/discours (narrative theory) 195–6,
    297, 303
Disney: Walt Disney Company 40; channel
    44; premises 145
DIT (Digital Imaging Technician) 89, 157,
    289
diversity 22, 204, **257–63**, 278, 301, 302
Dixon, Adele 12, 105
documentary 52, 102, 103, 162, 166,
    207–31, 267; documentary ethics 217,
    221, **223–29**; *Guardian* documentary
    unit 282–4, 302, 305, 307; *see also*
    cinema verité; direct cinema;
    observational
docu-soap 89, 211, 214, 308, 310–12
dolly 99–100, 289, 292, 299
DOP (Director of Photography) *see*
    cinematographer
drama 47–52, **185–206**, 186; directing 87;
    editing 156
drama-documentary/docu-drama 87,
    191–2, 246, 305, 313, 322
Drew, Robert 106, 289
drone (UAV) 99, 102, 268–9, 287, 289
dub 163, 170–1, 180, 289, 293, 297,
    299

Edge Hill University 84–5
Edinburgh International TV Festival 15, 31,
    187, 254, 277
Edison, Thomas 104
editing: edit decision list (EDL) 163, 289;
    editing picture **151–64**, 269; editing
    sound **165–71** styles of editing **159–62**
editor: edit producer (preditor) 77, 151,
    158; news 138, 235–7, 239–40; picture/
    video/VT 82–3, 89, 95, 180, 238, 288,
    300; social media 238; sound 125–6,
    165–6; *see also* commissioning: editor

editorial independence/guidelines 225, 233,
    242, 245
'educate, inform and entertain' 11, 50, 70
'effects' research 62
Eisenstein, Sergei 102, 154, 164, 303
electromagnetic spectrum *see* radio
    spectrum
Ellis, John 72, 119–20, 227; on 'realism'
    200–1
Endemol (production company) 29, 260,
    309, 317
ENG (electronic news gathering) 109, 289
enigma (narrative theory) 198, 290
entry-level jobs 260, 266, 271, 274, 295
EPG (Electronic Programme Guide) 19, 22,
    102, 146, 289
European Broadcasting Union (EBU) 163
Evolutions (post-production company) 151
EVS 182, 289
experts, researchers need to find 216–17

factual entertainment 50, 207, 211–12, 224,
    229–31, 270–1, 308, 310, 312, 314–15,
    322
factual research 216
fans/fan culture 37, 40, 46–7, 63, 72, 189,
    195, 215, 304
Farmer, Stephanie 254, 256
feminist writers/critics 60, 190, 204–5, 228,
    302, 306–7; film makers 14, 60, 204
Field, Syd 192, 197–8, 303
film researcher *see* archive research
Film4 24–5, 48, 320, 321
'filmed' programmes 70–1
Final Cut Pro (editing) 153
fine cut 82, 155, 158, 163, 289
fishpole boom *see* boom
Fiske, John 186, 188, 196, 198, 200–1,
    303
fixed rig 50, 71, 73, 134, 151, 155, 212,
    226, 290, 306, 312, 317, 321
fixer 248, 290
flood (light) 116, 290
flow/overflow (of television) 42–4, 46, 56,
    59–61, 71–2, 215, 290
focal length (lenses) 109–10, 290, 300
focus puller 89, 290
Foley 170, 290
format/formatted programmes 50, 53, 87,
    192, 211, **213–15**, 227, 229, 290; *see
    also* 'bible'

Fox News 16
Framestore 174
France TV 233
free-to-air 4, 16–17, 19–20, 27, 290
Freeman, John 94, 222, 313
Fresnel lens (for lighting) 117, 290
funding 14, 52, 297; of the BBC 20–1; of
    ITV 23; of Channel Four 258; sources
    of 282–3
Fuse TV (YouTube) 254
FX 290 *see* digital effects (dfx); sound
    effects, special effects, spot effects (sfx)

gallery (studio) 70, 73, 118, 137–9, **141–4**,
    148–9, 154, 291, 300; fixed-rig 212;
    news 236–7
Garnett, Tony 77, 187, 303
gaze: male 60, 204; opposed to 'glance'
    119–20
genre **47–53**, 162, 290; genre-specific
    channels 28; and realism 201;
    requirement to broadcast 13; Tunstall's
    21 genres 34, 51–2, 306; women's
    205, 304; *see also* documentary; news;
    factual entertainment; sport
gimbal 101, 291, 293
Glasgow Media Group 60, 303
Glastonbury Festival 6–7, 252–3, 254
globalisation **35–7**, 57, 291
grading *see* colourist
Graef, Roger 210, 319
Granada Television 23, 120–1, 186–7, 189,
    192, 211, 218, 246, 309, 311, 314–17,
    319, 322
graphics 154, 172–6, 291; playout operator
    144, 149; producer 237; *see also* CGI;
    visual effects
green screen 94, 138, 178, 287; *see also*
    chroma key
Grierson, John 209, 223, 225
Grierson, Ruby 98, 314
Grierson Trust 283
grip 68, 99, 141, 289, 291
gun mic 131, 134, 291

Hall, Tony 30, 38,
harm and offence 77, **225**, 233
HD (high definition television) 107–8, 291
Helmers, Maike 167, 171
Higson, Charlie 77
Hill, Brian 213, 219, 226, 311, 313, 317

HMI (hydragyrum medium arc iodide lamp)
    117, 291
Hoare, John 138
Hoggart, Richard 13
hot head (camera mounting) 100, 291
hypodermic needle theory 62

Iannucci, Armando 255
IBA (Independent Broadcasting Authority)
    13–14, 16
ident *see* channel identification
identity (cultural) 22, 60, **204–6**
ideology 55, 60, 202–3, 291; ideological
    text 203
independents/independent production
    companies/indies 13–16, 18–22, **28–35**,
    58, 76–7, 252, 258–9, 280–1, 291;
    see also PACT
ingestion 151, 155, 180–1, 291
interactivity (audience) 38, **46–7**, 174, 186,
    193, 195, 229, 255
intern/internship 149, 259, 266
internet 23, 243; channels 29, 35–40, 67,
    225, 276, 283, 287, 288; public service
    content 27, 34; streaming 17, 68; *see*
    also IPTV
interstitials **41–4**, 72, 103, 172, 292
intertextuality 46, 56, 204, 292
interviews: editing 157–61; filming 90–8,
    113–15, 120, 125, 132, 139, 143, 173;
    interviewees 216–18; for jobs 272–3;
    news 237–40; organising and research
    84; as paratexts 46; techniques **219–24**;
    types of 43, 49, 73
iPlayer *see* BBC iPlayer
IPTV (internet protocol television) 292, 297
Isaacs, Jeremy 58
ITA (Independent Television Authority) 12–14
ITC (Independent Television Commission)
    16–17
ITN (Independent Television News) 12, 23,
    233
ITU (International Telecommunications
    Union) 163
ITV (Independent Television): commissioning
    277, 281; ITV Hub 38; ITV PLC 23, 36;
    network 12–19, 22; schedule 43–4;
    sponsorship 225; training 239

Jarman, Derek 166, 309
Jenkins, Henry 467, 54, 62, 194, 305

jib/jimmy jib 99–100, 140, 292
Johnson, Catherine 22, 42, 44–5, 53
Johnston, Lisette 246
journalists/journalism 39, 49, 134, 155, 159,
    210, 231, **232–48**, 267; impartiality 225;
    undercover 213, 246; see also current
    affairs; news; UGC
Jurassica 269

K (as in 2k, 4K) see pixels
Katz, Elihu 62, 301
key light 115, 292
Klein, Leanne 30
Kodak 106
Kosminsky, Peter 102, 87, 192, 201, 317
Kuhn, Annette 205, 304

Lambert, Stephen 38, 211, 214, 313, 320
Lambie-Nairn, Martin 173
Lawford, Darren 33, 266
Leacock, Richard 100, 106, 289
LED (light-emitting diode) 118, 292
lenses (camera) **109–10**, 290; telephoto
    110, 298; zoom 110–11, 300
licence fee see BBC licence fee
Licklemor Productions 105, 260–1, 321
lighting: lights **111–18**, 286–99; personnel
    141–2, 296
linear: editing 155, 292; schedules 17,
    41–3, 62, 278, 290
Lintott, Chris 123
Little Fish Films 39
'live' programmes **69–70**, **136–7**; news
    234–40; streaming 243
Loach, Ken 201, 310, 321
local TV 25, 138, 281; London Live 33
location: filming 292; finding 81; producer
    (fixer) 248, 290; research 218
logging/logger 82, 157, 269, 271, 292
Longinotto, Kim 213
Love Productions 226
Lynch, David 166

M and E (music and effects track) 171, 292
MacDonald, Adam 278
McGovern, Jimmy 187, 189, 196,
McKee, Robert 192
McKenzie, Abigail 84–5
McLeod, Liz 280
McTaggart Lecture 254–5
Magna Carta 255

make-up 137, 139; digital 177
Maker studios 40
MAMA Youth Project 260–5
Manchester University 254
marxism/neo-marxist critical tradition 58, 60,
    193, 202–3, 292, 294
master control room 138, 149
matte 176, 288
MCN (multi channel network) 39–40
Mellows, Hannah 268–75
Meridian (ITV franchise) 32, 254
Mersey Television 77, 305
microphone/mic 120, **123–7**, 138;
    directional 130, 287, 291; personal/
    radio mics 123, 127–8, 132–3, 295;
    placement of 127–9, 133–4; selecting
    130–3; studio 141, 143, 147; see also
    cameras/camcorder; spectrum
mise-en-scene 73, 293
Mitchell, Denis 166, 209, 316
Mittell, Jason 189
mobile phone: 'captured' footage 213, 219;
    filming with 50, 71, 108–9, 243; for
    viewing 17, 233, 239, 294
Moffat, Steven 188
montage 164, 293; of attractions 154;
    editing 162
motion capture/motion control (digital
    effects) 176, 293
motivated/unmotivated (camera movement)
    98, 162, 293
MoVI (camera mounting) 101, 293
Mulholland, Siobhan 212, 277
multi-platform see platform
Mulvey, Laura 60, 193, 204–5, 305
Murch, Walter 160, 164, 165, 167
Murdoch, Rupert 15, 28, 30, 36–7
Murrell, Richard 236
music 49–50, 82–3, 120–2, 273, 314, 317;
    post-production 163, 166–7, 170, 292;
    recording 130, 133
MXF (material exchange format) 181, 293

narrative 86, 91, 153–4, 287, **185–206,**
    209, 289, 293, 297, 301, 303, 305–6;
    in editing 158–62; in formatted
    programmes 214; narrative functions
    198, 293
National Film Archive see BFI
National Geographic Channel 31, 213,
    245–6, 312

naturalism 153
Netflix 17, 35, 37, 38
Newman, Sydney 187, 309
news 49, **232–245**; agencies 242;
    balance/impartiality 12; editing 119–20,
    151, 155, 165; streaming/online 27, 39;
    see also ITN; Fox News; journalism; Sky
    News
News International/News Corporation 28
niche (programmes) 263, 293

OB (Outside broadcast) 69–70, 74, 84, 154,
    236, 254, 299
observational documentaries 50, 209–10,
    227, 230, 287, 293; editing 158, 162;
    filming 90–1; lighting 111; research 217;
    sound 130, 132; see also cinema verité;
    direct cinema
Ofcom (Office of Communications) 9, 16,
    19, 22, 25–8, 39; codes of practice 77,
    85, 179, 233, 225–6, 288, 300;
    complaints 233; and radio frequencies
    132–3; research/reports 57–8, 61–2
'oov' (out of vision) 234, 293
overnights (ratings) 52, 293, 295
ownership (of media) 16, 36–7, 40, 291

package (news) 234, 237–8, 240, 293
PACT 80, 281
Paget, Derek 192
palantypist see Sign Zone
pay-TV 16
paratexts **41–53**, 55, 69, 72, 215, 294
Parisio, Anne 77, 229–31
Peacock Committee 15
Performing Rights Society 170
PewDiePie 37, 39
Pilger, John 225
Pilkington Committee 13
pitch/pitching (a programme idea) 271,
    279–81, 294
pixels 107–8, 176, 292, 294; see also
    resolution
platform/cross-platform/multi-platform 4, 17,
    34, 35–47, 186, 204, 238–9, 294
Poliakoff, Stephen 166
pop filter (for a microphone) 125, 294
portable single camera (PSC) 88
postmodern/postmodernity 193–4, 203, 294
post-structuralism 193, 294
Potter, Dennis 187, 194, 203

precinct 214, 218, 294
preditor see producer (edit)
producer **76–8**, 146–9, 306; news **235–240**;
    digital 77, 191; edit 77, 151, 230;
    'producer choice' 16
Production Assistant (PA) 79, 85, 141, 148,
    270
production manager/management **78–83**,
    218
pro-filmic event 73, 294
programme metadata see XML
proxy 157, 294; see also rushes
PSC (portable single camera) 88, 294
psychoanalytic theory 55, 60, 193, 203–4,
    294
public relations (PR) 241, 243
public service: broadcasting (PSB) 11, 15,
    17, **18–31**, 34, 224, 294, 301, 302,
    304–5; genres 48, 52; ecology 14

quality control (QC) 163, 179, 180, 294
QVC 144, **145–50**

Radical Film Network 225, 283–4
radio (electromagnetic) spectrum 11, 15, 22,
    25–6, 286, 288, 295, 298; and radio
    mics 132–3, 295
radiophonic workshop 166–7
ratings 43, 52, 57, 61, 239, 241, 278, 285,
    295; see also overnights
raw file 157, 295
Rawstrone, Karl 155, 164
realism 103, 153, **200–4**, 287, 301, 305;
    see also classic realist text
reality programmes/constructed reality 75,
    159, 162, 211; genres 51–2, **213–15**;
    see also format
recce 218, 295
RedBalloon (production company) 107,
    254–6
redhead (light) 117, 295
Redmond, Phil 77, 101, 190, 305, 309,
    314; see also Mersey Television
regulation (television) 5, 12, **25–8**, 55–6,
    215, 218, 295; see also IBA; ITA; ITC;
    Ofcom
Reith, John 11, 20, 120, 294
representation (on screen) 60, 204, 227,
    295; see also identity; stereotype. For
    representation in the workforce see
    diversity

researcher: casting 171; factual
     programmes **215–19**, 261; ideas 279;
     news 237, 239–40; *see also* archive
     research
resolution (of the image) 106–8, 292, 295;
     see also pixels
Ridley, Vanessa 144–5, 147–50
Rose, Mandy 229
Rosenbaum, John 89, 103, 122, 129–30
Rouch, Jean 106, 162, 211, 287, 306,
     310
rough cut 82, 158, 309
Royal Charter *see* BBC
Royal Television Society (RTS) 247, 255,
     266–7
runner/logger 32–4, 84, 181, 265, 268–75;
     Facebook group 271
rushes 71, 79, 155–6, 157, 231, 292, 295
Russia Today (RT) 36, 233, 244

Salisbury Cathedral 255
Sankofa 258
satellite TV 17, 243
scheduling 18, **42–5**, 52, 70, 137, 149,
     188–9, 210, 225, 243, 276–8, 292, 296,
     304
Screen journal 59, 193, 294
'Screen 2' 48
scrim 117, 288
sd card 269
'segmented' television 71–2
semiotics (in film theory) 59, 193, 294,
     296–7
sensor: in a camera 107–9, 296; for motion
     capture 176, 293
sequence 71, 73, 89–91, 96, 100, 296;
     editing 152, 157
set designer 139, 142, 146
sfx: sound effects 169; special effects 177
S4C (Sianel Pedwar Cymru) 14, 20, 25
Shed Media Group 30
Shine Group 29, 265–6
Shklovsky, Viktor 199
shot 296, 298; shot, reverse shot structure
     91; types of 94–103
showreel 253, 296
showrunner 78, 86, 188, 296
Shub, Esfir 156, 312
Sign Zone 171, 293
'sizzle reel' 280
Skillset *see* Creative Skillset

Sky Academy 260, 265–6
Sky News 28, 109, 138, 225, 318
Sky Television 15–17, 28–9, 144;
     commissioning 208, 212, 277–8, 281;
     diversity 257; Sky 1 105, 260–3, 270,
     263; Sky Atlantic 284; Sky Sports 51;
     Sky UK 28, 36; *see also* BSkyB
skype 243, 296
Smyth, Barnaby 169
soaps/soap operas 43, 49, 52, 60, 70–1,
     77, 101, 112, 145, 187, **189–191**;
     narrative 196; 'women's genres' 205,
     302, 304–5; *see also* docu-soap
social media 242–3
Solent Productions 252
Sothinathan, Luke 180–2
sound 73; editing 155–63, **165–71**, 179;
     recording **119–36**, 218, 306; recordist/
     engineer 88, 132–3, 139, 141–3; sound
     control suite 139; sound presence 297;
     supervisor 162; *see also* audio design;
     studio; sync
sound effects (sfx) 120–2 128, 163, 169,
     285, 290, 296; spot fx 169, 171, 297
sound track 73, 285, 298
Southampton Solent University 252
sparks 112, 141, 297
spectrum *see* radio spectrum
Spicer, Phil 179
spin 241–2
sponsorship 42, 225, 296
sport 51, 182, 293; BBC Sport 84, 144;
     Sky Sports 28
spot (light) 116, 290
spun 117, 288, 297
stereotyping 80, 227–8, 297
steadicam 101, 297
Steyger, Tony 254
story (in narrative theory) 194–5; 'histoire'
     297
storyboard/storyboarding 72, 90, 96, 177,
     297
straps (on screen information) 237, 297
streaming 19, 21, 27, 35, 37–9, 45, 67,
     233, 243; *see also* IPTV
Street-Porter, Janet 173
structuralist theories 193
studio 8, 69–71, 73, 94, 99, **136–50**, 302,
     306; cameras 109, 140; graphics 175–6;
     lighting 112, 115, 117–18; sound 126,
     128, 133–4, 141, 169, 290; vision mixing

154, 299; *see also* gallery; OB; vision mixer
subwoofer 171, 297
sungun 118, 298
suture 91, 152, 161, 298
Svilova, Elizaveta 156
sync (synchronised sound) 124–6, 168–70, 298; 'syncing' rushes 157; *see also* clapper board

take 298; while filming 71, 90, 123, 296; in editing 158
'the talent' (on screen performers) 279–80, 298
Talent Team (BBC) 84–5
Talent Television/Talent South (production company) 33
Tarantino, Quentin 106
technical standards 163, 179, 294; *see also* EBU; ITU; quality control
technological determinism 3, 298
telephoto lens *see* lenses
telerecording 105, 298
Thatcher, Margaret 15, 36
themed seasons 45, 308
Thompson, Mark (BBC DG) 38
timecode 125, 157, 164, 180–1, 289, 292, 298
Tinderflint Productions 268–9
track laying 168, 170, 299
tracking (software for digital effects) 176, 293, 299
tracking shot 99–100, 298
trailer 22, 41–2, 46, 71–2, 138, 152, 172, 174, 292, 294, 299
training 6–7, 67–8, 75, **251–63**, **266–7**; The Hatch 265; *see also* Creative Skillset
transcript 157, 299
transmedia storytelling 194
True North (production company) 102, 280
Turner, George Jesse 247
Turner Long, Sophie 263
tungsten 117–18, 293, 299
Twitter 38, 44, 46, 60, 195, 227, 233, 238, 240–1, 243–4, 294, 299
'two way' (in news packages) 238, 299
Twofour (production company) 226, 312
TX (transmission) controller 138, 299
Tyler, Owen 151

UAV (unmanned aerial vehicle) *see* drone
UGC *see* user generated content
UHD (ultra-high definition) 108, 299
Ulleri, Giovanni 246–8
Unit List 251, 272, 276
user-generated content (UGC) 243–5, 299
'uses and gratifications' 62

verité style filming 161, 299; *see also* cinema verité; direct cinema
Vice Media 27, 39
video checker 181, 299
video journalist (VJ) 132, 238
'video space' 89, 91, 114, 122
video tape 106
Virgin 36
vision mixer 73, 138, 142–4, 154, 237, 291, 299
visual effects 172–9, 286
visual grammar 91–3, 299
vlogger 106, 300
VoD (video on demand) 38, 292; *see also* IPTV
voice (human voice in television programmes) 120–2, 221, 223, 317; editing 165–9, 171; recording 127–9, 132, 135; voice-over 126, 153, 162, 237, 300; *see also* ADR; commentary
vox pop (vox populi) 123, 300
Vertov, Dziga 98, 102–3, 154, 156, 203, 224, 303, 307
VT (video tape) 300; operator 262; technician 181–2;

Wall to Wall (production company) 30–1, 247
Warner Brothers 30–1
watershed 61, 179, 225, 300
Watson, Paul 89, 226, 312, 316
Wednesday Play 77, 187, 310, 321
white balance 117, 300
Whitehouse, Mary 12
wild track (recording) 126, 135, 300
wind gag/shield (for microphone) 125, 132, 300
Winston, Brian 228, 306
women in the television industry 6, 13–14, 156, 206, 257–8; experts 217; programme makers 205; women writers 205; *see also* feminist writers/ filmmakers

Women in Film and Television 60, 284
Women's Programmes Unit 48
women's representation (on screen) 60, 120, 204–5, 228, 295, 304; women's genres 190, 205, 304
Woodcut Media (production company) 29, 31–4, 265, 315
workshops (set up by C4) 14, 29, 121, 228, 258, 266, 269
wrangler/wrangling *see* DIT

Wurtzel, Alan *see* Rosenbaum, John

XML (Extensible Markup Language) 163, 179, 181, 300

Yapi, Jonny 264–6
YouTube 50, 36, **37–40**, 67, 238, 240, 282

Zoella 37, 40
zoom: shot 99; lens 110–11, 300